CONFLICTS AND NEW DEPARTURES IN WORLD SOCIETY

World Society Studies

Volume 3

Stiftung Weltgesellschaft
World Society Foundation
Zürich

Board

Volker Bornschier, President
Karl W. Deutsch †
Hans-Joachim Hoffmann-Nowotny
Hans-Peter Meier-Dallach

Address: Rämistrasse 69
CH•8001 Zürich, Switzerland.

CONFLICTS AND NEW DEPARTURES IN WORLD SOCIETY

World Society Studies

Volume 3

Edited by

**Volker Bornschier
Peter Lengyel**

LONDON AND NEW YORK

First published 1994 by Transaction Publishers

Published 2017 by Routledge
2 Park Square, Milton Park, Abingdon, Oxon OX14 4RN
711 Third Avenue, New York, NY 10017, USA

First issued in paperback 2017

Routledge is an imprint of the Taylor & Francis Group, an informa business

Copyright © 1994 by Taylor & Francis.

All rights reserved. No part of this book may be reprinted or reproduced or utilised in any form or by any electronic, mechanical, or other means, now known or hereafter invented, including photocopying and recording, or in any information storage or retrieval system, without permission in writing from the publishers.

Notice:
Product or corporate names may be trademarks or registered trademarks, and are used only for identification and explanation without intent to infringe.

ISSN: 0942-3087

ISBN 13: 978-1-138-50845-3 (pbk)
ISBN 13: 978-1-56000-129-4 (hbk)

CONTENTS

PREFACE — ix

INTRODUCTION

EMERGENCES AND CONFLICT DYNAMICS IN WORLD SOCIETY
Volker Bornschier and Peter Lengyel — 3

I PEACE AND WAR

1. THE DEMOCRATIC PEACE
   Bruce Russett — 21

2. WAR, POLITICS AND THE MARKET: REFLECTIONS AFTER THE GREAT POTLATCH
   Georg Kohler — 45

3. ARMAMENTS AND DISARMAMENT IN THE POST-COLD WAR PERIOD: THE QUEST FOR A DEMILITARIZED AND NUCLEAR-FREE WORLD
   Marek Thee — 61

4. THE ROLE OF THE UNITED NATIONS IN THE POST-COLD WAR ERA
   Johan Kaufmann, Dick Leurdijk, Nico Schrijver — 93

II CORE-PERIPHERY SITUATIONS

5 THE EMERGING HUMAN RIGHTS ENVIRONMENT
  IN THE ARAB WORLD
  Jill Crystal   113

6 THE WORLD BANK AND EXPROPRIATION
  DISPUTES IN AFRICA
  Adeoye Akinsanya   129

7 WORLD ECONOMIC INTEGRATION AND POLITICAL
  CONFLICT IN LATIN AMERICA
  Michael Nollert   159

8 GENESIS AND DYNAMICS OF POPULIST REGIMES
  AT THE PERIPHERY
  Christian Suter   181

9 THE CAUSES OF LATIN AMERICAN SOCIAL
  REVOLUTIONS: SEARCHING FOR PATTERNS
  IN MEXICO, CUBA AND NICARAGUA
  John Foran   209

10 MEXICO'S UNSOLVED CRISIS
   Hanspeter Stamm   245

11 SOCIAL PERCEPTION OF ENVIRONMENTAL
   PROBLEMS: DESTRUCTION OF TROPICAL FORESTS
   AND ETHNIC PROTEST MOVEMENTS IN BOLIVIA
   H.C.F. Mansilla   263

12 BETWEEN REFORM AND DISASTER: OPTIONS
    FOR SUB-SAHARIAN AFRICA IN THE EMERGING
    GLOBAL ORDER
    Julius O. Ihonvbere   295

III SOCIAL AND LABOR CONFLICTS

13 THE GLOBALIZATION OF SOCIAL CONFLICT
    James Mittelman   317

14 CYCLES OF HEGEMONY AND LABOR UNREST
    IN THE CONTEMPORARY WORLD SYSTEM
    Beverly J. Silver   339

15 GOVERNMENTAL BUDGETING: A COMPUTER MODEL
    OF CONFLICT AND BARGAINING
    Georg P. Müller   361

16 POLITICAL CONFLICT AND LABOR DISPUTES
    AT THE CORE: AN ENCOMPASSING REVIEW
    FOR THE POST-WAR ERA
    Volker Bornschier and Michael Nollert   377

PREFACE

Towards the end of our century people in the most diverse locations on earth and in the most varied of circumstances are becoming increasingly aware that the world is growing irrevocably together, into a world society. This emerging society faces every sort of problem, in its parts and as a whole. Yet it also represents a great challenge to humanity which thus attains a completely novel stage of its social evolution.

The *Stiftung Weltgesellschaft* • World Society Foundation offers its support to social scientists who wish to meet this challenge by making world society and its constituent phenomena more frequently the subject of their professional attention and reflection.

The financial means at the Foundation's disposal to support social scientific research on world society are limited. Moreover, it supports only such research projects as deal with social phenomena explicitly from the viewpoint of world society. It thus attempts, with its modest means, to contribute to a venture which will in future no doubt be pursued by an increasing number of participants.

The Foundation respects values of a scientific nature (communicational capacity about a subject), of comprehensibility (public communicational ability) and of pluralism (communication across cultures and schools of thought). It favors no particular school of thought, but is open to different theoretical and methodological approaches to the social scientific study of world society. Original formulations – including those that might deal with problems – which propose a specific research project on the basis of a clear research design are of interest to the Foundation.

The Foundation was established in 1982 by Peter Heintz (1920-1983) and endowed by him posthumously. Peter Heintz taught and conducted research in Europe, South and North America. Before returning in 1966 to

Zurich, to the university where he had studied, there to found the University Sociological Institute he was, between 1960 and 1965, director of the Facultad Latinoamericana de Ciencias Sociales (FLACSO) in Santiago de Chile. In conjunction with his activities in Zurich he was also professor at the Departamento de Sociología of the Fundación Bariloche in Argentina. The Foundation's Board feels committed by his conscious world citizenship and his professional dedication towards world society as a subject of research.

The sponsorship program of the Foundation was made known in 1984 through announcements in leading social science periodicals; since, a number of research projects supported by it have already been completed. Aside from supporting researchers, the Foundation also decided to contribute to the social scientific debate through a series which principally contains articles reflecting aspects of Foundation-supported research, supplemented by invited papers, staff papers and occasional outstanding scholarly contributions identified by colleagues or otherwise acquired. The articles in successive volumes are not intended as comprehensive reports on sponsored research, generally published as a book or as several journal articles. The series is designed rather to complement these other channels of communication. Instead of presenting summaries of what are often complex and lengthy research designs, and which would thus arouse but limited interest, we have chosen to publish more broadly informative texts arising out of scholarly efforts. Such articles, of varying length, can of course not cover the entire field of the research from which they spring.

Our third volume contains an invited contribution on the second European revolution and the end of the world order established at Yalta by Georg Kohler, a concluding review article on political conflict and labor disputes in core countries over a 35-year span in the post-war era and fourteen articles from Foundation-sponsored research. Two other research reports could not be included: one by Paolo Bellucci (Rome, Italy) on "Foreign Aid and Foreign Policy" and one by Richard L. Merritt, Robert G. Muncaster and Dina A. Zinnes (Champaign, Illinois, U.S.A.) on "Modelling International Interconnectedness".

The Foundation owes thanks to several persons whose dedication and help make it function and the series appear. First of all, the Board wishes to thank Marie-Thérèse Ficnar for her excellent services as the secretary of the Foundation since its beginning, and Peter Lengyel for his dedicated work as co-editor of the series. Furthermore, thanks go to Hildegard

Köhler and Rachel Matthey for their help on the manuscripts of the series and to Simon C.J. Bornschier for preparing the camera-ready copies. Starting with volume two the series is published by Transaction, New Brunswick (U.S.A.) and London (U.K.), whereas the first volume (ISBN 3–593–34309–6) – published in 1990 – came out at Campus Press (Frankfurt and New York). The Foundation wishes to point out that these volumes can lay no claim to any representative sampling of theoretical viewpoints or subject coverage of research into world society. The series, however, does convey a broad picture of research sponsored by the Foundation.

The Foundation's Board deeply regrets the loss of its member, Professor Karl W. Deutsch, who died in Cambridge, Mass. in 1992. Professor Deutsch became a Board member in 1984 after the death of the Foundation's founder, Professor Peter Heintz in 1983, left a seat vacant. Thus Karl W. Deutsch contributed essentially to the development and identity formation of the Foundation at a time when its activities were as yet hardly consolidated. His unusually wide knowledge and experience also influenced the formulation and application of policy guiding research funding. In Karl W. Deutsch the Board loses a colleague of international repute whose own world citizenship so excellently embodied the image which the World Society Foundation wishes to project.

Volker Bornschier, President
World Society Foundation

INTRODUCTION

EMERGENCES AND CONFLICT DYNAMICS IN WORLD SOCIETY

Volker Bornschier and Peter Lengyel

Conflicts and new departures – the theme of this volume – form a duality. New departures are born of conflicts, which themselves intensify as old orders collapse. Today, more than ever, the inhabitants of the globe and the governments of almost 200 sovereign states are being forced to share a common, universal fate, conditioned by economic interdependence, globe-spanning transportation and communication networks and, not least, the ecological crisis. Such a community is not automatically a peaceful one. It can only become so if some order for the so often adumbrated world society is found.

Surely, such an order must centrally involve politics and economics, power and its re-distribution. But such matters have to be preceded by a change in patterns of thought. Without fresh normative leads no sustaining institutions for a societal model which settles conflicts peacefully can be established. Looking back at our century, one essential new departure stands out. It occurred long ago and has for some time already exhausted its capacity to shape the social world: before the end of the century it must be renovated. Despite all the great achievements to be credited to this departure, the new societal model will have to accomodate the challenge of a pact for the survival and welfare of life on earth. We propose to recall briefly here certain major achievements, as also various shortcomings of the order that stands in such need of renovation, with reference to the different contributions to this volume.

The cleavage at the end of the Second World War, occasioned by this century's "Thirty Years War" and the confrontation of the liberal democracies with Nazi and fascist ideologies initially transformed the world system, through the order of the United Nations, agreed in San Francisco in 1945 under the leadership of the hegemonic United States, into a world society, albeit a weak one. Entry into a new era was celebrated enthusiastically by many throughout the 1950s and into the early 1960s. Yet it was fraught with many unsolved problems, amongst which the unfulfillable promises of development and opposition to the Western world order by the socialist states became the principal ones to define the North-South and East-West lines of conflict.[1]

And yet: the pioneering innovation of the new world order installed by the United Nations is the adoption, in 1945, of a superordinate codex of human rights, the creation of a supranational right through international agreement. The catalysing function of the horrors of war and of the Nazi regime in bringing this innovation about transpires clearly from the Preamble to the Charter of the United Nations. The United Nations Organization is historically linked to the wartime coalition of the Allies to counter the Axis powers: important normative elements underlying it can already be traced in the Atlantic Charter of 1941. It was this coalition, calling itself "United Nations", which, as early as 1942 and 1944, laid claim in different declarations to respect for human rights and basic freedoms. These were subsequently incorporated into the Charter of the United Nations, later to be spelt out in detail in the Universal Declaration of Human Rights in 1948.

The importance of this new departure can hardly be overemphasised. The universalistic order of sovereign states, based on the "equality of states" became a world society through the codification of human rights, which establishes the equality of all human beings through supra-national law. The world's inhabitants thus became direct bearers of rights. In this connection, it is to be underlined that these do not only include the classic basic freedoms, as well as social and economic rights, but also claims to a certain political order. For Article 28 of the 1948 Universal Declaration stipulates that "Everyone is entitled to a social and international order in which the rights and freedoms set forth in this Declaration can be fully realized." From this, the right to peace, to an intact environment and to development may, amongst others, be extrapolated.

Of course, we all know that the implementation of human rights and basic freedoms has been sadly deficient in many parts of world society since 1945, and still is. Jill Crystal, for example, describes difficulties encountered in the Arab world, in part owing to conflicts with basic Islamic ethics, below. Discrepancies between claims and implementations through the creation of conditions in which human rights may be enjoyed, frustrated by local, national and international power holders and spontaneous social processes, is an index of the weak social compact of the post-war era, a compact that was more binding until the 1960s than it has been in the 1970s and 1980s.

It is by now indeed apparent that the implementation of the new order has become deficient for the great majority of mankind. A form of social regulation which, in Emile Durkheim's sense, might have provided orientation, was attempted, but the contrast between the model and social reality soon created manifest strains, in the sense of Robert K. Merton. The dynamics at play here were made the subject of his research by Peter Heintz, the founder of the World Society Foundation. His theme was the value of development, for long a consensual one after the Second World War: he examined the institutionalisation of the sharply rising expectations thus aroused. The widespread failure to meet such aspirations, according to him, made the justification of differences in life chances and power holdings ever more difficult, leading to an anomic situation in the sense of Merton's strain theory. As a result, greater conflict-proneness was actually anticipated in sociological theory. And, in fact, since the mid-1960s, an increasing number of revolts occurred against authorities and against the West and its world order. While these were initially mainly of socialist inspiration, they were later of a fundamentalist or populist character as the developmental impulse began to disintegrate and disorientation spread.

Several of the contributors to this volume deal with such phenomena. Christian Suter sets up a structural approach to populism and traces the history of populist regimes in Latin America. John Foran sketches a theory of Third World social revolutions and seeks common patterns in the Mexican, Cuban and Nicaraguan cases. James H. Mittelman notes that "world society is entering a new era in the relationship between conflict and the division of labor" and goes on to illustrate this insight with several telling examples from East Asia. In a similar spirit, Julius O. Ihonvbere analyses the inadequate response of African regimes to globalization processes, leading to the desperate crisis which the continent must now face, mainly with its own resources. And Michael Nollert reports on an empirical test of the causal chains which link dependencies in world economic processes with levels of insurgency, coming to what he calls the "cynical" conclusion that greater domestic inequalities actually lead to lower levels of insurgency.

Failures at the institutional level are numerous. We may note some important ones. The Atlantic Charter of 1941, as the initial formulation of a new order, was couched not only in terms of political security but was also linked to the fundamentals of the democratic and welfare societal model of the 1930s. It declared these to be the politico-economic bases for a better world, specifying, in Paragraph Five the "desire to bring about the fullest collaboration between all nations in the economic field with the object of securing, for all, improved labor standards, economic adjustment and social security".

While the United States had already adopted the new Keynesian economic policies domestically in the 1930s, it stood in the way of a similar solution at the world level after the war. This attitude is encapsulated in the observation: "John Maynard Keynes at home, Adam Smith on the world market". It can only be explained in that the United States played the hand of the hegemonic power after winning the war. As a result, the principles of free trade and enterprise on the one hand, and those of a controlled economy (in the developing countries) or of central planning (in the socialist countries) to further lagging industrialization entered a collision course.

Alternatives to the world economic order according to the hegemonic power were already put forward in the later 1940s at trade conferences by representatives of Latin American and Asian states. Their acceptance through compromise by the Western core was no doubt also prevented by the distance then taken from the Stalinist Soviet regime. By reference to the normative world standard of human rights this was certainly correct since the deviation of the Soviet Union therefrom became clear in 1948 on the occasion of the final vote on the Universal Declaration at the UN. Though adopted without opposition, the Ukraine, Byelo-Russia, the Soviet Union and its satellites, Poland, Czechoslovakia and Yugoslavia, as also Saudi Arabia and South Africa abstained. At the same time, the distance taken from Stalinist state socialism also provided an excuse to deny any democratic elements or coordinated intervention to the world economy despite the fact that, domestically, such measures had been adopted with success over decades in the welfare-state core.

The adoption of free trade without compromise and its anchoring in the new world economic institutions, such as the World Bank, the IMF and the GATT by the United States, aroused resistance to the West and its world order, first by unsucessful opposition from the periphery, later by the counter-center backed by the military might of the Soviet Union. The rivalry between free enterprise and state socialism soon made the former allies in the fight against the world conflagration lit by Nazi terror into implacable foes in the Cold War. The formation of the new world order was thus marked by vigorous demarcation conflicts with the unacceptable Stalinist regime, creating the East-West rift from the very start.

The absence of a fresh developmental policy to stimulate lagging performances is a typical example of the weak insitutionalisation of the world society model. Mexico's unresolved crisis, elements of which date far back in history, described by Hanspeter Stamm, below, constitutes a case study of the results. The GATT is merely the surviving rump of what was mooted in the 1940s: an International Trade Organization (ITO) within the UN family, which was aborted. Another outcome are the expropriation disputes, especially in Africa, occasioned by ambiguous norms, and the position taken in them by the World Bank as the guarantor of financial orthodoxy expounded by Adeoye Akinsanya, below.

The opposition of the developing countries to the free trade regime led, in 1964, to the establishment of the UN Conference for Trade and Development (UNCTAD) as the voice of the South. But the missing organisational link, which an ITO might have provided, certainly contributed to the insufficiently constructive solution to the North-South confrontation as it escalated towards the end of the 1960s. It attained a peak resembling a class struggle on 1st May 1974, the date of the traditional workers' festival, which was to underline the parallels between the movements of the South and the struggle of the workers' movements in the northern industrial countries. Against the monolithic opposition of the Western core states, the Southern coalition (Group of 77 plus the non-aligned states) then forced through the adoption of the "Declaration for the Foundation of a New International Economic Order" and the "Action Program for the Introduction of a New International Economic Order"(NIEO) at the 6th Special Assembly of the United Nations. Aspects of labor-capital conflicts and world hegemony are analysed below by Beverly Silver, who comes to the conclusion that there is concurrence between rising labor unrest and a crisis of hegemony, the protagonists being primarily those who profited from the latest expansion of the world system. Volker Bornschier and Michael Nollert provide a broad picture of political conflict and labor disputes within the core for the post-war period, concluding that structural properties of states, including the phase of a societal model in which they may find themselves, substantially predict collective action.

The transformation of the world political economy for a dozen years brought about by OPEC through the pricing of that vital raw material, oil, was, at least initially, supposed to be a component of Third World resistance, though the consequences of the price hikes were later to be experienced painfully enough by the developing countries themselves. Other raw material cartels being desired in the 1970s by countries of the South to defend themselves collectively explains why they at first welcomed OPEC's policies as a decisive step towards the idea of Third World control over its own resources.

The confrontation by the South failed in face of the united stand by the Western core, and even the oil weapon finally proved blunt. The North-South developmental dialogue failed, too: retrospectively, it turns out that the 1981 North-South Conference of Cancun (Mexico) marked the end of conflictual reform attempts. In the 1980s, the core countries turned inwards to experiment with unconvincing, fundamentalist market doctrines which included de-regulation, de-nationalisation and the mysterious "supply side" approach, which was theoretically never systematically underpinned. They negotiated with the Third World principally about the settlement of debts, incurred partly through the recycling of petrodollars through Western banks only too eager to make dubiously secured loans, forcing many countries of the South into a financial straitjacket which, in turn, laid them open to the structural adjustments recommended by the IMF. Looking back, one may say that the departure of 1945 did not incorporate long-term, satisfactory conflict-resolution mechanisms within the newly created world society nor could that have been reasonably expected so long as the rivalry between the Western core and the Eastern counter-center offered so many opportunities for conflicts to become entrenched within the risky context of the Cold War escalating into a nuclear holocaust. Johan Kaufmann and associates, below, offer some suggestions for adapting the United Nations as a prominent institutional element of world society, more closely to post-hegemonic requirements, including a reform of the Security Council, new sources of finance and fresh approaches to so-called "domestic" conflicts the consequences of which tend increasingly to spill over boundaries.

Nevertheless, new ideas gradually surfaced in the 1980s, even before entirely unanticipated events transformed the entire world landscape at the end of the decade. For, at that time, the menace of nuclear holocaust, which had hung over world society for decades disappeared, as it were overnight, as a result of a thus far remarkably "silent" revolution. Between 1989 – the fall of the Berlin Wall – and the end of 1991, when the Soviet empire collapsed, the East-West conflict which characterised the entire post-war period was consigned to history, thus freeing mankind from the strategy of atomic overkill known as MAD (Mutually Assured Destruction), adopted by the super-powers for supposed security purposes. In his essay below, Marek Thee discusses the henceforth very different, but far from simple quest for a demilitarized and nuclear-free world.

Almost simultaneously, between 1985 and 1987, awareness of the ecological crisis takes on entirely novel proportions. The ozone hole and global warming, the two most prominent environmental problems, assume global urgency in the second half of the 1980s. Unlike, for example, the loss of biodiversity, forest destruction or the erosion of arable lands which, through their increasingly widespread appearance also constitute world problems, the transformation of the fragile atmospheric chemistry hits the entire Earth with equal impact to an extent hitherto unknown.

Thus, in 1989, the world again experiences a revolutionary year of epochal proportions as a result of which traditional signposts vanished with breathtaking speed. The confrontation between competing systems ends shortly after 1989 with the victory of the capitalistic market order over its chief challenger since the outset of the Industrial Revolution. This victory of the imperfect but open Western societal pattern is fundamental. Since the historic rival has been defeated there is no longer any alternative promise of progress and the improvement of human standards of living. Yet it transpires that the collapse of Communism and the end of the Cold War have not so far brought hoped-for peace as a dividend. Nationalisms and fundamentalisms seem to threaten a sort of world-wide civil war. While regrettable, this is not really surprising following the decay of ideological and power constellations serving orientational functions. Yet the chances for a wider peace in an increasingly democratic world would seem to improve, according to Bruce Russett's assessment below, since democracies shun wars with each other. Reaching back, like Russett, to Immanuel Kant's design for eternal peace, Georg Kohler also speculates along such lines, following the end of the simulated third world war in which the winner outbid the loser in weaponry squandering, which he likens to a gigantic potlatch. There is, after all, a very appreciable difference between the outbreak of local armed conflicts (often in the nature of civil wars, as in former Yugoslavia or the Transcaucasian region, based on ethnic rivalries) and the threat of world nuclear war. Local conflicts can be controlled by determined international effort and even terrorism has become less menacing now that many of its agents have lost their bases and sources of support in the former Soviet bloc, depending for them more on certain rogue regimes themselves the object of international opprobrium.

Prospectively the question is whether the victorious market societies of the West will find the means to correct the world welfare deficit as well as the threatening environmental crisis. To answer this question briefly we must first remember that fresh orientations start in the mind. Really significant departures always begin by making suddenly concilable what was hitherto considered irreconcilable. Environment and development have become known as the two urgent challenges. What attitude is being taken to them after the "victory of the market"?

Since the counter-culture movements, often dated as beginning in 1968, ecological and developmental concerns have featured on the agendas of opposition social and political trends rooted in the anti-authoritarian youth protests of the 1960s and diffused throughout broader intellectual strata. These have, since the 1970s, increasingly defined political landscapes, especially in the central societies, albeit winning but limited legislative representation. In such opposition movements, which are not free of fundamentalist limitations because they do not take sufficiently into account the need to act responsibly in politics and to win votes, the market and the environment on one hand, and the market and development on the other have long stood in diametrical contradiction. Yet the increasingly wide acceptance of such diagnoses together with the manifest "victory of the market" alter the framework for further thinking. The counter-project to market societies has missed its historic opportunity, not least because, in its real incarnation, it could not guarantee human rights, perverted the idea of social equality through self-inflicted shortages that had to be shared by too many and failed even more miserably than the market economies to grapple with environmental problems. H.C.F. Mansilla, in his detailed account below of the forces leading to the destruction of the Bolivian lowland forests, describes the cross-currents that determine the perception of environmental issues in a particular case that certainly has wider implications.

We propose now to broach briefly recent thinking with respect to the triad development, ecology and the market. Within the oppositional movement of the Group of 77 and the non-aligned states, which articulated its political claims through the NIEO, the traditional growth model was to be adopted in the interests of greater equity for the South through re-distribution, accompanied by interventions in the market, or even its total eradication. Environmental problems were neglected, being perceived as luxuries for the rich.

Such attitudes were also supported and politically endorsed by broad sections of the oppositional movements in the highly developed world. Yet ecological demands clearly originated in the core countries: they were an early part of youth agitation in the United States in favor of "the care and feeding of a small planet", according to one then popular motto. A fundamental critique of economic growth based on the plundering of the Earth's resources was issued in 1972, when Dennis Meadows' Club of Rome report, *The Limits of Growth* attracted much attention. This had, in fact, been preceded by warning from other quarters, not primarily focussed on the environment, such as E.J. Mishan's *The Costs of Economic Growth* (1967) and his *Growth: the Price We Pay* (1969) and was to be followed by an extensive literature, both technical and general, including E.F. Schumacher's best-selling *Small is Beautiful* (1973), with its impassioned anti-nuclear power stand and plea in favor of intermediate technology, which became a counter-culture bible. Ecological awareness was thus raised, amplified by the media, but for long the reconciliation of the contradiction between catching up with development and the finiteness of the world's resources remained baffling. The view that the distribution of life chances might be a zero-sum game did not open up any solutions to the puzzle of satisfying demands for participation in welfare while simultaneously attending to the urgency of protecting the natural bases of life.

In the same year in which Meadows' book appeared, there occurred another key event which was to focus the discourse on the linkage between development and ecology, the 1972 Stockholm Conference on the Human Environment.[2] Lobbies from the industrial core succeeded in placing environmental problems on the agenda of a conference originally sponsored by Sweden but organized under UN auspices, at a time when questions of re-distribution within the framework of the traditional growth model held the almost exclusive attention of the majority of the UN's members. It was in Stockholm that the first negotiations about environment and development took place. The linkage first remained weak though re-inforced by the formulation launched by the then Indian Prime Minister, Indira Gandhi: "Poverty is the biggest polluter."

The Stockholm conference decided to establish the UN Environmental Program (UNEP), endowed with but modest funding, to be located in Nairobi, a symbolic concession to the South. This was followed by such initiatives as the International Geophysical Year and the launching of the Man and the Biosphere Program (MAB) based at UNESCO. Key theoretical work was accomplished, such as pioneering notions of industrial metabolism and the "throughput economy" which stressed recycling, and systemic reasoning on dissipative structures and self-organizing systems. Many thinkers profoundly impressed by ecological imperatives became prominent, including the philosophical anthropologist Gregory Bateson, the ecologist Barry Commoner, the French agronomist, René Dumont, the culture critic Theodore Roszak, the economist Kenneth Boulding, the physicist Fritjof Capra as well as certain women's righters. The media, of course, amplified ecological discourses in a more or less spotty and anecdotal fashion in the West, much less elsewhere.

Despite such efforts, the environment remained a marginal world issue in the 1970s. The North-South Commission under the chairmanship of Willy Brandt began in 1977 to work on the then chief problem of a cosmopolitan domestic policy *(Weltinnenpolitik)* to stem the widening gap in welfare. In its reports of 1980 *(North-South: A Programme for Survival)* and 1983 *(Common Crisis North-South: Cooperation for World Recovery)* it recommended a global, developmental Keynesianism to extend a century's social-democratic achievements to the world at large by revitalising the traditional growth model through an injection of greater social equity. While perhaps a possible blueprint in its day, such an approach now seems outdated, for two reasons. In the first place, Keynesian management of the core economies is no longer working as it should, as witness high unemployment and other ills. To what extent this may be due to technological innovation, to inexperience in the running of a globalized economy or to other factors cannot be broached here. In the second place, however, the center of economic dynamism appears to be shifting fast from the traditional core countries particularly to the East Asian area. One may thus speculate that the traditional core may not remain the chief exporter of developmental stimuli for very much longer, these also coming from other sources. One result is that it is now certain East Asian countries that press for free trade, feeling confident that they can compete successfully on world markets, while the EC and the United States are turning warily to forms of protectionism in the face precisely of this offensive. The long and initially very slow progress from Stockholm in 1972 to the "Earth Summit" of Rio de Janeiro in 1992 leads via the UNEP meeting in Nairobi ten years after this body had been mandated with its task by the international community. The results were meagre and the Scandinavian countries in particular were highly critical. The Nairobi meeting led to the establishment of a committee of UNEP that was to set environmental perspectives to the year 2000 and beyond. The UN General Assembly then decided also to create a special World Commission on Environment and Development (WCED) chaired by the Norwegian Prime Minister, Gro Harlem Brundtland, who had the benefit of her experience as minister for the environment.

This Commission submitted its report, *Our Common Future*, in 1987. It marks a qualitative modification of the general approach. For a start, development and ecology were explicitly linked. Then the idea of development was newly formulated in "sustainable" terms, to secure future requirements to avoid the risk that coming generations might no longer be able to meet their needs. In the Brundtland report development is no longer simply equated with growth but rather interpreted in terms of a transformation of economy and society with the aim of satisfying human needs and aspirations. Unlike the earlier Brandt Commission reports, the Brundtland report's vision was not simply pigeonholed but rather served as a fundamental substantive input for the "Environmental Perspective" which the United Nations adopted in 1987 and which significantly influenced the "Earth Summit" of Rio in 1992, held under the leadership of Maurice Strong, a member of WCED and founder as well as first Executive Director of UNEP.

The concept of sustainable development represents a remarkable *Changing Course - Global Perspective on Development and Environment*, the title of an influential book by Stephan Schmidheiny with the Business Council for Sustainable Development (1992). Ecology and development are here amalgamated into ecodevelopment, to be pursued by means of market forces. The key notion is the internalization of environmental costs so that the pricing of goods and services will also provide guidance as to their environment sustainability. Not a restriction of the market but rather its extension is seen as the basis for sutainable development: in this way, the old principle of free trade is revived, albeit under fresh societal assumptions. It is further remarkable that an influential group of enlightened businessmen is prepared not merely to contemplate a radical transformation in the rules of the game but actually to participate therein. The Business Council for Sustainable Development has some 50 members across the world representing leading firms who are no doubt taking such steps in their own interests and in order not to lose political clout.

If ecological and economic aims are no longer viewed as antagonistic but integrated into a synthesis to create harmony between citizens and between mankind and nature then we are in the presence of a revolution in economic doctrine for which, in this century, there is only one equivalent: the Keynesian revolution which sought to make welfare, redistribution and stable growth compatible, a synthesis which earlier seemed beyond the grasp of bourgeois economics and subsequently became the ideological support for the successful welfare states of the highly industrialized countries.[3]

New departures need means as well as ideas: a realistic assessment of possibilities deserves brief consideration. The capital requirements for investments to pursue ecodevelopment in the developing countries alone has been estimated at $ 600 billion annually (cf. Kaufmann et al. below), a vast sum by comparison with the annual flow of some $ 65 billion in official aid. Part of this may be raised by limiting outlays on armaments by the needy developing countries which, with the end of the Cold War, no longer seems like mere wishful thinking. The reduction of tariffs by the core countries on exports from the periphery might raise the revenues of the latter by some $ 150 billion. That still leaves a considerable gap that needs to be filled by some scheme of global taxation which also would be market-driven, as mentioned below by Johan Kaufmann and his co-authors. Different weightings in the processes reflecting conflict and bargaining in government budgeting, as modelled by Georg Müller, below, will have to be adopted if there is to be even a remote chance of rasing such sums.

At the Rio "Earth Summit" (UNCED) of 1992 the interests of the center and the periphery still clashed markedly: there were also differences within each camp. The "Rio Declaration", originally prepared as the "Earth Charter", was to have been an epoch-making document comparable to the Universal Declaration of Human Rights. As the price of agreement many programs lost their teeth (Agenda 21) not least owing to concessions to the United States on the one hand, and Saudi Arabia, as the leader of the oil producers on the other. But in the United States there has since been a renunciation of the policies of the 1980s under President Clinton. A social democratic and ecologically inspired direction seems now to be taken in this leading country, without the participation of which little can be realistically accomplished. At any rate, the large number of ecologically active non-governmental organizations principally from the North, present at Rio was noticeable, an example of a world "civil society" which loudly championed the needs of the South. For, if the redistributional demands of the South were, during the 1970s, legitimated by the sins of colonialism, this changed in the 1990s. It is now argued that the industrial development of the North has consumed too great a share of the common environmental assets and that compensation for the South is only equitable. Also, as Julius Ihonvbere shows, below, there is greater readiness on the part of Third World countries to blame some of their miseries on their own mistakes.

If the wealthy have been reluctant to compensate generously for the deeds of their ancestors they are surely easier to convince if it is demonstrated that their own future is at stake. By the same token, however, the poor cannot allow themselves to wallow in righteousness and will have to tackle their problems with the energies that made the rich rich while profiting from the fact that they can get help and draw on advantages which have allowed certain latecomers to industrialization to become successful in record time. All of that, however, supposes that the Western economies can pull out of their current depression which certainly does not dispose politicians to favor external causes when so many needs cry out internally. Much, too, will depend on how well and how fast the formerly socialist countries, particularly the Commonwealth of Independent States, can become solvent and occupy an appropriate place in the international division of labor and world trade. For there can be little doubt but that the semi-autarky in which they dwelt for so long, the natural and human resources they squandered and the social decay created by decades of a totalitarianism that claimed to defend public interests as opposed to the allegedly selfish individualism of the market system have largely contributed to world imbalances. That the socialist bloc was for so long practically immune from criticism by the South on the grounds that it was an ally in confrontations with the West is one of those great ironies on which historians may dwell when some distance has been gained from our painful 20th century.

Yet, as Georg Kohler forcefully underlines at the end of his essay, the "victory of the market" cannot be taken entirely at face value. "The market and economic competition are themselves political institutions. They are never to be understood only as arrangements of the economic system ... politics can never be reduced to the economic dimension". In practice, this means that there will be continuing perplexities in optimal policy mixes for sustainable ecodevelopment in any context. Particularly, changing balances and trade-offs will need to be struck between the private and the public sectors as the logic of interdependence drives home. Mixed economies no doubt lie in the future, as they have been functioning in the past, though often but grudgingly acknowledged by devout supporters of free enterprise or socialism. Not all the values that need to inform world society can be met by market mechanisms, and some might even conflict with them.

Finally, it is essential to recall that, when a world society was initiated in 1945, the Earth's population stood at some 2.5 billion. It has more than doubled in only 50 years since, and may, according to certain UN projections, stand at around 10 billion by 2050, representing an annual growth rate of 1.7%. Obviously, this in itself exerts enormous pressure on environments and resources. If it was one thing to aspire to the extension of developmental benefits to the world population as it was in 1945, it is quite another thing today, not to speak of the numbers that lie ahead. On the contrary, the fear is now being fanned that the affluent countries may actually be overwhelmed by the poor masses, directly (eg. through uncontrollable migration) or indirectly (eg. through environmental degradation, resource exhaustion or commercial competition). Right-wing and nationalistic political movements are playing on these fears with some success. It is thus not too early to envision a final possible confrontation in world society: that between an ageing, besieged core, ever more inward-looking and defensive, and a desperate, youthful, armed and aggressive periphery at the end of its patience. If such a catastrophic scenario sounds too depressing to contemplate then perhaps the energetic curbing of our species' reproductive exuberance deserves, after all, to be placed squarely at the top of the ecodevelopmental agenda.

NOTES

1 Further details on these matters and the various sources for the following paragraphs are to be found in Volker Bornschier, "Gesellschaftsmodell und seine Karriere. Eine Anwendung auf die Weltgesellschaft," pp. 21-54 in Volker Bornschier et al. (eds.), *Diskontinuität des sozialen Wandels. Entwicklung als Abfolge von Gesellschaftsmodellen und kulturellen Deutungsmustern*, Frankfurt and New York: Campus, 1990.

2 In the following paragraphs we also draw on materials and sources collected by Andreas Missbach and Martin Anderhalden for their contributions to Bornschier's seminar on World Economy in winter 1992-93.

3 The evolution of the whole environmental debate can conveniently be followed in successive issues of the *International Social Science Journal*, "Controlling the Human Environment" (Vol. XXII, No. 4, 1970), "Man in Ecosystems" (No. 93, 1982), "Environmental Awareness" (No. 109, 1986), "Reconciling the Sociosphere and the Biosphere" (No. 121, 1989) and "Global Environmental Change" (No. 130, 1991).

I
Peace and War

1   THE DEMOCRATIC PEACE

Bruce Russett

The vision of a world society of democratically governed states at peace with one another has long been invoked as part of a structure of institutions and practices to promote peace among nation-states. Immanuel Kant (1795/1970) spoke of perpetual peace based partially upon states sharing "republican constitutions". His meaning was compatible with basic contemporary understandings of democracy. As the elements of such a constitution he identified freedom, with legal equality of subjects, representative government, and separation of powers. The other key elements of his perpetual peace were "cosmopolitan law" embodying ties of international commerce and free trade, and a "pacific union" established by treaty in international law among republics. Woodrow Wilson expressed the same vision for the twentieth century. His 1917 war message to Congress shows why he believed "a steadfast concert of peace can never be maintained except by a partnership of democratic nations:

> "We have no quarrel with the German people ... It was not upon their impulse that their government acted in entering this war. It was not with their previous knowledge or approval. It was a war determined upon as wars used to be determined upon in the old unhappy days when peoples were nowhere consulted by their rulers and wars were provoked and

---

This article (© Princeton University Press) is drawn from the research project "A Democratic and Therefore Peaceful World Society?" funded by the World Society Foundation. Bruce Russett is Dean Acheson Professor of International Relations and Political Science at Yale University, Department of Political Science, P.O. Box 3532 Yale Station, New Haven, Connecticut 06520-3532, U.S.A.

waged in the interest of dynasties or of little groups of ambitious men who were accustomed to use their fellow men as pawns and tools. Self-governed nations do not fill their neighbor states with spies or set the course of intrigue to bring about some critical posture of affairs which will give them an opportunity to strike and make conquest... Cunningly contrived plans of deception or aggression, carried, it may be from generation to generation, can be worked out and kept from the light only within the privacy of courts or behind the carefully guarded confidences of a narrow and privileged class."

The Spread of Democratic Peace

At the time of Kant, and even of Wilson, the hope for a world of democratic nation-states was merely that: a hope, a theory perhaps, but without much empirical referent. Europe in 1795 was hardly an area in which republics flourished. By Wilson's time there were more, in the new world as well as the old, but the dozen or so democracies of that era still were substantially in a minority. Since democracies were mostly few and far between, their failure to fight each other was little noticed. States need both an opportunity and a willingness (Most and Starr 1989) to go to war with each other. Non-contiguous democracies, unless one or both were great powers, had little opportunity to fight each other. States cannot fight unless they can exert substantial military power against each others' vital territory. Most states, if not great powers with "global reach" (large navies in this era), could exert such power only against contiguous states or at least near neighbors. Furthermore, states' willingness to fight depends in large part on issues over which they have conflicts of interest. Territorial disputes (over borders, or rights of ethnic groups whose presence is common to both) are rare in the absence of proximity (Diehl and Goertz 1992). Since relatively few democracies bordered or were even very near each other in the 1920s and 1930s, it is not surprising that they generally avoided war with each other. Thus the empirical fact of little or no war between democracies could be obscured by the predominance of authoritarian states and the frequent wars involving them.

Following World War II, however, and especially by the 1970s, increasing numbers of democracies emerged and the peace among them became harder to ignore. There were at one time by various counts 35 or so democratic states, and more of them were proximate to one another. Still there was little war, or even serious threat, of war, to be found in relationships among those democracies. The phenomenon of democratic peace more clearly extended beyond merely the rich industrialized countries belonging to the OECD. It began then to be more widely recognized, and by the end of the 1980s it had been widely accepted in the international relations literature, though not so easily explained. This research result is extremely robust, in that by various criteria of war and militarized diplomatic disputes, and various measures of democracy, the relative rarity of violent conflict between democracies still holds up.[1] By 1992 it had even passed into popular political rhetoric, with the international zone of "democratic peace" invoked in speeches by both American presidential candidates.

Wide recognition is not, however, synonymous with universal acceptance. It became confused with a claim that democracies are *in general*, in their dealings with all kinds of states, more peaceful than are authoritarian or other nondemocratically-constituted states. This is a much more controversial proposition than "merely" that democracies are peaceful in their dealings with each other, and one for which there is little systematic evidence.[2] Especially in the Vietnam era of U.S. "imperial overreach", it was politically charged and widely disbelieved.

Furthermore, some variants of the proposition took the form of statements like "democracies never go to war with each other", or even "democracies never fight each other". The latter, applied to relatively low-level lethal violence, is demonstrably wrong as a law-like "never" statement even for the modern international system. The former, limiting the statement to the large-scale and typically sustained form of organized international violence commonly designated as war, nonetheless begs the historically-minded reader to come up with counterexamples. And, especially with the key terms still largely undefined, it is not hard to identify candidate counterexamples.

Some Precision about Terminology

In a new book (Russett 1993) I establish the following: First, democratically-organized political systems operate under restraints that make them relatively peaceful in their relations with other democracies. Democracies are not necessarily peaceful, however, in relations with other kinds of political systems. Second, in the modern international system, democracies are less likely to use lethal violence toward other democracies than toward autocratically-governed states or than autocratically-governed states are toward each other. Third, peace between democracies is importantly a result of some features of democracy, rather than caused exclusively by economic or geopolitical characteristics merely correlated with democracy. The causal forces are a combination of structural and normative restraints, producing a set of conclusions: 1) Structural / institutional features of democratic systems constraints make it hard for democracies to go to war rapidly unless they are attacked, and hard to prepare for war in secret. 2) Two democratic states disputing with each other therefore need not fear sudden or surprise attack from each other, and thus know they have time to resolve conflict through peaceful means of negotiation and mediation ("Democracies need not fight each other"). 3) Each of two democratic states in a dispute knows that the other, like itself, follows and understands norms of compromise and peaceful conflict resolution, so the norms of peaceful conflict resolution can also operate between them ("Democracies should not fight each other").

Further discussion requires some conceptual precision. Without it everyone can – and often does – endlessly debate counterexamples while by-passing the phenomenon itself. We need to define what we mean by democracy and war, so as to be able to say just how rare it is for two democracies to go to war with each other. When we do so it becomes evident that such occasions virtually never arise.

Interstate war

War here means large-scale institutionally-organized lethal violence, and by large-scale we designate the threshold commonly used in the social scientific literature on war: 1000 battle fatalities (Small and Singer 1982). The figure of 1000 deaths is arbitrary but reasonable. It is meant to eliminate from the category of wars those violent events that might plausibly be ascribed to:

-"Accident" (e.g., planes that may have strayed across a national boundary by mistake, and been downed).

-Deliberate actions by local commanders, but not properly authorized by central authorities, as in many border incidents.

-Limited, local authorized military actions not necessarily intended to escalate to large-scale violent conflict but undertaken more as bargaining moves in a crisis, such as military probes intended to demonstrate one's own commitment and to test an adversary's resolve.

-Deliberate military actions larger than mere probes, but not substantially resisted by a usually much weaker adversary. The Soviet invasion of Czechoslovakia in 1968, which was met with substantial non-violent resistance but not force of arms and resulted in less than a score of immediate deaths, is such an example, and contrasts with the Soviet invasion of Hungary in 1956 which produced roughly 17 000 Hungarian and Soviet dead.

A threshhold of 1000 battle deaths rather neatly cuts off the above kinds of events while leaving largely intact the category of most conflicts that intuitively satisfy the commonsense meaning of war. (Not of course such rhetorical examples as a "war on poverty" or "war on drugs", or for that matter the boat seizures and very limited exchange of gunfire (no casualties) between Britain and Iceland in the 1975 "Cod War" over fishing rights.) It is also convenient that the 1000 battle-death threshhold provides a neat empirical break, with few conflicts between nation-states very near it on either side.

In many wars civilian deaths far out-number those of combatants. Deaths from hunger and disease may also far out-number battle-inflicted casualties, as surely happened in many nineteenth century wars and may well have been the case of the post-war sufferings of Iraqis after Operation Desert Storm. But the number of such deaths may be difficult or impossible to estimate reliably and may be more a consequence of medical and public health capabilities than military actions. Without minimizing their human consequences, it is simply less ambiguous to limit the definition to battle deaths.

A related problem is deciding which political units get to be listed as fighting in a war. Sometimes, in coalition warfare, most or all of the deaths will be borne by one or a few contestants, with other contestants formally but not practically engaged in combat. For the latter, especially in circumstances where a nominal combatant suffers few or *no* identifiable deaths at all, it seems strained to include it among war participants. Small and Singer (1982, ch. 4) use a criterion requiring a state either to commit at least 1000 troops to battle, or to suffer at least 100 battle fatalities in order to count as a participant.

This definition also excludes, on theoretical grounds, covert actions in which one government secretly undertakes activities, including the use of lethal violence and the support of violent actors within the other government's territory, either to coerce or to overthrow that government.

Such activities may not involve deaths on the scale of "wars", and when they do the foreign intervention is by its very covert nature hard to document (though one can often, if perhaps belatedly, discover the metaphoric "smoking gun"). But these activities, precisely because they are denied by the acting government at the time, imply very different political processes than does a war publicly and officially undertaken. Because they may be undertaken under circumstances when overt war is not acceptable they receive special attention in the book.

Theoretical precision demands yet another definition, of "interstate" war. Here that term means war between sovereign "states" internationally recognized as such by other states, including by major powers whose recognition of a government typically confers *de facto* statehood. Some such definition focussing on organized independent states is common in the social science literature, and is important here. It is meant to exclude "colonial" wars either for the acquisition of territory inhabited by "primitive" people as practiced by nineteenth century imperialism or, for the twentieth-century liberation of those people. War it may certainly be, but interstate it is not unless or until both sides are generally recognized as having the attributes of statehood. Applying this definition may display a Western cultural bias, but it is appropriate to the behavior of states which, in the period, are also defined as "democratic" by the admittedly Western standards spelled out below. Non-state participants do not meet these standards.

Wars of liberation – with one or both parties not yet recognized as a state – are in this respect similar to civil wars, in that one or both parties to the conflict fight precisely so as to be free of sharing statehood with the other. Such wars are fought to escape from the coercive institutions of a common state, and to include them would confuse rather than clarify the generalization that democracies rarely go to war with each other. A crucial element in that generalization depends upon the role of democratic institutions and practices in promoting peaceful conflict resolution within states. Intrastate conflicts that become so fierce that lethal violence is common often indicate that the institutions of the state have become the problem rather than the solution. For example, the United Kingdom and the Republic of Ireland have lived in peace with each other, as separate states, since 1922; the conflict in Northern Ireland arises precisely because many people there emphatically do not wish to be governed as part of the existing common political structure. Democracies are only slightly less likely than other kinds of states to experience civil war (Bremer 1992b).

Democracy

For modern states, democracy (or polyarchy, following Dahl 1971) is usually identified with a voting franchise for a substantial fraction of citizens, a government brought to power in contested elections, and an executive either popularly elected or responsible to an elected legislature, often also with requirements for civil liberties such as free speech.[3] Huntington (1991: 7, 9) uses very similar criteria: "a twentieth-century political system is democratic to the extent that its most powerful collective decision makers are selected through fair, honest, and periodic elections in which candidates freely compete for votes and in which virtually all the adult population is eligible to vote", identifying a free election for transfer of power from a non-democratic government as "the critical point in the process of democratization". Ray (1992) similarly requires that the possibility for the leaders of the government to be defeated in an election and replaced has been demonstrated by historical precedent.

A simple dichotomy between democracy and autocracy, of course, hides real shades of difference, and mixed systems share features of both. Moreover, the precise application of these terms is to some degree culturally and temporally dependent. Nineteenth century democracies often had property qualifications for the vote, typically excluded women, and the United States – democratic by virtually any standard of the day – disenfranchised blacks. Britain, with its royal prerogatives, rotten boroughs, and very restricted franchise before the Reform Bill of 1832, could hardly be counted as a democracy. Even that reform brought voting rights to less than one-fifth of adult males, so one might reasonably withold the "democracy" designation until after the Second Reform Bill of 1867, or even until the secret ballot was introduced in 1872. By then, at the latest, Britain took its place with the relatively few other states commonly characterized as democratic in the parlance of the era.

If in the middle and late nineteenth century we admit countries with as few as 10% of all adults eligible to vote as democratic (a criterion used by Small and Singer 1976; Doyle 1986 uses a cut of 30% of all males), by the middle-to-late twentieth century nothing less than a substantially universal franchise will suffice. The term "contested elections" admits similar ambiguities, but rather quickly it came to require two or more legally recognized parties in practice. States with significant prerogatives in foreign affairs for non-elected agents (e.g., monarchs) should be excluded as having non-responsible executives, even in the nineteenth century.

By the middle-to-late twentieth century the matter of guaranteed and respected civil rights, including rights to political organization and political expression, also become a key element in any commonsense definition of democracy (Dahl 1989). The exercise of such civil rights tends to be highly correlated with the existence of democratic institutions as just elaborated, but not perfectly so. The institutions may be found without the regular widespread exercise of the rights; the opposite (civil liberties assured, but not democratic institutions) is rarer. For purposes of the discussion here we will nevertheless not use civil liberties *per se* as a defining quality, and we shall also ignore the matter of free-market economic liberties. While there is very likely a causal nexus of economic liberties making possible secure political freedom, the relationship is complex and, unlike some authors (Rummel 1983, Doyle 1986) it will not be built into the definition here. In not including civil rights and economic liberty as defining qualities of democracy we are lowering the standards by which a country can be labelled a democracy. That is highly relevant to our next step, which is to look at a list of conflicts alleged by some scholars to be wars between democracies. By lowering the standards we are making it *more* likely that some events will be labelled wars between democracies – events which I and many other writers contend are, at most, exceedingly rare.

Theoretical precision, however, requires one further qualification: some rather minimal stability or longevity. Huntington (1991: 11) emphasizes, stability or institutionalization as "a central dimension in the analysis of any political system". Doyle (1986) requires that representative government be in existence for at least three years prior to a war for the war to count as one waged by a democracy. Perhaps that is a bit too long, yet some period must have elapsed during which democratic processes and institutions could become established, and both the citizens of the "democratic" state and its adversary could regard it as one governed by democratic principles. Most of the doubtful cases arise within a single year of the establishment of democratic government.

By application of these criteria it is impossible to identify unambiguously *any* wars between democratic states since 1815. A few close calls exist, in which some relaxation of the criteria could produce such a case. But to have no clearcut cases, out of about 71 interstate wars involving a total of nearly 270 participants, is impressive. Even these numbers are deceptively low as representing total possibilities. For example, as listed by Small and Singer (1982), 21 states count as participating on the allied side in World War II, with 8 on the Axis side. Thus in that war alone there were 168 pairs of warring states. Allowing for other multilateral wars, approximately 500 pairs of states went to war against each other in the period. Of these, fewer than a handful can, with any plausibility at all, be considered "candidates" for exceptions to a generalization that democracies do not fight each other.

Some Alleged Wars between Democracies

To see what these criteria produce, consider the list in Table 1 of wars that have sometimes been suggested as exceptions to the generalization that democracies do not go to war with each other.

TABLE 1 Some "candidate" wars between democracies

1. War of 1812, U.S. and Great Britain
2. Roman Republic (Papal States) vs. France, 1849
3. American Civil War, 1861
4. Ecuador-Colombia, 1863
5. Franco-Prussian War
6. Boer War
7. Spanish-American War, 1898
8. Second Philippine War, 1899
9. World War I, Imperial Germany vs. Western democracies
10. World War II, Finland vs. Western democracies
11. Lebanon vs. Israel, 1948
12. Lebanon vs. Israel, 1967

Three should be dismissed immediately because they clearly fall outside of the criteria established even for any kind of interstate war in the period. The first, the War of 1812, is easy to dismiss simply because it precedes the beginning date – 1815 – of the most standard compilation of all wars. That may seem like a cheap and arbitrary escape, but it is not. There simply were very few democracies in the international system before that date, and as already discussed, though Britain had moved quite far from royal absolutism it just did not fit the criteria either of suffrage or of a fully responsible executive.

Wars number 3 and 8 are also readily eliminated as plausible candidates by straightforward use of the definitions. Whatever it may be called below the Mason-Dixon line, number 3 was a civil war in that the Confederacy never gained international recognition of its sovereignty; as a war for separation or to prevent separation it comes under our rubric of wars induced by the frictions of sharing common statehood. War number 8 was a colonial war, in which the United States was trying to solidify control of a former Spanish colony it had acquired. The Philippine resistance constituted an authentic war of resistance against colonialism, but not on the part of an elected democratic government. This is not in any way to denigrate the resistance, but merely to insist on a distinction that is important. Especially by the standards of Western ethnocentric attitudes at the time, Philippine resistance was not widely regarded as "democratic" in a way that would induce either normative or institutional constraints on the United States.

The Boer War begun in 1899 also fails to fit the requirements for an interstate war. Small and Singer (1982) identify it as an extra-systemic war because the South African Republic was not generally recognized as an independent state. Britain recognized only its internal sovereignty, retaining "suzerainty" and requiring it to submit all treaties to the British government for approval. This, too, is properly an unsuccesful war for independence. Moreover, the two Boer Republics strained the definition of democracy, then as for almost a century subsequently. Suffrage was restricted not merely to the white male minority (roughly 10% of the adult population), but in the South African Republic – by far the larger – the electorate was further reduced, perhaps by half, by a property qualification and long-term residence requirements.[4] (Lacour-Gayet 1978: 168, 170, 182, 194.)

Others readily eliminated include numbers 10 (Finland's participation in World War II on the "wrong" side) and 12. Finland was actively at war only with the Soviet Union, in an attempt to wrest back the territory taken from it in the Winter War of 1939-40. Although nominally at war with the Western allies, there is no record of combat or casualties between Finland and democratic states that would even approach the rather low threshold specified above. In the Six Day War of 1967 Lebanon (still then a unified and fairly democratic state, which it was not when invaded by Israel in 1982) participated in "combat" only by sending a few aircraft into Israeli airspace; the planes were driven back with, apparently, no casualties at all.

Lebanon's participation in the 1948 war was well above the criterion used for a belligerent. Israel, however, had not previously been independent, and had not yet held a national election. While the authenticity of Israel's national leadership was hardly in question, Lebanon – itself only marginally democratic – could not have been expected to accredit it as a democratic state.

The 1863 conflict between Ecuador and Colombia also fits the criteria for war, but neither regime meets any reasonable requirement for democratic stability. Both governments came to power through revolution. Colombia's president governed with a new federal constitution promulgated only in May 1863; Ecuador's Gabriel Garcia Moreno became president two years earlier, but is described as heading an "autocratic regime" (Kohn 1986: 150) and governing "with absolute authority" (Langer 1972: 852). As for France against the Roman Republic, both parties were but ephemerally democratic. Following the revolution of early 1848, presidential elections took place under the new French constitution only in December of that year. The notion of democratic Papal States sounds oxymoronic. The Pope introduced a constitution with an elective council of deputies in 1848, but reserved veto power to himself and the college of cardinals. After an insurrection in November, he fled and the Roman Republic was proclaimed in February 1849. Within two months the Republic was at war with France.

The Franco-Prussian War can be eliminated simply by looking at France. Reforms ratified in the plebiscite of May 1870 could be interpreted as making the empire into a constitutional monarchy, but war began a mere two months later. In Prussia / Germany the emperor appointed and could dismiss the chancellor; a defeat in the Reichstag did not remove the chancellor from office. The emperor's direct authority over the army and foreign policy deprives the state of the democratic criterion of "responsible executive" on war and peace matters; Berghahn (1973: 9) calls the constitutional position of the monarchy "almost absolutist". Doyle (1986) rightly excludes Imperial Germany from his list of liberal states. Such a decision removes World War I from the candidate list.

The most difficult case is the Spanish-American War of 1898. Spain after 1890 had universal male suffrage, and a bicameral legislature with an executive nominally responsible to it. But the reality was more complex. The ministry was selected by the king, who thus remained the effective ruler of the state. Nominally competitive elections were really manipulated by a processes known as *caciquismo*. By mutual agreement, the Liberal and Conservative parties rotated in office; governmental changes preceded rather than following elections. Through extensive corruption and administrative procedures the king and politicians in Madrid controlled the selection of parliamentary candidates and their election. Election results were often published in the press before polling day. The meaningless elections were thus manipulated by the king and his close advisers; the system lacked the democratic quality of a responsible executive (Carr 1980: 10-15). None of the large-scale analyses of the question of democracies fighting each other (cited in footnote 1) puts Spain among the democratic countries, nor do most major long-term political surveys. (Vanhanen 1984, Banks 1971, Gurr et al. 1989 code it as sharing democratic and autocratic characteristics.)

It seems, therefore, best to treat it as a close call but probably not a refutation even of the strong form (i.e., democracies *never* make war on each other). Equally important, as we shall see later, is the matter of perceptions. The Spanish political situation was at best marginal enough for key United States decision-makers readily to persuade themselves and their audiences that it was not democratic. Consider, for example, the remarks of the two Republican Senators from Massachusetts. Senator Henry Cabot Lodge: "We are there because we represent the spirit of liberty and the spirit of the new time, and Spain is over against us because she is mediaeval, cruel, dying." Senator George Hoar: "The results of a great war [on which the U.S. was embarking] are due to the policy of the king and the noble and the tyrant, not the policy of the people." (*Congressional Record,* April 13, 1898: 3783, and April 14, 1898: 3831.)

Subsequent to my writing the above, Ray (1992) has presented a thorough review of these and other alleged cases of wars between democracies, and concludes that the generalization of no wars between democracies remains true. Whether one holds to the lawlike "never" statement or not may not really be very important. Almost all of the few near misses are in the nineteenth century, an era of generally very imperfect democracy by modern criteria.

Depending on the precise criteria, only 12 to 15 states qualified as democracies at the end of the nineteenth century. The empirical significance of the rarity of war between democracies emerges only in the first half of the twentieth century, with at least twice the number of democracies as earlier, and especially with the existence of perhaps 60 democracies by the mid-1980s. Since the statistical likelihood of war between democracies is related to the number of pairs of democracies, the contrast between the two centuries is striking: by a very loose definition, possibly three or four wars out of roughly 60 pairs before 1900, and no more than one or two out of around 1800 subsequent pairs.[5] As twentieth-century politics unfold, the phenomenon of war between democracies becomes impossible or almost impossible to find. Even the kind of crisis-bargaining that uses military force in a threatening manner becomes rare between democracies. Not quite absent, but extremely rare. And if there is crisis-bargaining, it does not escalate to the point of war.

Table 2 illustrates these facts in data on all militarized diplomatic disputes from 1946 to 1986. "Dyad" means a pair of states; the table counts each year of existence separately, thus Britain and France in 1946 constitute one

TABLE 2 Dispute behavior of politically-relevant interstate dyads, 1946-1986

Highest level of dispute	Both states democratic	One or both non-democratic	Total dyads
No dispute	3 864	24 503	28 367
Disputes:			
Threat of force	2 (5.6)	39 (35.4)	41
Display of force	4 (12.5)	116 (107.5)	120
Use of force	8 (23.3)	513 (497.8)	521
War	0 (4.3)	32 (27.7)	32
Totals	3 878	25 203	29 081
Escalation probabilities:			
To threat of force	0.05%	0.16%	
To display of force	85.70%	94.40%	
To use of force	57.10%	79.00%	
To war	0.00%	4.60%	

observation, and another in 1947. The highest level of conflict reached in the dispute between that pair of states is identified. (Disputes that spill over into two or more years are counted only in the year they began or escalated to a higher level.) Contrasting with the number of actual disputes in each cell is, in parenthesis, the number that would be "expected" if disputes were distributed randomly. The phrase "politically-relevant dyads" refers to all pairs of states that are contiguous or at least somewhat geographically proximate to each other, or where one of the states in the pair is a major power and hence has military "global reach". This recognizes, as noted above, that the majority of states in the international system lack the means or the interest to engage in militarized disputes with each other, and hence are irrelevant to a serious analysis.[6]

The information in this table has several rich implications. There were no wars between democracies, and even though the number of democratic dyads is relatively small, if they had fought wars as frequently with each other as chance would predict, there would have been four wars between democracies. Note also that in this period there were only 14 instances of disputing pairs involving even the threat of military force by one democracy against another. The odds that any pair of politically-relevant democratic states would have a militarized dispute, at any level, in a year during this period were only 1 in 276. By contrast, if one or both states in the pair was not a democracy, the odds were as short as 1 in 40 – seven times greater. Surely this is a very dramatic difference in behavior. The actual uses of military force are trivial occasions like the "Cod War", very minor fire by Israel against Britain during the 1956 Suez intervention – in which the British and Israelis were in fact accomplices – brief conflict between British and Turkish forces during a 1963 peacekeeping operation on Cyprus, and Turkish sinking of a Greek boat in 1978.

One can also use the tabular information to calculate "escalation probabilities" for militarized disputes that do occur. For democracies, the chances that any militarized dispute would progress to the point of display of force were consistently lower, at every level, than for pairs in which one or both states were not democracies. For example, only a little more than half of the few disputes between democracies resulted in the actual use of force, whereas more than 80% of all disputes by other kinds of pairs of states escalated to the use of force. For earlier periods (nineteenth century, and 1900-1945) the relationships for conflict-proneness and escalation appear to be in the same direction – democratic pairs of states dispute less – but much weaker than in the post-1945 era (Maoz and Abdolali 1989, Bremer 1992a).

The Emergence of Democratic Peace before World War I

A strong norm that democracies do not fight each other may have developed only towards the end of the nineteenth century. Certainly there were nineteenth-century instances of stable democracies engaging serious diplomatic disputes in which they threatened to use military force in a major fashion, including up to war, but without actually going to war. In the restraint of action short of war between democracies, and in the subsequent evaluation of the crisis by the peoples and elites involved, we can discern some important differences in the expectations and norms operating between democracies than when a democracy entered into an adversarial relationship with an authoritarian state.

During the 1890s Britain was engaged in a dispute with Venezuela over where the boundary between it and British Guyana should lie. Grover Cleveland, the American President, grew exasperated by British unwillingness to submit the matter to arbitration and, invoking the Monroe Doctrine, threatened war. The British, in turn, took four months to reply – and then rejected the United States position. Cleveland sought and obtained a congressional appropriation of funds for a boundary commission – in effect, enforced arbitration by the United States. In subsequent discussion the United States offered to exclude from arbitration areas settled by British subjects for at least two generations, or 60 years. Charles Campbell (1974: 185) says this "unexpected reversal virtually ensured an early termination of the controversy". With it the British in turn backed down, and agreed to arbitration which ultimately decided the issue by a compromise, but one generally favoring Venezuela. In doing so "Great Britain made almost all the concessions, and all the important ones" (A. E. Campbell 1960: 27). Then the United States pressured the Venezuelans to accept the decision.

Clearly the British Prime Minister, Lord Salisbury, misjudged the American government's determination, and he was not willing to fight a war. Of Cleveland's intention we cannot be certain, but his actions look more like those of a poker player who expected his bluff to work, and not to be called. Both sides "blinked" in some degree – especially the British, at a time when their relations with Germany were deteriorating and they did not need another enemy.

While important in preventing an Anglo-American war over this bagatelle, British strategic interests do not deserve all the credit for avoiding war. Stephen Rock, who has looked at this and other relationships at about this time, has some illuminating comments on the public and official discourse. On this one, he describes the milieu of the time – both during the crisis and then, over the next few years, as the participants stepped back from the brink and considered what they might have done: "The reform bills of 1867 and 1884, which extended the franchise in England, had largely dissolved" the American image of England as feudal and aristocratic. "Anglo-Saxonism emerged as a major force" in relations between two nations toward the end of the 19th century, and burst forth in the war crisis. Feelings of Anglo-Saxon kinship contained strong elements of racialism and social Darwinism, but they held a serious political component as well. Richard Olney, Cleveland's Secretary of State during the Venezuelan crisis, declared in 1896: "If there is anything they [Americans] are attached to, it is to ideals and principles which are distinctly English in their origin and development ... nothing would more gratify the mass of the American people than to stand ... shoulder to shoulder with England." Americans were expressing very different sentiments about Spain in 1898.

From the other side, British Colonial Secretary Joseph Chamberlain later declared that American "laws, their literature, their standpoint on every question are the same as ours; their feeling, their interest, in the cause of humanity and the peaceful development of the world, are identical with ours"; he had earlier praised the two countries' "common laws and common standards of right and wrong". Arthur Balfour claimed that America's "laws, its language, its literature, and its religion, to say nothing of its constitution are essentially the same as those of English-speaking peoples elsewhere, ought surely to produce a fundamental harmony – a permanent sympathy". According to Rock, this feeling of homogeneity of societal attributes "lay behind the initial outpouring of pacifist sentiment during the Venezuelan boundary controversy and was a central element in popular and official desires for the settlement of that and other issues ... First, it colored the perceptions of both Englishmen and Americans, causing them to underestimate the importance of the conflict of geopolitical and economic interests between the two countries and to discount the significance of the concessions necessary to achieve an understanding. Second, it led many persons to conclude that the benefits of avoiding a fratricidal war with "racial' kin outweighted the costs of the sacrifices required for this to be accomplished". (Material and quotations in this and the two preceding paragraphs are from Rock 1989: 49-56.)

In effect, an Anglo-American security community was becoming established; "the last serious threat of war between the two powers passed". (Russett 1963: 5) Allen (1955: 540) concludes that "the British public never looked like accepting war, the American public after the first fine careless rapture drew back from the prospect of making it". In the Spanish-American war shortly thereafter, British sympathies were overwhelmingly with the United States (C.S. Campbell 1957: ch.2).

Meanwhile and subsequently, British and then American relations with Germany deteriorated, ultimately to war. Kennedy (1980: esp. p. 399) contrasts Britain's attitudes toward Germany with its new "special relationship" with the United States. Rock (1989: 56) declares, "These effects were devastatingly absent – or reversed – in the Anglo-German and German-American cases". "While turn-of-the-century Britain was an industrial-capitalist, liberal, parliamentary democracy, imperial Germany was an autocratic, bureaucratic, authoritarian state ... These differences were appreciated, and even exaggerated, on both sides of the North Sea, and they colored the attitudes and perceptions of important segments of popular opinion as well as governmental leaders themselves. Englishmen, who could agree on practically nothing else, were in fact almost unanimous in their distaste for the German political system, its ideology, and its methods... Both of these nations [Germany and the United States] were rising imperial powers with growing navies. Both threatened British interests in various regions of the globe. Yet Britons, while they detested and feared Germany, almost universally admired the United States and felt minimal apprehension at her ambitions. Part of this was geographic ... But a large portion was ideological and cultural as well. Imbued as they were with a sense of Anglo-Saxon solidarity, the vast majority of Englishmen simply did not believe that Americans could wish or do them serious harm." (Rock 1939: 86-87.)

The Fashoda crisis of 1898 furnishes a harder case for our thesis. British and French interests had been advancing toward the Sudan, with Britain increasingly determined to control the area as protection for its major stake in Egypt. French forces, however, occupied the small fortress of Fashoda before the British could get there. When a much larger British force did arrive, heads of states had to decide what to do. The French were in no position to fight. Their forces at Fashoda were far weaker, Britain held unquestioned naval superiority, and the French had their hands full on the continent with Germany. The premier, Delcasse, admitted "the problem is how to combine the demands of honor with the necessity of avoiding a naval war which we are absolutely incapable of carrying through" (quoted in Sanderson 1965: 359). Thus he offered compromise in several forms, ultimately offering to quit the area in return for commercial concessions. The British, however, would have none of it. They refused to negotiate so long as French forces were in the area, and the British prime minister, Lord Salisbury, seemed ready to go to war if the French would not concede totally. Ultimately they did. The most recent scholarship on the crisis (Bates 1984: 153) concludes, "there is really no evidence in the archives in London and Paris that either government seriously considered going to war over Fashoda". In the French surrender, the impetus came from their military weakness and need to avoid isolation in their far graver quarrel with Germany. Salisbury wanted good relations with France to counter the growing threat he felt from Germany, and generally preferred diplomacy to force. In this crisis Salisbury was the poker player, against imperialist hawks in domestic politics as well as with the French. While he might have been willing to fight if he had to, he did not want war and knew how weak the French hand was – weakened further by governmental instability over the Dreyfus affair (Albrecht-Carrié 1970).

Considerations of any norm that these two nations should not fight each other were well in the background on both sides; war was avoided primarily for other reasons. Nevertheless, sober reflection on the crisis brought the norms forward: "Both Britain and France possessed a commitment to liberalism and representative government and were opposed to autocracy and absolutism. During the period of reconciliation, numerous references were made to this effect, and to the role of this similarity in drawing the two countries together." One Liberal party leader says, "Most Liberals regarded the Entente with France as the natural result of common democratic impulses". Though they played little role in settling the crisis itself, these feelings were catalyzed by Fashoda and fed directly into the emerging Anglo-French Entente (Rock 1989: 117-118).

As for the German and American political-economic systems, they were "two essentially different conceptions of the state: that of the economically-liberal laissez-faire state, in which one from the German side saw only disorder, egoism, and corruption, and the half-absolutist, neofeudalistic, bureaucratic state, which in American eyes destroyed the freedom of the individual and lacked democratic legitimation through the 'voice of the people'" (Christof 1975, quoted in Rock 1989: 141). For Americans, an earlier vision of Germany became "replaced by the picture of an increasingly repressive, militaristic, authoritarian, and autocratic society" (Rock 1989: 143). Such views were enhanced by the subsequent German war with Britain. Relationships based on type of political system reinforced strategic considerations. The ground was prepared for Wilson's vision of a world that could be at peace if and only if it were democratic. It seems likely that a norm against the use of force between democracies, and even the threat to use force, has emerged and strengthened over time.

My book lays out competing causal theories for the phenomenon of peace between democracies, and looks at the power of these competing theories during the post-World War II era – the time when, by far, the largest number of democracies and hence of possible warring democratic pairs existed. It shows that the rarity of lethal violence between democracies is not due to any apparent confounding influence, but to something in the nature of the democratic-to-democratic state relationship itself, and then begins to identify what that is. It also carries on that analysis in two domains very different from the modern global system. It looks at the world of ancient Greek city states, with a close analysis of who fought whom during the Peloponnesian War. Whereas a number of examples of warring democratic pairs of states emerge during that era, there are hints in the historical record of restraints as well as of the instances when the restraints failed. And an effort to widen the empirical net still further beyond the modern Western sphere looks at the experience of ethnographic units – usually pre-industrial societies, studied by anthropologists. It finds still further evidence that such units, when governed according to democratic "participatory" principles, do not often fight similarly-governed units.

Finally, my book considers all this evidence for glimmers into the future of a world in which, at present, half the states are democratic by criteria like those above (McColm et al., 1992). It addresses the emerging policy debate about whether further democratization, in addition to being a "good thing" for people in their relations within democratically-governed countries, might promote peace between countries. If so, by what principles can democracy best be advanced in a world of nationalism and ethnic hatred? What are the prudent possibilities for intervention – whether by economic means or by military force – to promote democracy? What are the prospects for building a world predominantly of democratic states that are able to live together – not without conflicts of interest, but without the large-scale lethal violence called war which has so blighted the human experience to date?

NOTES

1. The literature on this topic is voluminous; in addition to citations in the text here see the exhaustive listing in Russett 1993: ch.1. While common among writers in the United States, the finding has also been well recognized by European scholars, including Wallensteen 1973, Weede 1984, Gantzel 1987, Duroselle 1988, and Gleditsch 1992.

2. Virtually all the authors cited in Russett 1993 and in the text above agree that democracies are not in general markedly less likely to go to war than are other states. The principal dissenter is Rummel, whose empirical analysis (1983) is limited to 1976-1980 – a period that omits, among others, the Vietnam War and most postcolonial wars – and whose literature review (1985) has been overtaken and corrected by subsequent empirical analyses.

3. With some variations in the mix and in the precise empirical applications, these elements are common in the cross-national literature. By the middle-to-late 20th century the requirement for a responsible executive becomes largely redundant to the other conditions (Vanhanen 1990), but it certainly is not for the 19th century.

4. Rotberg (1980: 30) further reports that voters had to be "approved by the elders of the Dutch Reformed Church", but the constitutional provision requiring a voter to be a member of the Church was repealed immediately after its passage in 1858 (Eybers 1918: 368-369).

5. The formula for calculating the number of possible pairs is $N(N-1)/2$.

6. Definitions and sources are given in Maoz and Russett 1992 and Russett 1993. The militarized dispute data and information on contiguity were derived (without changing definitions) by Zeev Maoz from Gochman and Maoz 1984 and compilations of the Correlates of War project, and the codings of political system type are from Gurr et al. 1989.

REFERENCES

Albrecht-Carrie, René 1970. *Britain and France.* New York: Garden City.
Allen, H.C. 1955. *Great Britain and the United States: A History of Anglo-American Relations* (1783-1952). New York: St. Martin's.
Banks, Arthur S. 1971. *Cross-Polity Time-Series Data.* Cambridge, MA: M.I.T. Press.
Bates, Darrell 1984. *The Fashoda Incident of 1898: Encounter on the Nile.* New York: Oxford University Press.
Berghahn, Volker 1973. *Germany and the Approach of War in 1914.* New York: St. Martin's.
Eybers, G. W. 1918. *Select Constitutional Documents Illuminating South African History, 1795-1910.* London: Routledge.
Bremer, Stuart A. 1992a. "Dangerous Dyads: Conditions Affecting the Likelihood of Interstate War", 1816-1965, *Journal of Conflict Resolution* 36, 2: 309-41.
Bremer, Stuart A. 1992b. "Are Democracies Less Likely to Join Wars?" paper presented at the annual meeting of the American Political Science Association, Chicago, IL: September.
Campbell, A.E. 1960. *Great Britain and the United States 1895-1903.* London:
Campbell, Charles S. 1957. *Anglo-American Understanding 1898-1903.* Baltimore, MD: Johns Hopkins University Press.
Campbell, Charles S. 1974. *From Revolution to Rapprochement: The United States and Great Britain* 1783-1900. New York: Wiley.
Carr, Raymond 1980. *Modern Spain 1875-1980.* Oxford: Oxford University Press.
Christof, Horst 1975. *Deutsch-amerikanische Entfremdung: Studien zu den deutsch-amerikanischen Beziehungen von 1913 bis zum Mai 1916.* Warzburg: Julius-Maximilians Universitate, Ph.D. dissertation.
Dahl, Robert A. 1971. *Polyarchy: Participation and Opposition* (New Haven, CT: Yale University Press, 1971).
Dahl, Robert A. 1989. *Democracy and Its Critics.* New Haven, CT: Yale University Press.
Diehl, Paul F., and Gary Goertz 1992. *Territorial Changes and International Conflict.* London: Routledge.
Doyle, Michael 1986. "Liberalism and World Politics," *American Political Science Review* 80, 4: 1151-61.
Duroselle, Jean-Baptiste 1988. "Western Europe and the Impossible War," *Journal of International Affairs* 41, 2: 345-361.
Gantzel, Klaus Juergen 1987. "Is Democracy a Guarantor against War-Making Policy?" Working Paper No. 14. University of Hamburg, Institut für Politische Wissenshaft, Center for the Study of Wars, Armaments, and Development.
Gleditsch, Nils Petter 1992. "Democracy and Peace," *Journal of Peace Research* 29, 4: 369-376.

Gochman, Charles, and Zeev Maoz 1984. "Militarized Interstate Disputes, 1816-1975," *Journal of Conflict Resolution* 29, 4: 585-615.
Gurr, Ted Robert, Keith Jaggers, and Will Moore 1989. *Polity II Handbook*. Boulder: University of Colorado.
Huntington, Samuel P. 1991. *The Third Wave: Democratization in the Late Twentieth Century*. Norman: University of Oklahoma Press.
Kant, Immanuel. 1970. *Kant's Political Writings*, Hans Reiss, ed., H.B. Nisbet, trans. Oxford: Oxford University Press.
Kohn, George C. 1986. *Dictionary of Wars*. Garden City, NY: Doubleday.
Kennedy, Paul 1980. *The Rise of Anglo-German Antagonism*. London: Allen and Unwin.
Lacour-Gayet, Robert 1978. *A History of South Africa*. New York: Hastings House.
Langer, William L. 1972. *An Encyclopedia of World History*. Boston, MA: Houghton Mifflin.
Maoz, Zeev, and Nasrin Abdolali 1989. "Regime Types and International Conflict," *Journal of Conflict Resolution* 33, 1: 3-35.
Maoz, Zeev, and Bruce Russett 1992. "Alliance, Contiguity, Wealth, and Political Stability: Is the Lack of Conflict between Democracies a Statistical Artifact?" *International Interactions* 17, 3: 245-268.
McColm, R. Bruce, et al. 1992. *Freedom in the World: Political Rights and Civil Liberties 1991-92*. New York: Freedom House.
Most, Benjamin, and Harvey Starr 1989. *Inquiry, Logic and International Politics*. Columbia: University of South Carolina Press.
Ray James Lee 1992. "Wars between Democracies: Rare or Non-Existent?" *International Interactions* 18, 3.
Rock, Stephen R. 1989. *Why Peace Breaks Out: Great Power Rapprochement in Historical Perspective*. Chapel Hill: University of North Carolina Press.
Rotberg, Robert L. 1980. *Suffer the Future: Policy Choices in Southern Africa*. Cambridge, MA: Harvard University Press.
Rummel, R. J. 1983. "Libertarianism and International Violence," *Journal of Conflict Resolution* 27, 1: 27-71.
Rummel, R. J. 1985. "Libertarian Propositions on Violence within and between Nations," *Journal of Conflict Resolution* 27, 1: 419-455.
Russett, Bruce 1963. *Community and Contention: Britain and America in the Twentieth Century*. Cambridge, MA: M.I.T. Press.
Russett, Bruce 1993. *Grasping the Democratic Peace: Principles for a Post-Cold War World*. Princeton, NJ: Princeton University Press.
Sanderson, G. N. 1965. *England, Europe, and the Upper Nile, 1882-1899: A Study in the Partition of Africa*. Edinburgh: Edinburgh University Press.
Small, Melvin, and J. David Singer 1976. "The War-Proneness of Democratic Regimes," *Jerusalem Journal of International Relations* 1, 1: 50-69.
Small, Melvin, and J. David Singer 1982. *Resort to Arms: International and Civil Wars 1816-1929*. Los Angeles.

Vanhanen, Tatu 1990. *The Process of Democratization: A Comparative Study of 147 States 1980-88*. New York: Crane Russak.
Wallensteen, Peter 1973. *Structure and War: On International Relations 1820-1968*. Stockholm: Raben & Sjogren.
Weede, Erich 1984. "Democracy and War Involvement," *Journal of Conflict Resolution* 28, 4: 649-64.

2 WAR, POLITICS AND THE MARKET: REFLECTIONS AFTER THE GREAT POTLATCH

Georg Kohler

Introduction

1989 is the year of the second European revolution. Two centuries after the first one, it again marks the transition from one epoch to another. The collapse of the Soviet Union, barely two years after the fall of the Berlin Wall, demonstrates with blinding clarity what ended then: the world order as established at Yalta; hegemonic rivalry between the USSR and the United States; the societal model of state socialism; the idea of a communist world revolution, the secularised version of salvation.

Thus regarded as the termination of a process which began in 1945 or 1917, in the middle of the 19th century or even earlier, the significance of 1989 appears only in retrospect. But what meaning do the events of 1989 convey if they are regarded in a future-oriented perspective? What is the prospective message of the 1989 revolution? The victory of capitalism? The

---

This invited paper offers a fresh look at the great confrontation, for more than four decades at the center of world attention, and reflects the historic change following this risky rivalry. Georg Kohler teaches philosophy at the University of Zurich and presently holds the chair of political philosophy and theory at the Geschwister-Scholl-Institut for Political Sciences at the University of Munich, Ludwigstrasse 10, 8000 Munich 22, Germany.

primacy of the economy and economic dimensions over all politics? The triumph of Adam Smith's "invisible hand" over any conception of purposeful political intervention? Not a few intellectuals prefer to understand matters in that way. Given the ideological categories with which not least the dogmatists of real socialism operated such an interpretation is obvious. Which does not improve it. As a simple inversion of the viewpoint of their shipwrecked opponents it repeats its structural fault: it is blind to the difficult linkage between war, the economy and politics.

Yet, whoever reflects on the meaning of "1989" must reflect precisely about this linkage. Which is what I propose to do below, guided by two propositions:

a) 1989 represents a *historical stage* along the road to civilisation, notably through de-militarization and the infiltration of economics into politics.

By developing this proposition, I intend to show that, even following the demise of the Marxist utopia, progressive historical perspectives are still open. To be exact, that "Idea of a Universal History from a Cosmopolitan Point of View" which Immanuel Kant sketched out in a text dated 1784 and which points to a "general cosmopolitanism" under which war between states is domesticated through tribunals and appropriate sanctioning forces, or more precisely, in which war becomes "civilised" or "bourgeois". Yet this cosmopolitan condition is insufficient without orientation through political leadership and "world domestic" institutions. Hence the second proposition:

b) The state and politics are *necessary conditions* for the market, which cannot be understood as simply arising out of them. They ensure and formulate the assumptions and limits of autonomous market economies. The political element therefore cannot simply be reduced to market rationality.

I wish to make these two propositions plausible by starting from the world-wide hegemonic struggle which dominated the second half of our century, that conflict between the super-powers which, with pardonable trenchancy, one can describe as a "third world war".

War and the Market

The hegemonic struggle between the United States and the Soviet Union, which did not lead to open war but to a historically unprecedented rivalry in armaments assumed the shape of an enormous potlatch, a competition in the capacity to destroy ones own (weaponry) resources. The main logic of this conflict was determined by that of nuclear terror and the functional assumptions of the techno-industrial sphere. The historical outcome of this potlatch war – within the framework of the given conditions – is the victory of "the market" over "war". I wish to argue this assertion in three steps. Firstly, by commenting on the statement that the rivalry between the Soviet Union and the United States developed in the shape of a potlatch for reasons of strategic logic. Secondly, by looking at different phases of American security policy from Richard Nixon's presidency to the Reagan administration. Thirdly, through certain reflections on the fundamental connection between arming, war and the market economy in an era of permanent technological progress.

The logic of deterrence and of potlatch

According to Clausewitz (1989 [1832]) two aspects must be distinguished and seperately considered (Aron 1976, 1962) if the "nature of war" is to be correctly understood: the "closer meaning" of war and its "overall definition". The latter defines war as an instrument for a political purpose. This is encapsulated in Clausewitz's famous dictum "war is only the pursuit of politics by other means". The conclusion of this formulation is clear: it arises out of the instrumental nature of war. War is not autonomous: as a (political) instrument it relates to the purposes dictated by the current self-preservatory and hegemonic interests of the state. This defines and also limits war.

In other words, the instrument – war – must stand in a calculable and logical relationship to its end, otherwise it becomes useless and loses its meaning. For, in a *Realpolitik* perspective, war is a stake in a bet. How big a stake it is depends on the interests, political power and aims at play in the wager. Thus viewed under the primacy of politics, war is subordinated to a "modifying force" which can break that tendency towards inevitable extremes which arises from the specific certainty of the instrumentality of war. For this is the other aspect, the "closer meaning", expressed in the opening definition with which *On War* starts: "War is an act of force designed to oblige the opponent to yield to our will". Regarded seperately from everything that characterises it as a political instrument, war is simply a bloody, physical trial of strength. It conforms to the pure logic of fighting, to the mutual compulsion to escalate. Each contestant escalates military capacity in proportion to the other – and a little beyond – to the very extreme, war with all possible means. If, however, Clausewitz' basic formulation holds, ie. if political primacy is maintained, then the tendency to total war must not always and everywhere be pursued. Total war would thus break out only if it lies within the policy aims which legitimate waging war. Yet there are circumstances under which war can never be a policy instrumententality towards an end. Such are situations when the logic of war in its "narrower significance" would, of foreseeable necessity, destroy its very basic purpose, that is to say, the assumption concerning the logic of war according to the "total definition" and under the primacy of policy. That remains the situation today. Nuclear war is no longer the continuation of politics by other means and cannot be. The calculable logic of destructive potential leads to the *Realpolitik*-spirit of moderation (self-negating, but for powerful reasons) in the actual unleashing of this potential. Menace must replace action, deterrence the decision to use the weapons.

The "Cold War", ie. the entire period between Yalta 1945 and Malta 1989, is marked by the logically provable "impossibility of a great war" in its real sense, a conclusion which became apparent in the age of nuclear weaponry. Following Clausewitz it can therefore be demonstrated why the hegemonic conflict between the Soviet Union and the United States had to become, to an extent, a potential war, a simulated war and a war of simulation. For this is what transformed all the axioms of international (power) politics and upset all corresponding norms of action. The role of real war lost its traditional place in the co-ordinating system of international relations with the advent of the nuclear age and the certainty of mutual retaliation: it moved into a paradoxically marginal position which, in principle, threatened the whole just as it kept it at peace (Aron 1962). War was no longer an instrument in the mutual attempt by the super-powers to assert their positions or to extend them but either defined the limits of this struggle or its absolute end.

This is the strategic reason why, between 1945 and 1990, real war between the super-powers, which under all other historical conditions would probably have been unavoidable, was transformed into a simulated conflict. It became a vast armaments race, each contestant aiming to possess the most efficient weapons, a competition in the absurd capacity most perfectly to destroy the world. The victory in this contest to possess the ability to undo the world could not be won by the real use of weaponry but rather by the ability to destroy one's own weapons, ie. to make them obsolescent and to replace them by new, expensive ones, forcing the opponent to do the same. If the arms race and its effects is seen in this light it immediately becomes clear that the simulated war, which steered the hegemonic conflict between the two super-powers from beginning to end was not, in fact, adjusted to the direct but to the indirect effects of armaments: to the destruction of industrial resources, public capital and economic energies through the continuing need to modernise the military apparatus. Which can readily be compared with that peculiar competition in the art of squandering which anthropologists call "potlatch".[1]

"Potlatch" is a corruption of a word in the North American Chinook Indian language meaning "to give". Potlatches were originally no more than gift-distribution festivals celebrated along the entire north-western coast of North America. Nevertheless, they always had some societal function such as, for example, to determine who was to be the new tribal chieftain. The potlatch system of the Kwakiutls, who lived in the region of Vancouver, has been amply researched, if not entirely clarified.

"To simplify, a successor potlatch, for example, can be imagined as follows: after the death of a tribal chieftain, the clan elders quarrel about his succession. To secure his claim, one of them proclaims a potlatch to which his rival, along with his clan, are invited. Up until the festival takes place, the members of the host's clan produce a mass of goods and food which are lent to the potlatch giver, who thereby enters into a debt relationship. During the actual festival the host shows his goods and distributes them to the guest clan, carefully respecting hierarchy. The rival is now obliged to offer a potlatch, too. Through the distribution of goods during the second potlatch members of the first clan regain possession of their lent goods, or corresponding counterparts. Whoever is in the position to overwhelm the other with a bigger potlatch may inherit the contested rank. The potlatch system underwent considerable transformation during the 19th century. Through the decimation of the Indian population it became increasingly necessary to find successors to positions left open through death, which led to increasing numbers of those who experienced, or conquered upward social mobility ... A developing system of credit, investments and interest allowed for further multiplication of potlatch goods. Thus, in a certain village of 150 inhabitants, only 400 wool blankets (important potlatch goods) were counted. But the sum of mutually owed blankets reached 75 000. Interest rates of 100% became usual and the restitution of lent goods was expected within a year. In fact, interest was never paid since that would have led to "breaking the bank". An errant debtor naturally lost his prestige or was charged correspondingly higher interest. Credit was not supposed to bring profit, in our sense, but a claim to higher rank. The overheating of the potlatch system was manifested principally in the development of the destructive potlatch. In the rivalry between potlatchers, the ultimate way of humbling a contestant was the destruction of so-called "coppers", plates about 75 cm long hammered out of pure copper. A "copper" was something like a very high-denomination banknote, worth several thousand blankets. By throwing a "copper" into fire or the sea a potlatcher extinguished all the claims he had against others." (Bechtler-Vosecková and Gerber 1980: 54f.)

The outbidding mechanism is the same for the Kwakiutl potlatch and the allegedly rational defense planning of the super-powers. The only difference lies in the criterion adopted to determine what constitutes the decisive advantage in the bidding. With the Kwakiutl it was blankets and copper plates, with the war potlatch of the super-powers it was weapons, the properties and numbers of which could finally always be translated into available powers of destruction.

James Fallows, a former collaborator of Jimmy Carter and well-known American journalist has described the pattern of argument which kept the "armament potlatch" going on the American (and no doubt also on the Soviet) side: "What would happen if, by a surprise attack, the Soviet Union managed to neutralize not only all American intercontinental missiles in their silos but also developed a method to destroy the submarines and bombers which transport four-fifths of the American arsenal? What would need to be done so that not only the entire nuclear system, which represents an insurmountable deterrent, but also its different elements survive such a pre-emptive atomic blow? Such speculation led directly to the MX missile. Reflections of this sort are not merely based on hypothetical threats but lead to beautiful if fantastic suggested solutions ... Would it not be wonderful to direct an air battle from the ground instead of leaving it to a group of simple-minded pilots to determine, in the greatest heat of the battle, which enemy planes are to be destroyed, and which not? With a comprehensive, computerized radar system it would be possible, on the other hand, to distinguish cleanly between the "good" and the "bad" and to issue combat instructions with tactical precision to provide planes with orders and flight paths to the enemy. Visions of this type justified a 20 billion dollar radar system called 'SAGE' in the 1960s. After countless revisions the system ultimately broke down because it proved technically impossible to design a computer program that could distinguish between one's own and enemy planes" (Fallows 1981: 14).

James Fallows makes clear, firstly, the extent to which the coherence of the arms race during the Cold War – that see-sawing between catching up and preventive action, between anticipation and the anticipation of anticipation, between understandable deterrence and vast exaggeration – could become autonomous and perpetuate itself, or rather escalate, through self-generated justification. Secondly, Fallows explains how the functional sphere of the arms race, like that of real war or the logic of destructive potlatches necessarily confirms the tendency towards the extreme, as analysed by Clausewitz ([1832] 1980: 20ff). Thus, I come to a first conclusion: in the age of certain mutual thermonuclear destruction real war between the American and Soviet rivals became rationally impossible. Yet, since the prevailing hegemonic conflict had to be expressed in some way, competition in weapons production was transformed into an actual substitute for war, that is to say, into an arms race, the rules of which finally reproduce those of the archaic pattern of the potlatch.

Reagan's wager

How very risky this, albeit more civilised form of combat still remained was borne in on public consciousness when the question of stationing medium-range rockets and Cruise missiles on European NATO territory arose. These weapons were supposed to neutralize the corresponding opposite systems and further, thanks to the targeting accuracy of the American Pershing II, secure strategic advantages for NATO. But it was not only the European strategic arms round and the idea of an atomic war made "perceptible" through technological developments which led such informed and independent analysts as the physicist C.-F. von Weizsäcker to refer openly to the "dangers of the 1980s" (Weizsäcker 1981, Chap. vii). Rather, it was the general situation between the super-powers which made the years from 1980, when the Brezhnev era drew to a close, to 1986, when the Gorbachev reforms began, so particularly risky. For it gradually became evident that the Soviet Union would soon be unable to keep pace.

Historically, however, no "great power" (Paul Kennedy) had ever accepted its imperial decline without a last belligerent effort. The 1980s thus really became the final and decisive phase of the potlatch war, above all because the American government began to conceive of the rivalry with the Soviet Union precisely as a potlatch competition in order to win that way. At the White House, the model was picked up and factored into strategy. The popular motto became: arming to death. Before Reagan's presidency and the tenure of his Defense Secretary, Caspar Weinberger, the arms race was understood and accepted only by reference to real war.[2] President Nixon and Henry Kissinger thus developed a strategy of arms limitation with their "policy of détente" on the basis of the "balance of security interests of both powers" which, however, was also to persuade the Soviet Union to discipline itself in its foreign policy and to behave "peacefully", in the American understanding. This is what Kissinger called "linkage": the idea that the Soviet Union could only be trusted to maintain technical weapon parity in connection with an adaptation of its foreign policy.

President Carter's human rights policy was based on other assumptions. While the Nixon-Kissinger team pursued a primarily pragmatic line, Carter argued morality while acting in a *Real*-political manner. Carter's human rights policy was certainly aimed at the central weaknesses of the Soviet system: its oppressive practices towards its own peoples, and those of the satellite states, as well as the unlimited powers of the Communist Party, which was allegedly to bring social justice and real emancipation to men. Despite his ideological offensive, Carter also meant to pursue the easing of military tension. Thus, he tried to put through a precise conception in the arena of arms control (SALT II). But the Soviet Union countered Carter's policy in the same way as that of his predecessor: with the intention of extending its own sphere of influence and with undiminished arming. Hence the second attempt of an American administration to accomodate to a system of equilibrium with the Soviet Union failed (Czempiel 1986: 297). President Reagan aimed precisely to break out of this system. He and his advisors sought expressly to attain (once more) a position of hegemonic dominance. The arms control negotiations were put permanently on ice, while re-armament, begun under Carter, was massively[3] expanded, on land, on sea, in the air and in space. Under the conditions of a thermonuclear stalemate, which continued to exist (the projected anti-missile system based in space was never more than a military research program) such a re-armament policy could have only a single politico-strategic meaning: to force the opponent to keep pace until overwhelmed by political and economic ruin. In other words, the Reagan administration converted the arms race, which previously could be called a potlatch only ironically or metaphorically, into an effective and real potlatch war.

Obviously, one can hardly document that such a policy was expressly formulated in these terms. Nevertheless, Caspar Weinberger was supposed to have remarked (as reported by Rudolf Augstein in the German weekly, *Der Spiegel*) that, with the help of re-armament, "the Soviet Union would be forced to the wall until it squeaked". It is an incontestable fact that American military outlays increased by leaps and bounds at the beginning of Reagan's presidency. Compared to Jimmy Carter's last military budget that of 1985 nearly doubled (see Table 1).

TABLE 1

(figures in millions of current dollars)

	1980	1981	1982	1983	1984	1985
1. Defense Function	133995	157513	185309	209903	227413	252748
2. Veterans Benefits	17600	19236	20079	20952	21740	22510
3. International Security Assistance (1962-1991)	4763	5095	5416	6613	7924	9391
4. National Aeronautics and Space Adminstration	-	-	-	1089	534	732
5. Military Portion of Net Interest on Public Debt	40778	50752	60810	62967	75182	87908
Total Military Outlays	197136	232596	271614	301524	332793	373289

Source: Military Spending Research Services, 5855 Potomac Avenue, NW, Washington D.C. 20016.

Comment to Table 1: Measured in absolute dollar amounts the steep rise in outlays as compared to the foregoing year is clear. This rise becomes relative if compared to the overall U.S. economic performance. In the past thirty years much greater proportions of GNP were from time to time devoted to military purposes. At the beginning of the 1950s, the Korean War caused a jump in this proportion to over 13%. This was followed by a drop to around 7% until the beginning of the Kennedy administration. At the height of the Vietnam conflict, the proportion rose again to 9% and then fell to around 5% beginning with the era of Nixon and his détente policy until 1979. Still under Jimmy Carter's presidency a new rise occurred, not least in response to the Soviet invasion of Afghanistan, greatly accelerated after the electoral victory of Reagan in November 1980.

Paul Kennedy (1987), in his impressive study *The Rise and Fall of Great Powers. Economic Change and Military Conflict from 1500 to 2000* has described the extraordinary difficulties occasioned in Soviet politics and the economy by the final phase of the potlatch war. Kennedy detected this in 1987, before the end of the Soviet Union but at a stage when the general "overextension" (Kennedy's key concept) of the communist superpower had become manifest (Kennedy 1987: 488-514). Kennedy refers not only to narrower economic problems but also to the political and socio-psychological limits of the Soviet system, which stood in the way of Moscow's policy as soon as it became a question of importing advanced high technology to modernise the arsenal. "Star wars" was, in this perspective, the last and decisive American trump card which ended the whole thing. Reagan's wager, which seemed so reckless to many observers, myself included, paid off: the United States won the "Third World War". The opponent and his army have not been disarmed, but their normative-ideological identity has been destroyed, to such an extent that the state structure, which lived off this identity as much as it guaranteed its validity, literally burst asunder within a few years. Yet even the victor is impoverished. Nothing else can be expected after a violently conducted potlatch war. (Cf. Perkovich, 1991; Smith 1988; Mintz and Huang 1991.)

The victory of the market over war

The American victory means several basic things.

(a) Firstly, the decisive importance of the free market functioning according to the rules of the private economy. The West was in a position to "squander" more than its opponent under state socialism. The advantage of the free market societal model is demonstrated in its material and ideological resource superiority. Apparently, a societal order under the rule of law and democracy and with a decentralized free market disposes over greater financial potential and technological innovational capacity than a society organized along centralized, bureaucratic lines.[4]

(b) The more developed a modern techno-scientific civilisation, the less "interest" it has in waging a real war, for in the context of such a civilisation a war would in all probability destroy more than could be gained economically. Even in the perspective of so-called *Realpolitik* war can finally only be justified in the case of defensive self-assertion. That is the consequence of the evolutionary trend which became inescapable out of the logic of atomic deterrance. Yet the trend is not simply identical with that logic. One has only to imagine a conventional conflict, conducted by both sides with the most modern weaponry, to realize that general progress in armaments increasingly limits their use, if not proscribing it altogether. Even a conventional war between two "great powers" would make inevitable the widespread destruction of that civilian infrastructure which a country, a nation or a group of states needs in order to survive at all at today's level of civilisation.

In itself, this circumstance does not yet explain the "primacy of the market over war" but simply establishes that techno-scientific modernity and the political instrumentality of a great war tend to cancel each other out. One can only attain the specific "primacy of the market" through a combination of the reflections under (a) and (b), ie. an argument in five steps:

(1) In modern civilisation the *Real*-political place of war is marginalized. War is displaced from being a calculably applicable instrumentality to becoming the actual termination of all political calculation. From the center of the considered use of power war is pushed to its outer limit and beyond.

(2) In modern civilisation, free market democracies (as defined by Böckenförde, 1991) are evidently in a better position to maintain performing weaponry and combat-ready armies than any of their ideological opponents.

(3) In modern civilisation, free-market democracies avoid going to war with each other. This is statistically easily demonstrable, the reasons being many (cf. Lake 1992). Primarily, however, it is in free-market, democratic social orders that the general law which defines modern civilisation expresses itself in a particular way, namely, the more efficient weapons become, the lower the marginal utility of war.

(4) (2) and (3) being the case, modern civilisation has a strong tendency to tame, ie. to "economesticate" and de-militarize international relations. This tendency favors "cosmopolitan" regimes and institutions, supra-national tribunals and peace-keeping actions by world policing.

(5) The market (albeit only if it functions and is protected within the framework of a pluralistic democracy adhering to the rule of law) thus eliminates war itself from the political domain. It is this course of events in modern civilization to which the encapsulation "the primacy of the market over war" properly refers.

The 1989 revolution is the historical confirmation of this structural trend. Thus seen, it is also the empirical proof of Kantian historical philosophy or evolutionary theory of civilisation according to which

»der Krieg (selbst) allmählich nicht allein ein so künstliches, im Ausgange von beiden Seiten so unsicheres, sondern auch durch die Nachwehen ,die der Staat in einer immer anwachsenden Schuldenlast fühlt, deren Tilgung unabsehlich wird, ein so bedenkliches Unternehmen (wird), dabei der Einfluss, den jede Staatserschütterung in unserem durch seine Gewerbe so sehr verketteten Weltteil auf alle anderen Staaten tut, so merklich (ist); dass sich diese, durch ihre eigene Gefahr gedrungen, obgleich ohne gesetzliches Ansehen, zu Schiedsrichtern anbieten und so alles von weitem zu einem künftigem grossen Staatskörper anschicken, wovon die Vorwelt kein Beispiel aufzuzeigen hat« (Immanuel Kant 1784 (1912/23), 28).

("war (itself) gradually becomes not only an artificial undertaking but one, the outcome of which for both contestants is quite uncertain and which entails an ever greater debt burden for the state, the settlement of which becomes boundless. War thus becomes a dubious enterprise; every time it rocks states in our part of the world it influences all others closely linked to it through trade. These others, driven by the dangers to which they are exposed, and without formal authority, then offer their services as arbitrators: thus, everything points to a vast future state system such as was never seen before in history".)

In 1795, eleven years after writing the above text, Kant attempted to formulate the normative principles of this anticipated world citizenship in his *Perpetual Peace*. What Kant designs then is not the constitution of a world state but the mechanism of a League of Nations. Its core is the mutual and unconditional refusal to resort to violence amongst states, that is to say, the introduction of a general condition of peace based on binding international law. Indeed, Kant avoids postulating what might strictly be regarded as a world state (cf. Höffe 1990: 249-279). In case conflicts do continue to occur, his design includes neither common public laws nor a permanent court of arbitration with authorised sanctioning powers. That is an obvious shortcoming, and Kant appears to have rejected the undoubtedly Utopian visionary idea of a peace force on politico-pragmatic grounds. He nevertheless believed it to be really possible for belligerent conflicts to disappear from the comity of nations. The rule of international law which he suggested thus explains at the normative level what had already become urgent in reality: the avoidance of wars. The argument that there are opportunities in this direction is the same as that exposed in Kant's 1784 text:

„So vereinigt (die Natur) ... die Völker, die der Begriff des Weltbürgerrechts gegen Gewalttätigkeit und Krieg nicht würde gesichert haben, durch den wechselseitigen Eigennutz. Es ist der *Handelsgeist*, der mit dem Kriege nicht zusammen bestehen kann, und der früher oder später sich jedes Volkes bemächtigt." (Kant 1795 (1912/32), 368).

("Thus does [Nature]... unite nations through mutual self-interest, which would not have been secured by the notion of cosmopolitan outlawing of violence and war, it is *the spirit of trade* which cannot co-exist with war and which sooner or later conquers all nations.")

It is thus fundamental forces and processes of modern civilisation, and not merely the good intentions of reformers, which give substance to the idea of eternal peace. As epoch-making proof of the reality of such an evolution I point to the collapse of the Soviet Union and what it signifies in a systems perspective: an important step in the victory of the market over war. If such an actual development takes place, however, there is no reason why, at the normative-constructive level, that loop should not be closed which Kant left open in his design for an internationally peaceful order: the establishment of world domestic political authorities endowed with the powers necessary to ensure respect for treaties concluded and the prevention of larger-scale wars.[5]

Politics and the Market

Democratic market civilisation under the rule of law appears historically to be capable of de-militarizing politics. By no means coincidentally, wars and violence are thus increasingly stripped of their attributes as political instrumentalities. Such a value transformation from the belligerent national policies of the 19th century is expressly set out in the Charter of the United Nations, Article 2, paragraph 4. It forbids member states to adopt violent means to achieve political aims, only permitting them, under Article 15, in collective or individual self-defense. Declarations and *Realpolitik* are two different matters: nobody who refers to the Charter of the United Nations is likely to forget that. But declarations, too, constitute segments of reality. They mirror that evolutionary trend which inspired Kant. He promised that there would be a repetition, at the universal level, of what had always been the principle of politics at more restricted levels: the establishment of an order which forces conflicts to be settled through generally accepted rules of law. That such a task can be handled through political structures which do not necessarily result in an actual world state is now accepted. Non-hegemonic international "regimes" (cf. Krasner 1983 and Ruloff 1986) have evolved capable of forming the crystallization points for world domestic institutions to abolish the Hobbesian state of nature prevailing between states. In short, the idea of a "pax universalis" has long ago become more than a merely Utopian conception. And, at least in terms of its major objectives and fundamental behavioral norms, the New World Order can even be fairly concretely described (cf. particularly Czempiel 1992). That cannot be done here; instead, I propose to make a concluding remark about the relationship between the market and politics.

The market shapes societies which have interiorised its principles in all their aspects, naturally in accordance with the way their politics are run. But – and this is the essential point here – the market and economic competition are themselves political institutions. They are never to be understood only as arrangements of the economic system. They are based on rules of the game, laws and sanctions which always assume prior political structures and will. The motto of fair play, which should also apply to the free market, immediately reminds us of this: the market and competition do not sweep away the eternal political questions of justice and equality, of law and order, of basic democratic legitimacy: they lend them urgency. The market and competition can unfold their capacity to produce and distribute goods optimally only in the framework and on the basis of a regulating political order, recognized as legitimate in that capacity. That also means that politics can never be reduced to the economic dimension. For politics always obeys its own logic. This arises out of the particular interests which appear in the political arena: interests attaching to fundamental material and life-opportunity egalitarianisms which cannot be adequately apprehended or handled in the economic sphere, but the satisfaction of which precisely the capitalistic market economy system must, of course, ensure if it is to survive over the long run. That has held over time for the national policies of Western countries, for easily understandable reasons connected to the very nature of human sociability: thus it equally holds for any New World Order. [6]

NOTES

1 Marcel Mauss, who in his *Essai sur le Don* (1950) first extensively analysed the inner rationality of potlatch, himself established a connection between potlatch and war.
2 In what follows I am much indebted to Czempiel 1986.

3 Caspar Weinberger's "Program of military strengthening" which he sketched out to the Congress on 4 March 1985, is to be recalled. After Ronald Reagan's triumphant re-election at the end of 1984, the already adopted policy was to be continued in principle. Cf. Baldauf 1985 and Pordzik 1984.

4 This was not obvious in prospect. "For a remarkably long time, the outcome of the Great Contest, as Isaac Deutscher called it, was anything but clear. In view of the dreadful destruction wreaked by two world wars, a civil war and brutal collectivisation, not to mention the merciless, inescapable and massive domestic purges, it was an impressive achievement to turn Russia into a super-power which shared world supremacy, with an educated and diligent population, which was for a time even in the position of assuming the leading role in space research." (Gellner, 1992: 648).

5 All this holds true despite recent events, which meant the end of the eastern bloc. For the majority of them are wars in regions where the complex and fragile but welfare-producing civilisational structures which make any war seem unprofitable in advance do not yet exist. Furthermore, they are wars, as for example in former Yugoslavia, in which the military means are very unequally distributed. The Bosnian Muslims fight with guerrilla weapons against a more or less regular army. And after all, such conflicts, for various reasons, assume the character of civil wars, or at least contests on territories with uncertain state boundaries. In such cases it is already progress if the community of nations is in a position to prevent interested third parties from intervening on one side or the other in order to gain advantages. Should it be possible to neutralize conflicts in the territories of the post-Communist East to the extent that has already been done and to let them burn themselves out – dreadful though that is – then even the fact of such wars does not dispel the long-range hope for a "world citizenship" order.

REFERENCES

Aron, Raymond (1962), *Paix et guerre entre les nations*. Paris.
Aron, Raymond (1976), *Penser la guerre, Clausewitz*. Paris.
Baldauf, Jörg (1985), "Der amerikanische Verteidigungshaushalt für das Finanzjahr 1986". *Europa-Archiv*, Folge 21: 653-662.
Bechtler-Voseckova, Eva und Gerber, Peter (1980), *Nordamerikanische Indianer. Ihre Geschichte und ihre Kultur*. Völkerkundemuseum der Universität Zürich.

Böckenförde, Ernst-Wolfgang (1991), "Demokratie als Verfassungsprinzip". In Ernst-Wolfgang Böckenförde, *Staat, Verfassung, Demokratie Studien zur Verfassungstheorie und zum Verfassungsrecht*. Frankfurt.

Clausewitz, Carl V. (1832, 1980, Ullstein Materialien), *Vom Kriege*. Frankfurt, Berlin, Vienna.

Czempiel, Ernst-Otto (1986), "Gleichgewicht oder Hegemonie – zu den amerikanisch-sowjetischen Beziehungen". *Merkur*, 4, April 1986, No. 446: 289-301.

Czempiel, Ernst-Otto (1992), "Pax Universalis. Variationen über das Thema der Neuen Weltordnung". *Merkur*, 8, August 1992, No. 521: 680-693.

Fallows, James (1981), "Hochrüstung und Nachrüstung in den USA". *Der Monat*, 3, 1981, No. 280: 4-18.

Gellner, Ernest (1992), "Aus den Ruinen des Grossen Wettstreits". *Merkur*, 8, August 1992, Nr. 521: 647-656.

Höffe, Otfried (1990), *Kategorische Rechtsprinzipien. Ein Kontrapunkt der Moderne*. Frankfurt.

Kant, Immanuel (1784), "Idee zu einer allgemeinen Geschichte in weltbürgerlicher Absicht," cited according to *Kants gesammelte Schriften*, edited by the Königliche Preussische Akadademie der Wissenschaften, volume VIII, Berlin 1912/1923), pp. 15-32.

Kant, Immanuel (1795), "Zum Ewigen Frieden," cited according to *Kants gesammelte Schriften*, edited by the Königliche Preussische Akadademie der Wissenschaften, volume VIII, Berlin 1912/1923), pp. 341-386.

Kennedy, Paul (1987), *The Rise and Fall of the Great Powers: Economic Change and Military Conflict from 1500 to 2000*. New York.

Krasner, Stephan D. (ed.) (1983), *International Regimes*. Ithaca, N.Y.

Lake, David A. (1992), "Powerful Pacifists: Democratic States and War". *American Political Science Review*, Vol. 86, No. 1: 24-37.

Mauss, Marcel (1950), *Essai sur le don*. Paris

Mintz, Alex and Huang, Chi (1991), "Guns vs. Butter: The Indirect Link". *American Journal of Political Science*, Vol. 35, No. 3: 738-757.

Perkovich, George (1991), "Counting the Costs of the Arms Race". *Foreign Policy*, 1991-2, No. 85: 83-105.

Pordzik, Wolfgang (1984), "Der amerikanische Verteidigungshaushalt". *Politik und Zeitgeschichte*, 1984, Volume 22: 3-14.

Ruloff, Dieter (1986), *Weltstaat oder Staatenwelt. Über die Chancen globaler Zusammenarbeit*. München.

Smith, Dale L. (1988), "Reagan's National Security Legacy. Model-Based Analyses of Recent Changes in American Policy". *Journal of Conflict Resolution*, Vol. 32, No. 4: 595-625.

Weizsäcker, C.F. von (1981), *Der bedrohte Friede*. München.

3 ARMAMENTS AND DISARMAMENT IN THE POST-COLD WAR PERIOD
THE QUEST FOR A DEMILITARIZED AND NUCLEAR-FREE WORLD

Marek Thee

Continuity and Discontinuity of International Conflict

In historical perspective, the 20th century has been marked by ceaseless armament, enduring arms races and intermittant wars, hot and cold. But there have also been moments of hope, as after World Wars I and II, with the establishment of the League of Nations and the United Nations, which promised to free the world from the scourge of war. Alas, this did not materialize.

Likewise, at the end of the Cold War there were, for a twinkling, expectations of peace dividends and a peaceful New World Order. Then, the war in the Gulf and widespread nationalist-ethnic-religious violence in former Yugoslavia and elsewhere, as well as the many still raging local wars around

---

This is part of the research project "Role of Science and Technolgy in the Arms Race and Economic Development" funded by the World Society Foundation. Marek Thee was for many years editor of the quarterly *Bulletin of Peace Proposals* and conducted this research while Senior Research Fellow Emeritus of the International Peace Research Institute, Oslo. He is now Research Associate at the Norwegian Institute of Human Rights, St. Olavs gt. 29, 0166 Oslo 1, Norway.

the globe[1], shattered these rays of hope. Rather than "order", "disorder" appeared to be gaining momentum. Instead of a peaceful discontinuity with the turbulent past, in the post-Cold War period also we face continuity of conflict, armaments and political-military contention. Basically, international relations essentially remain power relations, with resort to military force still seen as the pursuit of politics by other means.

In the following I seek to trace the state of armament and disarmament in the post-Cold War period, focusing on the potential dangers as well as opportunities for peaceful change.

The Post-Cold War Politico-Military Landscape

With the end of the Cold War, the immediate danger of major hostilities between the big powers has disappeared. Yet the armaments drive, stimulated by latent and prevalent international strife, has not faded away.

One of the signal changes fraught with increased tension is the shift from a bipolar to a multipolar world, not unlike the constellation prior to World War II. In the process, the axes of conflict and the long-term military agenda tend to multiply. Apart from the unrest and agitation in the former Soviet empire, with internal and external implications, habitual conflicts of interests fuelled by the emergence in Asia and Europe of new economic giants such as Japan and Germany, with long-standing hegemonic aspirations and renewed competitive ability, are to be expected.

At the same time, South-North politico-economic resentment is becoming militarized, as indicated by the Gulf War. The North's status quo pursuit is being questioned and challenged by a destitute and increasingly assertive South, including China. In parallel, in the course of nation-building and maturation of intrinsic power-relations, the South itself is burdened by local and regional conflicts of tribal, hegemonial and religious natures. In the process, tangential points are emerging between tensions in the South and competitive major power interventions, framed and compounded by arms deliveries and politico-economic as well as military leverage.

The transition from the Cold War to a new politico-strategic equilibrium or disequilibrium has been characterized by intense strains. The world seems to remain on a socio-economic and politico-strategic boil.

What, then, of the post-Cold War armaments momentum?

Armaments and arms races are a multi-causal and multi-dimensional phenomenon prompted by inter-state, national, economic, technological and behavioral motive forces.

Many of these determinants are still present – especially those vested in the political economy of armaments; in constituency interests, military and industrial; in doctrinal-strategic and institutional bureaucratic rationales, as well as in the push power of modern technology. Yet a number of specific circumstantial stimulants, endemic and congruous to the post-Cold War period, are conspicuous in their impact.

Paramount among them is the general atmosphere of uncertainty and volatility stemming from the breakup of the former Soviet Union, with the convulsive system changes that have unsettled the lands of the former Soviet empire, from Central Europe through Central Asia to the Far East. This has brought with it an urge to keep open the lines of weapons development, production and deployment. Though felt mainly at the level of major powers, it also trickles down to lower hierarchies of local and regional state actors. Obviously, the dislocations and quandaries caused by the tremors on a large part of the Eurasian continent are of a protracted nature with no clear settlements in sight, the resurgence of power-hungry authoritarian and totalitarian regimes not excluded. Hence, contingency military planning and military preparedness, permeated by projection and design, remain the order of the day.

A particular impulse to contemporary armaments derives from the residues of the Cold War, including the indeterminate fate of the arms control accords so hastily concluded on the eve of the collapse of the Soviet empire. This concerns both the agreement on the reduction of Conventional Armed Forces in Europe (CFE) as well as the Strategic Armaments Reduction Treaty (START). Implementation of these accords – during the dismemberment of the Soviet empire, with new conventional military and nuclear actors on the scene, and a time-schedule running into the 21st century – raises many uncertainties. While the emphasis is on reduction, the concern is with proliferation of weapons, conventional and nuclear.

These apprehensions have been reinforced by the experience and lessons of post-Cold War armed conflicts, both of the level of major-power engagements and low-intensity guerrilla wars. The implications and lessons of the Gulf War in relation to successes and failures in the employment of the most advanced conventional weaponry constitute especially powerful technological inducements to modernize existing arsenals and forge new, more effective weapons and weapon systems. A new armaments spiral has ensued. In a different way and at a different level, lower-intensity conflicts, like the murderous one in former Yugoslavia, prompt endeavors to refine conventional arms suited for guerrilla-type warfare, as well as the taking of armed precautions by smaller countries which may feel vulnerable to military assault. The lessons of the Gulf War and spreading national-ethnic violence throughout the world, spur military preparedness and the development of increasingly sophisticated arms, both for defense and for offense. High on the armaments agenda is intensification of the work of military laboratories, research and development.

I will deal in greater detail below with the circumstantial determinants and daunting problems of contemporary armaments and disarmament. Suffice it to point out here that, in line with the upsetting and transformation of the politico-military landscape, sweeping changes are under way in military sectors, including planning, production and deployment. The current situation is characterized by flux and nervousness because of the crumbling of old patterns of strategic stability, and of the fragile transience inherent in shaping a new, power-based world order.

The Nuclear "Disarmament Race"

As a result of the demise of the Soviet empire – with the breakaway of the Central European satellite states, the dissolution of the Warsaw Treaty Organization (WTO) and the disintegration of the Soviet Union itself – nuclear arms control has undergone a remarkable acceleration. After nine years of tough and convoluted negotiations, the Strategic Arms Reduction Treaty (START) was signed on July 31, 1991 in Moscow by Presidents Bush and Gorbachev. Then, in a rush of unilateral, reciprocated moves by President Bush and Presidents Gorbachev and Yeltsin in September-October 1991 and January 1992, the START ceilings were to be drastically reduced, all ground-launched short-range nuclear weapons eliminated, strategic bombers removed from the alert posture, and ballistic missiles no longer to be targeted at each other. Finally, in an understanding still to be worked out in detail, concluded on June 1, 1992 in Washington, Presidents Bush and Yeltsin envisaged further deep cuts in strategic nuclear stockpiles.

It was evident that behind this haste, which created the impression of a nuclear "disarmament race", lay different apprehensions. On the one hand,

President Bush, who initiated the unilateral reciprocated measures, feared that the collapse of the Soviet Union, with the potential for weakened control over its huge nuclear arsenal, might jeopardize US security and world peace. Of particular concern was the proliferation of nuclear weapons, as Soviet deployments were dispersed (apart from those in the Federal Republic of Russia itself) in three other members of the new Commonwealth of Independent States (CIS) – Ukraine, Kazakhstan and Belarus. For its part, Moscow was keen to reduce the burden of armaments at a time of profound socio-economic and political crisis, simultaneously preserving a semblance of approximate nuclear parity with the United States, while all along also trying to limit US nuclear capabilities.

The START Treaty aimed at a new departure, not only in limiting the burgeoning and redundant growth of nuclear armaments but also in reducing the strategic nuclear buildup. The negotiations proved rather tortuous, especially as the notion of "reduction" was understood more in qualitative than quantitative terms, to be safeguarded by strict and intrusive verifications about which both parties had their reservations.

The outcome was a very long and complex treaty, with specific counting rules for warheads, which in some cases made it possible to exceed the actual number set down in the Treaty itself, and which imposed limits on their deployment modes. In broad outline, START awards to both parties aggregate and equal apportionments of 1600 strategic nuclear delivery vessels (SNDVs) comprising inter-continental ballistic missiles (ICBMs), submarine-launched ballistic missiles (SLBMs) and strategic bombers. These launchers may carry no more than 6000 START-countable warheads. Moreover, START imposes specific sublimits for these warheads. No more than 4900 warheads may be carried by ICBMs and SLBMs; no more than 1100 warheads on mobile ICBMs, and no more than 1540 warheads on 'heavy' ICBMs – with only the Soviet SS-18 classified as 'heavy' ICBMs. Implementation was to take seven years after ratification of the Treaty (which by the end of November 1992 had not yet passed either the US Congress or the parliaments of Ukraine, Kazakhstan and Belarus; the Russian Parliament ratified the Treaty on 4 November, 1992).

Originally, the START Treaty was to cut the strategic nuclear arsenals of the USA and the USSR by 50%. Following protracted negotiations, the goal slid significantly, with the greater onus on the Soviet stockpile. Ultimately, START provides for a cut, in the seven-year period after its entry into force, of 18% of US launchers (from 1947 to 1600), of 38% of US warheads (from

9745 to 6000); of 36% of Soviet launchers (from 9483 to 6000), and of 46% of Soviet warheads (from 11 159 to 6000) – all according to START counting rules.[2] Actually, the cuts on the CIS side are envisaged to be larger not only in quantity but also in quality, as they would include elimination of half of the CIS 'heavy' ICBMs.

On the whole, however, the implementation of the START Treaty would still far from solve the nuclear standoff. Indeed, it could lead to leaner yet more operational strategic nuclear forces. As emphasized by *SIPRI Yearbook 1992*:

> "The START Treaty permits the replacement and modernization of strategic offensive forces, except where specifically prohibited. Since both sides have modernisation programmes that take account of these prohibitions, none of these programmes will have to be scrapped to comply with START rules. The START Treaty permits both sides to make the required force reductions among older, less capable systems, thus preserving the most modern and accurate ones. The Treaty's impact on offensive nuclear capability is therefore rather limited... Both sides are left with sufficient nuclear weapons to cover the targets prescribed by their respective operational plans."[3]

We may recall here that the post-World War II nuclear buildup in its process of growth took for granted wide redundancies resulting from the thrust of innovation. As pointed out back in 1986 by former US Secretary of Defense, Robert McNamara and by the Nobel Laureate, Hans A. Bethe:

> "The 25 000 (nuclear) warheads that each nation [the US and USSR] possesses did not come about through any plan but simply descended on the world as a consequence of continuing technological innovation."[4]

Both in START and the subsequent unilateral reciprocated Washington-Moscow moves as well as in the June 1992 Bush-Yeltsin provisional agreement, the two parties proved to have a number of convergent and divergent points. First, there was unanimity that some of the weapons to be withdrawn would be destroyed while others would be removed and retained in storage. It is to be noted that the START Treaty contains provisions allowing the parties to recycle the warhead fuel from withdrawn missiles for new nuclear weapons, and to also reuse the missiles themselves.[5] Second, whereas the US pressed for reductions of land-based multiple-warhead ICBMs which may have a first-strike capability and in which the former Soviet Union prevailed, Moscow was more interested in limitations on sea-based multiple warhead SLBMs, also with a first-strike capability, in which the USA has maintained a decisive lead. Third, while the USA insisted on confining all mobile ICBMs to their garrisons and limiting the modernization of the Russian single-warhead mobile missiles, it at the same time sought to reserve for itself the right to modernize its single warhead long-range missiles. Fourth, while both sides agreed to withdraw from deployment the short-range ground-based tactical nuclear weapons which had lost their utility after the radical alteration of the European map, the USA was not willing to eliminate the more operational submarine and air-launched cruise missiles. There is actually a distinct trend to focus modernization on air- and sea-based systems with greater mobility and functionality.[6]

The final station of the Moscow-Washington deals was the 16 June, 1992 Washington arms control understanding initialed by Presidents Bush and Yeltsin. This provides for a reduction of the strategic nuclear forces of both sides, in two phases. By the year 2000 each party would retain 3800 – 4250 nuclear warheads on SNDVs, of which 1000 may be deployed on ICBMs. This would then have to be scrapped in the second stage by the year 2003 when the total limit for each party would be 3000 – 3500, with the Russians totally deprived of ICBMs and half of the US warheads deployed on invulnerable SLBMs on the Trident submarines.

There are a number of preconditions for the implementation of this accord. First, the text is still a makeshift memorandum which has yet to be translated into legal treaty language with all the detailed imponderables of the START format, especially as far as verification is concerned. Second, doubts have been expressed concerning Russia's technological-economic capability to dismantle and eliminate such a large number of missiles.[7] Third, though the three CIS states with heavy deployment of strategic nuclear weapons – Ukraine, Khazakhstan and Belarus – have signed a protocol adhering to the START Treaty, coordination and control of their arms may pose tough problems. And fourth, this all may depend on the very survival of the Yeltsin government or a like-minded successor administration during the long period of implementation.[8] Here it is worth noting that the START Treaty contains a clause according to which each party retains "a right to withdraw from the Treaty if it decides that extraordinary events related to the subject matter of this Treaty have jeopardized its supreme interests".[9]

But even after full implementation of the accord, there will, as pointed out by Lawrence Freedman, be "still enough warheads to go round",[10] – not to mention the nuclear stockpiles of China, France and the UK, which in 1991 amounted altogether to 856 strategic warheads.[11]

Essentially, the START Treaty and the subsequent unilateral reciprocated declaratory moves as well as the expedient June 1992 accord were rather past- than future-oriented. They related to balancing bilateral US-Soviet nuclear deterrence relations. But in the meantime, the breakup of the Soviet Union dramatically changed the very context and depth of the nuclear collision course. The bilateral confrontation has become amplified into a pentagonal spurt, with Ukraine, Kazakhstan and Belarus showing an interest in the indeterminate preservation of their strategic nuclear deployments as a deterrent to safeguard their independence.[12] A new nuclear deterrence configuration has thus emerged, with proliferation an acute issue.[13] While the danger of a major nuclear conflict has abated, the nuclear contest remains alive and the danger of exacerbation looms large. Nuclear overkill and the nuclear Sword of Damocles over mankind have been projected far into the future.

Nature of the Treaty on the Reduction of Conventional Armed Forces in Europe

Another residual armaments problem left over from the Cold War is the implementation of the treaty on the reduction of Conventional Armed Forces in Europe (CFE) signed in November 1990, as well as the supplementary CFE1A accord on limiting the strength of troops in Europe, concluded in July 1992.

The CFE Treaty, negotiated in a record period of 20 months, was originally structured as a bloc-to-bloc accord with equal arms ceilings, aimed at balancing the conventional weapons buildup in Europe between NATO and the Warsaw Pact (WTO) forces. But in its final 1992 version, following the unification of Germany, the dissolution of the WTO and the breakup of the Soviet Union, the balancing objective faded. When the Treaty was finally concluded, the area of application – initially shaped to cover 16 NATO and 7 WTO countries – comprised 29 countries from the Atlantic to the Urals. With the demise of the WTO and the disintegration of the Soviet Union, the arms contingent originally assigned to the WTO had to be reapportioned between Russia, its former Central European satellites (Poland, Czechoslovakia, Hungary, Romania and Bulgaria) and the newly established republics of the Commonwealth of Independent States (Ukraine, Belarus, Moldavia, Armenia, Azerbaijan, and the European part of Kazakhstan). The Baltic countries, which in the initial period of Soviet disintegration declared their independence, withdrew from participation in the CFE. In addition, not included in the CFE Treaty are former non-aligned and neutral countries in the middle of Europe, such as Yugoslavia, Sweden, Finland and Austria, as well as the Russian territories beyond the Urals. Ultimately, the CFE Treaty lost much of its initial purpose, with Russia itself landing in a much weaker position than originally contemplated.

Nevertheless, though the original balance model of the Treaty has now melted away, the reduction of substantial amounts and key types of conventional weaponry in the space from the Atlantic to the Urals, if fully implemented, may still contribute to the amelioration of the political climate in Europe and beyond. More important, perhaps, than the reductions themselves may be the confidence-building aspect of the CFE Treaty. On the other hand, CFE provides for the retention, within the Treaty area of application, of 40 000 active and stored battle tanks, artillery pieces, 60 000 armored combat vehicles, 36 000 armed infantry vehicles, 30 000 heavy armored combat vehicles, 13 600 combat aircraft and 4000 helicopters.[14]

The surplus would have to be destroyed or converted to non-military purposes, leaving an opening for redistribution of more modern armor within the military alliances or subzones as well as translocation of Russian assets east of the Urals or even for export. This, in practice, amounts to the elimination of obsolete and redundant weapons, equivalent to a process of arms modernization. Even after thorough implementation of the Treaty, the European continent will still contain the largest concentration of advanced conventional arms in the world. In case of conflict, there would certainly be no shortage of weapons, as fighting in Yugoslavia or the strife in some CIS lands underscores. In addition, the CFE1A accord on the reduction of military manpower in Europe, which is neither legally binding nor subject to legislative ratification, often sets troop limits higher than current levels; nor are there any limitations on paramilitary forces which, as proved on the battlefields of former Yugoslavia, can play a key role in ethnic-nationalist violence.[15]

In a military-political perspective, the radical transformation of the political map of Europe which occured together with the CFE negotiations has changed the very nature of the Treaty. Not only does the deterrence balance appear in a new light, but verification issues have also become much more tangled. In 1992 it was agreed that the CFE treaty should enter into force without re-negotiation, but it may prove highly intricate to implement at a time of broad military rearrangement, with the buildup of new national armies in the CIS countries and the pursuit of altered military doctrines, nuclear and conventional.

One of the dangers lies in trends to replace the reduction of conventional strength by greater reliance on nuclear arms. As pointed out by the Director of the London-based International Institute for Strategic Studies, Bo Huldt: faced with a general decline in the effectiveness of its armed forces, Russia could be tempted to rely more on nuclear weapons for deterrence. "This is thus really a more dangerous situation than we had before."[16]

The Technological Armaments Stimulus from the Gulf War

A powerful boost to post-Cold War armaments, especially in the domain of advanced military technology, has come from the Gulf War. Essentially an uneven contest between a leading superpower in alliance with other major powers on the one hand, and an ascending Third World country on the other hand, it offered the opportunity to test, in real battle conditions and on specific terrain, the most modern conventional weapons as well as military space gear developed in recent years. It was an extensive testing range for sophisticated arms – in space, air, land and sea – after the wars in Korea, Vietnam and Afghanistan.

This was the first computerized, real-time, grand battle to feature massive synchronized use of precision-guided munitions, long-range cruise missiles, invisible "stealth" and laser technology, electronic warfare, instant military communication, streamlined command and control, artificial intelligence, robot gun-carriers and resourceful armors – all combined with atrocious "surgical" bombardment, even though targets were often missed.

Certain lessons of the Gulf War were of extreme importance to military planners. It was proven that precision-guided, relatively small conventional weapons, "smart" bombs and cruise missiles can destroy targets that once would have required massive bombings or nuclear explosives. In World War II it took 9000 bombs and 300 unguided bombs in Vietnam to destroy a 'point target' such as an aircraft shelter, compared with one or two precision weapons in the Gulf War.[17] Target accuracy has thus improved dramatically.

First in the annals of history, in the Gulf War, airpower played a decisive role in determining its course, paving the way for a swift and almost unopposed ground battle of very short duration, with record low infantry casualties of the attacking forces. In the minds of the military, superior modern military technology has made war more manageable, reducing battle carnage to levels unthinkable before.

Also for the first time in war history, space technology became fully integrated with the planning and execution of the military campaign. The US made use of the largest number of multipurpose satellites ever in space simultaneously, with an all-weather capability and repeated daily cruising over the battlefields. They fulfilled basic tasks of reconnaissance, remote sensing, mapping, communication and weather prognosis. This employment of space systems marked a turning point in modern warfare. As stated in the *SIPRI Yearbook 1992:*

> "Desert Storm will be regarded as the first "space war", since it was the first occasion on which the full range of modern military space assets was applied to a terrestrial conflict... Proponents of military space systems will point to the outcome of Desert Storm as a sign of the decisive potential of military space systems."[18]

A particular experience of the Gulf War was the first use of Patriot anti-missile interceptors against SCUD launchers fired by the Iraqis at Israel and Saudi Arabia. First proclaimed as a great success, its effectiveness was later challenged.[19] Be this as it may, the very advent of a missile contest in the Gulf War caused a flurry of renewed interest both in ballistic missiles and anti-ballistic missile (ABM) defenses. The US Strategic Defense Initiative, having consumed from its inception in 1983 approximately US $25 billion with rather meagre successes, awakened to a new life. Attention turned on the one hand to ground-based ABM technology and on the other hand to anti-theater ballistic missiles (ATBMs). The SDI program was refocused to Global Protection Against Limited Strikes (GPALS) consisting of space- and surface-based sensors as well as interceptors based in space, on the ground or at sea. According to the US Secretary of Defense, following the Gulf War "ballistic missile defense has become far more urgent and immediately relevant than could have been projected from the perspective of the early 1980s".[20]

There were, of course, particularly ugly aspects to Desert Storm such as the US use of refined cluster bombs with lethal effects on humans and designed to spread devastation over wide areas, or fuel-air explosives producing both strong blast and intense fires.[21] There were also failures in the use of sophisticated military technology – such as effects much lower than expected in the employment of cruise missiles, of "stealth" aircraft or the Patriot anti-missile rockets. Moreover, command and control intelligence did not always work satisfactorily. Still, the effect of advanced new military technology employed by the coalition forces was staggering. The Gulf War marked a watershed in the history of modern wars. A main lesson drawn by the US military was a renewed emphasis on military R & D to reinforce the conventional and nuclear deterrent. As stated by the US Secretary of Defense:

> "While the requirement for the United States to deter Soviet strategic nuclear attack remains, the spread of military technology of increased sophistication and destructiveness is a development that must increasingly be considered as we develop military forces to be fielded in the 1990s... our modernization process is, and must remain a dynamic one."[22]

Translated into practice,

> "In the aftermath of the Gulf War, new battle lines have been drawn in the world of U.S. military planning. On one side are military planners in the Pentagon and at the war colleges. On the other side are a group of civilian weapons scientists and strategists who work for the Defense Advanced Research Projects Agency (DARPA), the Defense Science Board, the national laboratories, and a bevy of contractors... At issue is a new generation of "brilliant" weapons – crewless tanks, cruise missiles that behave like kamikaze robots, advanced air-defense missiles, and anti-missile satellites... The leading military concept of the new era might be called "cyberwar", in which robots do much of the killing and destroying without direct instructions from human operators. The weapons would be "autonomous", to use one of the weapon designers' words...."[23]

The lessons learned from the Gulf War have spread globally to military establishments of major and minor state actors. A new spiral in the race in military technology has ensued, both in the intensification of military R & D and in the arms trade in most modern weapons. The first statement of the new Russian military doctrine published in May 1992 in the military journal *Voennaya Mysl*, as reviewed in the RFE/RL *Research Report*,

> "shows respect for the way in which the US and UN coalition conducted the Gulf War. It states that first strikes may begin in air and space, not by land; that coordinated simultaneous operations by air, air defense, naval and highly mobile assault landing groups aimed at strategic objectives will be carried out; and that precision weapons will be used in great depth, accompanied by the simultaneous or preemptive use of electronic warfare. Then, in subsequent stages, large ground forces may be introduced under powerful air cover... It should be noted that the use of the word "may" in this last instance is the first indication in the country's formal doctrine that modern, long-range, conventional weapons might be decisive in war without the commitments of large ground formations".[24]

The excitement over weapon modernization caused a flurry in the international arms trade, with producers eager to sell and even minor countries eager to acquire the most modern weapons. Pointing to the armaments fever in Asia, the *International Herald Tribune* notes:

> "The leading sellers are American and European firms anxious to recoup profits lost in traditional markets where tensions have been greatly reduced. Their main selling point is the record of high-tech weaponry in the Gulf."[25]

Thus the USA has been showing little restraint in competing in weapon sales with other major powers. Two such deals – the sales of combat jets to Saudi Arabia and to Taiwan totalling US $14.8 billion, announced in September 1992 – outstrip the value of US arms sales to all nations of the Third World in 1991.[26] At the same time Russia, in a rush for foreign currency, has been offering a variety of sophisticated weapons to countries around the globe, even to the Chinese adversary. As emphasized by Russian foreign minister, Andrei V. Kozyrev, arms "is one of the few commodities left by the former Soviet Union which can be competitive on the world market".[27] On the other hand, China has assumed the role of one of the main purveyors of rather unconventional arms to the Third World.[28]

Coming at a time of flux in international relations, this race in modern military technology prompted by the experiences in the Gulf War has contributed substantially to perpetuate the widespread politico-military malaise and to speed up armaments.

Armaments and Military Expenditures in Times of Transition

A distinct feature of armaments and military expenditure in the post-Cold War period is the process of accommodation to the erratic times of transition – some temperance on the one hand and long-term planning on the other hand. In line with the START and CFE treaties, obsolete and redundant weapons are being eliminated and new deployment patterns initiated. At the same time, in the strategic-doctrinal domain, armed forces are being restructured and new deterrent and contingency planning is taking shape. In armaments themselves there is a clear tendency away from serial production of weapons which are costly and may in no time become antiquated, towards greater emphasis on military R & D and test modelling of readily-available new generations of weapons and weapon systems – more efficient in speed, range, accuracy, versatility, target acquisition, penetration and non-detectability. Available weapon production capacities are filled by arms trading.

The idea of getting rid of superfluous overkill weapons and slowing down their production, while concentrating on R & D innovation, is something the military scientific-technological community has been advocating since the demise of the Cold War. In spring 1990 two prominent scientists of the Los Alamos National Laboratory, Joseph F. Pilat and Paul C. White, pleaded:

> "If one believes that the world is poised on the threshold of a military-technological revolution, and that the prospect of East-West conflict in the next ten years is low, than greater emphasis should be placed on R & D and modernization than on maintaining current active force levels. Traditional Western reliance on technology will grow, not diminish in the years ahead... Prudence dictates a shift in emphasis from deployed to deployable forces, entailing an R & D program designed to provide a range of rapidly producible and deployable weapon systems."[29]

It is well known that military laboratories and R & D have long been working hard to develop new weapon technologies which would revolutionize the art of warfare. As the 1990 *Jane's Strategic Weapon Systems* noted:

> "The range of new technologies currently under study is very wide and includes both directed and kinetic energy weapons. The first of these include lasers, neutral and charged particle beams and radio frequency beams. The kinetic energy weapons are the kind we are already used to, but they now come with precision guidance and will soon have the very high velocities provided by electromagnetic propulsion. All these weapons will eventually have the option of space-basing to increase their versatility and hence promise, or threaten, new military options. The real concern is ... that they will spread their capabilities to all theatres of weaponry, including offensive systems."[30]

Commenting on the shift in armaments expenditure in the 1992 US military budget, the *New York Times* wrote:

> "The Pentagon plans to suspend production of most new weapons after developing test models... There would not be an automatic move from design to production of future generations of weapons still on the drawing board, or in the imagination of engineers... The Pentagon would suspend production until the weapon was needed and was affordable. Ideally, the weapons could then be produced on short notice to meet crises."[31]

This orientation is fairly well reflected in the US military budget. Overall, US military expenditures in the post-Cold War period fell by approximately

4% annually, amounting in FY 1992-93 to US $274.5 billion (not counting expenditures for the Gulf War covered largely by contributions from Japan, Germany and the Gulf states). In comparison to the high rate of military expenditures in 1980, US national defense outlays for 1992, at constant prices, grew by 36.2%.[32] Yet in comparison to 1980, projected real change in US defense expenditure for research, development, testing and evaluation (RDT&E) shows an even greater increase: by 1992 it grew by 79% and for defense energy (nuclear weapons) by 139%.[33] Budget authority for military RDT&E grew from 1982 to 1991 from 9.2 to 12% of the national defense budget, and the percentage share for defense energy grew from 2.2 to 4%, together reaching US $46.1 billion in 1991.[34]

Within military RDT&E budgetary expenditures, the shares for the Strategic Defense Initiative and the Tactical Missile Defense Initiative show an increase in current prices from US$ 3119.6 in 1991 to US $5657.0 billion in 1993.[35] While US investments in current-generation weapons systems in FY 1992 decreased on the average by 10%, investments in next-generation weapons systems increased at the same time by 13%.[36] It is to be emphasized that much US military expenditure is invested in secret "black budget" programs mainly devoted to weapon modernization. Such programs amounted in 1989 to US $36 billion;[37] increasing in the post-Cold War period, they were estimated in 1992 to comprise approximately 18% of the defense budget.

Reliably comparable figures from Russia are lacking. It is, however, known that in the years 1991-1992 military production was reduced considerably, though "there were still many reports of weapon modernisation and continuing military R & D".[38] In fact, Moscow's new military doctrine "commits Russia to reducing its procurement of mass-produced weapons and equipment but to retaining a sufficient level of production capability and research and development".[39]

Similar patterns of preserving defense production capabilities with special attention to military R & D are apparent also in Western Europe. Perhaps even more than in the USA, European countries are sensitive to the flux in the international situation at a time of turbulence in the neighboring East. The aggregate military expenditure of European NATO countries remained almost unchanged in 1991 as in 1990, stabilizing at about US $150 billion at 1988 prices. According to UN sources "the process of developing new and sophisticated weaponry has not been halted".[40]

Most conspicuous are trends towards a renewed arms race in the Asian-Pacific region with military technology on the ascent. This area is emerging as the zone with the fastest rise in military expenditures. In 1991 China increased its military budget by 12% in real terms and again in 1992 by 10%. According to Japan's Mid-Term Defense Plan for the years 1991-1995, military R & D is to be doubled in relation to the 1991 level and trebled in relation to mid-1980, increasing annually by US $1.5-2 billion at 1990-1991 prices. More than in any other country, Japan's military R & D interacts closely with civilian R & D dualpurpose technologies.[41] There is growing concern in Asia about the danger of proliferation of weapons of mass destruction. Advanced conventional weapons are becoming readily available, and many Asian countries are enhancing their conventional arsenals. Ballistic missile technologies are spreading to India, Pakistan and North Korea. Advanced combat fighters and warships with modern missile systems are becoming commonplace. The risk of an intense regional arms race is growing.[42]

The post-Cold War transition period, with a future as yet unknown, is fraught with a new armaments momentum of perilous proportions.

Contingency Planning

The precarious atmosphere of transition from the Cold War to a future still in the balance is proving a fertile breeding ground for speculative thinking and contingency planning. Prompted by wary vigilance, this posture tends to incite hasty overreaction in military preparedness. Eventually, excess programming may slide into a self-fulfilling prophecy, with a return to renewed hostility.

As the world order is being re-arranged, an integral element of the politico-military environment, is a scramble for new positions of authority on the part of old and new national actors, both major powers and ascendant regional states. National interests are being redefined and deterrence postures refocused, all with the aim of coping with fresh strategic challenges and guarding against new threats. Force structures of national armies and military alliances are being amended to suit new strategic conditions.

With the imminent threat from the East receding, and new sources of tension and violence surfacing elsewhere throughout the world, feverish efforts are being made in favor of an adequate military rebuttal, in competition and cooperation. The United States and NATO are striving to build up rapid reaction forces to intervene in crisis areas within Europe and beyond. Europe's 9-country Western Union, awakened to new life, is aiming to set up a military force to shield European security, with Germany and France currently engaged in forming a joint military corps as the nucleus of a European army. The Conference on Security and Cooperation in Europe (CSCE) is seeking to perform peace-keeping and peace-enforcing operations in cooperation with NATO forces. Both Germany and Japan seem eager to restore their military muscle, if only under the mantle of UN peace-keeping and peace-enforcing units to begin with. And Russia, trying to halt the decomposition of its empire, is laboring hard to reconstruct the military-political cohesion of the lands of the former Soviet Union within the framework of the CIS. In many ways, previous military alliances and new military groupings resemble heroes in search of new roles.

The atmosphere of political and military strain and uncertainty is well reflected in the nervous contingency planning in US military corridors. A distinct example was the draft US Defense Planning Guidance for the fiscal years 1994-1999 which was leaked to the press in February 1992. It contained a number of scenarios for possible future military engagements around the globe, with the main fiat being that whatever gravitational pull may arise in the shift from a bipolar to a multipolar world, the USA should strive to ensure that no rival power challenge its dominant superpower position. With visions of a unipolar world, the aim was to contain not only "resurgent / emergent global threat" (acronym REGT), a euphemism for the possible rise of a resurgent authoritarian Russia, but also, in the longer perspective, the ascent of other rival industrial powers with possible nuclear capability such as Germany and Japan.[43]

Reports of these strategic Pentagon designs met with a critical reaction from the Congress and the US press. Subsequently, the Defense Planning Guidance was redrafted in tone, omitting direct references to Germany and Japan as potential military rivals. Yet the most substantial passages of the February draft survived.[44] As stated in editorial comment of the *Washington Post:* "The music is now being changed, but the earlier force plans remain in effect".[45] In an atmosphere of uncertainty and instability on the international politico-military scene, and with the disappearance of the old force equilibrium, military planners seem inclined to prepare for the worst. A crucial ingredient for such planning is the preservation and enhancement of military strength.

In less detail but in a more comprehensive way, the Russian military have set about addressing their new tasks in a world where they face the dilemma of accommodating to a much reduced imperial profile on the one hand, while retaining sufficient military vitality, nuclear and conventional, for a conceivable comeback as a major power on the Eurasian continent on the other hand. For the moment, the emerging new Russian military doctrine, expressly drafted for the "transitional period"[46], out of circumstantial exigencies, seems inner- rather than outward-oriented, defensive rather than offensive, mainly oriented to regain cohesion and dominance over the lands of the former Soviet Union, within the framework of the CIS. Tasks like finding a way out of the slump, restoring fighting capabilities, defending borders and territorial integrity are predominant. The new doctrine in this context recognizes political, economic, territorial, religious and ethnic disputes as possible sources of war. But it also indicates grimly that peace can be endangered by the aspirations of foreign powers for world and regional hegemony, and the stationing of powerful armed formations near Russia's borders, as well as military blackmail of Russia and violation of the rights of Russian citizens in the former republics of the USSR.[47]

In a broader world-view, turning to "the strategic nature of possible war", the current Russian military doctrine excludes neither a nuclear nor a large-scale conventional conflagration which may grow out of regional conflicts.[48] Taking as a point of departure a vague and sketchy notion of "sufficiency" in strategic and general purpose forces, Russia would then aim to preserve the strategic balance, maintain the capability of force generation, and keep troops at appropriate levels of readiness, with an emphasis on forming rapid-reaction forces.[49] A central tenet, parallel to the dominant US and NATO doctrine, is deterrence, which assumes the command of "sufficient" conventional and nuclear forces able to deter any adversary.[50]

In sum, judging from dominant politico-military thinking and military planning in East and West, we must conclude that world peace and war horizons remain rather gloomy. An old force equilibrium has gone, and a new balance or imbalance cannot as yet be discerned. In the meantime armament continues.

Nuclear Testing and Nuclear Proliferation

Continued nuclear testing was long interpreted as a sign of the on-going modernization of nuclear weapons and adherence to the defensive-offensive strategy of nuclear deterrence. Officially, the nuclear powers viewed testing as necessary to ensure the safety and reliability of nuclear stockpiles. It has, however, for years been established by reputable scientists that sufficient knowledge and experience has accumulated for the maintenance of safety and reliability of nuclear arsenals by non-nuclear and chemical means in combination with computer simulation.[51] Given also the ominous environmental effects of nuclear testing,[52] strong pressures for a comprehensive test ban (CTB) became manifest in international opinion. The main message is to get rid of nuclear weapons altogether. In its appeal to Presidents Bush and Yeltsin in June 1992, the Pugwash Conference on Science and World Affairs emphasized:

> "Nuclear testing nourishes the impression that these weapons have legitimate military application for which the most advanced military powers envision a continuing and evolving need. This cannot fail to reinforce beliefs in the usability of nuclear weapons, hence will increase the chance of their use, not least because of their acquisition by additional nations."[53]

Mounting opposition to continued nuclear testing and favour for a CTB coincided with the demise of the Soviet empire. The Soviet Union and its successor state, Russia, were also the first to declare a moratorium on nuclear testing. Following 48 Soviet tests conducted in the years 1987-1990, President Gorbachev announced in October 1991 a one-year moratorium, which was extended in October 1992 by President Yeltsin until mid-1993.[54] The call for a moratorium was then picked up by France. Having conducted 36 tests in the years 1987-1991, France declared a moratorium in April 1992 until the end of 1992. But neither China or the UK, nor the United States accepted the challenge for a halt in testing. Apparently they ranked the technical modernization benefits of testing higher than moral and political compulsion. In 1992 China conducted two tests – one of them, in May 1992, with an explosive power of several hundred kilotons, much higher than the 150 kt limit established by the US-USSR Threshold Test Ban Treaty (TTBT) of 1974. The UK conducted one test annually in the years 1989-1991, using as testing ground the Nevada desert in the US West. The USA conducted altogether 54 tests in the years 1987-1991, and an additional six nuclear tests in 1992. But bowing to pressure from public opinion and the US Congress,

President Bush signed on 2 October, 1992 a bill which provides for a maximum of 15 tests between 1 July, 1993 and 30 September, 1996, with a maximum of five tests annually and a halt to testing as from September 1996, provided that Russia does not resume testing.[55]

US Administrations have a long record of opposing a CTB, all the while repeating that a CTB remains a "long-term" objective. The US position has been made plain at major international fora dealing with nuclear weapon testing and nuclear proliferation. Thus at the September 1990 Fourth Review Conference of the 1968 Nuclear Non-Proliferation Treaty (NPT), the United States and the UK categorically rejected demands for a CTB. For the first time in the history of the NPT Review Conferences, the 1990 meeting failed to arrive at a Final Declaration reaffirming the basic commitment of the NPT "to pursue negotiations in good faith on effective measures relating to the cessation of the nuclear arms race at an early date and to nuclear disarmament".[56] Also, the Partial Test Ban Treaty (PTBT) Amendment Conference, convened in January 1991 with the aim of converting the PTBT into a Comprehensive Nuclear Test Ban, ended in failure. A majority of conference participants supported the amendment, but it encountered strong opposition from the USA and the UK. In the end, the motion for an amendment was not even put to the vote.

The US position in the post-Cold War period has even seemed to be hardening. On the one hand the strategy of nuclear deterrence, as pursued by the US administration, has become crucial as the main pillar of military predominance in what is to be a unipolar world. On the other hand, there has been agitation for modernization and research for new generations of nuclear weapons to suit the wide-ranging contingency scenarios of an unstable world. In particular, following the Gulf War experience, there has been a trend to conventionalize nuclear weapons, to make them usable not only in large-scale warfare but also in Third World, low-intensity engagements. In line with this, nuclear weapon laboratories seem to be concentrating on the development of specific types of new weapons with extremely small nuclear yields of very high accuracy and little collateral damage. These include mini- and micro-nukes to be used as pinpoint earth penetrators against particular targets as well as other exotic technology warheads to paralyse enemy movements and concentrations.[57]

There is also an interconnection between nuclear testing and the SDI program. Indeed, it has been officially admitted that "a number of new classified (SDT) weapon concepts were in the early stage of development and could not be tested if nuclear testing was limited to establishing only the safety and reliability of weapons".[58]

Does, then, the October 1992 bill on the limitation of nuclear testing and a CTB accord in 1996 herald a new US position on nuclear testing?

There is certainly no shift regarding reliance on nuclear weapons for deterrence purposes. But would a CTB in 1996 only confirm that problems of safety and reliability of the nuclear stockpile do not require nuclear explosions and can be assured by laboratory technology? Would the objective of modernization of nuclear weapons be abandoned? Or are we rather on the threshold of breakthrough new laboratory technology which would not only assure safety and reliability of the nuclear arsenal but also open ways to modernize weapons by laboratory means?

In this context, it is worthwhile to recall the circumstances under which the Partial Test Ban Treaty (PTBT) was concluded in 1963. The conclusion of the PTBT was, like the current pressures for a CTB, preceded by an outcry of public opinion concerned about the adverse impact of atmospheric nuclear tests on air pollution and human health. But the USA and USSR finally agreed on the PTBT only after they had mastered the technology of underground tests. After the PTBT, testing simply moved underground, and was even intensified.[59]

Can a parallel be drawn between the circumstances of abandoning atmospheric nuclear testing in 1963 and current endeavors for a CTB? Technological advances in laboratory nuclear testing are making rapid progress. These advances may include so-called inertial confinement fusion (ICF) by which laboratory micro-explosions would be triggered by laser or particle beams combined with computer simulations.[60] Should these R & D exertions succeed fully, we may face a situation where a CTB would be followed by a proliferation of laboratory nuclear weapon testing and modernization, with implicit vertical and horizontal nuclear proliferation. It is thus high time that the call for a CTB be extended and specified to include the commitment to get rid of nuclear weapons altogether – including the production of weapons-grade fissile materials.

In this context we may note that only recently, recalling the 1962 Cuban missile crisis, "replete with examples of misinformation, misjudgement, miscalculation", former US Secretary of Defense Robert S. McNamara came to the conclusion that "we should seek to return to a non-nuclear world".[61]

In the meantime, however, nuclear proliferation is on the ascent.[62] Though China and France in 1992 acceded to the 1968 Nuclear Non-

Proliferation Treaty (NPT), bringing the number of NPT signatories to 144, the non-proliferation regime remains precarious.[63] The case of Iraq, an NPT member which had accepted its safeguards, is a striking example of the feasibility of evading control and trying in secret to develop nuclear weapons. More and more countries are ready to supply nuclear state-of-the-art technology, equipment and services to nations aspiring to nuclear capability – which may undermine nonproliferation efforts.[64]

As long as the major nuclear powers view nuclear weapons as useful for deterrence, for defense and offence, weaker actors in the international community will strive to follow suit and acquire nuclear weapons as a shield against stronger neighbors or world powers.[65] Some local actors would even argue that nuclear proliferation may stabilize the regional balance similar to the deterrence effect in major power relations.[66] On the horizon there is even the spectre of Germany and Japan, with sufficient knowledge and equipment to produce nuclear weapons, "propelled" to nuclear capability. Indeed, Japan is already causing apprehension among Western experts by taking steps to amass the world's largest stockpile of plutonium.[67] And Germany, in the wake of the disarray in the former Soviet Union, may have second thoughts about deterrent assurance of its national security.[68]

The danger of nuclear proliferation increased considerably with the disintegration of the Soviet Union and the joining of the nuclear club by Ukraine, Belarus and Kazakhstan.[69] A number of Third World countries aiming to go nuclear may now find it easier to get access to nuclear production know-how and even procure highly enriched uranium and plutonium.[70] It is to be noted that Kazakhstan holds one of the greatest nuclear complexes of the former Soviet Union – the Semipalatinsk testing site – which may include large facilities for the assembly of nuclear weapons. And Kazakhstan is located rather near the arc of countries in the Middle East and South Asia, with crypto-nuclear and threshold states eager to get full nuclear capability.

Closely related to the problem of nuclear proliferation is the spread of ballistic missiles with a potential to carry nuclear warheads and other weapons of mass destruction. It is estimated that a total of 26 countries either possess ballistic missiles or may possess them by the year 2000.[71] As the linkage with nuclear proliferation is clear, the concept of banning ballistic missiles now ranks high on the arms control agenda.[72]

Both the problem of a CTB and banning of ballistic missiles are intimately linked to controlling and taking the edge off the modern military technology thrust. In trying to formulate an agenda for a nuclear-free and demilitarized world, a crucial question is transparency of the huge science-based military technological sector[73] and redeeming military R & D for humane purposes.

Ingredients of an Agenda for a Demilitarized World

With the armaments momentum again on the ascent, is it possible to revive the vision of a peaceful New World Order?

The end of the Cold War still offers a unique opportunity to move from a polarized and militarized world to a cooperative endeavor in pursuit of non-violent, civilized relations between nations and human beings. The way to proceed in questions of armament and disarmament is no longer to revert to convoluted Cold War arms control designs. The aims and substance of arms control, atuned to Cold War conditions, did little to restrain armaments. Essentially, arms control aimed at joint steering of armaments to abet the strategic balance of major powers, while offsetting attempts at quantitative arms reductions by qualitative weapon modernization.[74] Arms control was intimately tied to the technological momentum. What is now needed is change of direction. The over-arching long-term objective, posited by the United Nations, must be a revival of the idea of General and Complete Disarmament (GCD).[75]

A new agenda for associative progressive advance towards GCD and human security needs to be set up. In fact, the broad lines of the program of action for disarmament, adopted by the UN General Assembly in 1978, retain their basic validity.[76] A timely goal should be "the complete elimination of nuclear weapons"[77], with an ulterior GCD aspiration,

> "to ensure that war is no longer an instrument for settling international disputes and that the use and the threat of force are eliminated from international life, as provided for in the Charter of the United Nations... General and complete disarmament under strict and effective control shall permit states to have at their disposal only those non-nuclear forces, armaments, facilities and establishments as are agreed to be necessary to maintain internal order and protect the personal security of citizens and in order that states shall support and provide agreed manpower for a United Nations peace force..."[78]

The blueprint for GCD was laid down in the September 1951 US-Soviet Joint Statement on Agreed Principles for Disarmament Negotiations.[79] As further developed in the US "Outline for Basic Provisions of GCD in a

Peaceful World" and in the Soviet "Draft Treaty"[80], GCD provided for the establishment of an International Disarmament Organization (IDO), within the UN framework, to coordinate, supervise and exercise control over the execution of the Treaty's assumptions. The US Outline specifically pointed to the need for

> "full international cooperation in the fields of scientific research and development, and to engage in full exchange of scientific and technological information and free interchange of views among scientific and technical personnel."[81]

The Soviet Draft Treaty added that

> "All scientific research in the military field at all scientific and research institutions shall be discontinued... Inspectors of the IDO shall exercise control over these measures."[82]

Alas, negotiations on GCD proved unsuccessful. Underlying the failure was the explosion in the early 1960s of novel military technology, with the development and deployment of supersonic bombers, of ICBMs and SLBMs, of guided missiles, military satellites and new generations of nuclear weapons. The impulse of science-based military technology created an impasse in the GCD negotiations. In fact, interference from burgeoning military technology was to become a recurrent feature of disarmament and arms control negotiations in the Cold War period. It reflected the structural, dynamic nature of the pushpower of the unfolding innovative military technology.[83] With the beginning of the 1960s came a shift in negotiations from efforts at disarmament to the design of arms control.

At the opening of the 1990s, military R & D was employing globally approximately one and a half million persons, of whom at least one million were scientists and engineers with academic degrees.[84] It consumed globally up to US $140 billion.[85] Moreover, the influence of military R & D extends far beyond its own borders, penetrating civilian R & D in a spin-on or spin-in bid to make use of available accomplishments in the civilian sector for military purposes. A symbiotic interface between military and civilian technology has developed, with dual-purpose civil-military applications a central issue. Since modern science-based technology is today a decisive determinant for human development, the activities and feats of military technology not only affect the sphere of armaments but also the fundamentals of human life and society.

If we are to aim for a peaceful, open and kind world, we shall have to pay special attention to the workings and role of military R & D. A basic precondition for success in restraining military technology is greater transparency and openness in the exertion of contemporary science and technology, with particular heed to the performance of military laboratories and military R & D.[86] In our search for a disarmed and convivial world, we must endeavor within the framework of comprehensive disarmament to convert military R & D for peaceful use – not to serve armaments but to help satisfy unmet basic human needs.

Achieving General and Complete Disarmament, and restructuring the workings of science and technology – this is certainly a tall order. During the Cold War, military R & D was the sacred cow of national security. With the end of the Cold War, we need to adopt a new attitude and embrace new thinking. This will require political resolve and persistence. Either we face this challenge, or we lose an historical chance to bring about creative change.

NOTES

1. See Birger Heldt, Peter Wallensteen and Kjell-Åke Nordquist, "Major armed conflicts in 1991" in *Sipri Yearbook 1992, World Armaments and Disarmament,* Oxford University Press 1992, pp. 417-456. In 1991 major armed conflicts (with battle-related deaths of at least 1000 persons) were waged in 30 sites in different parts of the world.

2. See tables on US and Soviet strategic forces with START counting rules, in *The Military Balance 1991-1992,* The International Institute for Strategic Studies, London 1991, pp. 219-220. For greater details on START see *ibid,* pp. 216-218, and in Regina Coven Karp, "START Treaty and the future of strategic nuclear arms control", *Sipri Yearbook 1992,* op.cit., pp. 13-66.

3. *SIPRI Yearbook 1992,* op.cit., p. 28.

4. Robert MacNamara and Hans A. Bethe, "Reducing the Risk of Nuclear War", *Bulletin of Peace Proposals,* Vol. 17, No. 2, 1986, p. 127.

5. There have been reports that nuclear warheads from Pershing II missiles being eliminated under the Intermediate-Range Nuclear Forces (INF) Treaty were being converted into new nuclear bombs. Cf. Robert S. Norris and William M. Aricin, "Beating Swords into Swords", *The Bulletin of the Atomic Scientists,* Vol. 46, No. 9, November 1990, pp. 14-16.

6 President-elect Bill Clinton also stressed this orientation. While emphasizing in his Veteran Day speech the need "to keep this country the strongest in the world", he said that he favored increasing the nation's aircraft and sealift capability "because in this uncertain world we may never know where we are needed". See "Clinton Pledges 'Strongest' Military Despite Cuts" (The Associated Press). *International Herald Tribune*, November 12, 1992,p.2.

7 Cf. Peter Pringle, "Doubts raised in Moscow on arms deal", *The Independent*, June 18, 1992, p. 12. See also Christopher Paine and Thomas B. Cochran, "So little time, so many weapons, so much to do", *The Bulletin of the Atomic Scientists*, Vol. 48, No. 1, January-February 1992, pp. 13-16.

8 Cf. Thomas L. Friedman, "US-Russian Talks Snagged. Moscow Raises Questions on Missile Pact", *International Herald Tribune*, October 16, 1992, p. 5. See also Michael R. Gordon, "Keeping an Eye on Warheads. Democrats Now Want Verification of Russia's Stockpile", *International Herald Tribune*, July 4-5, 1992, p. 3.

9 See text of the START Treaty in *SIPRI Yearbook 1992*, op.cit. Art. XVII.3, p. 57.

10 Laurence Freedman, "Still enough warheads to go round", *The Independent*, June 18, 1992, p. 29.

11 See table 2.8 on world strategic nuclear weapon arsenals 1985-1991, *SIPRI Yearbook 1992*, op. cit. p. 82.

12 In a speech to the Ukrainian Parliament on 30 September, 1992, President Leonid Kravchuk said that Ukraine "does not want to keep its finger on the nuclear button. but it should give the world community guarantees that the nuclear weapons stationed on its territory will not be used by a third state". He reaffirmed his country's commitment to maintaining substantial control over the weapons on its territory and over their elimination. He also rejected the idea of Ukraine's joining any defense alliance formed by member countries of the Commonwealth of Independent States. See *RFE/RL Research Report*, Vol. 1, No. 41, 16 October, 1992, p. 53.
It has also been reported that an agreement was reached in August 1992 between Russia and Kazakhstan on keeping Russian strategic nuclear weapons in Kazakhstan for seven years. See *RFE/RL Research Report*, Vol. 1, No. 35, 4 September, 1992, p. 41.

13 Fedor Burlatsky, adviser to Nikita Khrushchev, recalling the circumstances of the 1962 Cuba missile crisis, warned in October 1992: A security crisis could again occur, this time involving Russia, Ukraine, Belarus and Kazakhstan, where nuclear missiles are based... The most immediate problem is controlling missiles. It cannot be ruled out that separatists and extremists might seize them for blackmail. Observation

points manned by American officers in the four nuclear states, with the approval of these states, could provide a barrier against such adventurism and a future missile crisis. See Fedor Burlatsky, "Recall How Things Can Go Too Far", *International Herald Tribune*, 27 October, 1992, p. 4

14 See Table 12.3 Subzonal ceilings of the 1990 CFE Treaty, *SIPRI Yearbook 1992*, p. 469.

15 See Michael Z. Wise, "Pact to Limit Troops in Europe is Ready", *International Herald Tribune*, July 7, 1992, p. 3

16 "Hard Times Lead Russia to Cut Navy" (Reuters), *International Herald Tribune*, 9 October, 1992, p. 2.

17 Cf. Barton Gellman, "Reassessment of Stealth Jet and Cruise Missiles", *International Herald Tribune*, April 11-12, 1992. p. 6.

18 John Pike, Sarah Lang, and Eric Stambler, "Military Use of Outer Space", *SIPRI Yearbook 1992*, op.cit., p. 121.

19 Cf. R. Jeffrey Smith, "U.S. Anti-Missile Testers Reportedly Exaggerated Successes", *International Herald Tribune*, September 17, 1992, p. 1.

20 Dick Cheney, *Annual Report to the President and the Congress*, U.S. Government Printing Office, Washington, D.C., January 1991, p. 58.

21 Cf. Paul F. Walker and Eric Stambler, "The dirty little weapons", *The Bulletin of the Atomic Scientists*, Vol. 47, No. 4, May 1991, pp. 21-24.

22 Secretary of Defense, *Annual Report to the President and the Congress*, op. cit., pp. 58/60.

23 Cf. Erich H. Arnett, "Welcome to Hyperwar", *The Bulletin of the Atomic Scientists*, Vol. 48, No. 7, September 1992, pp. 14-21.

24 Scott McMichael, "Russia's New Military Doctrine", *RFE/RL Research Report*, Vol. 1, No. 40, 9 October 1992, pp. 47-48.

25 R. Jeffrey Smith, "Armaments Fever Spreads in Asia as it Ebbs in Europe", *International Herald Tribune*, March 10, 1992, pp. 1/4.

26 Cf. Michael R. Gordon, "Russian Sales Fuel Arms Race", *International Herald Tribune*, October 19, 1992, pp. 1/4.

27 Interview with Michael Richardson, "Russian Far East Warms to Neighbors", *International Herald Tribune*, July 27, 1992, p. 2. See also Von Ole Diehl, "Russland als Waffenbasar", *Europa Archiv*, 47. Jahr, 20. Folge, 25. Oktober 1992, pp. 603-609; Peter Almquist and Edwin Bacon, "Arms Exports in a post-Soviet Market", *Arms Control Today*, July-August 1992, pp. 12-17.

28 Cf. Richard A. Bitzinger, "Arms to Go: Chinese Arms Sales to the Third World", *International Security*, Vol. 17, No. 2, Fall 1992, pp. 84-111.

29 Joseph F. Pilat and Paul C. White, "Technology and Strategy in a Changing World", *Washington Quarterly*, Vol. 13, No.2, Spring 1990, pp. 84-85.

30 Duncan Lennox, Foreword to *Jane's Strategic Weapons Systems*, Couldson, Surrey, UK, 1990.

31 Eric Schmitt, "Pentagon Plans Deep Cutbacks in New Weapons, Big Savings Sought in Shift to Buying Test Models Only", reprinted in *International Herald Tribune*, 25-26 January, 1992, p. 1.

32 See US national defense outlays, 1980-96, *SIPRI Yearbook 1992*, op.cit., table 7.3, p. 197.

33 See "Projected real change in US defense expenditures, budget authority, 1992 and 1995", *ibid*, table 7.9, p. 203.

34 See "Allocations of US national defense budget authority, FY 1982-91", *ibid*, table 7.4, p. 198.

35 See "Budgetary expenditure on the Strategic Defense Initiative and the Tactical Missile Defense Initiative, FYs 1991-93", *ibid*, table 7.2, p. 195.

36 See "US investment in current and next-generation weapon systems, FY 1992", *ibid*, table 7.8, p. 202.

37 Robert Pear, "Congress Moves to Control Secret Military Funding", *International Herald Tribune*, 2 November, 1990, p. 3.

38 Saadet Deger and Somnath Sen, "World military expenditure", *SIPRI Yearbook 1992*, op.cit., pp. 226-227.

39 Scott McMichael, "Russia's New Military Doctrine", *RFE/RL Research Report*, Vol 1, No. 40, October 1992, p. 48.

40 Cf. Barry James, "Awaiting Europe's Arms Cuts", *International Herald Tribune*, August 13, 1992, p. 11; and Deger & Sen, *SIPRI Yearbook 1992*, op.cit., pp. 226-227.

41 Cf. Marek Thee, *Science and technology: between civilian and military research and development*, Geneva: United Nations Institute for Disarmament Research, Research Papers No. 7, 1990, pp. 18-19.

42 Cf. *SIPRI Yearbook*, op.cit., pp. 240-250; see also Paul Dibb, "Asia-Pacific Security: Act Now to Avoid a Regional Arms Race", *International Herald Tribune*, August 26, 1992, p. 4; Michael Richardson, "Asia Sees a Risk In Tokyo-Beijing Military Rivalry", *ibid*, October 20, 1992, pp. 1/5; Gerald Segal, "Managing New Arms Races in Asia/Pacific", *The Washington Quarterly*, Vol. 15, No. 3, Summer 1992, pp. 83-101; Douglas M. Johnson, "Anticipating Instability in the Asia-Pacific Region", *ibid*, pp. 103-112.

43 Cf. Patrick E. Tyler, "The Seven Deadly Scenarios: Pentagon Plans for Theoretical, but Costly Emergencies", *International Herald Tribune*,

February 18, 1992, pp. 1/4. Also: Patrick E. Tyler, "Pentagons New World Order: US to Rein Supreme", *ibid*, March 9, 1992, pp. 1-2; Leslie H. Gelb, "World Cop: Daydreams of Grandeur", *ibid*, 10 March, 1992, p. 8; Patrick E. Tyler, "Pentagons 'No Rivals' Plan Draws Fire", *ibid*, 11 March, 1992; Patrick E. Tyler, "Top Officials Thrash the 'No Rivals' Plan", *ibid*, 12 March, 1992.

44 Cf. Barton Gellman, "For Pentagon, Thwarting New Rivals Is No Longer Primary Aim", *International Herald Tribune*, 25 May, 1992, pp. 1/6.

45 "A New Pentagon Plan", *International Herald Tribune*, May 28, 1992, p. 6.

46 Scott McMichael, "Russia's New Military Doctrine", op. cit. p. 45.

47 *Ibid*, p. 46.

48 *Ibid*, p. 47.

49 *Ibid*, p. 48.

50 *Ibid*, p. 49.

51 Cf. Marek Thee, "The Pursuit of a Comprehensive Nuclear Test Ban", *Journal of Peace Research*, Vol. 25, No. 1, 1988, pp. 1-15. See also Ray L. Kidder, CTB: *The Way Ahead*, paper presented at the 42nd Pugwash Conference on Science and World Affairs, Berlin, September 1992.

52 In conjunction with nuclear arms production, the environmental consequences are alarming. Over 40 years of nuclear testing and production have resulted in the accumulation of immense amounts of radioactive nuclear waste. It is estimated that the costs of cleaning up of the nuclear arms mess in the USA alone would amount to US $300 billion. Redressing similar environmental problems in the former Soviet Union may be even more daunting. Russian environmetal experts report that facilities in the key nuclear complex Chelyabinsk-40 have produced radioactive waste in even greater quantities than those released by the Chernobyl disaster. See George Perkovich, "Counting the Costs of the Arms Race", *Foreign Policy*, No. 85, Winter 1991-92, pp. 58/87.

53 *Pugwash Newsletter*, July 1992, p. 1.

54 For data on nuclear explosions 1945-1991, see *SIPRI Yearbook 1992*, op. cit. pp. 117-119

55 For details see *Trust and Verify*, N. 32, October 1992, pp. 1-2.

56 Art. VI of the NPT. For the text of the NPT see *Arms Control and Disarmament Agreements*, Washington, D.C.: US Arms Control and Disarmament Agency, pp. 91-95.

57 Cf. William M. Arkin and Robert S. Norris, "Tiny Nukes for Mini Minds", *The Bulletin of Atomic Scientists*, Vol. 48, No. 3, April 1992, pp. 24-25.
58 Cf. Michael R. Gordon, "U.S. Cancels Last Test of SDI Laser Weapon", *International Herald Tribune*, July 22, 1992, p. 2.
59 See details in Marek Thee, "The Pursuit of a Comprehensive Nuclear Test Ban", op. cit., pp. 8-9. Cf. also "Chronology of Comprehensive Test Ban", *Arms Control Today*, November 1990, pp. 31-35.
60 Cf. Gsponer André, Bhupendra Jasani, and Sümer Sahin, "Emerging Nuclear Energy and Nuclear Weapon Proliferation", *Atomenergie-Kerntechnik*, Vol. 43, No. 3, pp. 169-174.
61 Robert S. McNamara, "Conclusion, 30 Years On: Better a Non-Nuclear World", *International Herald Tribune*, October 15, 1992, p. 4.
62 Cf. Jennifer Scarlott, "Nuclear Proliferation after the Cold War", *World Policy Journal*, Vol. VIII, No. 4, Fall 1991, pp. 687-710.
63 Cf. Leonard S. Spector, "Repentant Nuclear Proliferants", *Foreign Policy*, No. 88, Fall 1992, pp. 21-37.
64 Cf. William C. Potter, "The New Nuclear Suppliers", *Orbis*, Vol. 36, No. 2, Spring 1992, pp. 199-210.
65 Cf. Jasith Singh, "Nuclear Weapon Proliferation in Asia", *Strategic Analysis*, Vol. XIV, No. 2, March 1992, pp. 1345-1360; and Ali Sarvar Naqvi, "Don't Blame Proliferation on Pakistan", *International Herald Tribune*, July 22, 1992, p. 6.
66 Cf. Joseph F. Fitchett, "Atomic Weapons: Might Security Lie in Proliferation?" *International Herald Tribune*, March 3, 1992, pp. 1/6.
67 Cf. David E. Sanger, "Plutonium Stock Gives Japan Nuclear Lever", *International Herald Tribune*, November 10, 1992, pp. 1/7.
68 Cf. Joseph Fitchett, "Bomb's Allure for Bonn and Tokyo", *International Herald Tribune*, March 10, 1992, p. 1/6.
69 Cf. John M. Deutsch, "The New Nuclear Threat", *Foreign Affairs*, Vol. 71, No. 4, Fall 1992, pp. 120-134. Also "Nuclear Security and the Soviet Collapse", Daniel Ellsberg, interviewed by Jerry Sanders and Richard Caplan, *World Policy Journal*, Vol. IX, No. 1, Winter 1991-92, pp. 135-156.
70 Cf. Joseph Fitchett, "Specter of 'Instant' Powers Haunt Post-Soviet World", *International Herald Tribune*, March 3, 1992, pp. 1-2.
71 *SIPRI Yearbook 1992*, op. cit., p. 130.
72 Cf. Alton Frye, "Zero Ballistic Missiles", *Foreign Policy*, No. 88, Fall 1992, pp. 3-20.

73 Cf. Marek Thee, *Science and technology: between civilian and military research and development*, op. cit. pp. 1-21.
74 On the nature of arms control, see Marek Thee, "The Impact of Military Technology on Disarmament and Peace in Europe", *END Papers Nineteen, Spokesman 57*, Spring 1989, pp. 44-53.
75 See Final Document of the 1978 Special Session of the UN General Assembly Devoted to Disarmament, para 19; text in Marek Thee (Ed.), *Armaments, Arms Control and Disarmament*, A UNESCO Reader for Disarmament Education, Paris: UNESCO, pp. 217-239.
76 *Ibid.*
77 *Ibid*, para 47.
78 *Ibid*, para 19 & 111.
79 *Ibid*, pp. 240-241.
80 Texts in *Documents on Disarmament*, Washington DC: United States Arms Control and Disarmament Agency, 1963, Vol. I, pp. 351-382, and Vol. II, pp. 913-938.
81 *Ibid*, Vol. I, p. 379.
82 *Ibid*, Vol. II, p. 931.
83 Cf. Marek Thee, *Whatever Happened to the Peace Dividend?* Nottingham: Spokesman for European Labour Forum, 1991, pp. 54-83.
84 *Ibid*, p. 42.
85 *Ibid*, pp. 42-47.
86 Cf. Marek Thee, "The Quest for Openness Versus Secrecy in Science and Technology", in Rainer Rilling et al. (Eds.), *Challenges: Science and Peace in a Rapidly Changing Environment*, Bonn: Schriftenreihe Wissenschaft und Frieden, 1992, Vol. II, pp. 197-200.

4 THE ROLE OF THE UNITED NATIONS IN THE POST-COLD WAR ERA

*Johan Kaufmann, Dick Leurdijk
and Nico Schrijver*

"Present demands on the United Nations have no precedent in its history. The presence of the Organization is being more intensely felt world-wide as it helps people in danger, need or despair. The United Nations is constantly at work: from Security Council meetings and consultations on an almost continuous basis, to peace-keeping operations in four continents; from good offices and quiet diplomacy, to essential humanitarian missions and responses to emergencies all over the world; from major economic and social conferences, such as the Earth Summit, to technical cooperation activities in practically every developing country." (B. Boutros-Ghali, *Report of the Secretary-General on the Work of the Organization,* United Nations, New York, September 1992.)

This article is part of the research project "State of the United Nations Systems, Role and Readiness to Deal with Important International Issues" funded by the World Society Foundation and undertaken by Johan Kaufmann and Nico Schrijver with the cooperation of Dick Leurdijk. Nico Schrijver is head of the International Law Department, Institute of Social Studies, The Hague, Netherlands. Johan Kaufmann – a former Cleveringa Chair professor at the University of Leiden – was Dutch Ambassador to the United Nations and to Japan. Address: A. Godelweg 25, 2517 JE The Hague, Netherlands.

Introductory Remarks

In a world still groping for some kind of "new order", the United Nations is increasingly becoming the focal point in the search for new approaches to world problems. Can the world community stand by idly when, in the name of ethnicity, innocent groups within a country are subjected to cruel treatment? If a civil war threatens to destroy a country and leave its inhabitants exposed to mass famine and disease, should not the United Nations undertake some kind of action? Should the United Nations more vigorously than formerly undertake peace-making and peace-keeping missions? Can preventive diplomacy play a role in avoiding international or "domestic" conflicts? These and other questions confront humanity and raise issues on the appropriate role of the United Nations.

Here we endeavour to summarize the role of the United Nations in the post-cold war era as follows:
- the composition and functioning of the UN Security Council;
- the Gulf Crisis and the future of collective security arrangements;
- the future of conflict resolution, peace-keeping and nation-building;
- the UN system and its ability to deal with existing and emerging issues;
- the challenge of economic security and interdependence;
- towards new sources of finance;
- the sovereignty issue: fragmentation versus integration.

For most of these there exists a considerable gap between words and acts. The United Nations can do no more than the collective wisdom (or folly) of its member States will permit it to do. It must be hoped that wisdom will prevail.

Composition and Functioning of the Security Council

In recent years there has been consistently close cooperation among the five permanent Security Council members, particularly between the United States and the Soviet Union / Russian Federation. This dates back to the consultations leading to the adoption of resolution 598 (1987), imposing a truce between Iran and Iraq in order to terminate this "Gulf war".

The Permanent Five have been wise enough to stress repeatedly that their conclusions do not commit the Council as a whole and remain open to amendment. Yet, there is a real risk of a "directorate" role of the permanent members, not only vis-à-vis the non-permanent members but also vis-à-vis two other principal organs of the United Nations, the General Assembly and the Secretary-General. This has raised the question of the representativeness of Council decisions and hence discussions on the composition of the Security Council, especially with respect to the permanent members (each holding veto power) selected on the basis of the power relations and military capacities prevailing in 1945.

Four issues arise:

(a) Should the size of the Council be enlarged from its present membership of 15?

(b) Should states other than China, France, the Russian Federation, the United Kingdom and the United States be given permanent membership?

(c) Should the veto powers of the present five permanent members be abolished or modified?

(d) Given that economic and military conflicts are often closely linked, should the Security Council be given tasks in the wider area of economic issues and for environmental security?

Enlargement of the Council raises the question of its efficiency. Enlarged membership would make consensus-seeking more cumbersome and time-consuming.

Granting permanent membership to additional states (as has been proposed from time to time for Brazil, Germany, India, Japan, Nigeria and others) obviously raises very difficult questions of choice.

Modifying the present veto system implies the risk that the largest powers might be tempted to take action outside the Security Council and, by implication, outside the United Nations generally, while the present system can be seen (under favorable circumstances such as those since the end of the Cold War) as an incentive to achieve big power consensus and to pursue a multilateral approach in the context of the United Nations.

Giving wider attributes to the Security Council cannot be separated from the role of various existing organs, especially the Economic and Social Council.

Yet, while these observations would point to keeping things as they are, it is likely that the representativeness of the Council will come increasingly under attack, as recently illustrated by the Secretary-General's outburst on the Council's one-sided attention to wars of the rich (Gulf region, Yugoslavia), while neglecting wars of the poor (Somalia).

Amongst the many proposals and suggestions made, one of the most sensible seems to be to enlarge the Security Council by five permanent seats but without the right of veto. These new seats could be allocated to Brazil, Germany, India, Japan and Nigeria. This would greatly enhance the representativeness of the Council and *thus underscore the authority of its decisions,* without excessively compromising its efficiency. A related, interesting and additional variant is that, in the future, the European Community is to occupy only one permanent seat, occupied on a rotating basis by France, Germany and the UK. No doubt such changes in composition involve the cumbersome, time-consuming procedure of amending the UN Charter. But this could be avoided if an international consensus emerges on the necessity for such a change, as in 1963, when the number of non-permanent members was enlarged from 6 to 11 in order to reflect changes in the international community as a result of the decolonization process.

The Gulf Crisis and the Future of Collective Security Arrangements

Collective sanctions

The Gulf crisis led to an unprecedented series of important decisions by the Security Council. Most important were the imposition of a comprehensive trade and financial embargo on Iraq and occupied Kuwait and military action by an alliance of states to achieve the withdrawal of Iraq from Kuwait and restoration of peace in the region. In 1992, sanctions were also imposed upon Somalia, former Yugoslavia and Libya. Until recently, there was only limited use of collective economic sanctions, the trade embargo on Southern Rhodesia (1966-79) and the arms embargo on South Africa (1977 to the present) being the main examples. So far, the mandatory sanctions against Iraq have been the most important ones. Since Iraq and occupied Kuwait were very interwoven with the world economic and financial system, a whole network of trade, financial and human relationships became seriously affected. The overall impression is that the sanctions against Iraq were complied with remarkably well and more strictly than anyone dared to predict about collective economic sanctions imposed by the Security Council. They had a major negative impact on the Iraqi economy and civilian population. In this particular case it remains a matter of speculation how long it would have taken before (if at all) the Iraqi regime would have withdrawn its forces from Kuwait if only the embargo weapon had been imposed. An important lesson from the Gulf crisis is that, under specific circumstances, the international community is willing to join in collective sanctions against an aggressor State. However, another important lesson is that effective sanctions can result in unintended shifts in trade and financial flows to the serious detriment of many countries. The concept of collective burden-sharing under Chapter VII should also include compensation to innocent victims of a crisis and of enforcement measures; the hundreds of thousands of migrant laborers in the Gulf area and their home countries have been inadequately compensated for their severe sufferings.

Collective enforcement action

The military enforcement action against Iraq in January-February 1991 was not directly a United Nations operation (as provided for, *inter alia,* in Articles 42 to 47 of the UN Charter at the behest of the Security Council), but rather a collective self-defense action by Kuwait and "Member States co-operating with the Government of Kuwait" under Article 51 of the UN Charter. The Security Council had earlier forsaken resort to the use of force in the period till 16 January 1991, thus providing "a goodwill pause" and "one final opportunity" for Iraq to withdraw its forces from Kuwait (Resolution 678).

In the aftermath of the Gulf war, a major challenge relates to the future of collective enforcement action under Chapter VII of the UN Charter. Is the United Nations heading towards a position in which a more assertive Security Council quickly reacts to threats to, and breaches of, the peace, and to acts of aggression, but delegates to *ad hoc* coalition forces action to be taken "by all necessary means"? Does this authorization imply that the *collective* security arrangements of Article 42 remain dormant? Or could the UN's reaction to the Kuwaiti crisis serve as a first step towards reviving the Chapter VII provisions on collective security arrangements? Although speculations on such matters may be very challenging, one should not lose sight of the uniqueness of the Kuwaiti crisis. The naked aggression and the usurpation of the authority of a neighboring sovereign State has no precedent in the history of the United Nations (it can best be compared with the annexation of Austria and other countries by Germany in the late 1930s). Such an act of aggression is not likely to be repeated in the near future, because a potential aggressor would be deterred by the case of Kuwait. Also, the nearly unanimous stand of the world community and the management of the crisis by the Security Council are without parallel (only the Korean case bears some similarities). It is not appropriate to make sweeping statements and forecasts on the future of collective security, yet, if the Gulf crisis results in enhanced and steady willingness of the international community to channel its reactions to major crises through the Security Council rather than resorting to often controversial and escalating unilateral action, much will have been gained.

The Future of Conflict Resolution, Peace-Keeping and Nation-Building

Peace-keeping activities "old style", whether initiated by the Security Council (e.g. Cyprus), by the General Assembly (e.g. UNEF I) or by the Secretary-General (e.g. UNGOMAP, the UN Good Offices Mission in Afghanistan and Pakistan), will no doubt continue. Peace activities "new style" can relate to:
- Aid in preparing for nationhood (Namibia, Western Sahara);
- Supervision of domestic elections or referenda (Nicaragua, Haiti);
- Aid in overcoming domestic strife, including civil war (e.g. Cambodia, Central America, Angola);
- Verification of respect for human rights (El Salvador);
- Aid in coping with disasters and providing protection to UN humanitarian relief operations (Sudan, Iraq, Somalia).

Recently, the idea of a permanent UN "Police and Peace Force", replacing present ad hoc arrangements, has once again been put forward, among others in the UN Secretary-General's report 'Agenda for Peace' (June, 1992). Based on military and civilian contingents made permanently available to the UN by member states (with perhaps a core contingent instantly available) such a force could be deployed by the Security Council, or by the Secretary-General. Obviously, rules would have to be worked out to prevent arbitrary use of the UNPPF and to delimit the competencies of the Security Council, the General Assembly (with its budget power!) and the Secretary-General (the chief administrator). Very gradually the community of nations may be ready to accept such a drastic change in the organizational set-up of peace-keeping operations. In the short term it seems likely that *ad hoc* arrangements more or less akin to those at present will be continued, with probably a more conspicuous role for the Security Council.

It is worthwhile to point out that, in some cases, specialized organs can make their own contribution, perhaps not to conflict solution, but to conflict mitigation. Thus, the World Food Programme was able to negotiate, in December 1990, an agreement to re-open the port of Massawa, Ethiopia, for shipments of emergency food relief. This required separate negotiations, undertaken at the request of the UN Secretary-General, with the government of Ethiopia and the Eritrean People's Liberation Front. In 1989 UNICEF was able to negotiate an agreement with the government of Sudan and the opposition movement in the south of that country, on the safe passage of food etc. In El Salvador, several times each year of the conflict, a zone of tranquillity was created to permit vaccination and other health services for children. Something similar happened in Angola. The commitment of governments towards "periods of tranquillity" and "corridors of peace" in war-torn areas has been enshrined in the World Declaration on the Survival, Protection and Development of Children (paragraph 8 of point 20), and the accompanying Plan of Action (paragraph 25). Recent examples of what could be called micro-peace-keeping are the "blue routes", established by the UN Humanitarian Centers (UNHUC's) in Iraq, especially in the Iraq / Turkey and Iraq / Iran border areas, and the airport of Sarajewo and immediate surroundings in Bosnia.

The UN System and Its Ability to Deal With Existing and Emerging Issues

The present set-up of the UN and its Specialized Agencies is not well equipped to deal with many existing and emerging issues and problems. One dimension of unsolved continuing problems is the low status of women, with illiteracy, lack of access to family-planning and health services, maternal mortality, malnutrition, exclusion from agriculture and economic development programs all serving to delay and retard broader policy objectives. The United Nations made an important beginning through the UN Decade for Women with the development of information on women and on policies for governments and international organizations to tackle gender discrimination.

An example of a new issue is migration, especially from the South to the North. Large-scale, often unexpected migration has caused problems of economic and social readjustment, human rights and discrimination issues, etc. In the UN system these problems are dispersed, in terms of responsibility, amongst such agencies as the UN High Commissioner for Refugees, the UN Human Rights Center, Geneva, the new office for Humanitarian Affairs in the UN Secretariat (New York), the UN Population Fund (UNFPA) and to some extent the International Labor Organization (ILO) and the World Health Organization (WHO). An organization outside the UN system (the International Organization for Migration (IOM)) has done pioneer work on migration and related issues. A strong case can be made for the appointment of a single coordinator, whose competence would extend throughout the UN system and even include (as proved effective in the case of the humanitarian consequences of the Gulf conflict) non-governmental organizations like the International Committee of the Red Cross, to deal with all aspects of migration, refugees, human rights, especially in contacts with a government (or governments) considered to be largely responsible for the problem(s) at hand. In the case of the Kurds vis-à-vis Iraq the appointment of Prince Sadruddin Aga Khan as the overall coordinator on behalf of the UN system worked well. It can be argued that as long as the UN has not set up an effective coordinating system for dealing with the consequences of natural disasters, these should also be part of the coordinating authority of the "human problems coordinator". It is worth mentioning that the 45th session of the General Assembly adopted an important draft International Convention on the Protection of the Rights of All Migrant Workers and Members of their Families (res. 45/158).

The Secretary-General's formal and informal relations with different parts of the UN system also need to be strengthened. At present, a major restructuring of the UN Secretariat takes place for this very purpose. The Specialized Agencies have usually resisted any increased influence of the UN Secretary-General on their activities, claiming that they are responsible only to their own governing bodies. In practice specific situations may modify this point of view. The leadership of the UN in humanitarian activities in the Gulf conflict was not disputed. Certain formal developments are also worth mentioning. The revised General Regulations of the World Food Program stipulate that it may provide relief assistance at the request of the UN Secretary-General, such assistance to be fully coordinated with the UN system and NGO efforts. Another example relates to the various requests of the Security Council to the IAEA to assist in inspecting nuclear installations in Iraq.

The heads of the Specialized Agency secretariats together with the Secretary-General of the UN could constitute a cabinet-type commission, with a mandate considerably wider than that of the coordination that is now vested in the Administrative Committee on Coordination. The "cabinet of executive heads" could draft memoranda and possible action proposals for an Economic Security Council, ensuring an integrated approach. This would require that the executive heads be of the highest calibre, and their staffs capable and efficient. Like government ministers in practically all countries, executive heads are now elected largely on the basis of a political process, which does not put sufficient emphasis on competence. There is an obvious need to change procedures for electing the executive heads of the Specialised Agencies.

The Challenge of Economic Security and Interdependence

Recent years – aside from the valuable work done through several Specialized Agencies – have not seen much real progress on multilateral cooperation for economic security. The 1992 UN Conference on Environment and Development (UNCED) resulted in the adoption of two conventions, on climate change and biodiversity. The ambitious "Agenda 21 program" requiring a huge increase in external aid to developing countries, may have raised expectations which cannot be met. Much will depend on whether the Commission on Sustainable Development, to be established by the UN General Assembly, to oversee the activities and commitments agreed upon at UNCED, will be an effective, relatively small body or a large cumbersome council where debate will tend to overwhelm action. Concepts like 'global partnership', 'interdependence', 'meeting the challenges of environment and development', 'integration of environment and development concerns' abound in declarations and texts, including the "Agenda 21" document adopted at UNCED.

The growing North-South gap and allegedly inadequate responses by the "rich countries" to the problems of less developed nations present a major challenge closely linked to the maintenance of peace. It is now generally agreed that "sustained growth" is inextricably linked not only with measures safeguarding the environment, but also with general national economic and political policies. Among these (child and adult) literacy, an adequate population policy, the right health policies, appropriate financial policies, and correct incentives to private business are significant. Minimal human rights standards, both civic and economic / social, are a recognized pre-condition for achieving accelerated growth and sustainable development. Similarly, avoidance of environmental pollution is not only important for its own sake, but also to facilitate other policies leading to sustainable development. We are confronted with a number of vicious circles, e.g. the fact that a correct population policy and indeed all policies intended to promote development and preservation of the environment, require that adults be able to read and write. An additional problem is that most resources are going to the richer developing countries, leaving the poorest countries with an inadequate flow of external capital. There is no lack of ideas on how to overcome, or at least to diminish the North-South gap.

One difficulty is that governments confront problems mainly on the basis of short-term considerations. For democratic governments, the decision-making horizon is often no further away than the next election. Policy reports by international commissions often get no further than middle-level officials or the minister directly concerned with their substance, e.g. the minister for development cooperation. Exceptionally, a report may attract government-wide attention; this was the case with the Brundtland Report on environmental problems. Perhaps the time has come to ask the Secretary-General to make a summary of the many reports of the last decades on development and environment, with emphasis on those recommendations that are still valid (in other words a comprehensive up-date of all these reports), and request him to indicate their main policy implications for the UN system, both substantively and institutionally.

The UN system is essentially organized along functional lines. The FAO deals with food and agriculture, the WHO with health, UNICEF with children, etc. Most contemporary problems, however, cut across such neat divisions. Numerous inter-agency committees and working groups are to some extent an answer to this problem. Since each agency usually aims at maximizing its share in activities on any given problem, the end result, in terms of solving the problem at hand, will not always be optimal. Most governments are similarly organized along functional lines, so that, normally, a ministry of agriculture will give support to proposals of the executive head of the FAO. An important consideration must be that political, economic, environmental and certain other issues and problems should be looked at in an integrated way, taking into account the many cross-influences which are a fact of everyday life.

Towards New Sources of Finance?

No reform of either the intergovernmental set-up or the secretariats will be successful if adequate finance is lacking. The action program for children accepted at the "Children's Summit" of September 1990 alone would require $20 billion per year. At the present time, financing of international agencies and programs is based either on assessed budgets (with problems because many governments are in arrears) or on so-called voluntary contributions. The latter method has meant that many executive heads spend a considerable part of their time travelling around the world seeking additional funds for special or general programs. It seems logical that urgent consideration should be given to new "automatic" sources of finance. Among the proposals advanced are a tax on deep-sea-bed mining, a tax on armaments produced and / or internationally traded and a tax on telecommunications. There are several proposals for some sort of autonomous international finance for environmental purposes. For example, there could be internationally agreed levies on carbon dioxide and sulphur emissions, with part of the proceeds going to projects in developing countries. Another idea is that of a "special international fund" for joint implementation of internationally agreed measures: developed countries, rather than taking additional measures at home, would make funds available for the cleaning-up or renovation of outdated coal or nuclear energy plants or for the preservation of tropical rain forests in Brazil or Africa, and thus contribute to the global reduction of carbon monoxides and greenhouse gases.

In the early 1970s, the UN Environment Programme (UNEP), advised by a group of experts, endeavoured to arrange autonomous financing for a multi-billion dollar anti-desertification program for the countries south of the Sahara. The UN General Assembly rejected such a revolutionary idea. Ironically, economic losses due to desertification and external assistance from developed countries amounted to a multiple of the sum that would have been raised by autonomous financing.

On the subject of finance for urgent environmental and development needs one must note the failure of UNCED to come through with anything new. The text on "financial resources and mechanisms" adopted at UNCED as chapter 33 of the "Agenda 21 document", is partly full of platitudes, such as the observation that 'The cost of inaction could outweigh the financial costs of implementing Agenda 21', partly a rehash of sometimes long-standing recommendations. On the target of transferring 0.7% of GNP for official development assistance, agreement "to augment ... aid programmes in order to reach that target as soon as possible" is retrograde compared with what was adopted earlier, e.g. at the seventh special session of the UN General Assembly in 1975 or the International Development Strategy for the Third UN Development Decade (DD III) in 1980. Moreover the world's largest donor, the United States, has consistently refused to accept the target, while almost all other countries, except the Nordic ones and the Netherlands, have remained far below 0.7%.

As sources of financial implementation UNCED lists numerous financial institutions, programs and mechanisms. One might have hoped for something constructive under the heading "innovative financing". However, the "use of economic and fiscal incentives...", the "feasibility of tradeable permits" and "new schemes for fund-raising...through private channels..." can hardly be called new. A little hope lies in the notion of "the reallocation of resources presently committed to military purposes", but the Rio document indicates no agreement on how this reallocation is to be achieved. Even a modest decision that "in principle", at least 10% of the 'peace dividend' should be allocated to the development / environment programs of developing countries, would have been useful. Regrettably the idea of some sort of international tax (on airline tickets, telecommunications, arms transfers, or anything administratively possible and controllable) is totally absent from the UNCED document.

This vagueness on methods of finance is in somewhat strange contrast to the apparent precision of the secretariat's estimate of $600 billion per year (average for the period 1993-2000) needed to implement the "Agenda 21" program in developing countries. Such a large sum may not encourage governments to look seriously at specific sources of finance.

The 'Sovereignty Issue': Fragmentation Versus Integration

For conflicts threatening international peace and security and for many economic / financial matters, there exist agreed ways to involve the UN system. For crucial questions related to possible autonomy or independence for separatist groups within states there is a distinct vacuum of internationally agreed procedures. However, there is a trend towards a new kind of involvement of the United Nations in advising on and supervising domestic elections. In the past the UN has assisted in organizing plebiscites related to the decolonization process. Similarly, on the basis of Chapter XI of the UN Charter the United Nations supervised the administration of Non-Self Governing Territories and monitored the progress towards a "full measure of self-government" (cf . G.A. Res. 1514 – the landmark Decolonization Declaration – and G.A. Res. 1541 of 14-15 December 1960). There may equally be a UN role in an orderly process leading to the autonomy or independence of parts of a country. These issues cannot be separated from the changing significance of the nation-state. The following, partly contradictory tendencies can be observed:

a) The clear distinction between states, groupings of states and non-state actors is becoming less important in the light of the complexity of issues, and the great range of influences of different actors. Under an "hegemonic order", with one state dominating the international scene, there was a more or less orderly international system, with some accepted division of activities between the nation-state, specialized and regional organizations, and global bodies including the UN and the specialized agencies. The role of each actor is either generally accepted, or challenged in a clear "linear" way (e.g. decolonization and liberation movements). Under such an "hegemonic order" the nation-state plays a central role. In what has been called the "post-hegemonic world" the role of the state as the promoter of welfare and the guardian of security is challenged by various often unpredictable external actors, factors and situations, whether economic, political or social. As a result, tendencies towards globalization are sometimes at cross-purposes with regional, religious, linguistic or other ambitions. The post-hegemonic world may be characterized by an increasingly important role for the UN and its affiliated agencies. However, we cannot automatically assume that the trend towards tackling issues globally be linear. In terms of creating a "world order" progress will probably alternate with setbacks.

b) The impetus in several parts of the world towards regional economic and / or political integration ("supra-regionalism"), on the one hand, and trends towards subregional, linguistic or religious rights and / or autonomy ("infra-regionalism") on the other hand constitute an important modification of the "existing order of things". Efforts towards regional economic and political integration in all parts of the world are of great significance.

Infra-regionalism manifests itself not only in the former Soviet Union, but in many countries throughout the world, e.g. the former Yugoslavia, Ethiopia, Sri Lanka, and India. If infra-regionalism is expressed in civil war, this is not only harmful for the peoples concerned, but also constitutes a serious impediment to regional integration, as events in Central America show. Theoretically, a referendum, under UN auspices could have helped to determine the future of the Kurds, not only in Iraq, but also in adjoining countries, constituting a freely expressed majority view. The constraints of Article 2, paragraph 7 of the UN Charter, the efforts of numerous nation-states to suppress rebellious minorities claiming autonomy and the Yugoslav-type warfare in nations falling apart, may be controlled if the international community at last decides that UN member States can no longer determine for themselves what is or is not "essentially within their domestic jurisdiction".

Intervention by the UN for broadly humanitarian reasons is bound to remain on the international agenda. This will require, if not an amendment to the UN Charter, agreement to interpret it in ways commensurate with conditions prevailing in a turbulent era in world history.

What was exceptional in the past (e.g. Security Council resolution 421 (1977) on a UN arms embargo against South Africa), may become the rule. On the positive side, the 1989 Operation Lifeline Sudan and the 1991 UN Inter-Agency Humanitarian Program for Iraq may serve as creative precedents for future humanitarian initiatives and show how to come to terms with the tension between human suffering and sovereignty by infusing the latter with humanitarian concerns.

An innovative interpretation of the UN Charter and of Article 2.7 in particular, as well as universal acceptance and a gradually expanding interpretation of the UN Human Rights Covenants would enhance the internationalization of "domestic" conflicts. The basic question will remain: can and should the United Nations get involved in member States' internal affairs and in political movements striving towards self-determination of parts of existing member States? Could the United Nations, at the request of a population aiming at autonomy, play some role in having the entire process evolve peacefully and democratically? Should a special UN task force on the spot make sure that a request for autonomy is authentic, not "fabricated" by a minority? The plight of the Kurds has shown how political and tactical constraints are at cross-purposes with lofty ideals towards a world order in conformity with the UN Charter.

Although enforcement measures under Chapter VII may not be prejudiced by the domestic jurisdiction clause of Article 2, paragraph 7 of the UN Charter, it seems to be a fact of international life that the Security Council is only willing to intervene in "domestic affairs" in exceptional cases. Despite compelling humanitarian reasons, Security Council involvement under Chapter VII with the plight of the Kurdish people or the Shiites, beyond the merely hortatory Resolution 688, adopted April 5, 1991, appears to be unlikely.

In trying to safeguard the rights of minorities, the introduction of UN Humanitarian Centers (UNHUC's) and the UN Guards Contingent in Iraq may constitute an innovative approach to allow minorities to contemplate solutions other than full nationhood. Some governments might consider this a dangerous precedent for future Security Council meddling with their domestic affairs, examples being the USSR / Baltic states, China-Tibet, India Punjab / Kashmir, UK-Northern Ireland, conflicts. On the other hand, a government faced with regional or ethnic autonomy movements may find it useful to have the UN conduct or supervise a plebiscite. The results, if they go against the government's position, would provide an element of face-saving. If they endorse the government's position, international approval for action against "rebellion" would seem to be justified.

The cases of Cambodia and former Yugoslavia put into focus the kind of new problems the U.N. is facing. In Cambodia the U.N. has a mandate consisting of a multiplicity of tasks: supervision of the cease-fire, demobilization of armed forces, refugee resettlement, temporary replacement of the government for most of its essential tasks, organization of elections. The former Yugoslavia poses multiple problems on the role of UN peacekeeping forces, of conflict resolution under the joint auspices of the European Community and the United Nations (in an unprecedented way), of action to be taken in the light of serious human rights infringements, etc.

It is evident that only close inter-action between the Security Council, the Secretary-General and the governments concerned (in many cases the world community as a whole) can provide adequate responses to what may otherwise turn out to be insuperable problems.

c) The powers of the nation-state are increasingly affected by non-governmental entities. A positive example is the growing status of non-governmental organizations in such fields as human rights, environment and assistance to developing countries. But the nation-state, represented by its government, may also be negatively influenced by private pressures. An apparently generally acceptable text for the 1982 UN Convention on the Law of the Sea had been painstakingly negotiated over a period of nine years. At the last moment the United States government raised serious objections on a number of important points, mostly related to the international regime foreseen for the exploitation of "the common heritage of mankind". This U.S. government attitude reflected powerful lobbying by private interest groupings, which feared that their freedom to exploit the minerals of the deep seabed would be impinged upon.

d) Determined obstruction by a single state, acting in defiance of the UN Charter, constitutes another factor playing havoc with an "orderly" world system. Iraq's aggression against Kuwait will remain the prime example for a long time.

e) Unsolved, continuing problems add to the difficulties arising from the factors outlined above. The still growing economic and social gap between North and South related to what must be called the inadequate response of the North to problems of the South, remains a major issue. Relatively new problem areas are the degradation of the environment, drug abuse, AIDS, and massive often unexpected movements of people, many as (economic or political) refugees, the UN system has shown that it can respond flexibly to a great variety of often unpredictable new events and circumstances. However, without the full cooperation of the member States and the many non-state actors, many problems cannot be fully solved.

Concluding Observations: Towards a New World Order?

The phrase "new world order" introduced by President Bush in the aftermath of the 1990-91 Gulf War has created much confusion, and also distrust. A "new world order" is widely considered to include a "renaissance" of the United Nations, but otherwise remains a concept the details of which have yet to be defined. Perhaps we are confronted with a "fallacy of misplaced concreteness" (Whitehead). The dramatic series of Security Council resolutions on the Gulf conflict and the ensuing U.S.-led military action indicate on the one hand that things will never be the same again, but on the other hand do not ensure that United Nations principles will be rigidly enforced in the future.

As of September 1992 the world is obviously still struggling with the exact contents of a new world order. This article has endeavoured to make clear the several options and the many uncertainties concerning the role of the United Nations, in particular of the Security Council and in regard to peace-keeping and conflict resolution operations, and to humanitarian intervention.

With a civil war and ethnic cleansing in former Yugoslavia, armed strife in the former Soviet Union, and ethnic uprisings in various parts of the world, the "new world order" may well remain elusive for a long time.

In the meantime Secretary-General Boutros Boutros-Ghali, in a report largely neglected by the world media ("An Agenda for Peace – Preventive diplomacy, peacemaking and peacekeeping" of June 1992), has made a number of proposals on strengthening the principal activities of the UN. They relate to such matters as early warning, preventive deployment, the utilization of peace-enforcement units, improved training of peace-keeping personnel. It is to be hoped that these proposals will receive early and positive attention.

Thus, in the post Cold War era the UN system could be the cornerstone of a "new world order" if its human rights activities receive a fresh impetus, if the economic and technical work of the United Nations system is strengthened through better management, if governments are willing to accept order rather than disorder in their behavior, and internationally agreed legislation on subjects like the environment that are international by definition. These "ifs" are many and demanding, requiring new attitudes.

NOTE

This article is based on the following two reports written for the Academic Council on the United Nations System:
Johan Kaufmann and Nico Schrijver, with Dick Leurdijk, *Changing Global Needs: Expanding Roles for the United Nations System*. Academic Council on the UN System, Reports and Papers 1990-5, ACUNS, Watson Institute, Brown University, Box 1983, Providence, RI 02912-1983, USA.
Johan Kaufmann, Dick Leurdijk and N. Schrijver, *The World in Turmoil: Testing the UN's Capacity*. ACUNS, Reports and Papers 1991-4, address as above.

SELECTED REFERENCES

An Agenda for Peace, Preventive Diplomacy, Peacemaking and Peacekeeping. Report of the Secretary-General, doc. A/47/277, United Nations, New York, June 17, 1992.

P.R. Baehr and L. Gordenker, *The United Nations in the 1990s*, London: Macmillan, 1992.

Th. C. van Boven "The Security Council: The New Frontier", in International Commission of Jurists, *The Review*. June 1992.

B. Boutros-Ghali, *Report of the Secretary-General on the Work of the Organization*, doc. A/47/1, 11 September 1992.

Changing Concepts of Sovereignty: Can the United Nations Keep Peace? 27th UN of the Next Decade Conference 1992, the Stanley Foundation, 216 Sycamore Street, Muscatine, Iowa, 52761-3831, U.S.A., 1992.

R.W. Cox, "Multilateralism and world order", *Review of International Studies*, (1992), 18.

D.P. Forsythe (ed.), *The United Nations in the World Political Economy, Essays in Honour of Leon Gordenker*, London: Macmillan, 1988.

M.H. Halperin and D.J. Scheffer with P.L. Small, *Self-determination in the New World Order*, Carnegie Endowment for International Peace, Washington D.C.

J. Harrod and N. Schrijver (eds), *The UN Under Attack*, Aldershot: Gower, 1988.

J. Kaufmann, *Conference Diplomacy. An Introductory Analysis*, 2nd rev. ed., Dordrecht: Martinus Nijhoff, 1988.

B. Urquhart, "The United Nations in 1992: problems and opportunities", *International Affairs*, London, April 1992.

II
CORE-PERIPHERY SITUATIONS

5 THE EMERGING HUMAN RIGHTS ENVIRONMENT IN THE ARAB WORLD

Jill Crystal

The Arab world has seen an explosion of human rights activity over the last ten years. From North Africa to the Levant and the Gulf, civil and political rights have begun to appear prominently on the agenda of oppositions and, reluctantly, on the agenda of governments as well. Following riots in 1988, Algeria introduced new restrictions on state control of information, new constitutional protections of human rights and rights activists, and even appointed the region's first human rights minister. In Jordan, following parliamentary elections in 1989, the new government liberalized press laws and took the first steps towards the abolition of martial law. In 1989-90 a prodemocracy Constitutionalist Movement appeared in Kuwait, engaging the government in a dialogue over the reinstatement of the National Assembly and constitutional provisions guaranteeing basic liberties of speech and assembly.

This article is part of the research "Liberalization and its Limits: State Formation and State Violence in the Middle East" funded by the World Society Foundation. Jill Crystal received a Ph.D. from Harvard University and is now assistant professor of political science at the Department of Political Science, University of Michigan, 5602 Haven Hall, Ann Arbor, Michigan 48109, U.S.A.

At the regional level, many groups began documenting human rights abuses and engaging in advocacy work. Amnesty International, which only began reporting on the region in the 1970s, set up local branches in the area in the 1980s. Other international groups became more systematic in their reporting. New groups such as Middle East Watch, appeared for the first time, as did a handful of local organizations. In 1983 when a group of Arab intellectuals formed the Arab Organization for Human Rights to protest the erosion of civil and political rights in their home states, they were condemned by a wide spectrum of Arab regimes which joined together to deny them the consultative status at the United Nations that they sought. Yet, by the end of the decade the organization had succeeded in reversing this opposition, establishing a place for itself as a regional human rights group, and acquiring observer status as a nongovernmental organization at the United Nations.

This level of organizing constituted a dramatic recent change in the political environment. With the wave of liberalization following the fall of autocratic regimes in the Soviet Union and Eastern Europe and the end of the security state atmosphere which the Iran-Iraq War had engendered, human rights activists in the region were optimistic.

Then came the Iraqi invasion of Kuwait, the second Gulf War, heightened tension in the region and, with it, the resurgence of the security state. The Kuwaiti experiment faltered; the Algerian experiment stalled. In Iraq, the reign of terror returned. In order to understand whether this setback is a serious reversal of efforts to constrain state violence or a temporary obstacle on the path to greater liberalization, it is necessary to understand those factors that first allowed the movement to emerge.

Human Rights Issues

If a human rights movement developed in the 1980s in the Middle East it was, in part, because one was needed: the movement was a response to patterned state violence. Outside observers have long focused on state violence in the region. Journalists seem particularly intrigued with it. Comparative studies have often highlighted it. Robert Wesson, in his *Democracy: a Worldwide Survey* rates no Arab state except Lebanon ("partial democracy") above "limited authoritarianism".[1] No Arab state ranks above the world average in Charles Humana's *World Human Rights Guide*.[2] Arab states do equally poorly in Raymond Gastil's annual *Freedom in the World* rankings.[3]

Comparative evaluations must, of course, be interpreted cautiously. Often they are apparent quantifications of the anecdotal (even outside the Middle East, efforts formally to compare violations sometimes produce odd results).[4] Frequently studies of state violence are shaped to fit prior political agendas. Often they reflect an ignorance of research in and on the Middle East.[5] And certainly, state violence is not unique to the Middle East: all states use coercion and force.

However, even those writers, including many from the region, who are more careful, draw a fairly dark picture.[6] Whether the regional situation is better or worse than others, it is bad enough. Human rights violations are documented in the reports of monitoring groups such as Amnesty International and Middle East Watch. The Arab Organization for Human Rights concluded its 1989 report, the last before the war, on a note of pessimism: "As a whole, most of the Arab states remained affected by widespread violations of civil, political, economic, social and cultural rights."[7] It noted the deadly government suppression of bread riots in Jordan, iron and steel workers' strikes in Egypt, and student demonstrations in the Sudan. It reported deaths by tortures in Morocco, Libya, Egypt, the Yemens, Saudi Arabia, and Iraq. It noted detentions, often under deplorable conditions, throughout the region and more frequent disappearances in Lebanon, Morocco, and Iraq. It documented the continuing restrictions on opinion and expression, freedom of political association, and the judicial process.

Naseer Aruri sums up the observation of many when he writes: "The region is a disaster area in terms of human rights. Irrespective of the type of government, ideological coloration or foreign policy orientation, whether pro-Western or pro-Soviet, conservative or 'progressive', theocratic or secular, nearly all regimes have displayed a thorough disregard for individual human rights."[8] A human rights movement emerged in some significant part because a human rights problem existed.

The human rights situation accounts in part for the human rights activity it generated. The problem alone, however, cannot account for the new freedom and support that human rights workers were experiencing in the 1980s. To understand that, it is necessary to examine a number of broad transformations in the post-World War II Arab world. The human rights movement reflects extensive structural changes that have occurred in the region over the last forty years.

Economic Transformations

The first relevant change was the economic transformation of the region, and particularly the development of the postwar oil industry which brought unprecedented wealth to the several Arab states exporting oil. Contrary to the early predictions of the modernization literature and those who followed that tradition, economic development, at least measured by steady growth in per capita GNP, did not prompt any automatic increase in either political participation or political freedom in these states. At first, oil revenues actually reduced political participation, as rulers with external revenue sources found themselves less dependent on internal sources and thus free from the political demands that had historically accompanied financial support.[9] A rise in materialism initially prompted a general retreat to private life and withdrawal of those previously most politically active.

In time, however, the oil revenues, invested in social infrastructure, health and education, gradually and quietly produced a population of well-educated citizens increasingly armed with the money and leisure to engage in the sort of sustained political activity conducive to human rights organization. Then, as oil revenues fell with the decline in oil prices after 1986, the governments' ability to meet the expectations that made private life so satisfying to this now educated population also declined. As public satisfaction fell, public participation rose, and with it a concern for the human rights protections that sustained political participation required. As some wealth had trickled down to private hands, a few patrons even emerged, able to finance these concerns. Human rights activists began to appear. This occurred most dramatically in the 1989-90 Constitutionalist Movement in Kuwait, but, as the increased political mobilization during the Gulf War would demonstrate, the impulse was growing in Saudi Arabia as well.[10]

If oil produced an educated and financially comfortable population in certain states of the region, it did not do so in the poorer Arab states. True, significant revenues did trickle down to most of these states in the form of remittances, foreign aid, and Arab investment, at least initially. But such regional redistribution of wealth did not occur on a scale sufficient to resolve the growing economic crises. These crises, exacerbated in the late 1980s by declines in income from remittances following the fall in oil prices, prompted governments to turn towards economic liberalization and limited privatization and denationalization, and consequently to adopt austerity programs which in turn exacerbated the plight of the poorest of the poor.[11] These policies, reversing many of the states' postwar efforts to address inequalities through public policy (such as land reform and expanded social services) increased inequality and economic privation among the poorest, who expressed their dissatisfaction in bread riots.

Regimes responded politically in one of two ways. The initial response was often to increase government repression in order to silence public objections to these new economic policies. Those who protested faced heavily armed police. But closing political space increased human rights abuses just when a retreat to private life was becoming economically less attractive. A second response was thus to open the political system in order to implicate the opposition in the adoption of difficult austerity measures and to legitimize these measures by offering the population a deal: a trade of political participation in exchange for acceptance of a degree of economic hardship. This was the choice made most notably by Jordan in 1989.

For oppositions, opening up political space offered an opportunity publicly to reassess governments' record on rights. From the governments' viewpoint, a new human rights debate offered the rulers an opportunity to address popular discontent without spending much money. In a period of austerity, human rights issues had one unusual advantage: they were cheap, issues which could be addressed, it seemed, on a budget. Creating jobs, subsidizing food, building adequate housing – these were all extraordinarily expensive undertakings. Opening jail doors, releasing prisoners, cutting back on torture – these were inexpensive measures. In a time of economic crisis, human rights became a financially more attractive proposition to governments. Thus, in rather different ways, both increasing wealth and increasing poverty contributed to a new openness to human rights issues.

Social Structural Transformations

Structural social changes also transformed the human rights environment. The rise of the state as the primary employer, especially in the oil states, weakened class as the basis for political organization. Communal solidarities – whether of tribe, sect, or ethnic group – also weakened, although not as dramatically, in the postcolonial period as a result of political changes, as regimes began to attack communal identities and structures contenders for loyalty – as part of a larger effort to create state-patriotic identities in their disparate populations.

Because so many claims on government and, more importantly, protections from the excesses of government were historically lodged in these communal groups, such change affected rights in the region. This was true of ethnic and tribal groups and of religious and sectarian minorities, which had enjoyed some historical autonomy from the state owing to their special status as *millets* under the Ottoman Empire. Even to the majority Sunnis, religious organizations had historically formed an important bulwark against the state. The rise of ethnically organized opposition, such as the Kurdish opposition in Iraq, and of Islamic opposition throughout the region, was in part a reaction to state destruction of the rights these communal organizations defended. As communal groups ceased to protect their members, both the need for and openness to the issue of individual rights rose.

Institutional Transformations

Institutional transformations also laid the groundwork for a human rights opposition. The steady growth of the state and the concomitant increase in its ability to monitor opposition and to use its power (ranging from employment in its huge bureaucracies to its technologically more able security apparatus) to control dissent increased state repression. Greater dependence of the population on the state for jobs, social services, and subsidies meant that people could more easily be coopted or silenced by the state.[12] As states became stronger, as their coercive capacity became increasingly institutionalized, their very strength precipitated a new politicization of even formerly quiescent elements of the population in reaction to the states' new ability to meddle in everyday life.

These changes were not conducive to human rights activism. However, although the extension of the state, and especially of its security apparatus, prompted a deterioration in the human rights situation, they also facilitated, in unintended ways, the emergence of a human rights-based opposition by producing a new bureaucratic elite from whose ranks human rights activists emerged. Many of them came to the movement after long service, often at high levels, in the state bureaucracies. They were able to build on their familiarity with government and their personal contacts with high-level officials to engage governments in dialogue.

Ideological Transformations

Ideological transformations in the postwar period also allowed the emergence of a human rights debate, which, in both its origins and evolution, is a Western discourse, even if the issues underlying it are cross-culturally valid. The major contribution of the Third World to the human rights discussion has been to introduce a focus on collective rights. The United Nations, often the arena for discussion of rights issues, has tried to avoid a debate over which set of rights, individual or collective, is more important by calling for simultaneous and equal implementation of both the individual and the collective rights which its resolutions demand. In practice, however, regimes have either used this plea for evenhandedness to justify little progress in either direction, or they have ignored it.[13] One sort of rights usually receives ideological priority. For historical reasons governments and oppositions in the region have, in practical terms, favored collective over individual rights. The interwar anticolonial nationalist struggles necessarily emphasized collective rights, as did the struggle against the landowing classes associated with the colonial powers, classes unwilling or unable to respond to growing demands for social justice. These struggles produced Arab socialist and nationalist regimes which emphasized collective rights, both economic and cultural.

The efforts of the postwar Arab regimes to address collective social injustice were in some ways successful, certainly in eliminating some of the greatest inequities in land ownership. But, by the 1970s, certainly by the 1980s, these regimes had run their course, both in terms of harnessing resources that could easily be redistributed and in terms of stimulating economic growth and achieving the developmentalist victories that formed the core of their collective promise to the population.

The most powerful ideological response to the failure of collective pan-Arab socialist and other developmentalist ideologies was Islamist. While Islamist ideologies were quite good at addressing collective concerns, both issues of social justice and identity, they did not address individual rights in any serious way, at least initially. Indeed, Islamists were in principle somewhat hostile to the human rights movement. They were not, of course, hostile to human rights or to protecting them: after all, Islamists were usually the first to suffer state violence. Nor did they engage in the odd debate carried on outside the region over whether any human rights, and if so which ones, are sufficiently basic to be cross-culturally meaningful. They took as given that Islam was universally valid, not merely appropriate for the Middle East. That, in fact, was the core of their disagreement with the human rights activists. Islam, an Islamist government relying on Islamic law, would provide both a necessary and sufficient protection of rights.

Those in the human rights movement, however, took their bearings not from Islam but from the United Nations declarations on human rights, notably the three documents which together comprise the International Bill of Human Rights, the cornerstone document of the international human rights movement: the Universal Declaration of Human Rights, adopted in 1948 and the two supplements to the Declaration added in 1966 – the International Covenant on Economic, Social, and Cultural Rights and the International Covenant on Civil and Political Rights. Many Islamists did not feel comfortable with that approach. Most were at least troubled by the rights groups' exclusive reliance on humanistic sources, and Western ones at that. The United Nations documents are built on a premise of secularism that restricts religion to the private domain of individual and personal choice.[14] They are the product of a discussion Western in origin and evolution. Many Islamists felt they did not need to import norms when they already had, in Islam and the Islamic movement, a superior defense of human rights.

There were also particular points of conflict. These included the Declaration's insistence on equal treatment before the law of women and members of different religions (Islamic law, the Shar'iah, grants different legal status to Muslims and non-Muslims and to women and men in family law, court testimony, and eligibility for high state posts), its prohibition of slavery (which the Quran accepts and regulates) and its condemnation of cruel, inhuman, and degrading treatment, which some feared could be interpreted to restrict certain Shar'iah punishments.[15]

There was considerable variation in the way Islamists interpreted and applied the Shar'iah in connection with human rights issues.[16] The widespread arrest of so many Islamists in the 1980s sensitized them to these issues in a new way. And, in practice, Islamists and others could in fact reach considerable consensus on what constituted abuse: they agreed that the state ought not to pull people from their beds in the middle of the night, ought not to torture its citizens, ought not to imprison children to coerce their parents. They shared a belief that the state could engage in behavior that was just and legitimate and in behavior that was not, and the belief that people could distinguish between the two. Although the vocabulary, the form of discourse, varied, Islamists and other dissidents could often identify a core set of human rights, involving freedom from the state's routine use of coercive control over political speech, action, assembly, organization, and movement and its use of violence: forcible political detention, torture, and murder.

The establishment of an Islamic Republic in Iran and the emerging political pluralism under many Arab regimes fostered new practical discussions in the 1980s about the kind of dissent it would tolerate. These discussions prompted new thinking about human rights, leading some Islamists to develop an argument specifically addressing human rights but that grew out of Islam and stressed Islam's historic emphasis on knowledge, learning, choice, and toleration. Many Islamist groups were also, like the governments, reluctant to reject the United Nations Declaration out of hand. Understanding and respecting its international legitimacy, they preferred to minimize differences between the Shar'iah and the Declaration. Nonetheless, despite some movement in this direction, most Islamists remained philosophically suspicious of, hence distant from, human rights issues. Their reluctance to tackle these issues directly left an opening for non-Islamist dissidents looking for an issue that could broaden their constituency.

Many Arab nationalists, in their own way suspicious of an historically Western movement, now began to rethink this position. Although there was some effort to reconcile the historical collectivist goals of pan-Arabism with the individualist goals of the human rights movement, it was these individualist goals which provided the opportunity to refashion Arab nationalism and put forward a progressive response that could perhaps halt some of the defections to Islamist ideologies by the Arab nationalists disheartened by developmentalist failure, and possibly even draw in new supporters.[17]

The new human rights movement's emphasis on political and civil rights was thus an expression of dissatisfaction with the historical emphasis that Arab regimes and their opponents had placed, and continued to place, on social and economic rights as collective rights, at the expense of individual rights. Economic crises in the 1980s offered concrete evidence both that economic development was not automatic, and that efforts to achieve economic development would not automatically lead to greater political freedoms. With this came a deepening awareness that there might not be a natural priority of rights, with collective rights, economic and social, preceding and naturally prompting civil and political rights. Indeed, perhaps the priority ought to be reversed: political activity might be the precondition for economic change. At a minimum both economic and political needs had to be addressed: civil and political rights deserved their own attention. Activists saw in human rights a potentially popular ideological issue which neither the old Arab nationalists nor the Islamists had truly addressed. Ideological changes thus contributed to the emergence of a human rights movement, the most important change being disillusionment with the ability of collective rights, especially as they had been defined by Arab regimes, to address the full spectrum of political concerns and the emergence, in this gap, of Islamist opposition and the subsequent efforts of human rights groups to put forward a credible answer to both the governments and the Islamist opposition, based on individual rights.

The International Environment

Finally, the changing international environment contributed to the emergence of a human rights movement in the 1980s. Three factors were important. The first was the decline of authoritarianism and central state power in the Soviet Union and Eastern Europe. The fall of single-party regimes and their rulers was eagerly followed throughout the Middle East. The rise of human rights issues on the left in the Soviet Union and Eastern Europe encouraged Arab progressives also to reexamine them.

The second factor was the Intifadah which, especially in its heady early days, inspired the human rights movement in the example it offered of a population overcoming fear and standing up to a regime. The Intifadah had some demonstration effect as people saw Palestinians take on an opponent who appeared tougher than their own governments. It was an opposition movement in which human rights groups played a role.[18] The Intifadah also allowed Arab nationalists to link human rights issues to the central, historically pan-Arab issue of Palestine.

The third factor was the international human rights movement. Human rights groups drew their inspiration from international organizations, especially Amnesty International, now active in the region, and from the more tolerant atmosphere these organizations encouraged. These factors, then, domestic and international, contributed to an opening up of the political environment in which human rights groups emerged.

The Iraqi Invasion and the Gulf War

The Iraqi invasion of Kuwait and the Gulf War of 1990-91 created a new environment less favorable to human rights. True, the rhetoric of human rights was invoked by several parties to the conflict. President Bush condemned Iraqi atrocities in occupied Kuwait while opponents of U.S. policy pointed to human rights abuses in preinvasion and post-liberation Kuwait and in Saudi Arabia to justify opposition to military support for these regimes. Even Saddam Hussain raised the issue of the rights of the Palestinians and Lebanese.[19] Although these public statements focussed new media attention on human rights groups, they did so in a somewhat unwelcome way, politicizing and, in at least one case (the infamous incubators), embarrassing human rights monitoring groups.[20] The attention was partisan in a way these groups had always sought to avoid.

The immediate post-war environment saw still further setbacks for the human rights movement. Although the war had a very different impact depending on the role any particular state played during the conflict, nonetheless some common themes emerged. Whether by increasing military spending, limiting American aid, or (in Iraq and Kuwait) destroying much of the country's infrastructure, the war introduced a sense of renewed economic deprivation that forced governments to face more directly the choice between repression and increased political incorporation of a mobilized and angry population. By elevating the role of the military and creating the security state atmosphere that so often accompanies the military's engagement in domestic politics, the war increased the power of those institutions most resistant to curbing human rights abuses. The popular sense of crisis and strategic vulnerability made it easier for rulers to invoke an appeal to national unity that is hard to reconcile with the continuing, institutionalized pluralism that lies at the heart of democracy. By increasing the popularity of the Islamist opposition groups (and of the Islamic Republic of Iran, which alone was able to claim historical opposition to *both* the Iraqi and United States governments) which were particularly able to mobilize the sense of vulnerability to American attack that the war raised, the war generated a surge of Islamist support that prompted a government backlash in the form of increased human rights abuses. Wars and war footing are not generally good for democracy or human rights. Although the international events of the 1980s were supportive of the human rights movement, the transformations of the 1990s have been less so.

Nonetheless, the postwar environment was not uniformly bleak. Throughout the region the conflict demonstrated the dangerous policies that could emerge when leaders were unrestrained by public opinion. In Kuwait the opposition argued the government to a standoff, scheduling elections for October 1992. In Saudi Arabia, in response to public pressures, the government introduced a new package of reforms, including an advisory council, aimed at adding a greater degree of transparency, although not necessarily of participation, to the political process. In Jordan, the government pressed ahead with reforms, eliminating the remaining elements of martial law in 1992. The war was a setback, but not necessarily a longterm reversal of the changes of the 1980s. It transformed the domestic circumstances of the moment and it certainly changed the international environment, but it did not reverse the decades of economic, social structural, institutional and ideological transformations that allowed the movement to emerge in the first place.

Conflict in World Society: Lessons from the Arab World

Human rights and basic freedoms are critically important to the expansion of political participation and to the dissemination of information on which the democratic process rests. The experience in the Arab world suggests a degree of caution in conventional evaluations of political liberalization that measure democratization primarily by the growth in participatory institutions without paying sufficient attention to the necessarily concomitant decline in authoritarian ones. In addition to focusing on the development of parliaments and participatory institutions, analysts would be wise to be alert as well to the retreat of the security state and the growth of organizations and groups, such as those of the human rights movement, that check its activities. Indeed, to most people, formal political participation is probably important less for its own sake than for the protections that an elected legislative body can provide from the arbitrary actions and violence of an otherwise unchecked state.

The experience of the Middle East suggests several factors that contribute to the environment in which human rights groups as organizations that challenge state violence, are more likely to thrive. The first is a changed economic environment. Although wealth, even great wealth, does not necessarily limit the growth of the security state, it does encourage the emergence of a population better able to check it. Both the experience of the oil exporting and importing states suggests that transitions, especially sudden declines in state wealth, are important in creating decisive watersheds where regimes are more likely to become either far more or far less repressive. Changes in social structure and state-society relations involving the weakening of class and communal solidarities have also played a role. As collective groupings have weakened and failed, after attacks by the state, to provide protection for their members, these members have sometimes sought protection in individual rights. Third, broad institutional changes, including the emergence of large bureaucratic states, have paved the way for the movement. Although the expansion of the state has generally been a threat to human rights, the ability of former members of the state elite to join forces with those who would restrict state violence has emerged as a force countering that trend. The fourth factor is a change in the ideological atmosphere involving a decline in the undisputed hegemony of collective rights and a parallel opening of space for individual civil and political rights. The final factor is a supportive international environment. An analysis of these factors and the human rights activity they promote increases our understanding not only of the dynamics of political change in the Middle East, but also of the broader worldwide process of political liberalization and of the forces that limit that process.

NOTES

1 Robert Wesson, ed., *Democracy: a Worldwide Survey* (New York: Praeger, 1987).

2 Charles Humana, *World Human Rights Guide* (London: Hutchinson, 1983).

3 Raymond Gastil, *Freedom in the World* (New York: Greenwood, annual).

4 See Robert Goldstein, "The Limitations of Using Quantitative Data in Studying Human Rights Abuses," *Human Rights Quarterly* 8 (1986).

5 Although the Middle East has not been prominently covered in the recent literature on democratic transitions, human rights and democratization are

issues of considerable concern to scholars of and especially from the region. On human rights see, for example, Saad Eddin Ibrahim, "The Future of Human Rights in the Arab World," in Hisham Sharabi, ed., *The Next Arab Decade* (Boulder: Westview), pp. 38-52; Adib Al-Jadir, ed., Special Issue of Human Rights in the Arab World, *Journal of Arab Affairs 9 (1990)*; and the special issue on human rights in *Middle East Report* (November-December 1987). Recent secondary works include Ann Elizabeth Mayer's *Islam Human Rights: Tradition and Politics* (Boulder: Westview, 1991) which includes the Sudan among its mostly non-Arab cases and Kevin Dwyer, *Arab Voices: the Human Rights Debate in the Middle East* (Berkeley: University of California Press, 1991) which looks at North Africa and Egypt. The related issue of democratization has generated more scholarly concern, although much of the work is still in progress. For an overview of work underway, see Louis Cantori, "Democratization in the Middle East: Report, American Political Science Association," *American-Arab Affairs* 36 (Spring 1991), which summarizes papers from the 1990 San Francisco American Political Science Association annual meeting, Michael Hudson, "The Democratization Process in the Arab World: an Assessment," from that conference, and his "After the Gulf War: Prospects for Democratization in the Arab World," Middle East Journal 45 (Summer 1991), and the essay by Muhmamad Muslih and Augustus Richard Norton, who are working on a larger project on the same topic, "The Need for Arab Democracy" *Foreign Policy 83 (Summer 1991)*.

6   See, for example, Muthir Anabtawi, "Dawr al-nakhbah al-muthaqafah fi ta ziz huquq al-insan al- arabi, (The Role of the Cultural Elite in Strengthening Human Rights in the Arab World)" *al-Mustaqbal al-Arabi* 52 (1983), 3-31.

7   Al-munathamah al-arabiyyah li-huquq al-insan (The Arab Organization for Human Rights), huquq al-insan fi al-watan al-arabi, 1989 (Human Rights in the Arab World, 1989) (Cairo: Arab Organizations for Human Rights, 1990), p. 9.

8   Naseer Aruri, "Disaster Area: Human Rights in the Arab World," *Middle East Report* (November-December 1987), p. 7.

9   A point I develop at length in *Oil and Politics in the Gulf: Rulers and Merchants in Kuwait and Qatar* (Cambridge: Cambridge University Press, 1990). See also Hazem Beblawi and Giacomo Luciani, eds., *The Rentier State* (London: Coom Helm, 1987).

10 On Kuwait, See Jill Crystal, *Kuwait: The Transformation of an Oil State* (Boulder: Westview, 1992), chapter 5; on Saudi Arabia, see F. Gregory Gause, III, "Saudi Arabia: Desert Storm and After," in Robert Freedman, ed., *The Middle East Since the Iraqi Invasion of Kuwait* (Miami: Florida International University Press, forthcoming).

11 See, generally, Alan Richards and John Waterbury, *A Political Economy of the Middle East* (Boulder: Westview, 1990).

12 A point made by F. Gregory Gause III, in "Revolutionary Fevers and Regional Contagion: Domestic Structures and the 'Export' of Revolution in the Middle East," *Journal of South Asian and Middle Eastern Studies* 14: (Spring 1991), pp. 1-23.

13 Mohamed El Sayed Said, "Human Rights in the Third World: the Question of Priorities," *Journal of Arab Affaires 9 (1990)*, pp. 62-3; Jack Donnelly, "Human Rights at the United Nations 1955-85: The Question of Bias," *International Studies Quarterly* 32 (1988), pp. 275-277.

14 See Jan Hjarpe, "The Contemporary Debate in the Muslim World on the Definition of 'Human Rights'," in Klaus Ferdinance and Mehdi Mozaffari, eds., *Islam: State and Society* (London: Curzon Press, 1988), p. 28.

15 See Hjarpe, pp. 28-31 and Mayer, passim.

16 See Mayer and Abdullahi An-Na'im, "Religious Minorities under Islamic Law and the Limits of Cultural Relativism," *Human Rights Quarterly* 9 (1987), pp. 1-18

17 There have been several efforts to develop a uniquely Arab notion of human rights, in the tradition of the 1981 African Charter on Human and People's Rights or the 1950 European Human Rights Convention to replace a 1970 draft convention of the Arab League's largely inactive Human Rights Commission, which remained largely unratified after twenty years of desultory consideration. In 1986 a group of human rights activists drew up such an Arab human rights charter. However, although the preamble and subsequent sections gave the document an Arab flavor, it still drew heavily on the International Bill of Human Rights, incorporating parts verbatim. Munzer Anabtawi, "The Draft Charter on Human and People's Rights in the Arab World: Background and Analytical Description," unpublished manuscript, International Human Rights Institute, Strasbourg, July 21, 1987, p. 4; Interview, Munthir Anabtawi, Geneva, May 26 1989, "Draft Charter on Human and People's Rights in the Arab World," (Siracusa, Italy: International Institute of Higher Studies in Criminal Sciences, 1985); "International Conference: Criminal Justice: Education, Reform, and Human Rights Protection in the Arab World," (Siracusa, December 1-7, 1985), distributed by Aim Communications International, Chicago, April 1986.

18 See Nabeel Abraham, "Human Rights Briefing," *Middle East Report* (September-October 1990), pp. 41-42 for a discussion of these groups.

19 See Naseer Aruri, "Human Rights and the Gulf Crisis: the Verbal Strategy of George Bush," in *Beyond the Storm: A Gulf Crisis Reader* (Brooklyn: Olive Branch Press, 1991).

20 In 1990 the story that Iraqi forces had taken premature Kuwaiti babies from incubators and left them to die was widely circulated by journalists and some human rights groups (among them, and unfortunately, given

its generally excellent reporting record, Amnesty International). Although other stories of Iraqi human rights violations were amply documented, the incubator story appears groundless. See "Kuwait's 'Stolen' Incubators: The Widespread Repercussions of a Murky Incident," *Middle East Watch* 4: 1 (February 6, 1992).

6 THE WORLD BANK AND EXPROPRIATION DISPUTES IN AFRICA

Adeoye Akinsanya

INTRODUCTION

Few areas of international law have engendered so much controversy and acrimony as the expropriation of privately-owned property. If a sovereign State, in the exercise of its power of *dominium eminens* (eminent domain), takes over alien-owned property, terminates concession agreements or State contracts with aliens or socialises the means of production and distribution, it is expected to discharge its obligations under customary international law by providing a measure of compensation.[1] While the United States and other capital-exporting countries maintain that the legality of an expropriatory measure is contingent on the payment of "prompt, adequate and effective compensation", the less-developed countries take the position that the question of compensation is to be settled under the domestic law of the

---

This article reports on findings of the research project "The World Bank and Expropriation Disputes" partly supported by the World Society Foundation. Adeoye Akinsanya was born in Lagos, Nigeria, and graduated from the University of Chicago. He conducted research at the Department of Government and Public Administration of the University of Ilorin, Nigeria, and is presently professor at the Department of Political Science, University of Calabar, P.O. Box 94, Ikenne LGA, Ogun State, Nigeria.

nationalising State and by its tribunals. Although Calvo clauses in concession agreements and State contracts have generally not been accorded any recognition by a majority of jurists and Western European governments and although the United States and Western European governments have taken the position that an alien cannot bargain away the right to diplomatic protection of his government without its consent,[2] the implication of Article 2 (2) (c) of the Charter of Economic Rights and Duties of States is that alien investors must abide by the decisions of the courts of the taking States, and cannot invoke the right to diplomatic protection of their governments in the event of investment disputes.[3] Despite the position of LDCs on the Charter, they have enacted investment laws or signed bilateral investment treaties with capital-exporting countries guaranteeing an international minimum standard of treatment to private foreign capital.

This article is divided into three parts. Part I focuses on terminology while Part II examines economic nationalism in Africa as manifested by nationalisation, expropriation, 'creeping' expropriation, indigenisation or unilateral termination of concession agreements and/or State contracts with aliens. Part III examines the responses of the World Bank to expropriation disputes in Africa.

PART I

The terms "expropriation", "nationalisation", "indigenisation", "requisition", and "confiscation" are very often used in the literature to refer to various forms of intervention or involvement by the State in the 'enjoyment' of privately-owned property, but unfortunately in overlapping, different, and sometimes, conflicting senses.

"Expropriation" is very often used interchangeably with "nationalisation". In the classic sense, nationalisation is

> "the transfer to the State, by a legislative act and in the public interest, of property or private rights of a designated character, with a view to their exploitation or control by the State, or to their direction to a new objective by the State."[4]

While there is no clear-cut definition of "nationalisation", it obviously implies that privately-owned property acquired out of "public necessity" is transferred to the State ostensibly for public use.

Confiscation is the taking of private property by the State without any compensation.[5] While owners may well regard any government interference with property as confiscatory, the State may regard such measures as legitimate exercises of "police" powers to regulate "public morals, health and safety" or to make private interests "subservient to the general interests of the community".[6]

Where compensation is provided and paid by the State, the term "expropriation" may be used, although there is some controversy on the question of whether compensation must be paid if the taking is to be regarded as "expropriation". Some scholars and capital-exporting countries maintain that "the taking of property without compensation is not expropriation. It is confiscation".[7] Others, such as Friedman, hold the view that compensation is a separate category.[8]

It seems to be established that the State must provide some compensation when exercising its "eminent domain" power but that no compensation is necessary when exercising "police" power. Where a State exercises its powers to expropriate or confiscate private property, such property is, in both cases, nationalised.

Expropriation sometimes occurs not through a direct action but as an indirect result of some other governmental action, for which the term "creeping expropriation" has been used. Of late, the term has been used to describe measures having a similar effect as direct expropriation, including

"discriminatory or confiscatory taxes, fines, currency devaluation, regulation of prices or utility rates, withdrawal of residence permits and licenses, refusal to renew residence permits, limitations on profits or ... on the right to transfer / remit profits abroad, and limitations on imports and the use of foreign exchange earnings."[9]

Undoubtedly, "creeping expropriation" may be more difficult to recognise than "direct" expropriation if only because the measures indicated above are, *prima facie*, lawful exercises of the powers of government. Thus, Herz has noted that it may be extremely difficult to determine where normal regulation ends and expropriation begins.[10]

The State can, for the time being, and for its own use, take possession of private property with or without compensation, for which the term "requisition" may be used, though the distinction between "expropriation" and "requisition" is very tenuous.

Finally, the term "indigenisation" is often used to refer to the process by which a government limits the participation in certain sectors of the economy to its nationals (indigenes) and thus compels aliens operating in these sectors to divest. Where a host government acquires majority equity interests in foreign enterprises, particularly local subsidiaries of multinational corporations, the term "indigenisation" or "nationalisation" may be used.

Expropriation will be used in this study to mean:

(1) the taking over by the State of foreign-owned enterprises out of public necessity; (2) the acquisition by the host government of majority equity interests in foreign enterprises or the reservation of the operation of certain economic activities for indigenes; (3) the unilateral termination, repudiation or alteration of concession agreements or State contracts with aliens; and (4) the imposition of restrictive maintenance / operational conditions or the taking of other actions which have the effect of expropriating property.

We have noted that, when a State expropriates foreign property in the exercise of its power of eminent domain, it is expected to discharge its obligations under customary international law by providing some compensation to the dispossessed owners. In certain cases such compensation may be far from adequate; in others, the taking State may assert that it is under no obligation to make any reparations for expropriations of a "general" and "impersonal" character or maintain that aliens are not entitled to any compensation if this right is denied to its own nationals, implying that aliens are only entitled to "national treatment" as opposed to any "international minimum standard".[11]

It is only when a taking State refuses to provide a certain compensation, when compensation is illusory or when there is a "denial of justice"[12] that the investor State, as a matter of right and duty (as espoused by the World Court in the *Mavrommatis Jerusalem Concession Case*, the *Chorzow Factory (Indemnity: Merits) Case*, the *Nottebolm Case (Second Phase)* and the *Barcelona Traction Case*[13]) calls on the taking State to discharge its obligations under customary international law.

Thus, an expropriation dispute is deemed to have occurred when a sovereign State, in exercising its eminent domain power:

1. takes over majority equity interests in foreign-owned enterprises;

2. repudiates, terminates, alters or takes steps to alter, repudiate or terminate concession agreement or State contracts with aliens;

3. limits foreign capital participation in certain economic activities, thus, compelling aliens to divest;

4. imposes restrictive maintenance or operational conditions or takes other actions which have the effect of expropriating property

and fails within a reasonable period to take appropriate steps (which may include arbitration) to discharge its obligations under international law or customary international law to aliens (natural / juridical) or fails or neglects to take steps to provide relief from restrictive maintenance or operating conditions.

PART II

The year 1960 was perhaps the most crucial date in Africa's international relations. It was a year of independence: more than fifteen African colonial territories obtained freedom. Not unnaturally, the immediate post-independence era witnessed a flurry of activities by African leaders, the formulation of Development Plans and the creation of new investment regimes. Investment laws enumerated and classified "pioneer", "infant" or "approved" industries. More often than not, they provided the framework for government policy: they described the executive authority responsible for examining, approving and supervising investments. Usually, they incorporated conditions of entry of foreign capital, procedures for investment dispute settlement, repatriation of capital and profits, employment of nationals, tax incentives, nationalisation and rules of compensation. In essence, investment laws served not only to facilitate and attract direct foreign investments but also to create a recognizable structure of the relationships involved.

One major factor influencing the investment climate in many LDCs has been the fear of nationalisation. Public policy on nationalisation in several African countries has been made manifest in official statements, investment laws or Constitutions. The Investment Code of Dahomey (now Benin) makes provision for the payment of "equitable" compensation while the Approved Enterprises (Concessions) Act 1956 of Sudan stipulated that:

"if any time any property belonging to an approved foreign enterprise is compulsorily acquired by the Sudan Government in furtherance of nationalisation, the said compensation shall be remitted out of Sudan".

These investment laws are consistent with customary rules of international law relating to expropriation of foreign property.

Legal guarantees of international minimum standards of treatment of private property have been provided in the Constitutions of many African countries, including Libya, Ethiopia and Nigeria. For example, Section 30 (1) of the Nigeria (Constitution) Order-in-Council 1960 states *inter-alia:*

"No property, movable or immovable, shall be taken possession of compulsorily and no right over or interest in any such property shall be acquired compulsorily in any part of Nigeria except by or under the provisions of a law that

(a) requires the payment of adequate compensation therefor : and

(b) gives to any person claiming such compensation a right of access, for the determination of his right in the property and the amount of compensation, to the High Court having jurisdiction in that part of Nigeria".

In effect, the constitutional provision relating to the safety or security of private property or the payment of "just" or "adequate" compensation in the event of expropriation applies to nationals and aliens alike. Policy statements guaranteeing an international minimum standard of treatment to foreign enterprises especially MNC subsidiaries were made by several African leaders.

One major reason why LDCs cannot attract direct foreign investments is because alien investors have difficulties in repatriating their profits in convertible currencies. In this respect, the investment laws of many African countries reflect two main tendencies: while one group places no restrictions on the repatriation of funds except the procedural requirement of permission, another group consisting of Algeria, Ghana, Guinea, Libya, Niger, Somalia, Senegal and Tunisia impose certain conditions before any foreign remittances can be made by alien investors.

Some countries in the former group, notably Côte d'Ivoire, Nigeria and Madagascar allow free transfer of currency to a particular monetary zone – Nigeria to the Sterling Zone, Côte d'Ivoire and Madagascar to the Franc Zone. For Nigeria, a prior permission of the Federal Minister of Finance must be obtained for "non-resident" capital investment and "approved status". African countries providing free transferability include Benin, Ethiopia, Gabon, Tanzania, Morocco, Senegal, Mauritania, Chad and Liberia.

The investment regimes created by African countries in the post-independence era have attempted to minimise obstacles to Direct Foreign Investment (DFI) and have encouraged DFIs through special incentives (tax rebates, repatriation of capital and profits, etc.) and guarantees (non-discrimination, "fair" or "equitable" compensation in the event of nationalisation and dispute settlement especially the acceptance of the jurisdiction of the International Centre for Settlement of Investment Disputes as a means of resolving investment disputes).

As a further guarantee of the security of DFIs, many African countries have concluded bilateral investment treaties for the reciprocal protection and promotion of investments with major capital-exporting countries. A typical bilateral investment protection treaty thus provides that:

> Property of nationals and companies of either Party shall not be taken within the territories of the other Party except for a public purpose nor shall it be taken without prompt payment of just compensation. Such compensation shall be in an effectively realizable form and shall represent the full equivalent of the property taken; and adequate provisions shall have been made at or prior to the time of taking for the determination and payment thereof.[14]

With respect to investment dispute settlement, Article VII (3) of the Treaty between the United States and Senegal Concerning the Reciprocal Encouragement of Investment of December 6, 1983, which is typical of several bilateral investment protection treaties, states that

(a) Each Party hereby consents to submit any dispute between such Party and a national or company of the other Party to the Centre for settlement by conciliation or binding arbitration .....

(b) Conciliation or binding arbitration of such disputes shall be done in accordance with the provisions of the Convention and the Regulations and Rules of the Centre.[15]

Article VII (1) of the Treaty defines an investment dispute as one involving

(a) the interpretation or application of an investment agreement between a Party and a national or company of the Other Party;

(b) the interpretation or application of any investment authorization granted by the competent authority of a Party to such a national or company; or

(c) an alleged breach of any right conferred or created by this Treaty with respect to such an investment.

These bilateral investment protection treaties make provisions for most-favored nation treatment, "just" compensation in the event of expropriation and settlement of investment disputes through diplomatic negotiations, conciliation or binding arbitration. Table 1 shows the major capital-exporting countries which have concluded investment protection treaties with African countries between 1959 and 1992.

TABLE 1 Bilateral investment treaties for the promotion and protection of investments between African countries and capital-exporting countries 1959-1992

MAJOR CAPITAL-EXPORTING COUNTRIES	NUMBER OF AFRICAN COUNTRIES CONCLUDING BILATERAL INVESTMENT PROTECTION TREATIES
1. Belgium-Luxembourg	8
2. Denmark	3
3. France	8
4. Federal Republic of Germany	34
5. Italy	5
6. The Netherlands	10
7. Sweden	5
8. Switzerland	24
9. United Kingdom	8
10. United States of America	5

Sources: Athena J. Pappas, "References on Bilateral Investment Treaties", *Foreign Investment Law Journal* 4 (Spring 1989): 194-203; International Center For Settlement of Investment Disputes, *News from ICSID* 2 (Winter 1985): 12-20; Id; *News from ICSID 3 (Winter 1986): 10-11; News from ICSID* 3 (Winter 1986): 9; Letter from the Swiss Embassy, London, 9th June, 1978.

In addition to concluding bilateral investment treaties which contain provisions relating to the ICSID Convention with ten major capital-exporting countries as shown in Table 1, forty-one African countries are signatories to the ICSID Convention with Ethiopia, Guinea-Bissau and Zimbabwe yet to deposit Instruments of Ratification, as shown in Table 2.

TABLE 2 Parties to the World Bank Convention on settlement of investment disputes: The Africa Group as at May 28, 1992

COUNTRY	SIGNATURE	DEPOSIT OF INSTRUMENT OF RATIFICATION	ENTRY INTO FORCE OF CONVENTION
Benin	September 10, 1965	September 6, 1966	October 14, 1966
Botswana	January 15, 1970	January 15, 1970	February 14, 1970
Burkina Faso	September 16, 1965	August 29, 1966	October 14, 1966
Cameroon	September 23, 1965	January 3, 1967	February 2, 1967

Centr.Afric.Rep.	August 26, 1965	February 23, 1966	October 14, 1966
Chad	May 12, 1966	August 29, 1966	October 14, 1966
Comoros	September 26, 1978	November 7, 1978	December 7, 1978
Congo	December 27, 1965	June 23, 1966	October 14, 1966
Côte d'Ivoire	June 30, 1965	February 16, 1966	October 14, 1966
Egypt	February 11, 1972	May 3, 1972	June 2, 1972
Ethiopia	September 21, 1965		
Gabon	September 21, 1965	April 4, 1966	October 14, 1966
Gambia	October 1, 1974	December 27, 1974	January 26, 1975
Ghana	November 26, 1965	July 13, 1966	October 14, 1966
Guinea	August 27, 1968	November 4, 1968	December 4, 1968
Guinea-Bissau	September 4, 1991		
Kenya	May 24, 1966	January 3, 1967	February 2, 1967
Lesotho	September 19, 1968	July 8, 1969	August 7, 1969
Liberia	September 3, 1965	June 16, 1970	July 16, 1970
Madagascar	June 1, 1966	September 6, 1966	October 14, 1966
Malawi	June 9, 1966	August 23, 1966	October 14, 1966
Mali	April 9, 1976	January 3, 1978	February 2, 1978
Mauritania	July 30, 1965	January 11, 1966	October 14, 1986
Mauritius	June 2, 1969	June 2, 1969	July 2, 1969*
Morocco	October 11, 1965	May 11, 1967	June 10, 1967
Niger	August 23, 1965	November 14, 1966	December 14, 1966
Nigeria	July 13, 1965	August 23, 1965	October 14, 1966
Rwanda	April 21, 1978	October 15, 1979	November 14, 1979
Senegal	September 25, 1966	April 21, 1967	May 21, 1967
Seychelles	February 16, 1978	March 20, 1978	April 19, 1978
Sierra Leone	September 27, 1965	August 2, 1966	October 14, 1966
Somalia	September 27, 1965	February 29, 1968	March 30, 1968
Sudan	March 15, 1967	April 9, 1973	May 9, 1973
Swaziland	November 3, 1970	June 14, 1971	July 14, 1971**
Togo	January 24, 1966	August 14, 1967	September 10, 1967
Tunisia	May 5, 1965	June 22, 1966	October 14, 1966
Uganda	June 7, 1966	June 7, 1966	October 14, 1966
Zaire	October 29, 1968	April 29, 1970	May 29, 1970
Zambia	June 17, 1970	June 17, 1970	July 17, 1970
Zimbabwe	March 25, 1991		

* Until Mauritius attained its independence on March 12, 1968, it was covered by the ratification of the United Kingdom.
** Until Swaziland attained its independence on September 6, 1968, it was covered by the ratification of the United Kingdom

Source: International Centre for Settlement of Investment Disputes, *List of Contracting States and Signatories of the Convention, ICSID/3* (Washington D.C.: ICSID, n.d.), pp. 1-3.

TABLE 3 Parties to the World Bank Convention on the multilateral Investment Guarantee Agency: The Africa Group as at August 9, 1991

COUNTRY	SIGNATURE	DEPOSIT OF INSTRUMENT OF RATIFICATION	SUBSCRIPTION AS A % OF AUTHORISED CAPITAL
Angola *	September 19, 1989	September 19, 1989	0.187
Benin	April 17, 1986		0.061
Botswana *	August 31, 1989	September 25, 1989	0.050
Burkina Faso *	October 2, 1987	November 2, 1988	0.061
Cameroon *	January 27, 1988	October 7, 1988	0.107
Cape Verde	September 28, 1989		0.050
Congo	June 7, 1988	July 5, 1990	0.065
Côte d'Ivoire *	May 26, 1986	June 7, 1988	0.176
Egypt *	June 6, 1986	September 21, 1987	0.459
Equat.Guinea	April 7, 1986		0.050
Ethiopia	September 21, 1990	February 21, 1991	0.070
Ghana *	June 25, 1986	April 29, 1988	0.245
Guinea	September 25, 1989		0.091
Guinea-Bissau	September 27, 1990		0.050
Kenya *	October 2, 1987	November 28, 1988	0.172
Lesotho *	December 22, 1986	January 30, 1987	0.050
Madagascar*	May 27, 1987	June 8, 1988	0.100
Malawi *	February 12, 1987	May 14, 1987	0.077
Mali	October 5, 1990	October 5, 1990	0.081
Mauritania	April 10, 1991		0.063
Mauritius *	November 4, 1988	October 19, 1990	0.087
Morocco	April 11, 1986		0.348
Namibia *	September 25, 1990	September 25, 1990	0.107
Nigeria *	September 23, 1986	March 8, 1988	0.844
Rwanda	October 27, 1989	October 27, 1989	0.075
Senegal *	October 30, 1985	May 10, 1987	0.145
Sierra Leone	December 4, 1985		0.075
Sudan	March 10, 1987		0.206
Swaziland *	September 25, 1989	April 2, 1990	0.058
Tanzania	September 24, 1990	January 24, 1991	0.141
Togo *	May 30, 1986	April 15, 1988	0.077
Tunisia *	October 1, 1986	June 7, 1988	0.156
Zaire *	March 26, 1986	February 7, 1989	0.338
Zambia *	October 7, 1986	June 6, 1988	0.318
Zimbabwe	September 27, 1989		0.236

* Investments into these member countries made by investors from these countries or from developed member countries are eligible for MIGA guarantees.

Source: Multilateral Investment Guarantee Agency, *List of Signatures and Ratifications of the Convention Establishing the Multilateral Investment Guarantee Agency* (Washington, D.CV.: MIGA, n.d.), pp. 1-5.

Apart from being signatories to the ICSID Convention which entered into force on October 14, 1966, several African countries (Congo, Benin, Burkina Faso, Egypt, Ghana, Madagascar, Niger, Senegal, Sudan, Tunisia and Zaire) have incorporated in their investment laws provisions accepting, upon request from an investor, to submit investment disputes to conciliation or binding arbitration under ICSID. Furthermore, while forty-one African countries are signatories to the ICSID Convention, thirty five are signatories to the Multilateral Investment Guarantee Agency (MIGA) Convention formulated under the World Bank's auspices as shown in Table 3. It is significant that Senegal and Sierra Leone signed the MIGA Convention a few days after it was opened for signature.

The MIGA Convention which entered into force on April 12, 1988, following its ratification by the United States and the United Kingdom, seeks to encourage increased international capital flows by issuing guarantees to investors against non-commercial risks and to provide a wide range of research, technical and advisory services to help create conditions conducive to investments contributing to the development of LDCs. Undoubtedly, the ICSID and MIGA Conventions are intended to balance the interests of host states and investors, provide modern ways to depoliticise investment disputes by offering the parties suitable neutral international facilities to settle disputes and arrive at amicable settlements and thus avoid government-to-government confrontation.[16]

Certainly African leaders were anxious in the immediate post-independence years to attract DFIs because they saw MNCs as "engines of development", though not unaware of their dire effects. The result of the capacity to attract substantial DFI was that the economies of several African countries were dominated by their former colonial masters by the end of 1967 as shown in Table 4. In countries not under colonial tutelage, notably Ethiopia, Liberia and South Africa, the ownership structure of DFI is shown in Table 5. Liberia is unique. Independent since 1847 and ruled by Afro-Americans until the military *coup d'état* which toppled the government of President William Tolbert, Liberia, not unnaturally, had the greatest share of DFI provided by United States-based MNCs such as Firestone and Bethlehem Steel Corporation.

By the late 1960s, some African leaders had grasped the sobering fact that political independence is not synonymous with economic independence, that alien investors not only dominated their economies but also that the developed

TABLE 4 Direct foreign investment in Africa by former colonial powers by 1967

COUNTRY	STOCK AT END OF 1967($M)	OWNERSHIP STRUCTURE OF DIRECT FOREIGN INVESTMENT IN AFRICA (%)		
		(1)	(2)	(3)
UNITED KINGDOM				
Botswana	3	UK 88.0	Neth. 12.0	
Egypt	58	Italy 26.7	US 70.7	
Gambia	2	UK 87.0	US 4.3	
Ghana	260	UK 59.1	US 24.6	
Kenya	172	UK 78.8	US 8.7	
Lesotho	5	UK 60.0	US 20.0	
Malawi	30	UK 92.7	US 6.7	
Nigeria	1 109	UK 53.8	US 16.4	Neth. 14.5
Sierra Leone	68	UK 84.4	US 13.2	
Sudan	37	UK 74.9	Neth. 13.6	
Swaziland	29	UK 96.6	US 3.4	
Tanzania	60	UK 46.7	Italy 18.2	Denm. 12.9
Uganda	48	UK 48.1	Cana. 31.3	US 4.2
Zambia	421	UK 79.6	US 19.2	
Zimbabwe	237	UK 88.3	US 4.2	
BELGIUM				
Burundi	14	Belg. 84.5	Cana. 7.1	
Rwanda	15	Belg. 86.8	Italy 6.6	
Zaire	481	Belg. 87.8	Neth. 4.4	
PORTUGAL				
Angola	193	UK 48.6	Port. 28.5	US 17.6
Mozambique	102	UK 50.1	Port. 37.2	
ITALY				
Libya	578	UK 10.9	US 77.7	
Somalia	13	Italy 83.3	US 7.9	
FRANCE				
Algeria	703	France 71.7	US 16.4	
Benin	18	France 57.0	Italy 25.7	
Cameroon	150	France 75.1	UK 11.9	
Central Afr.Rep.	37	France 91.8	US 8.4	
Chad	18	France 80.4	Neth. 8.4	
Congo	90	France 83.4	Belg. 6.1	
Djibouti	5.5	France 90.9	Neth. 8.4	
Gabon	265	France 73.4	US 10.9	
Guinea *	93	France 23.1	US 38.5	Switz. 20.5
Ivory Coast	202	France 80.0	US 3.7	
Madagascar	72	France 76.5	US 8.3	
Mali	7	France 76.9	US 7.7	
Mauritania	101	France 68.8	UK 16.2	Port. 28.5
Morocco (Spain)	179	France 48.6	US 17.6	Port. 28.5
Niger	23	France 95.7	US 2.9	
Senegal	154	France 87.4	US 4.4	

Togo	42	France 56.6	US	30.7		
Tunisia	135	France 39.2	Italy	28.5	Swed.	28.5
Upper Volta	16	France 75.3	US	12.3		

* Guinea left the French Community in 1958 when Sekou Touré opted for independence. As a result, the French government removed everything that was valuable including office files, electric bulbs. France also influenced her Western allies not to recognise the Sekou Touré regime. Nkrumah's Ghana saved the situation with a N20 million loan.

Sources: C. Widstrand, ed., *Multinational Firms in Africa*, New York: Africana Publishing Co., 1975, pp. 83, 84; United Nations, *Multinational Corporations in World Development*, New York: UN Publication Sales No. E. 73 11, A. 11, 1973, pp. 182, 183.

TABLE 5 Ownership structure of Direct Foreign Investment in non-colonial African countries

COUNTRY	STOCK AT END OF 1967 ($M)	OWNERSHIP STRUCTURE OF DIRECT FOREIGN INVESTMENT IN AFRICA (%)		
Ethiopia	50	US 23.9	France 43.7	UK 15.9
Liberia	300	US 57.8	Swed. 21.7	
South Africa	NA	US 15.8	UK 54.2*	

Source: B. Rodgers, *White Wealth and Black Poverty: American Investment in Southern Africa*, Westport, Conn.: Greenwood, 1976, p. 123.
*Estimates are made from 1970 data.

countries of the North still control the production and distribution of the world's resources.

It is small wonder then that African countries joined others of the South in calling for an effective control over their economic resources and the establishment of a New International Economic Order which found expression in the Declaration and Programme of Action on the Establishment of a New International Economic Order and the Charter of Economic Rights and Duties of States adopted by the United Nations General Assembly by Resolutions 3201 (S-VI) of 7 May, 1974, 3202 (S-VI) of 16 May 1974 and 3281 (XXIX) of 12 December, 1974 respectively.[17] Article 2(1) of the Charter of Economic Rights and Duties of States provides, *inter alia*, that:

Each State has and shall freely exercise full permanent sovereignty, including possession, use and disposal, over all its wealth, natural resources and economic activities.

The drives by African leaders to assert control over foreign-owned enterprises have found expression in several United Nations resolutions on permanent sovereignty over natural resources. These drives have been manifested in the politics of economic nationalism, ranging from expropriation of alien-owned enterprises, particularly local MNC subsidiaries; indigenisation of foreign-owned enterprises; termination, renegotiation and/or restructuring of concession agreements or State contracts with aliens, to "intervention".

The late 1960s and early 1970s witnessed a rash of eminent domain seizures in several African countries, falling into three categories:

(1) Large extractive enterprises owned by MNCs.

(2) Local subsidiaries of MNCs – banks, insurance, petroleum production and distribution companies.

(3) Small / medium-scale enterprises owned by resident aliens (particularly Indians, Pakistanis, Syrians, Lebanese, Greeks, and Portuguese, sometimes lumped together as "Asians").

Some expropriatory measures do not fall neatly into these categories. Socialist expropriations (in Zambia, Tanzania, Ethiopia, Somalia, Benin, Congo, Guinea, Uganda, Algeria and Libya) cover almost every sector of the economy: public utilities, retail / wholesale trade, buildings, insurance, banks, petroleum production and distribution, agriculture and manufacturing. Nevertheless, these "socialist" States continue to attract DFIs for "approved" projects.

Many African countries have witnessed one take-over or another, if only because there is an attractive target. Perhaps, the exceptions are Côte d'Ivoire, Gambia, Liberia, Gabon, Cameroon, Burundi and Rwanda where there are only minor or no actions at all, indeed, where there are no significant eminent domain seizures that would attract international attention. Mention must be made of attempts by the government of Liberia to renegotiate concession agreements. An example is the Liberian American-Swedish Minerals Company (LAMCO) Agreement which not only brought increased revenue to Liberia but also other benefits to the country (i.e. infrastructures).

Extractive and petroleum enterprises have been nationalised or indigenised in Nigeria (60%), Zaire and Zambia (51%), Mauritania (99%), Ghana (55%),

Sierra Leone (51%), Senegal (50%), and Togo (100%). Extractive enterprises are natural targets for nationalisation, first, because they are highly visible, rich, and apparently profiting at the expense of the local inhabitants. Secondly, various political groups, trade unionists, intellectuals and student bodies are disturbed that an MNC is taking from "their soil" an irreplaceable natural resource. Thirdly, other LDCs have established a pattern for their seizure: Mexico (1938), Iran (1951), Guatemala (1954), Cuba (1959, 1961), and Brazil (1964). In any event, some African leaders believe that they can operate the mines and oil wells with little external assistance. The service sector (banking, insurance, petroleum distribution) is equally a target because of the need to control what is essential for running the economy. Public utilities (power, telecommunications, water, transportation) are nationalised because these are usually publicly-owned in Western Europe and North America. There have not been significant expropriatory measures in the manufacturing sector, particularly because it is not considered feasible to nationalise manufacturing.[18]

There have been comprehensive programs of indigenisation in Nigeria, Ghana, Zaire, Kenya, Morocco, Uganda and Zambia, with varying degrees of success. Despite these expropriatory measures, comprehensive programs of indigenisation and renegotiation of concession agreements or State contracts with aliens, various African countries have continued to make efforts to attract private foreign investments; joint ventures have been encouraged between host governments and alien firms while nationals have been encouraged to enter into joint ventures with alien investors. Legal guarantees of international minimum standard treatment for DFI have been given: non-discrimination, fair compensation and in hard currency; repatriation of capital and profits and settlement of disputes through binding arbitration. Because various expropriatory actions have been accompanied with payments or promise of payments, alien investors have not moved their investments elsewhere but rather to less politically sensitive areas of the economy.

PART III

The World Bank and its two affiliates (the International Finance Corporation and International Development Association) were established respectively in 1945, 1956 and 1960 with the aim of raising the living standards in LDCs by channelling financial resources from developed countries to them. The World Bank, whose capital is subscribed by its member-governments as shown in Table 6, finances its lending operations from loans from the capital markets, retained earnings and the flow of repayments from its loans.

TABLE 6 World Bank: Subscriptions to Capital Stock and Voting Power as at June 30, 1990

MEMBER / GROUP	SUBSCRIPTIONS		VOTING POWER	
	SHARES	% OF TOTAL	NUMBER OF VOTES	% OF TOTAL
AFRICA **	57 061	5.51	69 311	6.41
EEC +	322 554	31.07	324 359	30.24
JAPAN	93 770	9.03	94 020	8.74
CANADA	31 543	3.04	31 793	2.95
CHINA	34 971	3.04	31 793	2.95
INDIA	31 692	3.05	31 942	2.97
SAUDI ARABIA	25 140	2.42	25 390	2.35
SOUTH AFRICA	13 462	1.30	13 712	1.27
SWEDEN	14 974	1.44	15 224	1.41
UNITED STATES	162 523	15.65	162 773	15.12
AUSTRALIA	21 610	2.08	21 860	2.03
BRAZIL++	14 000	1.35	14 250	1.32
KOREA++	9 372	0.90	9 622	0.89
PHILIPPINES++	3 841	0.39	4 091	0.38
SINGAPORE++	320	0.03	570	0.05

* Expressed in Thousands.
** Excludes South Africa which has 1.30% of the shares and 1.2% of voting power.
+ The voting power of the member-States of the EEC stands at Germany (6.7%), United Kingdom (6.47%), France (5.15%), Netherlands (3.32%), Italy (2.36%). Belgium (2.34%), Spain (1.58%), Denmark (0.98%), Portugal (0.58%), Ireland (0.51%), Luxembourg (0.14%) and Greece (0.11%).
++ So-called Newly-Industrialising Countries (NICs).

Sources: International Bank for Reconstruction and Development, *Financial Statements*, pp. 194-7; Chike Akabogu, "Can the UN be democratised?", *Sunday Concord,* (Lagos), October 20, 1991, p. 22.

Undoubtedly, a major purpose of the World Bank is the promotion of direct foreign investment. That perhaps explains why it has been concerned about "member governments that have in the past dealt unfairly with investments".[19] It also explains why some observers have criticised the World Bank for

> "leaning towards the view and policies of certain of its major shareholders... (and) using its considerable power to enforce a standard of compensation for expropriated foreign property which no longer represents generally accepted international law."[20]

We shall come back to these issues later.

True, the World Bank is often regarded as a multilateral institution for the provision of loans for productive purpose in its member-States. However, the principal function of the Bank is "to encourage international investment by private investors". This has found expression in Article I of the Articles of Agreement emphasizing the role of the Bank in "facilitating the investment of capital for productive purposes" and describing the promotion of private foreign investments as one of its principal objectives. Certainly, the Bank has been able to pursue this objective in many ways and through three institutions exclusively designed for the promotion of direct foreign investments: the International Finance Corporation, the International Center for Settlement of Investment Disputes (ICSID) and the Multilateral Investment Guarantee Agency (MIGA).

While it is obvious that the Bank is not vested, under its Articles of Agreements, with the power to settle investment disputes, the authors of the ICSID and MIGA believe that the settlement of investment disputes

> "is clearly a way to improve investment conditions and thus stimulate increased flows of international investment."[21]

As one observer has noted: "The existence of unresolved disputes is an obstacle to the smooth transfer of resources from the developed to the less developed world through... MNCs... The prospect that disputes can... be resolved not only allows the MNC greater confidence in investing in developing countries but might act as a deterrent to host countries and MNCs in wrangling or arbitrary behaviour."[22] The Executive Directors of the World Bank, in submitting their Report on the ICSID Convention to member-States on March 18, 1965 "for consideration with a view to signature and ratification, acceptance or approval",[23] had hoped that

> "the creation of an institution designed to facilitate the settlement of disputes between States and foreign investors can be a major step toward

promoting an atmosphere of mutual confidence and thus stimulate a larger flow of private international capital into those countries which wish to attract it."[24]

They added, and this is very significant:

"Private capital will continue to flow to countries offering a favourable climate for attractive and sound investments, even if such countries did not become parties to the Convention or, having joined, did not make use of the facilities of the Centre. On the other hand, adherence to the Convention by a country would provide additional inducement and stimulate a larger flow of international investment into its territories, which is the primary purpose of the Convention."[25]

It has been said that the World Bank has an "institutional interest in promoting the settlement of investment disputes". According to Shitata

"an unresolved investment dispute involving one of its borrowing countries can jeopardize the economic interests of the borrower which the Bank is intended to serve, and eventually might affect the Bank's own access to capital markets. The settlement of investment disputes in a smooth and orderly manner can assist the Bank in its borrowing and, therefore, in its lending operations."[26]

Table 7 shows direct involvement of the World Bank or its President in investment disputes between 1951 and 1985.

And, in 1985, the Bank provided technical advice to assist the Argentine State-owned gas company and a Dutch company to resolve their disputes. In general, where the Bank was involved directly in the settlement of investment disputes, it only provided its "good offices" to assist the parties concerned to resolve their disputes. However, where the president was involved, he acted as a mediator or conciliator.

Obviously, direct involvement by the Bank or its President in the settlement of investment disputes had been "cost-effective and highly efficient". However, several factors do not permit "a wider involvement by the Bank or its President in the settlement of investment disputes".[27] President Eugene R. Black was aware of the limitations of the Bank, as a financial development institution, in facilitating the settlement of investment disputes. Addressing a Joint Annual Meeting of the World Bank and the International Monetary Fund in September 1961, the President announced that he would examine the possibility of establishing a machinery for conciliation and arbitration which would serve the common interests of States and investors alike. That announcement heralded the birth of the International

TABLE 7 Direct involvement of the World Bank or its President in investment disputes 1951-1985

PERIOD OF INVESTMENT DISPUTES	CAUSE OF INVESTMENT DISPUTES	SETTLEMENT OF INVESTMENT DISPUTES
1. 1951-1952	Iranian nationalisation of Anglo-Iranian Oil Company (owned by BP)	The Bank provided a basis for the settlement of Iranian oil nationalisation crisis: (August 1954) Oil Consortium.
2. 1956	Egyptian nationalisation of the Suez Canal Company (owned by British and French nationals).	The Bank mediated the settlement of claims by the Government of Egypt
3. 1956	Nationalisation and sequestration of British assets following Anglo-French invasion of Egypt.	The President of the Bank assisted in the settlement of claims in 1959
4. 1958	Dispute between the City of Tokyo and certain holders of City of Tokyo bonds.	The President of the Bank, pursuant to a Conciliation Agreement of 1958, proposed a plan in 1960 resolving the controversy between the parties.
5. Late 1950s	Nationalisation of electric power assets by the Tunisian Government	The President of the Bank served as a Conciliator between the parties in 1965.
6. Late 1960s	Nationalisation of certain mining interests by the Government of Zaire	The President of the Bank provided his good offices in reaching an amicable settlement between the government and certain investors in 1968.

Sources: Akinsanya, *Multinationals in a Changing Environment,* New York: Praeger, 1984, pp.232-242; Anthony Sampson, *The Seven Sisters*, London: Hodder and Stoughton, 1978, pp. 144-152; Shitata, pp. 99-100.

Center for Settlement of Investment Disputes created by the Convention on the Settlement of Investment Disputes between States and Nationals of Other States. The question of the desirability and practicability of establishing institutional facilities, sponsored by the Bank, to resolve investment disputes between States and investors through conciliation and arbitration, was placed before the Seventeenth Annual Meeting of the Board of Governors in September 1962.

Recognising the usefulness of creating a machinery for resolving investment disputes within the framework of a multilateral agreement, the Bank directed its staff to prepare working papers and drafts for the consideration of its Executive Directors. Because the Preliminary Draft of the proposed Dispute Settlement Convention prepared by the office of the General Counsel of the Bank, Mr. Aron Broches, raised several technical questions which do not lend themselves to full discussion by the Board of Governors, the Executive Directors directed the President to convene regional meetings of legal experts "designated by member-governments" to consider the draft Convention.

The consultative meetings attended by legal experts from eighty-six countries were held on a regional basis: Addis Ababa (December 16-20, 1963), Santiago de Chile (February 3-7, 1964), Geneva (February 17-21, 1964), and Bangkok (April 27-May 1, 1964). Armed with the Report of the General Counsel and Vice-President of the Bank who chaired the regional consultative meetings, the Executive Directors informed the Board of Governors at its Nineteenth Annual Meeting in Tokyo in September 1964 that it

"would be desirable to establish institutional facilities envisaged, and to do so within the framework of an intergovernmental agreement."[28]

Thereupon, the Board directed the Executive Directors on September 10, 1964 to formulate an Investment Dispute Settlement Convention. To assist the Executive Directors in their assignment, member States were urged to send representatives to a Legal Committee, which met for three weeks (November 23-December 11, 1964).

After finalising the text of the Convention and agreeing on the language of the Report accompanying it, the Executive Directors submitted them to the member-governments on March 18, 1965.

The ICSID Convention, which came into force on October 14, 1966 following ratification by twenty countries, established the International Center for Settlement of Investment Disputes

"to provide facilities for conciliation and arbitration of investment disputes between Contracting States and nationals of other Contracting States."[29]

While a detailed examination of the provisions and aspects of the ICSID system need not detain us here, we must note the unique effectiveness of the ICSID system. True, parties are free to avail themselves or not of the facilities provided by the Center. However, once they have consented to submit disputes to ICSID conciliation or arbitration, neither party can unilaterally revoke its consent.[30]

While a State refusing to comply with an ICSID award runs the risk of being declared an international derelict, by and large, ICSID arbitration

"offers a degree of finality which, combined with the relatively low cost of ICSID arbitration, makes it an attractive alternative to other forms of international arbitration."[31]

Table 8 shows that twenty-six investment disputes were submitted to date to the International Center. The two conciliation proceedings were terminated following agreements between the parties. Of the arbitration cases, eleven were settled by the parties on agreed terms; in one of these the settlement was embodied in an award. Arbitral awards have been given in ten cases. There have been three annulment and resubmission proceedings. One annulment

TABLE 8 Submission of disputes to the International Center for Settlement of Investment Disputes by type and region 1966-1991

REGIONS OF THE WORLD	CONCILIATION PROCEEDINGS	ARBITRATION PROCEEDINGS
North America	-	-
Latin America Caribbean	1	3
Europe	-	1**
Africa	1*	15
Middle East	-	-
Asia excluding Japan	-	4
Oceania	-	1+
Total	2	24

* *SEDITEX Engineering v. Government of the Democratic Republic of Madagascar* (Case No. CONC/82/1).
** *Swiss Aluminium Limited and Iceland Aluminium Company Limited v. Government of Iceland* (Case No. ARB/83/1).
+ *Mobil Oil Corporation, Mobil Petroleum Company, Inc. and Mobil Oil New Zealand Limited v. New Zealand Government* (Case No. ARB/87/2).

Source: International Center for Settlement of Investment Disputes, *ICSID Cases*. ICSID/16/Rev.2, November 15, 1991, (Washington, D.C.: ICSID, 1991), pp. 1-21.

and three other ICSID proceedings are yet to be determined and awards rendered.[32]

These cases are related to investments in the agriculture, banking, construction, energy, health, industrial, mining and tourism sectors.

Obviously, the success or effectiveness of the ICSID system should not be measured by the number of investment disputes submitted to, or settled by the Center but by the degree of willingness of governments and investors alike to accept ICSID conciliation and arbitration proceedings. To be sure, the small number of arbitration cases reinforces the belief that the very existance of a binding arbitration arrangement acts as a powerful incentive for the amicable settlement of investment disputes.

We have stated elsewhere that most eminent domain seizures or expropriatory measures in Africa have engendered little or no acrimonies between the expropriating – and investor States. While the threat of foreign-aid sanctions by the United States Government under the Hickenlooper Amendment and Trade Act of 1974 compelled the Somali and Benin governments to compel "good faith" negotiations with United States-based multinational oil companies leading to compensation settlements, the expropriation disputes arising from the Algerian oil and natural gas expropriations were only resolved as a result of the "good offices" of the United States Government.[33]

It has been said that the World Bank has acted as a spokesman or an instrument of private or corporate interests of one or two of its major shareholders, notably the United States and the United Kingdom. The fact that the World Bank or its affiliates at various times suspended loan disbursements or suspended consideration of loan applications or rejected loan applications of countries having expropriation disputes with the nationals of its five largest shareholders seems to lend credence to this charge: Algeria (1964), Bolivia (1971), Chile (1970), Egypt (1960s), Ethiopia (1977-1980), Guyana (1971), Indonesia (under Sukarno), Iraq (1972-3), Peru (1968-1975), Tanzania (1971) and Zaire (1960s).[34]

Table 9 shows occasions on which the United States failed to support (by abstaining from voting) or voted against loans being sought because the proposed recipients had expropriated United States-owned enterprises without compensation.

Certainly, World Bank loans have been denied to member-governments that have embarked on eminent domain seizure without "a fair and equitable settlement." The position is made more explicit:

TABLE 9 United States "no" votes and abstentions on multilateral loans as a result of expropriation disputes 1969-1980

COUNTRY	YEAR OF DISPUTE	INSTITUTION	PROJECT	AMOUNT ($M)
Peru	1968	Inter-American Dev. Bank	Power	9.5
Bolivia	1971	Inter-American Dev. Bank	Transportation	0.5
Guyana	1971	World Bank	Sea Dikes	5.4
Iraq	1972	World Bank	Education	12.9
Iraq	1973	World Bank	Irrigation	40.0
Peru	1973	Inter-American Dev. Bank	Mining	6.0
Syria	1973	International Dev. Assoc.	Water Supply	15.0
Peru	1973	World Bank	Education	24.0
Congo	1976	World Bank	Education	8.0
Ethiopia	1977	African Dev. Fund	Transportation	5.5
Ethiopia	1978	African Dev. Fund	Agriculture	24.0
Ethiopia	1979	African Dev. Fund	Water Supply & Sewage	7.9
Ethiopia	1980	African Dev. Fund	Rural Roads	9.7
Ethiopia	1980	African Dev. Fund	Tea Industry Expansion	9.0

Source: Lars Schoultz, "Politics, Economics, and U.S. Participation in Multilateral Development Banks", *International Organization* 36 (Summer 1982): 550, 554-8.

"The Bank is charged under its Articles of Agreement, to encourage international investment. It has, therefore, a direct interest in the creation and maintenance of satisfactory relations between member countries and their external creditors. Accordingly, the normal practice is to inform governments who are involved in such disputes that the Bank or IDA will not assist them unless and until they make appropriate efforts to reach a fair and equitable settlement."[35]

In 1971, the World Bank restated its policy:

"The Bank will not lend for projects in a country if it considers that the position taken by that country with respect to alien owners of expropriated property is substantially affecting its international credit standing. Nor will it appraise projects in a country unless it has good grounds for believing that the obstacles to lending will soon be removed."[36]

Three years later, the Bank's position was made more forceful:

"The Bank, charged under its Articles to encourage international investment and itself a creditor, has a direct interest in the creation and maintenance of satisfactory relations between its members and their foreign creditors. Where the Bank or IDA are contemplating lending to a member country whose credit is impaired by the existence of a dispute over a default on its foreign debt or over compensation for foreign-owned property which has been expropriated, it must first be satisfied that the government is making reasonable efforts to reach a settlement."[37]

What the management of the World Bank is saying in essence is that the World Bank would *only* provide assistance, in whatever form, to any country which provides a favorable and conducive atmosphere for direct foreign investment. Whether such a position reinforces the values or mores which the United States seeks to protect or promote is not our present concern. It would appear that the World Bank is the only multilateral financial institution that has taken a policy position in this area, and significantly, a policy position which is not at variance with that of the United States dating to the early 1960s when the Congress enacted the Hickenlooper Amendment to the Foreign Assistance Act of 1962 in the wake of expropriations of United States-owned properties in Latin America. Such a position was restated more forcefully by the Nixon Doctrine on the protection of American DFI announced on January 19, 1971 at the height of Chilean expropriations.[38] Public policy linking economic assistance and promotion of United States DFI seems to have found expression in the Gonzalez Amendment to the Foreign Assistance Act.[39]

The position taken by the United States, shared by the World Bank and its other major shareholders is that an uncompensated eminent domain seizure, if left unchallenged, would create a domino effect, and would be the death-knell of private property in the expropriating country. While the "coercive" nature of the Hickenlooper and Gonzalez Amendments linking foreign assistance to compensation for direct foreign investments (when expropriated out of public necessity) is inconsistent with the provisions of the United Nations Charter and the Charter of the Organisation of American States of which the United States is a member, and while records show that the World Bank has suspended loan disbursements, suspended consideration of loan applications or rejected loan applications of countries having expropriation disputes with alien investors, some observers have wondered why the World Bank has not enjoined parties to expropriation disputes to take advantage of the facilities provided by the International Center for Settlement of Investment Disputes for conciliation or arbitration.

Expropriation disputes in Algeria, Tanzania, the United Arab Republic and Zaire in the 1960s prevented World Bank or IDA loans from being made, disbursed or loan applications considered. But the World Bank or its President had been directly involved in the resolution of investment disputes in Tunisia, the United Arab Republic and Zaire as Table 7 indicates. The International Center for Settlement of Investment Disputes had provided conciliation or arbitration facilities for the resolution of sixteen investment disputes involving twelve African countries as shown in Table 8.[40] Latin America and the Caribbean only recorded four ICSID cases (one conciliation and three arbitration proceedings), three of them against the Government of Jamaica following its disputes with United States-based aluminium corporations, largely because several countries in Latin America and the Caribbean are not signatories to the ICSID Convention, as can be seen in Table 10. This is significant not so much because certain Latin American countries are traditionally hostile to international arbitration but principally because a considerable proportion of world-wide DFI is concentrated in this region and owned largely by United States-based MNCs.

Table 9 indicates that the World Bank or the Inter-American Development Bank suspended consideration of loan applications by Peru, Bolivia and Guyana because of unresolved expropriation disputes with alien investors who are largely United States nationals. The American Executive Director of the World Bank or IDB had either voted against the application or abstained from voting, thus, technically killing the application. The World Bank also suspended loan disbursements or rejected loan applications of Iraq, Peru, Bolivia, Indonesia (under Sukarno) and Chile (under Allende) because of expropriation disputes with alien investors, thanks to the pressure of the American Executive Director of the World Bank.

How does one explain the difference in the positions taken by the World Bank in respect of expropriation disputes in Africa vis-à-vis Latin America and the Caribbean? First, there is the policy position of the World Bank in respect of unsatisfactory compensation settlements. The decision to deny loans to countries that embarked on eminent domain seizures without "a fair and equitable settlement", whatever that phrase means, is consistent with Article I of Bank's Articles of Agreement to encourage international investment.

Second, there is the position of the United States, the Bank's largest shareholder. Mention has been made of the Nixon Doctrine enunciated at the height of the debate within the Administration as to the appropriate response

TABLE 10 Parties to the ICSID Convention: Latin America and the Caribbean 1965-1992

COUNTRY	SIGNATURE	Deposit of Instrument of Ratification	Entry into Force of Convention
Argentina	May 21, 1991	-	-
Barbados	May 13, 1981	November 1, 1983	December 1, 1983
Belize	December 19, 1986	-	-
Bolivia	May 3, 1991	-	-
Chile	January 25, 1991	September 24, 1991	October 24, 1991
Costa Rica	September 29, 1981	-	-
Ecuador	January 15, 1986	January 15, 1986	February 14, 1986
El Salvador	June 9, 1982	March 6, 1984	April 5, 1984
Grenada	May 24, 1991	May 24, 1991	June 23, 1991
Guyana	July 3, 1969	July 11, 1969	August 10, 1969
Haiti	January 30, 1985	-	-
Honduras	May 28, 1986	February 14, 1989	March 16, 1989
Jamaica	June 23, 1965	September 9, 1966	October 14, 1966
Paraguay	July 27, 1981	January 7, 1983	February 6, 1983
St. Lucia*	June 4, 1984	June 4, 1984	July 4, 1984
Trinidad & Tobago	October 5, 1966	January 3, 1967	February 2, 1967

*Until St. Lucia secured independence on February 22, 1979, it was covered by the ratification of the United Kingdom on June 10, 1966.

Source: International Center for Settlement of Investment Disputes, *List of Contracting States and Signatories to the Convention as of May 28, 1992*, ICSID/3 (Washington, D.C.: ICSID, 1992), pp.1-4.

to uncompensated eminent domain seizures. The position of the United States is to deny support for loans "under consideration in multilateral development banks" to countries expropriating United States', and direct foreign investments without "taking reasonable steps to provide adequate compensation". Most direct American foreign investments are concentrated in Latin America and the Caribbean. The 1960s and early 1970s witnessed a rash of expropriations, take-overs, "interventions", "creeping expropriations" and termination of concession agreements by several countries in that region. Since the American view, shared by the World Bank, is that uncompensated or unsatisfactory eminent domain seizures, and they would be legion if unchallenged, would encourage a domino effect in other areas, this certainly explains reactions to eminent domain seizures in Latin America and the Caribbean.

But the World Bank did not have much of a problem with eminent domain seizures in Africa, partly because most compensation settlements proved to be very satisfactory to alien investors; partly, because expropriation measures by several African countries have been taken within the framework of a capitalist path of development; partly because almost all African countries are parties to the ICSID Convention and partly because African countries have learnt from the experiences in respect of expropriation disputes and were able to reach amicable settlements with alien investors rather than risk the sanctions of the World Bank and major capital-exporting countries.

NOTES

1. cf. Adeoye A. Akinsanya, *The Expropriation of Multinational Property in the Third World*, New York: Praeger, 1980, pp. 16-48.
2. cf. Akinsanya, "Permanent Sovereignty Over Natural Resources and the Future of Foreign Investment," in: *Nigerian Journal of International Affairs* 5 (1979), 91, Notes 51, 52 and 53.
3. Richard Lillich, "The Diplomatic Protection of Multinational Corporations," in: *The New Sovereigns: Multinational Corporations as World Powers*, A.A. Said and I.R. Simmonds (eds.), Englewood Cliffs, N.J.: Prentice-Hall, 1975, pp. 108-109.
4. A. Akinsanya, *Illusion of State Power: International Corporations and Indigenisation of African Economies,* Ibadan: Social Science Council of Nigeria, 1988, p. 9.
5. Pieter Adriaanse, *Confiscation in Private International Law*, The Hague: Martinus Nijhoff, 1956, p. 8.
6. J.F. Williams, "International Law and the Property of Aliens", *British Yearbook of International Law*, 9, 1928, 26.
7. J.E.S. Fawcett, "Some Effects of Nationalization of Foreign Property", Ibid., 27, 1950: 369. See also Ben A. Wortley, *Expropriation in Public International Law,* Cambridge: University Press, 1959, p. 2.
8. Samuel Friedman, *Expropriation in International Law*, London: Stevens, 1953, p. 3.

9 Williams, op. cit., p. 12; Wortley, op. cit., pp. 108-9; Ian Brownlie, *Principles of Public International Law*, Oxford: Clarendon Press, 1973, pp. 523-25.
10 J. Herz, "Expropriation of Foreign Property", *American Journal of International Law*, 34, 1941: 243.
11 Akinsanya, op. cit.
12 See Brownlie, pp. 514-6.
13 H. Steiner and D. Vagts, *Transnational Legal Problems*, Mineola, N.Y.: Foundation Press, 1976, pp. 205-243, 414-8.
14 See *International Legal Materials* 2 (1963): 1099.
15 See International Centre for Settlement of Investment Disputes, *Convention of the Settlement of Investment Disputes between States and Nationals of Other States*, ICSID/2, Washington, D.C.: ICSID, n.d.
16 See Akinsanya, "International Protection of Direct Foreign Investments in the Third World," *International and Comparative Law Quarterly* 36 (1987): 58-75; C.F. Amerasinghe, "Dispute Settlement Machinery in Relations Between States and Multinational Enterprises. With Particular Reference to the International Center for Settlement of Investment Disputes," *International Lawyer* 11 (1977): 45-59; Id., "The International Centre for Settlement of Investment Disputes and Development Through the Multinational Corporations," *Vanderbilt Journal of Transnational Law* 9 (Fall 1976); 793-816; Ibrahim F.I. Shitata, "The Settlement of Disputes Regarding Foreign Investment: The Role of the World Bank With Particular Reference to ICSID and MICA," *The American University Journal of International Law and Policy* 1 (Summer 1986): 97-116.
17 The Declaration was adopted without a formal vote on the floor. Reservations were entered by the United States, France, Japan, the United Kingdom and the Federal Republic of Germany. See *International Legal Materials* 13 (1974): 744-766. The Resolution was adopted with a vote of 120-6, with 10 abstentions (Austria, Canada, France, Ireland, Israel, Italy, Japan, the Netherlands, Norway and Spain). Belgium, Denmark, the Federal Republic of Germany, Luxembourg, the United Kingdom and the United States voted against the Resolution. Malvides and South Africa did not participate in the voting. See *International Legal Materials* 14 (1975): 265; G.M. White, "A New International Economic Order," *Virginia Journal of International Law* 16 (Winter 1976): 323-345; Akinsanya, "The United Nations Charter of Economic Rights and Duties of States," pp. 64-104.
18 L.R. Rood, "Nationalisation and Indigenisation in Africa," *Journal of Modern African Studies* 14 (1976): 435.
19 White, "Wealth Deprivation: Creditor and Contract Claims," in: *International Law of State Responsibility for Injuries to Aliens*, edited by

Richard B. Lillich (Charlottesville, Va.: University of Virginia Press, 1983), p. 167.
20 Ibid., p. 168
21 Shitata, op. cit. 98.
22 Amerasinghe, "The International Center....", p. 794.
23 International Center for Settlement of Investment Disputes, *Convention on the Settlement of Investment Disputes between States and Nationals of Other States. Documents concerning the Origin and the Formulation of the Convention,* Vol. II, Part 2 (Washington, D.C.: ICSID, 1968), p. 1071.
24 Ibid., p. 1073
25 Ibid.
26 Shitata, op. cit., pp. 98-99
27 Ibid., p. 100.
28 International Center for Settlement of Investment Disputes, *Convention on the Settlement of Investment Disputes between States and Nationals of Other States. Submitted to Governments by the Executive Directors of the International Bank for Reconstruction and Development and Accompanying Report of the Executive Directors,* ICSID/2 (Washington, D.C.: ICSID, n.d.), p. 3.
29 Art. 1 (2) of the Convention.
30 Art 25 (1) of the Convention.
31 Shitata, op. cit. , p. 105.
32 International Center for Settlement of Investment Disputes, *ICSID Cases,* ICSID/16/Rev. 2, November 15, 1991 (Washington, D.C.: ICSID, 1991), p.i.
33 Akinsanya, op. cit., pp.284-300.
34 White, op. cit., p. 202 n.97; Akinsanya, op. cit., pp. 115-177, 284-300.
35 White, p. cit., p. 167.
36 Ibid. P. 168.
37 The World Bank Group, *Policies and Operations* (Washington, D.C.: World Bank, 1974), pp. 44-45.
38 United States, White House, "Policy Statement. Economic Assistance and Investment Security in Developing Nations," *International Legal Materials* 11 (1972): 241.
39 Akinsanya, "United States Economic Assistance and United States Direct Foreign Investments in the Third World: Lessons for Africa," *Nigerian Journal of International Studies* 15 (November 1991); 30-62.

40 These include Cameroon (1), Congo (2), Côte d'Ivoire (1), Egypt (2), Gabon (2), Guinea (2), Liberia (1), Madagascar (1), Morocco (1), Nigeria (1), Senegal (1) and Tunisia (1).

7 WORLD ECONOMIC INTEGRATION AND POLITICAL CONFLICT IN LATIN AMERICA

Michael Nollert

Introduction

For the last three decades Latin America has been one of the most conflict-prone areas in the world. Yet, data from the *World Handbook of Social and Political Indicators* (Taylor 1985) suggest that the cross-country variations in political violence and protest were even ampler than those in the group of Western European democracies. Thus, for example, population-deflated levels of political violence in Colombia during the 1950s and in Argentina during the 1970s were significantly higher than in the average Western core country, whereas Costa Rica or Mexico experienced postwar levels of conflict similar to those of Finland or Norway (cf. Nollert 1991/1992).

Third World theorists generally agree in arguing that the logic of the world economy is an important factor in explaining the political and social conditions in a less-developed country. Nevertheless, the approaches differ in

---

The article reports on the research project "World Economic Integration, Politco-economic Interest Mediation and Conflicts in Latin America" which was supported by the World Society Foundation. Michael Nollert took his Ph.D. from the University of Zurich and is senior member of Bornschier's team at the Sociological Institute of the University of Zurich, Rämistrasse 69, CH-8001 Zurich, Switzerland.

assessing the effect of economic openness on political conflict. While proponents of liberal neo-classical modernization theory suggest that investments by transnational corporations, for instance, pave the way to economic success and social stability, dependency and world system theorists prefer to assume negative effects of foreign influences. They reject the optimistic position of modernization theorists that integration into the world economy automatically furthers the extension of political rights, economic growth and the reduction of inequality in the distribution of material goods. Instead, economic, political and military dependencies linked to peripheral status in the world economy are regarded as causes of repressive authoritarianism, poor economic performance and sharp socioeconomic inequalities. In short, it is postulated that strong world economic integration incites insurgency.

Although modernization theory and dependency / world system approaches obviously differ in assessing the effects of economic openness on the level of domestic conflict, both schools agree that democratic institutions, high economic growth and narrow income inequality help stabilize political regimes. In considering the Latin American context in the 1970s, this premise, however, must be confronted with two historical facts. On the one hand, the breakdown of democratic regimes in Chile, Uruguay and Argentina indicates that, in peripheral states, civil and political rights are not sufficient to ensure political stability. On the other hand, contrary to cross-national findings based on world samples, political conflict in Latin America during the 1970s was most pronounced in countries characterized by below-average socioeconomic inequalities.

In the first part of this article, I sketch out the debate on the linkage between world economic integration and political conflict. Current theoretical approaches will be examined with the object of ascertaining (1) whether integration into the world economy fosters or dampens conflict, and (2) which causal relationships they suggest. As a result, three major causal chains linking external dependencies and levels of conflict will be discussed. The first major causal chain focuses on the role of political regimes. I conclude that regimes which peacefully accommodate business and labor interests should incite less social unrest than authoritarian regimes which oppress trade unions, or democratic regimes in which policy formation is dominated by multi-party politics.

Two other major causal chains suggest that world economic integration directly affects levels of economic growth and of socioeconomic inequality, which are in turn linked to the level of conflict. After summarizing the debate between modernization and dependency / world system theorists on the effects of economic openness on growth and inequality, I focus on the linkage between socioeconomic performance and conflict. Applying the *deprivation* approach one can, in principle, state that low growth and high inequality incite insurgency. Yet, the *resource mobilization* paradigm would take the opposite view. Thus, it seems plausible to suppose that especially in peripheral states, collective action against the state is mobilized by affluent, well-educated people rather than by poor and relatively deprived actors.

In the second part of the article the resulting causal model will be cross-nationally tested. I use four measures of world economic integration: penetration by transnational corporations, debt service, direct foreign investment and the export ratios. After calculating the bivariate correlations between these four measures and the level of political conflict in the 1973-1977 period, political conflict is regressed according to the major world economic predictor (export ratio), economic growth, and three types of regime. In a second step, I investigate whether the effects of economic openness are transmitted by the regime type and economic growth. Due to lack of data on socioeconomic inequality for five of the 21 Latin American countries included in the empirical analyses, two separate multiple regression models finally show whether the effect of economic openness on conflict is also transmitted by inequality in disposable income and in land-ownership.

The Debate on the Impacts of Economic Openness

Conventional theories of economic development and modernization postulate that Third World nations become developed by passing through a series of evolutionary stages (Rostow 1960). Successive economic stages are therefore expected to benefit populations, which in turn should foster the legitimacy of political regimes. World integration helps to modernize the economy since foreign influences would liberalize both the political and the economic system. As a result, Third World countries are to become as affluent and democratic in the long run as the highly developed countries are already. One can consequently argue that the high level of political conflict in Latin America points to a lag in modernization.

In the 1970s the modernization perspective was fundamentally challenged by dependency and world system approaches. Their starting point was the observation that the gap between poor and affluent nations was increasing rather than narrowing as the proponents of conventional development theory had projected. In addition, democratic regimes broke down in Argentina, Chile and Uruguay, which did not conform to the view that economic development automatically leads to political development. According to dependency theory, both events reflect a global structure of dominant and dependent states (e.g. Chirot 1977, Cardoso and Faletto 1979), while world system theory regards failure in economic development, political violence and repression as an outcome of the international division of labor (e.g. Wallerstein 1974, Bornschier and Chase-Dunn 1985). In short, both opponents of the modernization approach argue that foreign involvement in peripheral countries benefits the population at the core and local elites at the periphery but frustrates mass claims of the population at the periphery. Indeed, the prevalence of authoritarianism, retarding growth rates and the sharp socioeconomic inequalities linked to poverty in dependent Third World countries clearly supports this view. The Latin American countries in particular exhibit below-average growth rates and sharp inequalities in the distribution of income and landed property in the second half of the 20th century. In addition, the United States strongly contributed to the breakdown of the democratically legitimated regimes in Guatemala and Chile.

According to both modernization and dependency / world system theory it is possible to argue that world economic integration is either directly or indirectly linked to political conflict negatively or positively. Indeed, both schools use arguments to show that domestic political and socioeconomic structures transmit foreign influences at the level of conflict. Three variables may simultaneously be externally determined, and determine the level of political conflict: (1) the political regime, (2) economic growth, and (3) socioeconomic inequality.

The role of regime type. Both modernization and dependency / world system approaches argue that the effect of economic openness on political conflict is transmitted by the type of regime. Modernization theory suggests that foreign investment supports the shift from traditional authoritarianism to democracy. By contrast, dependency / world system approaches postulate that transnational corporations favor regimes which may oppose the demands of workers. Hence, world market integration is assumed to promote authoritarian rather than democratic polities.

For heuristic reasons, it seems useful to construct a regime typology (Figure 1) which encompasses two dimensions: (1) extent of freedom to articulate discontent, and (2) extent of incorporation of capital and labor interests into the process of policy formation.

The vertical dimension distinguishes between democratic and authoritarian regimes. Ideally, under democratic regimes, citizens have the opportunity to change their government, whereas authoritarian ones principally rely on repression to maintain power. Depending on which actors are incorporated into the process of policy formation, the horizontal dimension distinguishes between regimes which formally take into consideration both business and labor demands, regimes in which labor interests are ignored or even repressed, and those in which economic actors are not directly involved in decision-making.

If the democracy / authoritarianism dichotomy and the three degrees of incorporation of interest organizations are cross-tabulated against each other, six regime types can be distinguished (Figure 1).

FIGURE 1 A typology of regimes according to political rights and incorporation of interest organizations in the process of policy formation

Political Rights
extensive

pluralism	liberal corporatism	democratic corporatism
traditional authoritarianism	exclusive corporatism	inclusive corporatism

limited

      weak   labor organizations excluded   labor organizations included

Incorporation into the process of policy formation

In line with Stepan (1978) one can first distinguish between two modes of corporatist interest mediation. "Exclusive" corporatism refers to regimes which (1) incorporate the interests of capital into the process of policy formation and (2) exclude labor interests by suppressing trade unionism (see Erickson 1977, Moreira Alves 1989, Ruiz-Tagle 1989). The residual authoritarian regimes ruled by small landed elites or family dynasties can be labelled traditional authoritarian.

Both types of authoritarian corporatism correspond to what O'Donnell (1973) and Collier (1979) call bureaucratic or new authoritarianism. In addition, exclusive corporatism is mostly legitimized by a conservative Catholic development model which argues that the revitalization of medieval corporatism offers a third, non-capitalist and non-Marxist road to economic modernity (see Wiarda 1982).

According to the debate on corporatism in the democratic core countries (see Nollert 1992), regimes combining democracy and the incorporation of capital and labor interests are called *democratic* corporatist. Other current labels for this type would be *societal* corporatism (Schmitter 1974) or *social* corporatism (Katzenstein 1985). Regimes which combine democracy and corporatism restricted to business organizations are called *liberal* corporatist. Finally, in "pluralist" polities neither unions nor employers' organizations are incorporated, policy formation being a result of interparty competition.

According to dependency / world system theory one can expect that transnational dependencies favor authoritarian regimes, while modernization theory assumes foreign investment to have a liberalizing effect (Rothgeb 1989). Generally supposing that authoritarian regimes are more conflict-prone than democratic ones, modernization theorists thus expect world economic integration to have a positive effect on political conflict, while the critical view suggests a negative one. Referring to the distinction between exclusive and inclusive modes of corporatism, one can furthermore state that transnational capital supports exclusive corporatist or "bureaucratic-authoritarian" regimes (see Evans 1979). Finally, the debate on the effects of a tripartite accommodation of employer and labor interests on conflict patterns at the core (see Nollert 1992: ch. 6) suggests that both democratic and inclusive corporatism should exhibit less political unrest than the four other regime types. Assuming that the stability of democratic pluralism in peripheral polities depends strongly on economic performance, I even conclude that authoritarian incorporation of interest groups into the process of policy formation and implementation is more important in explaining below-average political unrest in Latin America than the presence or absence of democratic rights.

The role of economic growth and socioeconomic inequality. Third World theory also argues that the effect of economic openness on political unrest is transmitted both by variations in economic growth and in social inequality. The optimistic liberal view argues that foreign investment creates high growth rates and reduces socioeconomic inequalities, while dependency / world system theory predict exactly the opposite. Contrary to Olson (1963) who hypothesized destabilizing effects of economic growth in developing countries, both schools generally support the view that low growth incites social unrest. Also, they agree that high land-tenure and income inequality provoke domestic rebellion (Zimmermann 1980). Hence, foreign economic influences are depicted as either dampening or promoting political conflict. Although there are many case studies supporting the view that social unrest in Latin America is rooted in poverty and inequality (e.g. Roberts and Midlarsky 1986, Brockett 1988), in recent years the relative deprivation thesis (cf. Gurr 1970 and Davies 1978) has been challenged by the resource mobilization theory (Tilly et al. 1975). According to this perspective, low growth and high inequality should contribute to political demobilization rather than to collective action in the context of developing countries (see Zwicky 1989).

Finally, one must be aware of the possible impacts of the political regime on growth rates and inequality. Along the dimension of political rights one can expect first that democratic legitimacy promotes both economic growth (Bornschier 1988) and reduces inequality (Lenski 1966). Also, acknowledgement of labor interests in policy formation should in principle create higher growth rates and less inequality. Unfortunately, there is no space here to discuss both the linkage between economic openness and a specific regime type and the linkage between regime types, growth and socioeconomic inequality (see Nollert 1991).

The causal model. Since there is obviously no agreement about the nature of the relationships between the five variables mentioned above, the summarizing causal model (Figure 2) does not indicate the directions of the proposed paths. Challenging the view that economic openness directly affects political insurgency, it shows the indirect paths suggested above. On the one hand, variations in world market integration may be transmitted by variations in regime type, in economic growth and in socioeconomic inequality. On the other hand, two-step causal chains are possible. Thus the regime type may also affect conflict indirectly through differences in growth and inequality.

Since the causal model does not anticipate direct effects of world economic integration on political conflict and includes the type of regime as an intermediate variable, there is no empirical study to which I can refer. Yet, there are cross-national studies focussing on the linkage between dependency and political conflict. While the results of Timberlake and Williams (1987) and Boswell and Dixon (1990) tend to support our model, London and Robinson (1989) reject the view that the effect is transmitted by variations in income inequality. Yet, Rothgeb (1989) reports a negative, linear relationship between economic openness and conflict. However, his analysis is restricted to foreign investment as measure of world economic integration and neglects the three suggested intervening variables. Finally, the findings of Jagodzinski (1983) support the proposed negative, linear effect of economic growth on political conflict.

FIGURE 2 A summary of the argument

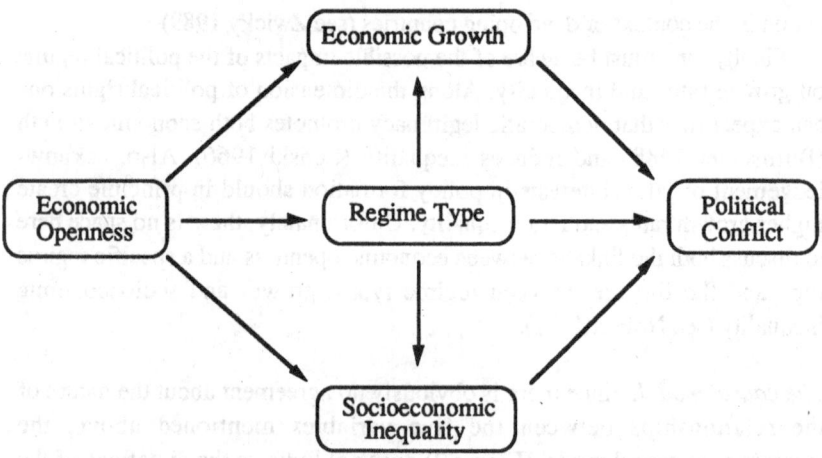

A Cross-National Test of the Causal Model

The causal model proposed above is tested in three steps. In a first step, the empirical linkage between various measures of economic openness and political conflict are investigated in a multivariate analysis based on data on 21 Latin American countries. In a second step, the significant relationships are controlled for the three intervening variables in the model. If the effect of world economic constraints is, as expected, an indirect one, only the effects of the regime type and the growth rate should be significant. Due to missing data on agrarian inequality for 5 cases, the question of whether socio-economic inequality transmits effects of world economic constraints and the regime type will be addressed in a separate subsection.

Measurement of the variables

Political conflict. The level of domestic conflict is measured by the index of political instability constructed by Gupta (1990). I take the mean annual levels in the 1968-1972 and in the 1973-1977 period. The index is based on seven indicators of political conflict provided by Taylor (1985): number of demonstrations, riots, political strikes, deaths from political violence, political assassinations, armed attacks, and political executions. In addition, the index reports whether there were coups d'état, whether they were successful and whether the regime was authoritarian or democratic.

Economic openness. Since economic openness is a multidimensional concept, four different indicators of dependency are used: (1) Export dependence is measured by the export ratio (exports as a % of gross domestic product) (Bornschier and Chase-Dunn 1985). (2) Dependence on transnational corporations is indicated by the level of TNC penetration in 1967 (Bornschier and Chase-Dunn 1985). (3) A measure of investment dependence is the flow of foreign investment in the 1967-1973 period, as a share of the average gross domestic product 1965-1970 (Bornschier and Chase-Dunn 1985). (4) The debt service ratio 1970 provided by the *World Development Report* (World Bank 1988) is included as a measure of "debt dependence". It indicates the percentage of total exported goods and services which are used for long-term debt reduction.

Regime type. Applying the regime typology above (Figure 1) to classify 21 Latin American regimes in the 1973-1977 period, three dummy variables (democratic - corporatist-authoritarian - tripartite) are constructed: (1) Coded as democratic in the 1973-1977 are the pluralist regimes of Argentina, Costa Rica, the Dominican Republic, Jamaica, the elitist liberal corporatist regime of Colombia (see Bailey 1987, Hartlyn 1989) and the democratic corporatist regimes of Mexico, Trinidad and Tobago, and Venezuela. (2) Authoritarian-corporatist (exclusive and inclusive corporatist) regimes prevail in Brazil, Chile, Uruguay, Peru (Stepan 1978) and Uruguay. Tripartism (democratic corporatism or inclusive corporatism) is found in Costa Rica, Ecuador, Mexico, Peru and Venezuela. (3) Classified as traditional-authoritarian are the regimes of Bolivia, El Salvador, Guatemala, Haiti, Honduras, Nicaragua, Panama, Paraguay.

Economic growth. In order to compare our results with those of prior research, the measure of economic growth is taken as the annual growth rate of per capita gross domestic product (GDP), 1965-1977 (Bornschier and Chase-Dunn 1985).

Socioeconomic inequality. Two measures are used in the analyses. (1) The level of income inequality is indicated by the size of the share of personal income accruing to the top quintile of recipients at about 1970. Although many studies on the linkage between inequality and political conflict used the Gini coefficient, I prefer the income share because it is (i) less sensitive to inequality in the middle of the distribution and (ii) has more meaning than the Gini coefficient. The data are taken from Hoover (1989). The values for Nicaragua, Guatemala, El Salvador are provided by Simpson (1990), and those for Jamaica stem from Muller and Seligson (1987). (2) Agrarian inequality is measured by the Gini coefficient of land concentration (Muller and Seligson 1987). The data refer to the 1966-1975 period and were collected by the Food and Agriculture Organization (FAO).

Findings

In the first analysis political conflict is regressed on a set of measures of the variables included in the causal model and on the level of conflict in the 1968-1972 period. Due to above-average collinearity among the world economy measures, only those indicators are adopted which significantly correlate with political conflict in the 1973-1977 period. The export ratio appears to be linked more strongly to political conflict than to any other world economy variable. However, the correlation of $r = -.49$ completely contradicts dependency theory. In short: highly integrated countries show lower levels of conflict than poorly integrated ones. Because of the low correlation with political conflict (r = .17), the level of economic development was eliminated in the original model.

Table 1 below shows that the inverse correlation between the export ratio and political conflict is still signficant if other variables are controlled. In line with deprivation theory there is also a significant impact of economic growth on political conflict. As expected, high growth dampens rather than inciting social unrest. However, democracy does not reduce political conflict, whereas both authoritarian corporatism and tripartism are significantly related to its level in the 1973-1977 period. According to this result, one may conclude that authoritarian corporatism generally fosters insurgency, while the incorporation of labor interests stabilizes the political economy. In short: the level of conflict in Peru and Ecuador would have been higher if labor interests had been excluded.

TABLE 1 Predictors of Political Conflict 1973-1977

Democracy	.44	a
	.26	b
Authoritarian Corporatism	.98**	
	.51	
Tripartism	-.64**	
	-.33	
Export Ratio 1970	-.03**	
	-.36	
Growth of GDP in % 1965-1977	-.25**	
	-.42	
Political Conflict 1968-1972	.76**	
	.55	
Intercept	1.28	
N	21	
Adjusted R^2	.66	
F and (p)	7.4	(0.001)

a unstandardized regression coefficient; ** = p< 05
b standardized regression coefficient (β)

Although the missing effect of democracy and an inverse effect of the export ratio have been detected, up to now the results tend to support our expectations. While the regime type and economic growth matter, the world economic measures aside from the export ratio do not directly affect the level of social unrest. This finding accords with our causal model. However, if economic openness is *indirectly* linked to the level of political conflict, there have to be significant effects of world economic measures on either the regime type, the growth rate or the level of socioeconomic inequality.

The role of the political regime as mediating variables. First, let us look at the relationships between world economic measures and types of regime. The simple correlation matrix (not shown) suggests that world economic integration measures generally fail to predict the regime type in the 21 countries during the 1973-1977 period. Only the emergence of authoritarian-corporatist regimes appears to be a function of a low export ratio ($r=-.38$) and high debt service ($r=.28$). A separate analysis (also not shown) testing interaction effects among the four predictors yielded further support for this finding. Authoritarian corporatism seems to reflect a combination of an export ratio below 18.5% and a debt service above 20%. This statistical tendency is perfect if only four outlying cases are dropped from the 21-country sample. Two cases, Argentina and Mexico, bias the estimates because they are classified as democratic, though their export ratios are low (8.2% and 9%) and their debt service is above-average (51.7% and 44.3%). The two other cases, Brazil and Ecuador, depart from the empirical tendency for they combine authoritarian corporatism and relatively low debt service (12.5% and 14.1%). The reason why the case of Argentina outlies may be that its regime must be classified both in the previous (1968-1972) and in the subsequent period (after 1977) as authoritarian-corporatist. Probably, in the 1973-1977 period the Mexican PRI regime may also not have been as democratic as those in Costa Rica or Venezuela (cf. Stamm 1992). The outlying case of Brazil points to the fact that our test design ignores long-run effects. Indeed, Brazil's democratic regime already broke down in 1964. Therefore, its low external debt may reflect the success of the subsequent exclusive corporatist regime. Finally, Ecuador's low debt service may stem from the availability of natural resources.

To test the well-known argument that democracy and corporatism mirror a high level of economic development (e.g. Lipset 1959, O'Donnell 1973, Rueschemeyer et al. 1991), simple correlations between regime types and the real gross domestic product per capita have also been calculated. In short: The level of development fails to explain variations in the three regime types considered in the analysis. Only the traditional-authoritarian type appears to be significantly linked to low economic development.

Different growth rates as an intervening variable. Up to now the results do not consistently support the hypotheses of foreign determination of regime type. Although authoritarian-corporatist regimes may primarily emerge in highly indebted countries, high export dependence prevents rather than promotes the breakdown of democracy in the 1970s. In addition, there are no significant impacts of any world economic variable on the three other regime types. However, both liberal development theory and dependency / world system approaches also argue that economic openness contributes to either high or low economic growth.

Table 2 indicates the results of the regression of the growth rate in the 1965-1977 period on our four world economy measures. Applying the test design of Bornschier and Chase-Dunn (1985), their measure of gross domestic investment (investment divided by the mean of gross domestic

TABLE 2 Predictors of the Economic Growth Rate 1965-1977

TNC Penetration 1967	-.0001	a
	-.25	b
Foreign Direct Investment	.0001**	
	.44	
Gross Domestic Investment	.0016**	
	.62	
Export Ratio 1970	-.123**	
	-.84	
Debt Service 1970 ln (1+x)	-1.11**	
	-.54	
Intercept	5.23	
N	21	
Adjusted R^2	.45	
F and (p)	4.3	(0.013)

a unstandardized regression coefficient; ** = p< 05, * = p<.10
b standardized regression coefficient (β)

products 1965, 1970, and 1973) is added as a control variable. In sum, there are strong but surprising external influences on the growth rate. First, there is no significant association between high TNC penetration and retarded growth. Although this rejects the causal model, it replicates Bornschier's and Chase-Dunn's (1985: 95) finding that the association does not hold in Latin America. Second, high debt service appears to impede economic growth. Since the level of indebtedness is measured in the middle of the growth period, however, high growth may also have limited excessive indebtedness. Third, foreign investment positively affects economic growth. This corresponds to previous findings by Rothgeb (1989), supporting the view of liberalizing effects of world economic integration. Fourth, a high export ratio appears to be a big impediment to growth. As expected, in the 1965-1977 period relatively weak dependent countries with strong states (e.g. Brazil) are economically far more successful than highly dependent, weak states (e.g. Jamaica). Finally, the often-reported effect of domestic investment reaches significance in our regression model.

All in all, the results broadly support the general view of dependency / world system approaches that retarded growth and consequently above average political conflict in peripheral states reflect the unfair logic of the world economy. Nevertheless, it is noteworthy that low growth rates are found in countries with high export vulnerability and high indebtedness as well as in countries where foreign investment is low. In addition, our findings reject the view that external factors directly contribute to different levels of internal conflict. There are only moderate simple correlations between world economy measures and political conflict, whereas our regression models show several significant effects of external factors on the growth rate (Table 2) and a significant inverse effect of the growth rate at the level of political conflict (Table 1). The most interesting exception is the ambigious effect of dependence on exports. Thus, high export dependence appears to inhibit high growth (Table 2), which in turn incites insurgency, while it helped prevent authoritarian corporatism, which in turn results in low political conflict.

Socioeconomic inequalities as intervening variables. After having focussed on the question of whether world economy variables directly or indirectly, mediated by either regime type or different growth rates, contribute to different levels of political conflict, I turn to the role of socioeconomic inequality as a mediating variable.

According to dependency / world system approaches the effects of world economy measures are also to be mediated by different levels of inequality. In addition, I argued that the effect of the regime type may also be mediated by inequality. Since agrarian and income inequality are weakly intercorrelated (r=.14), political conflict is regressed on both measures simultaneously, and on the two regime types which are significantly linked to political conflict (cf. Table 1). Control variables are the export ratio and the level of conflict in the preceding period. The economic growth rate is not included since it is not related either to regime type or to inequality measures.

The regression coefficients of the two inequality measures in Table 3 clearly reject relative deprivation theory. If the two outliers Honduras and Jamaica are dropped from the sample the findings suggest that political conflict is lower rather than higher in countries with grave socioeconomic inequalities. While the effect of agrarian inequality slightly misses the 10%-level of significance, our measure of income inequality predicts low rather than high levels of conflict in Latin American countries.

TABLE 3 Socioeconomic Inequality and Political Conflict 1973-1977

Gini of Land Distribution	-2.30	-5.02	a
ca. 1970	-.17	-.37	b
Income Share of the	-.04*	-.07**	
Top 20% ca. 1970	-.30	-.48	
Authoritarian	.23	.19	
Corporatism	.13	.10	
Tripartism	-.14	.29	
	-.08	.18	
Export Ratio 1970	-.03*	-.06**	
	-.42	-.66	
Political Conflict	.94**	1.09**	
1968-1972	.71	.79	
Intercept	4.93	8.80	
N	16	14	
		(Honduras, Jamaica excluded)	
Adjusted R^2	.73	.87	
F and (p)	7.9 (0.004)	14.9 (0.011)	

a unstandardized regression coefficient; ** = p<.05, * = p<.10
b standardized regression coefficient (β)

Contrary to the argument of relative deprivation theory, in both samples (N=16, N=14) there is a significant negative correlation between the share of income of the top 20% and level of political conflict in the 1973-1977 period. In line with resource mobilization theory this finding suggests that social inequalities in peripheral states inhibit political mobilization of grievances. By comparison to Table 1, the effect of the export ratio is even stronger but in the unexpected direction once more. In contrast, the effects of both regime types are not replicated. Authoritarian corporatism does not incite political unrest nor does tripartism inhibit conflict.

To examine the question of whether the effects of the two regime types and world economy variables are actually mediated by variations in income distribution, the %-share of the top quintile was regressed on regime types, world economy measures and the level of economic development (cf. Kuznets 1955) measured by the real (purchasing power disparities adjusted) per capita gross domestic income in international dollars of 1970 (Summers and Heston 1984). Several regression estimations not shown here indicated that the effect of tripartism is mediated rather by agrarian inequality than by

TABLE 4 Economic Openness, Regime Type and Income Distribution

Authoritarian Corporatism	3.5 .26	5.8** .43	a b
Democracy	1.8 .15	-1.4 -.11	
Export Ratio 1970	-.06 -.10	-.13 -.21	
TNC Penetration 1967	.0003 .15	.001** .54	
Real Gross Domestic Product per capita 1970	-.008** -.84	-.007** -.79	
Intercept	69.66	64.68	
N	18	16 (Chile, Mexiko excluded)	
Adjusted R^2	.40	.69	
F and (p)	3.25 (0.04)	7.52 (0.004)	

a unstandardized regression coefficient; ** = p< 05
b standardized regression coefficient (β)

income inequality (see Nollert 1991). Also, TNC penetration proved to be the only significant external factor.

Table 4 summarizes the main evidence of these analyses. Beside authoritarian corporatism and TNC penetration, three control variables are included in the model. Though often mentioned as determinant of socioeconomic inequality (e.g. Lenski 1966, Simpson 1990), democracy is not linked to inequality in Latin America. By comparison with the sample of core states, the export ratio is also not related to income distribution. In contrast, economic development on the one hand significantly reduces the share of the richest quintile. As predicted by Bornschier and Chase-Dunn (1985), an intensive penetration of the domestic economy by transnational corporations, on the other hand, increases the income gap between the rich and the poor. However, this finding holds only if the cases of Chile and Mexico are dropped from the sample. Considering that inequality is inversely linked to political conflict (Table 3), one has thus to conclude that transnational corporations incite conflict by impeding economic growth, whereas they dampen conflict by increasing the income gap. Finally, the significant positive impact of authoritarian corporatism on income inequality affirms our hypothesis. Yet, this finding rejects the conclusion derived from Table 1 suggesting that authoritarian-corporatist regimes are more conflict-prone than the other regimes. Now one has to note that this strong direct effect may be weakened by their above-average inequality. Due to different sample sizes in the multivariate models one cannot decide whether the direct positive or the indirect negative effect prevails.

All in all, the empirical findings presented above thus suggest that authoritarian corporatism is the only regime type which is partially determined by world economic integration (high debt service and low export ratio), and linked to the level of political unrest. Contrary to their proponents, however, the group of five regimes (Brazil, Chile, Uruguay, Ecuador, Peru) does not indicate above-average economic performance net of other explaining factors but sharp income gaps. In the three countries with stable exclusive corporatist regimes the socioeconomic inequalities may even have grown in the 1970s. Data on political conflict in Brazil, Chile and Uruguay for the 1978-1982 period which indicate a lower level than in the 1973-1977 period thus tend to support the cynical conclusion derived from my cross-national findings that *trickling up* of income and wealth pays off in political demobilization.

Conclusions

My cross-national test of modernization and dependency / world system hypotheses on the linkage between economic openness and political conflict in Latin America shows inconsistent findings. However, it supports the view that the impact of world market integration on the level of insurgency is not direct, but transmitted by the regime type, different growth rates and variations in levels of inequality in the distribution of privileges.

Some peculiar results must deserve attention in future research. Regime types cannot be predicted by external constraints. The only exception is the authoritarian corporatist type which appears to reflect the interaction of high indebtedness and a low export ratio. In contrast to a high penetration of transnational corporations, a high export ratio and high indebtedness, foreign direct investment furthermore promotes rather than inhibiting economic growth. Whereas no regime type is significantly linked to economic growth, authoritarian corporatism as well as TNC penetration promote income inequality. Since the relative deprivation view which argues that socio-economic inequality incites insurgency is totally rejected, however, both factors thus indirectly contribute to below-average levels of political conflict.

These empirical results have two implications. First, although the role of economic openness in explaining variations in political conflict is supported by the analyses, theory should pay more attention to endogeneous factors. One must be aware that types of regime are only weakly linked to world economic integration. In addition, the finding that the repressive exclusive corporatist regimes mainly emerged in countries with low export dependency and strong states (Brazil, Chile, Argentina) implies that independent political actors do not necessarily satisfy the demands of the domestic population. The case of Costa Rica even shows that strong dependency can be accompanied by low political insurgency if there exists a democratic accommodation of capital and labor interests.

Second, the inconsistent empirical effects of the selected measures of economic openness imply that "dependency" is a multidimensional concept. Hence, in empirically testing their hypotheses proponents of either the optimistic or the critical assessment of foreign influences should refer to several dependency measures. Finally, both modernization and dependency / world system theorists should be aware of the fact that, in the context of Latin American countries, high socioeconomic inequality is unexpectedly linked to low political conflict. Therefore, a comprehensive theoretical model must reveal that world economic integration may have two different impacts on the level of political unrest. It may incite conflict by impeding economic growth, while at the same time it may reduce insurgency by increasing the gap between the rich and the poor.

REFERENCES

Bailey, John J. (1977): "Pluralist and Corporatist Dimensions of Interest Representation in Colombia" in: James M. Malloy (ed.) *Authoritarianism and Corporatism in Latin America,* Pittsburgh: University of Pittsburgh Press, 259-302

Bollen, Kenneth A. (1983): "World System Position, Dependency, and Democracy. The Cross-National Evidence" *American Sociological Review* 49, 468-479.

Bornschier, Volker, Chase-Dunn, Christopher (1985): *Transnational Corporations and Underdevelopment,* New York: Praeger.

Boswell, Terry, Dixon, William J. (1990): "Dependency and Rebellion: A Cross-National Analysis" *American Sociological Review* 55, 540-559.

Brockett, Charles D. (1988): *Land, Power, and Poverty. Agrarian Transformation and Political Conflict in Central America,* Boston: Unwin Hyman.

Cardoso, Fernando, Faletto, Enzo (1979): *Dependency and Development in Latin America,* Berkeley: University of California Press.

Chirot, Daniel (1977): *Social Change in the Twentieth Century,* New York: Harcourt, Brace, Jovanovich.

Collier, David (ed.) (1979): *The New Authoritarianism in Latin America,* Princeton: Princeton University Press.

Davies, James C. (1979): "The J-Curve of Rising and Declining Satisfactions as a Cause of Revolution and Rebellion." in Hugh D. Graham and Ted R. Gurr (eds.) *Violence in America,* Beverly Hills: Sage, 415-436

Davis, Charles L., Coleman, Kenneth M. (1989): "Political Control of Organized Labor in Semi-Consociational Democracy: The Case of Venezuela" 247-273 in Edward C. Epstein (ed.) *Labor Autonomy and the State in Latin America,* Boston: Unwin Hyman.

Dix, Robert H. (1987): *The Politics of Colombia,* New York: Praeger.

Erickson, Karl P. (1977): *The Brazilian Corporative State and Working-Class Politics,* Los Angeles: University of California Press.

Evans, Peter B. (1979): *Dependent Development: The Alliance of Multinational, State and Local Capital in Brazil,* Princeton: Princeton University Press.

Evans, Peter B. (1985): "Transnational Linkages and the Economic Role of the State: An Analysis of Developing and Industrialized Nations in the

Post-World War II Period" in: Peter B. Evans, Dietrich Rueschemeyer and Theda Skocpol (eds.) *Bringing the State Back In,* Cambridge: Cambridge University Press, 192-226

Gupta, Dipak K. (1990): *The Economics of Political Violence,* New York: Praeger.

Hartlyn, Jonathan (1988): *The Politics of Coalition Rule in Colombia,* Cambridge: Cambridge University Press.

Hirschman, Albert O. (1979): "The Turn to Authoritarianism in Latin America and the Search for Its Economic Determinants." in: David Collier (ed.) *The New Authoritarianism in Latin America,* Princeton: Princeton University Press, 61-98.

Hoover, Greg A. (1989): "Intranational Inequality: A Cross-National Dataset" *Social Forces* 67, 1008-1026.

Jagodzinski, W. (1983): "Ökonomische Entwicklung und politisches Protestverhalten, 1920-1973" in: *Politische Vierteljahresschrift,* Sonderheft "Politische Stabilität und politischer Konflikt", Opladen: Westdeutscher Verlag, 18-43.

Katzenstein, Peter (1985): *Small States in World Markets. Industrial Policy in Europe,* Ithaca, N.Y.: Cornell University Press.

Kuznets, Simon (1955): "Economic Growth and Income Inequality" *American Economic Review* 45, 1-28.

Lenski, Gerhard (1966): *Power and Privilege,* New York: McGraw-Hill.

Lipset, Seymour M. (1959): "Some Social Requisites of Democracy" *American Political Science Review* 53, 69-105.

London, Bruce, Robinson, Thomas D. (1989): "The Effect of International Dependence on Income Inequality and Political Violence" *American Sociological Review* 54, 305-308.

Moreira Alves, Maria Helena (1989): "Trade Unions in Brazil: A Search for Autonomy and Organization" in: Edward C. Epstein (ed.) *Labor Autonomy and the State in Latin America,* Boston: Unwin Hyman, 39-72

Muller, Edward N., Seligson, Mitchell A. (1987): "Inequality and Insurgency" *American Political Science Review* 81, 425-451.

Nollert, Michael (1990): "Social Inequality in the World System: An Assessment" in: Volker Bornschier and Peter Lengyel (eds.) *World Society Studies, Vol. I,* Frankfurt / Main: Campus, 17-54

Nollert, Michael (1991): *Weltwirtschaftliche Verflechtung und politischer Konflikt in Lateinamerika. Eine vergleichende Studie,* final report to the World Society Foundation (available from the author).

Nollert, Michael (1992): *Interessenvermittlung und sozialer Konflikt,* Pfaffenweiler: Centaurus.

O'Donnell, Guillermo (1973): *Modernization and Bureaucratic-Authoritarianism. Studies in South American Politics,* Berkeley: University of California.

Olson, Mancur (1963): "Rapid Growth as Destabilizing Force" *Journal of Economic History* 23, 529-552.

Roberts, Ken, Midlarsky, Manus I. (1986): "Inequality, the State, and Revolution in Central America" in: Manus Midlarsky (ed.) *Inequality and*

Contemporary Revolutions. Denver: Graduate School of International Studies, 11-33
Rostow, Walter (1960): *The Stages of Economic Growth: A Non-Communist Manifest,* Cambridge: Cambridge University Press.
Rothgeb, John M. jr. (1989): "Direct Foreign Investment, Repression, Reform, and Political Conflict in Third World States" in: William P. Avery and David P. Rapkin (eds.) *Markets, Politics and Change in the Global Economy. International Political Economy Yearbook, Vol. IV.* Boulder Co.: Rienner, 105-125.
Rueschemeyer, Dietrich, Stephens Huber, Evelyne, Stephens, John D. (1991): *Capitalist Development and Democracy,* Cambridge: Polity Press.
Ruiz-Tagle, Jaime (1989): "Trade Unionism and the State under the Chilean Military Regime." in: Edward C. Epstein (ed.) *Labor Autonomy and the State in Latin America,* Boston: Unwin Hyman, 73-100
Russett, Bruce M. (1964): "Inequality and Instability. The Relation of Land Tenure to Politics" *World Politics* 16, 442-454.
Schmitter, Philippe C. (1974): "Still the Century of Corporatism?" *Review of Politics* 36, 85-131.
Simpson, Miles (1990): "Political Rights and Income Inequality: A Cross-National Test" *American Sociological Review* 55, 682-693.
Stamm, Hanspeter (1992): *Krise und Anpassung in Mexiko.* Saarbrücken - Fort Lauderdale: Breitenbach.
Stepan, Alfred (1978): *The State and Society: Peru in Comparative Perspective,* Princeton: Princeton University Press.
Summers, Robert, Heston, Alan (1984): "Improved International Comparisons of Real Product and Its Components: 1950-1980" *Review of Income and Wealth* 30, 207-262.
Taylor, Charles L. (1985): *World Handbook of Political and Social Indicators,* Third Edition. Köln: Zentralarchiv für Empirische Sozialforschung.
Tilly, Charles, Tilly, Louise, Tilly, Richard (1975): *The Rebellious Century, 1830-1930,* Cambridge, Mass. Harvard University Press.
Timberlake, Michael, Williams, Kirk R. (1987): "Structural Position in the World-System, Inequality and Political Violence" *Journal of Political and Military Sociology* 15, 1-15.
Wallerstein, Immanuel (1974): *The Modern World System, Vol. I,* New York: Academic Press.
Wiarda, Howard J. (1981): *Corporatism and National Development in Latin America,* Boulder: Westview Press.
World Bank (1988): *World Development Report,* Oxford University Press.
Zimmermann, Ekkart (1980): "Macro-comparative Research on Political Protest" in: Ted R. Gurr (ed.) *Handbook of Political Conflict.* New York: Free Press, 167-237
Zwicky, Heinrich (1989): "Income Inequality and Violent Conflicts in Developing Countries" *Research in Inequality and Social Conflict, Vol. 1,* 67-93.

8 GENESIS AND DYNAMICS OF POPULIST REGIMES AT THE PERIPHERY

Christian Suter

Introduction

The genesis of populist regimes has often taken place in times of intense social and political conflict. Broad mobilization of political and social groups hitherto excluded from political and economic participation as well as participatory demands in opposition to elite groups articulated by populist leaders and movements have been associated with violent conflicts sometimes even culminating in revolutions. Once in power, the maintenance of political stability was, however, undermined by the previously pursued mobilization policies. Populist regimes often got trapped between excessive popular demands and the opposition of powerful traditional elite groups. Hence it is no surprise that populist regimes were usually removed from political power by force.

This article addresses two principal research questions: the first refers to the theoretical and empirical characterization of populism and the second to

---

This article draws on the results of the research project "Populism in the Third World" funded by the World Society Foundation. Christian Suter took his Ph.D. in Sociology from the University of Zurich. He is presently working on a larger research project on political and social change in Latin America and is affiliated to Bornschier's research team at the University of Zurich, Sociological Institute, Rämistrasse 69, 8001 Zurich, Switzerland.

the occurrence of populist phenomena. (1) Populism is a fairly vague concept. As a result of considerable variation of populist phenomena, there is much theoretical confusion about their characteristics. This problem is approached by a focus on structural features and the specific variables of populism. (2) The literature suggests a close relationship between the occurrence of populism and stages of development, to be examined by an empirical analysis of the emergence of Latin American populist regimes during the twentieth century.

Towards a Structural Approach to Populism

Academic disciplines have applied the concept of populism to an extremely wide range of political and social phenomena in different zones and at different epochs of world society and economy. The term has been employed to characterize social and political movements, ideologies, political leaders, parties, multi-class coalitions, rhetorical techniques as well as procedures of direct democracy. Hence, quite contradictory manifestations like political dictators and radical grass roots movements have been lumped under this label. Such bewildering diversity must be attributed in part to the existence of three different but mostly unrelated theoretical strands, each concerned with different temporal and spatial contexts.

(1) *Historical populism*. The first and most original approaches are historical studies on radical rural movements. A large body of literature exists since the 1930s discussing farmer radicalism in the 1890s in the U.S. South and West (e.g. Hofstadter 1956, Goodwyn 1976). There are also studies dealing with the revolutionary *narodnik* movement in Tsarist Russia and the rise of peasant movements in Eastern Europe after World War I (e.g. Walicki 1969, Narkiewicz 1976).

(2) *Contemporary core populism*. A second and the most recent theoretical discussion deals with contemporary instances of populism in Western democracies. The conservative reorganization in the 1980s and the emergence of authoritarian (or reactionary) populism is the starting-point of these. This literature discusses populist techniques and ideologies of right-wing governments and leaders (e.g. Thatcherism, Reaganism, the German CDU/CSU). The concept has also been applied to radical right-wing (and to a lesser extent also left-wing) protest movements (cf. Hall 1980, Birnbaum 1986, Boyte et al. 1986, Elfferding 1986).

(3) *Peripheral or "Third World" populism*. The third group of studies focuses on "Third World" populism (cf. Hennessy 1969, Worsley 1969). Since the present article proposes an approach to study such populist regimes this theoretical strand is of special importance. While there are only a few attempts to study African or Asian experiences (Low 1964, Saul 1973, Jeffries 1975) an intensive discussion took place during the 1960s and 1970s among Latin American sociologists and political scientists (e.g. di Tella 1965, Ianni 1975, Laclau 1977, Drake 1978, Germani 1978, Quintero 1980, Stein 1980). Most of this research is concentrated on the so-called populist period of Latin American politics, from about 1920 to 1965. The discussion is characterized by three factors: first, by contrast to studies dealing with historical populism, it emphasizes the urban character of populist phenomena. Second, the examination of populist regimes, i.e. of populist movements and leaders that have achieved political power, represents a prominent topic. Third, scholars stress the transitory nature of populism and claim its close association with stages of economic and political development (e.g. O'Donnell 1973, Ianni 1975, Germani 1978, Cardoso and Faletto 1979). With the rise of authoritarianism during the 1970s the study of Latin American populism lost much of its initial vigor. Social scientists like Drake (1982: 217) even diagnosed the "death" of populism and began to speculate on its "autopsy". Yet, as recent developments in Latin America have demonstrated populism is still very much alive. Hence, a new theoretical assessment is required.

The literature on populism is rich in case studies, including several in-depth analyses of Latin American movements, leaders and ideologies, and regimes (e.g. Ianni 1970, Weffort 1973, Rock 1975, Drake 1978, Germani 1978, Sharpless 1978, Quintero 1980, Stein 1980). Yet, the impressive empirical material provided by these case histories is hardly used for comparative studies.[1] The diversity of populist phenomena together with the lack of comprehensive and systematic comparative research has contributed to the fragmentation and vagueness of the theoretical disscussion. While some scholars suggest a broad and flexible theoretical framework emcompassing all the varieties of related political and social phenomena others restrict themselves to specific circumstances (e.g. rural radicalism or manipulative forms of mass mobilization) or even choose to abandon populism due to its ambiguity.

Several attempts have been made to identify constituent elements of populism (e.g. Wiles 1969, Canovan 1981, Conniff 1982). While this facilitates coping with the large variety of populist phenomena it also helps localize more clearly the boundaries of populism. Yet, the specification of such features has remained rather descriptive, as for instance the list of twenty-four elements suggested by Wiles (1969), and has therefore been of scant theoretical value. The present study proposes three definitional elements or criteria to clarify the concept of populism: (1) appeal to the people in combination with the articulation of a basic antagonism between the people and the elite, (2) the multi-group and multi-class character of the social base and, (3) the existence of charismatic authority. These three features are to be understood as structural variables and must not be interpreted as uni-dimensional characteristics.

(1) *Appeal to the people and articulation of people / elite antagonisms*. This fundamental and most important element has been elaborated by Laclau (1977) whose analysis contains the most significant theoretical contribution to the study of populism. The appeal to the people is not addressed to specific social classes or interest groups but to the "common man", the small producers and consumers. Hence, populist ideologies strongly oppose the class concept and ideologies articulating class interests.[2] There is, however, a wide range of possible conceptualisations of "the people" as well as of the "ruling elite". These terms may be defined socially, economically, politically, culturally, or racially, being mostly a combination of two or more of these aspects.

Along a socio-economic dimension "the people" refers to ordinary folk, to the poor or to specific, economically underprivileged social groups (e.g. small rural producers, urban poor, "the proletariat"). Politically and culturally, "the people" may be defined as members of a single nation and culture (in the sense of common political tradition, history, language, cultural traditions and religion). Nationalism, therefore, represents an important and powerful resource exploited by populist ideologies. Along another dimension the notion of "the people" is related to specific races or ethnic groups. *Indigenismo*, emphasized by the literature and often found in populist ideologies may be considered a combination of a social, cultural and ethnic definiton of "the people".

At the same time, the identification of "the people" depends upon the specific construction of the basic antagonism between them and the elite. Thus, elite groups condemned in the populist discourse may constitute the political elite (e.g. the political establishment, dominant parties, parliamentary institutions), the economic elite (e.g. large landowners and agricultural producers, financial establishments, big corporations), or the intellectual elite (e.g. lawyers, the scientific community, the arts). Moreover, the people / elite-antagonism is not restricted to domestic groups but may also be directed towards foreign forces, particularly in the case of the articulation of an economic or political anti-elitism (e.g. opposition to transnational corporations, to foreign political control). Anti-imperialism and a critique of neo-colonialism is the most important ideological strand.

Often, the concept of "the people" is not only created by defining antagonistic elite factions but also by excluding marinal groups (e.g. immigrants, foreigners, ethnic and religious minorities). This combination of a people / elite antagonism with a people / minorities antagonism is a characteristic of contemporary right-wing populism in Western core countries (cf. Laclau 1977, Keller 1992).

The articulation of a specific people / elite-antagonism is strongly associated with participatory demands, which may include political participation (e.g. extension of civil and political rights, access to political decision-making) or economic and social participation (e.g. extension of social rights, access to welfare benefits, participation in national development).

In reality, the specific combination of "the people" with forms of anti-elitism and participatory demands is, of course, not arbitrary. Rather, specific clusters dominate: for example the combination of a predominantly socio-economic definition of "the people" with the articulation of opposition to the economic elite and demands for economic participation related to such antagonism (e.g. classical U.S. farmer radicalism considering farmers and laborers as "the people", railroad corporations, banks, "big business" as the antagonistic elite and access to credit and to railway facilities as principal participatory demands); the combination of national and nativistic definitions of "the people" with anti-elitist attitudes directed towards foreign political, cultural and economic elites (e.g. African Socialism, the Jamaican rastafari movement); or the combination of socio-economic and national definitions of "the people" related to opposition to the political and intellectual elite (e.g. *ibañismo* in Chile, *velasquismo* in Ecuador).

(2) *Multi-class character*. As outlined above populist movements or ideologies do not identify themselves with specific social classes or groups. Typically, they are based on multi-class coalitions of different social groups, a feature emphasized particularly by the Latin American literature (e.g. di Tella 1965, Germani 1978). Yet, as stressed by Dix (1985) one must differentiate among different sectors of the lower class (e.g. peasants, skilled

and organized labor, urban "marginals") as they may constitute specific types of populism. The leading role in populist coalitions is sometimes played by marginalized sectors of the traditional ruling elite. Other important leadership groups are sectors of the middle class such as professionals, intellectuals, ranking military officers or industrialists (cf. di Tella 1965, Dix 1985).

(3) *Charismatic leadership*. Due to their heterogeneous social base populist movements and alliances are rather loosely institutionalized. To overcome this organizational weakness they have to rely on charismatic leadership as an alternative integrative mechanism. According to Max Weber (1956) charisma is the extraordinary quality of a personality to whom supernatural or exceptional forces are attributed and who is thus elevated to leadership. Holiness, heroism and exemplary conduct are relevant features of such a quality. Accordingly, populist leaders refer to personal attributes and to their style of life to emphasize these elements.[3] Charismatic authority is often conferred on the leader through mass contact (e.g. mass rallies). Therefore, populist leaders generally seek direct contact with the people, not mediated by political institutions such as parties or a parliament.

As recognized by several scholars the considerable variations among populist phenomena may be explained by combining different elements and attributing them to types or syndromes of populism. There are, however, substantial differences among the three basic groups of approaches with regard to such typologies. Thus, Hall (1980) in his analysis of political change in Western democracies distinguishes between authoritarian and popular-democratic populism while other authors refer to reactionary (or right-wing) and progressive (or left-wing) populism (e.g. Boyte et al. 1986, Elfferding 1986). Canovan (1981) who deals with an extremely wide range of instances (e.g. historical and contemporary as well as "Third World" populisms) offers a rather broad typology with two main categories – agrarian and political populism – and seven variants. Subtypes of agrarian populism are: farmers' radicalism (in the nineteenth century United States), peasant movements (in early twentieth century Eastern Europe), intellectual agrarian socialism (in Tsarist Russia); subtypes of political populism are populist dictatorship (e.g. Peronism), populist democracies (i.e. calls for referendums, recalls and initiatives), reactionary populism (e.g. George Wallace), and politicians' populism (e.g. multi-class coalitions, opposition to the political establishment). As the list demonstrates this typology is purely descriptive and rather heterogeneous.

For "Third World" (basically Latin American) populism di Tella (1965: 55) suggests a typology based on the social composition of the middle class sector included in the populist alliance (e.g. the bourgeoisie, the military and the clergy versus intellectuals and lower middle class groups) and on the degree of marginalization of these groups with respect to their own class. Similarly, Germani's (1978) specification of liberal populism (e.g. *yrigoyenismo*) and national populism (e.g. *peronismo*) takes into account the social composition of the populist alliance (predominantly middle class-based lower class-based) and the character of the participatory demands on the ruling elite (political participation versus demands for social and economic participation). Other typologies refer more specifically to the leadership group (e.g. "military populism") or to the dominant ideologies of populist movements and regimes. The most elaborate classification scheme has been set up by Dix (1985) whose distinction between authoritarian and democratic populism relies on four dimensions (social composition of the mass base and of leadership groups, ideology, and organization).

Identifying types of populism represents a considerable conceptual improvement. Yet, it has two major shortcomings: first, since the classifications are mostly based on the description of concrete situations (i.e. "real types" rather than "ideal types" in the sense of Weber) their conceptual value is rather limited. Second, most typologies are reductionist. The varieties of populism are limited to only a few forms (usually two contrasted types) which are mostly defined uni-dimensionally. Yet, as suggested by the theoretical reasoning above, any particular manifestation of populism represents a specific combination of different elements or dimensions.

Hence, the empirical analysis of Latin American populism presented in the next section will take into account different structural features and variables for the characterization of populist phenomena, confined to populist regimes, i.e. to populist movements and coalitions that succeeded in achieving control over the state apparatus. The major advantage of this restriction is the relatively easy determination of the beginning and the duration of incidences of populism. Furthermore, properties specific to regimes such as state policies and modes of political dominance directly relevant for the pattern of populism can be taken into account. Thus, state resources may be used to reward certain social groups supporting a given populist regime or to build up clientelistic networks and corporatist structures. The pact of dominance underlying a given regime need not only be formal but can amalgamate formal and informal elements.

# Empirical Analysis of Populist Regimes: The Latin American Case

Occurrence of populist regimes

The theoretical and empirical discussion on Latin American populism is dominated by the experiences of a few "classic" cases which include Argentine radicalism (*yrigoyenismo*) and Peronism (Rock 1975, Germani 1978, Navarro 1982, Tamarin 1982), Brazilian *getulismo* (Ianni 1970, Weffort 1973, Erickson 1977, Mendes 1977, Conniff 1981), Bolivia's *Movimiento Nacionalista Revolucionario*-MNR (Dandler 1977, Mitchell 1977), Peru's *Alianza Popular Revolucionaria Americana*-APRA (Stein 1980, 1982) and Venezuela's *Acción Democrática*-AD (Ellner 1982). Although there are some recent analyses of less known or less typical populist phenomena, like Mexico's revolutionary and post-revolutionary period (Basurto 1969, 1982), *grovismo* and *ibañismo* in Chile (Drake 1978, Grugel 1992), *velasquismo* in Ecuador (Quintero 1980, Cueva 1982), *gaitanismo* and *rojismo* in Colombia (Sharpless 1978, Dix 1985), the Puerto Rican *Partido Popular Democrático* (Pantojas-Garcia 1989) or the short-lived Peruvian government under Guillermo Billinghurst (Blanchard 1977), there are numerous instances of populism which have not yet been considered. Thus, the concept is virtually absent in the literature on Central America and the Caribbean. Against the background of several populist movements and regimes in these regions this is rather surprising.[4]

The widespread occurrence of populist regimes is confirmed by a systematic coding of populist regimes based on Latin American case studies and research on individual countries: from the early twentieth century onwards some 70 cases of populist regimes may be identified. Populist regimes have been defined according to the three criteria set up in the previous section, i.e. the articulation of people / elite antagonisms, multi-class alliances of mass-based political forces and the existence of charismatic leadership and authority. Several cases which only show a weak articulation of these features have been coded as "weakly articulated populist regimes".[5]

Figure 1 shows a rise of populism from the 1920s until the 1960s and a decline during the 1970s. Yet, contrary to conventional assumptions, populist regimes already occurred before 1920 (e.g. Yrigoyen in Argentina, Billinghurst in Peru, Batlle y Ordóñez in Uruguay). One may even argue that

FIGURE 1 Number of populist regimes assuming political power per decade

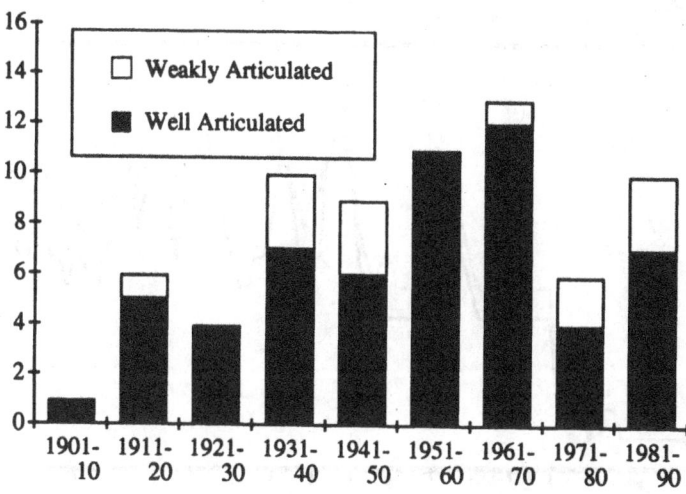

there are instances of proto-populism during the nineteenth century. Thus, according to Lynch (1979: 2-3) the regime of Juan Manuel de Rosas (1829-52) in Argentina showed vague elements of populism. More important is that a complete collapse of populism during the late 1960s and the 1970s cannot be observed. This may be illustrated by the emergence of "military populism" in Peru (Velasco) and Panama (Torrijos), by Michael Manley's "Democratic Socialism" in Jamaica, and by the temporary restoration of Peronism in Argentina. Furthermore, Figure 1 even suggests a resurgence of populism in the 1980s (e.g. García's APRA in Peru, the Sandinistas in Nicaragua, Siles Zuazo in Bolivia, Alfonsín and Menem in Argentina).

The indicator used in Figure 1 focuses on the assumption of power of populist regimes. Yet, the life span of individual regimes varies substantially. Hence, a more adequate measure for the occurrence of populism might be the number of countries ruled by populist alliances in a given year. This indicator has been computed in Figure 2. The data reveals a rise in the number of populist regimes until the early 1930s and a subsequent stabilization until the end of the decade. During the early 1940s the number of countries ruled by populist regimes increases again, with a peak of 10-12 countries in 1946-47

FIGURE 2 Number of Latin American countries ruled by populist regimes, 1900-1990

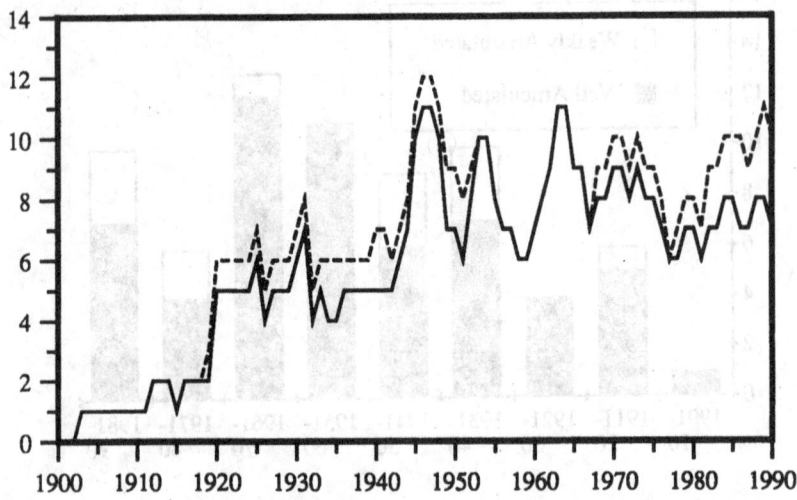

Notes: Solid line indicates well articulated regimes only; broken line: total number of populist regimes; for sources cf. Appendix.

and in 1963-64. Until the late 1970s there is a certain decline, though less pronounced than might be expected from the literature. As already mentioned this can partly be explained by the occurrence of new populist regimes. Moreover, there are several quite stable and long-lasting populist regimes which survived the rise of authoritarian military governments of the 1970s, such as the Mexican *Partido Revolucionario Institutional*-PRI (e.g. Echeverría), the Venezuelan AD (e.g. Pérez), or the Costa Rican PLN (e.g. Figueres). Figure 2 also confirms the increase of populist regimes during the 1980s. This is mainly due to less-pronounced cases which include some typical former populist parties and leaders (e.g. Paz Estenssoro and the MNR in Bolivia, Michael Manley's *People's National Party*-PNP in Jamaica, the Dominican PRD). A more detailed analysis suggests that the weak populist shaping of these regimes must be attributed to difficulties in articulating the traditional antagonism particularly between "the people" on the one hand and domestic and foreign economic elite groups on the other, partly due to the policies of IMF-sponsored programs of economic adjustment and export promotion pursued by these governments in the context of economic crisis.

Structural characterization of populist regimes

As suggested by the theoretical reasoning there is considerable structural variability among populist regimes. The following discussion characterizes them with respect to several inter-related structural dimensions and features. The variables selected refer to the definitional criteria of populism (i.e. the nature of the people / elite antagonism, the social composition of the multi-class alliance and the leadership group) as also to dimensions specific to political regimes (i.e. state policies, modes of political domination). The basic structural dimension is the social composition of the populist coalition. Accordingly, I argue that the nature of the social base of populist regimes structures the articulation of the people / elite antagonisms, state policies and techniques of political domination.

a) Structure of multi-class alliances. As already mentioned a populist coalition may be based on different social groups of the middle and the lower classes. Using Portes' (1985) definition of the Latin American class structure one may distinguish between a bureaucratic-technical class (i.e. civilian and military state bureaucracies, professionals), the formal proletariat (i.e. organized urban and rural labor with contractual employment and protected wages), the informal petty bourgeoisie (small urban entrepreneurs and small commercial farmers) and the informal proletariat (urban and rural "marginals", i.e. casual labor with irregular wages partly engaged in

TABLE 1 Latin American populist regimes and the structure of their mass support (number of regimes)

	Bureaucratic Technical Class	Informal Petty Bourgeoisie	Formal Proletariat	Informal Proletariat
Regimes with *significant* support from respective social classes	28	23	23	27
Regimes with *weak* support from respective social classes	9	6	8	2

Notes: Figures are confined to well articulated populist regimes (N=55); for sources cf. Appendix.

subsistence production). The figures presented in Table 1 indicate that Latin American populist regimes receive support from all four basic classes.

Since a populist regime is defined as multi-class-based one must distinguish between different class coalitions. A rough distinction made by the literature is that between regimes where middle class groups provide the main mass support and these where lower class groups form the principal social base (cf. Germani's typology of liberal and national populism). Populist regimes based on middle class support will be defined as having significant support among the bureaucratic-technical class and the informal petty bourgeoisie but with only weak ties to the formal and informal proletariat. Conversely, lower class populism mainly relies on segments of the formal and / or informal proletariat, in addition to support from middle class groups (e.g. the military, the intelligentsia).

The classification of 55 regimes on which sufficient data was available reveals 18 middle class-based and 37 lower class-based populist regimes. As shown in Figure 3 the occurrence of middle class-based populist regimes

FIGURE 3 Number of Latin American countries ruled by middle class populist regimes (broken line) and lower class populist regimes (solid line), 1900-1990

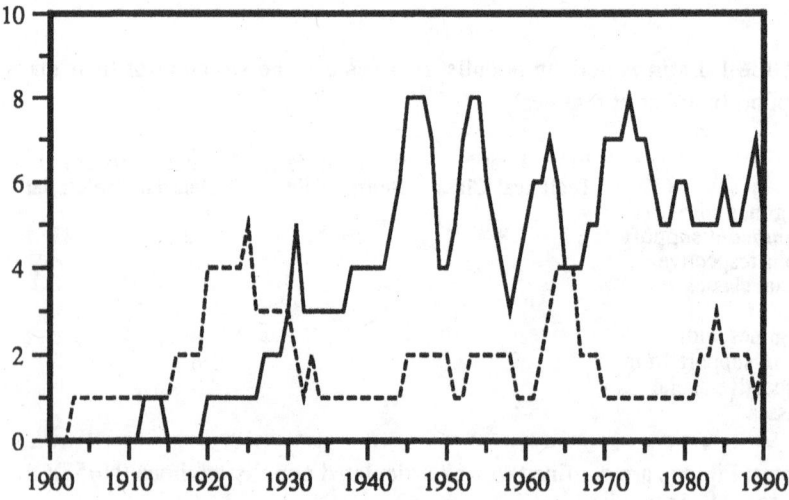

clusters during the 1910s and 1920s (e.g. Batlle y Ordóñez in Uruguay, Yrigoyen in Argentina, Saavedra in Bolivia). Two further, although less pronounced peaks fall into the mid-1960s (e.g. Belaúnde in Peru, Frei in Chile) and into the 1980s (e.g. Alfonsín in Argentina, Hurtado in Ecuador, Alwyn in Chile). Lower class-based populist regimes, by contrast, emerged from the early 1930s onwards. Their number peaks in the mid-1940s and mid-1950s with 8 regimes each. An additional peak occurred in the early 1970s. Thus, the already mentioned surprisingly high level of populist incidence during the 1970s has to be attributed to lower class populism.

b) Leadership structure. Several authors have stressed the relevance of the social composition of the leadership group for the characterization of populism (e.g. di Tella 1965, Dix 1985). Unfortunately, comparative data on this matter are rather scarce. As a rough measure the social background of top leaders of populist regimes has been classified according to the criteria suggested by Dix (1985), who distinguishes between military leadership and that by intellectuals and professionals. The provisional empirical evidence regarding some 20 regimes suggests a dominance of "intellectual" leadership in middle class-based regimes whereas lower class populism is characterized by both "military" and "intellectual" leadership.

c) Structure of the people / elite-antagonism. The people / elite-antagonism articulated by Latin American populist regimes is chiefly directed towards

FIGURE 4 Forms of anti-elitisms articulated by Latin American populist regimes (number of regimes)

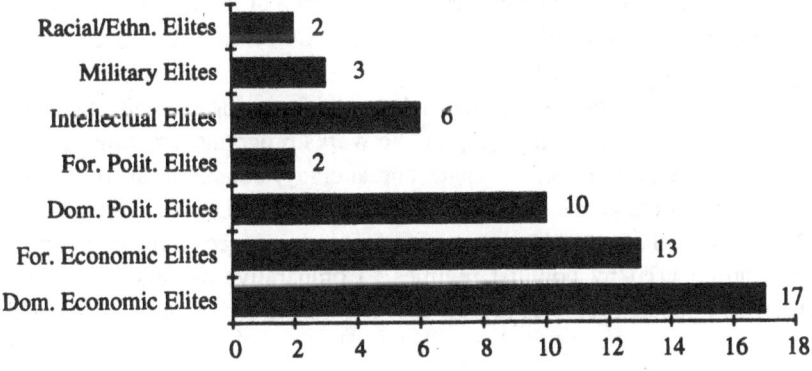

both foreign and national economic elite groups. As shown in Figure 4 there are also several instances of political anti-elitism confined largely to the national political establishment. Only two cases – the Jamaican independence movement led by Bustamante and the regime of Torrijos in Panama aiming at restoring national sovereignity over the U.S. controlled Canal Zone – significantly refer to foreign political elites. Intellectual, military and racial / ethnic anti-elitisms are rarely articulated.

d) State policies and modes of political dominance. Due to their articulation of participatory demands the policies of populist regimes are expected to be reform-oriented. In fact, Latin American populist regimes substantially expanded political participation by broadening the electorate.[6] In addition, considerable social and labor legislation has been enacted: empirical evidence is available for 12 cases. Constitutional reforms and social legislation have been carried out by both middle and lower class-based populist regimes. Advocating basic reforms to alter the social and economic structures, however, is largely confined to regimes receiving lower-class support. Thus, all 9 populist regimes (out of a total number of 43 cases for which data were available) that implemented relatively successful and comprehensive land reform schemes are based on the lower classes (receiving significant support from rural lower-class groups; e.g. Mexico under Cárdenas, Guatemala under Arbenz, Cuba under Castro, Bolivia under the MNR, Sandinist Nicaragua). Similarly, comprehensive programs of nationalization (of foreign assets) were chiefly advocated by lower class-based regimes articulating antagonisms between the people and foreign economic elite groups. This is demonstrated in Table 2 which shows that 12 out of 13 regimes engaged in nationalization schemes are based on lower class support. A notable example in this respect is the nationalization of the foreign-controlled oil sector carried out by regimes of this type (e.g. Perón in Argentina, Busch in Bolivia, Vargas in Brazil, Cárdenas in Mexico, Velasco in Peru, Pérez in Venezuela).

The implementation of political and social reforms together with a general expansion of state activities (e.g. public works programs, creation of state enterprises, expansion of the state bureaucracy) constitute an important source of patronage for the cooptation of middle and lower class groups. Hence, clientelism may be expected to be a relevant technique of political domination used by populist regimes.[7] Comparative evidence for Latin American populist regimes reveals that clientelism is present in at least 19

TABLE 2 Number of Latin American middle and lower class-based populist regimes nationalizing foreign assets (number of regimes with row percent in brackets)

	Nationalizations	No Nationalizations	N
Regimes with *middle class* support	1 (8%)	11 (92%)	12 (100%)
Regimes with *lower class* support	12 (63%)	7 (37%)	19 (100%)
Total	13 (42%)	18 (58%)	31 (100%)

Notes: Chi-Square=9.1, level of significance=.01; for sources cf. appendix.

cases. Two subforms are prominent among populist regimes, namely bureaucratic clientelism and mass clientelism.[8] Bureaucratic clientelism refers to the relationship between state bureaucrats or state entreprises and their clients. The clientelistic exchange consists in the access to state services and programs, jobs etc. for the client in return for political support. Mass clientelism refers to situations where patron-client relationships lose their face-to-face element while nevertheless remaining personalized; the good which the patron (i.e. the charismatic leader) controls is usually the legislative process through which he is able to benefit his followers through subsidies, regional development programs, appropriate labor policies etc.[9]

Modern clientelistic networks, and particularly those based on mass clientelism, are rather unstable. Thus, clients may switch to a patron who promises more favors or clientelistic networks may rapidly disintegrate due to declining sources of patronage.[10] Hence, mass clientelism usually marks only a transient stage in the history of a regime, and bureaucratic-clientelistic relations are often embedded in a larger network of state corporatism. Good examples are the policy of the Velasco administration in Peru towards the urban poor or the domination model of the PRI in Mexico. State corporatism is a pattern of interest representation in which interest associations, such as parties and labor unions, are structured, subsidized and controlled by the state (cf. Stepan 1978). Comparative evidence shows that only few populist regimes (7 out of 26 on which data was available) relied on corporatist techniques of political domination, all of them being lower class-based. Idealtypically, the implementation of corporatism is characterized by three phases: mobilization, incorporation into a corporatist structure, and demobilization (cf. Stepan 1978: 64, note 46). During the first phase, broad mobilization is achieved, built around a mass movement and charismatic leadership figures. During the incorporation phase control over the state is used, on the on hand, for a reformist policy designed to meet the aspirations of the masses previously mobilized (mass clientelism). On the other hand, these groups are bound to the regime by control over state resources to erect a state corporatist structure of a bureaucratic-clientelistic character. As soon as incorporation is completed, mass mobilization is no longer needed for the maintenance of the regime and participatory institutions are revert from a mobilization to a control function (demobilization phase).[11]

FIGURE 5 Failure of corporatist policies: Relationship between the regime of Velasco and the formal proletariat (in bracket years)

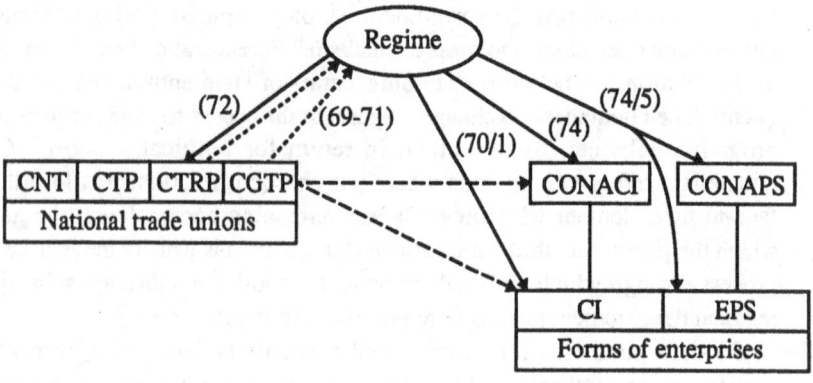

Explanations:
——— Institutional relationship
······· Regime support
– – – – Penetration of state corporatist institutions by labour class

Notes and sources: Brackets indicate the years during which a relationship was most important. CNT: Confederación Nacional de Trabajadores, CTP: Confederación de Trabajadores del Perú, CGTP: Confederación General de Trabajadores Peruanos, CTPR: Confederación de Trabajadores de la Revolución Peruana, CI: Comunidad Industrial, EPS: Empresa de Propiedad Social, CONACI: Confederación Nacional de Comunidades Industriales, CONAPS: Comisión Nacional de Propiedad Social. For sources see Pfister and Suter (1991)

The paradigmatic example illustrating the successful implementation of corporatism is provided by the case of Mexico. Mass mobilization of peasants and workers began during the revolutionary years of 1911-19. After a partial demobilization during the 1920s new mass movements among peasants and urban lower classes were encouraged under the government of Cárdenas (1935-40). As a result of his reformist policies (implementation of a land reform program, wage increases for urban workers, nationalization of foreign capital) Cárdenas was able to organize workers and peasants into separate official unions and to bind them as well as the state bureaucracy, youth and women's movements closely to the state and the ruling party. The demobilization is illustrated by the fact that the land reforms slowed down after the peasants had successfully been incorporated (from 1939 onwards). Similarly, urban wages declined as labor's autonomous organizational capabilities weakened during the 1940s (cf. Basurto 1969, Pfister and Suter 1989).

Other populist regimes did not manage to pass successfully through the three stages of the corporatist mode of domination. Some failed to build effective corporatist structures during the period of structural reform; as a consequence, the regime remained continuously dependent on distributive policies.[12] Others were unable to build a mass movement. As a consequence, corporatist policies had but weak success. It seems that particularly regimes characterized by military leadership and emanating from a middle class military coup have suffered this fate. A notable example is Peru under Velasco who failed to develop strong institutional links to the union movement.[13]

This is illustrated by Figure 5 which shows that the regime initially obtained support from the Communist labor movement. In 1972 Velasco established his own union movement with the foundation of the CTRP. This and increasing competition among the different national union movements stimulated the mobilization and unionization of the labor class and led to a marked increase in strikes. The failure of the regime to monopolize interest articulation and representation of the union movement led to incorporation attempts at the level of enterprises. These redistributive policies included the establishment of Industrial Communities and Social Property Enterprises and the creation of workers' participation at the level of enterprises. The individual enterprises were linked to the regime by corporatist-structured national associations which, however, were penetrated by the autonomous union movement. Eventually, the regime was forced to dissolve its corporatist institutions and resorted to repression (from 1976 onwards).

Regime transition

The analysis of state policies and modes of political dominance developed above has demonstrated the relevance of processes of political change for the analysis of populist regimes. The following discussion on regime transition will concentrate on two issues, namely, the structural preconditions for the genesis of populist regimes and the breakdown of populist regimes together with the consequent transformation of the political system. The basic concept used for this analysis is regime sequence, i.e. the specific transition to and from populist regimes (cf. also Hischier 1987, Suter 1992). Applying the definition of political regimes as the dominant alliance between the social classes and groups that underlies a given administration, two main types of political regimes relevant in Latin America during the twentieth century namely, capitalist regimes and disarticulated periods and regimes, may be identified in addition to populist regimes.

Under *capitalist regimes* political power rests in the hands of the class controlling the means of production and deriving its incomes from them. In peripheral economies, the export bourgeoisie, i.e. groups based on export production (cash crops, meat, minerals) and associated service activities (trade, banking) are usually the dominant elements of the bourgeoisie. The classic era of export bourgeoisies was the period when Latin America was integrated into the rapidly expanding world-economy during the second half of the nineteenth and the early decades of the twentieth centuries. A second variant of capitalist regimes which, however, occurred relatively rarely in Latin America is based on industrial interests often allied with technocratic elements of the state bureaucracy.

Disarticulated regimes try to keep social conflict under control through a forced disarticulation or demobilization of political interests. At the same time, political issues are objectified and handed over to a team of specialists or simply to the state administration for resolution or palliation. The social base of a disarticulated regime is not linked to productive relations; it consists mainly of the control over the repressive apparatus exerted by a faction of the state bureaucracy (usually the armed forces) or an alliance of several small elite groups. A good example of this regime type is Chile under Pinochet.

TABLE 3 Types of political regimes preceding the installation of middle and lower class-based populist regimes (number of cases; mean year of regime transition and standard deviation of mean year in brackets)

	Export Bourgeoisie	Middle Class Pop.	Lower Class Pop.	Disart. Regimes	Disart. Periods	N
Middle Class Populist Regimes	8 (1932/23)	0	0	2 (1987/4)	1 (1958)	11 (1944/29)
Lower Class Populist Regimes	8 (1942/18)	5 (1962/22)	3 (1963/10)	3 (1954/9)	15 (1955/19)	34 (1954/19)
Total of Populist Regimes	16 (1937/20)	5 (1962/22)	3 (1963/10)	5 (1967/20)	16 1955/19)	45

Notes: Sequences with less than 3 cases with respect to the total number of populist regimes have been excluded; for sources cf. appendix.

Similar to disarticulated regimes, *disarticulated periods* are marked by the absence of a viable pact of dominace among broad political forces. However, in contrast to disarticulated regimes, there is no group present capable of exploiting this situation to attain power. Rather, disarticulated periods are characterized by unstable structures of political power. Under certain circumstances, latent or overt civil war may even prevail (e.g. the revolutionary years in Mexico).

The different types of political regimes preceding and following populist regimes together with their time of appearance are shown in Tables 3 and 4. For the emergence of populist regimes two principal trajectories may be distinguished: first, the sequence from export bourgeoisies and, second, the sequence from disarticulated periods (for both sequences N=16). The sequence from export bourgeoisies to populist regimes, the oldest regime transition (mean year of regime change = 1937), is well known in the literature on Latin American political change (cf. O'Donnell 1973, Germani 1978). With the exception of one case the transition from disarticulated periods to populist regimes is confined to lower class populism. This reflects the often rather conflictual nature of the attempt to take power of such coalitions (e.g. the Mexican, the Bolivian or the Sandinist revolutions). In addition to these two principal trajectories there are two minor transitions of more recent date, i.e. the transitions from populist and disarticulated regimes.

The relevance of populist discourses in the context of recent redemocratization processes is illustrated by the transition from disarticulated regimes to middle class-based populist regimes (2 cases, mean year of sequence = 1987).

TABLE 4: Types of political regimes succeeding middle and lower class based populist regimes (number of cases; mean year of regime transition and standard deviation of mean year in brackets).

	Export Bourgeoisie.	Lower Class Pop.	Disart. Regimes	Disart. Periods	N
Middle Class Populist Regimes	0	5 (1961/22)	2 (1948/25)	1 (1931)	8 (1954/22)
Lower Class Populist Regimes	8 (1946/16)	4 (1968/16)	4 (1968/13)	8 (1946/13)	24 (1953/17)
Total of Pop. Populist Regimes	8 (1946/16)	9 (1964/19)	6 (1961/19)	9 (1944/13)	32

Note: Sequences with less than 3 cases with respect to the total number of populist regimes have been excluded; for sources cf. Appendix.

As shown in Table 4 no typical regime can be observed to follow populist regimes. Thus, the change from populist to disarticulated regimes is much less pronounced than might be expected from the literature on bureaucratic authoritarianism. There are four sequences with a similar frequency which, however, differ in their temporal appearance: the transition of populist regimes to export bourgeoisies and to disarticulated periods occurs rather early (mean year of sequences during the 1940s) whereas the change to disarticulated regimes and to lower-class populism has taken place relatively recently (mean year during the 1960s). The two types of populist regimes show rather different regime transitions: the dominant sequence from middle class populism goes to lower-class populism; this transition which is also shown in Table 3 may be interpreted in the context of changing participatory demands (e.g. from political to social participation; cf. also Germani 1978). The transition of lower-class populism back to disarticulated periods and export bourgeoisies (i.e. to the types of political regime where populism mostly originates) suggests the existence of certain vicious cycles. The conflictual nature of transition from lower class-based populist regimes is confirmed by comparative evidence about the cause of regime breakdown: the ruling populist coalition was replaced by force (e.g. military coups) in 27 cases (of which 21 were lower class populist regimes). Only 17 regime changes (of which 8 from lower class populist regimes) took place within a constitutional framework.

Concluding Remarks

The empirical evidence from Latin America clearly demonstrates that the occurrence of populism is not confined to specific historical periods or stages of development. Rather, one may argue that different patterns or syndromes of populism are associated with specific socio-economic, political and cultural structures.

As a result of deep economic crises and the consequent need to pursue economic stabilization policies Latin American populist regimes of the 1980s and early 1990s suffer from fragile links to their mass base. The populist coalition, therefore, often disintegrates rapidly after the regime has assumed power (e.g. García in Peru Pérez in Venezuela, Paz Estenssoro in Bolivia, Borja in Ecuador, Manley in Jamaica). At the same time, emerging populist reform movements may threaten existing populist regimes (e.g. the *Frente Democrático Nacional* of Cuauhtémoc Cardenas in Mexico). In order to cope with this situation populist regimes have gradually turned from the articulation of economic to political and military anti-elitism. The first variant may be illustrated by Fujimori's campaign against political parties and the parliament in Peru or Salinas' anti-corruption campaign against (official) union leaders and civil servants in Mexico. Opposition towards the military combined with an emphasis on the preservation of democracy and a liberal constitutional framework has recently been articulated, among others, by Pérez in Venezuela.

By contrast to populist phenomena in other zones Latin American populist regimes show several structural peculiarities. First, the emergence of charismatic authority is supported by the Latin American tradition of *caudillismo*. Second, *indigenismo* is relatively weakly articulated in Latin America (especially compared with African and Asian populist regimes). Some nativistic elements were present in Argentina (*gauchismo*), Cuba,

Jamaica (rastafari cult), Mexico (*zapatismo*) and Peru (e.g. Belaúnde's *cooperación popular*). The relative lack of strong nativistic ideologies may be attributed to the extreme social inequality and the cultural barriers between (predominantly rural) Indians on the one hand and (urban) Creoles and *mestizos* on the other. A third structural peculiarity of Latin American populism is the prevalence of forms of economic anti-elitism articulated against both domestic and foreign elite groups. Asian and African populism, by contrast, mainly relies on political anti-elitism to foreign political powers whereas contemporary core populism generally articulates a people / elite-antagonsim with respect to the domestic political establishment together with antagonism between "the people" and marginal groups. These features may be explained by the specific economic, social and political developments in these zones. Thus, Latin American countries achieved their political independence already in the early nineteenth century and were strongly integrated into the world economy at the periphery. In Asia and Africa, on the contrary, a colonial structure of political dominance survived until the 1950s and 1960s. Western core countries, finally, are characterized by the absence of foreign economic and political elites but are confronted with massive immigrant movements from peripheral and semi-peripheral countries.

NOTES

1. The most notable exceptions are van Niekerk (1974), Ianni (1975), Canovan (1981), Conniff (1982) and Dix (1985).
2. This point may be aptly illustrated by the following statement of a spokesman of the Argentine Radicals during Yrigoyen's first term: "Nor do we accept class differences, or that there are any classes in the Argentine republic; (...) we do not accept that there is a proletarian or a capitalist class, even if 95% of the Argentines were to fall into what in Europe is called the proletariat" (cited in Rock 1975: 78).
3. Examples are Rojas Pinilla's qualification to be "God's candidate" (Dix 1985), Michael Manley's Joshua image or Velasco Ibarras cultivation of an ascetic way of life which he explains as follows (cited in Cueva 1982: 91): "I am as poor as you and want to remain poor to love nothing but the ideal and the struggle toward the ideal (...) I seek nothing for myself.

I do not want comforts or money. I want to remain poor to have a revolutionary soul". A further illustration is the following characterization of Marmaduke Grove, leader of the short-lived socialist republic in Chile during the 1930s, by a socialist party pamphlet (cited in Drake 1978: 254): "(...) this soldier (...) who has not felt a muscle in his face tremble before death (...) who listens to threats of shooting with a smile on his lips, this man (...) made of steel (...) often has the tenderness of a child, when listening to a worker describe his poverty. More than once Grove has dried a tear from his eyes, taking upon his shoulders the misfortune of the humble".

4 E.g. the Cuban revolution of 1933 and the succeeding regimes of Grau San Martín, Batista and Prío Sacarrás as well as the 26th July Movement and Castroism, the *Partido Revolucionario Dominicana*-PRD and the short-lived government of Juan Bosch in the Dominican Republic, the Jamaican experience of competing populist coalitions led by the two charismatic leaders Bustamante and Manley, Estimé's and François Duvalier's black nationalism in Haiti, the urban-based *calderonistas* during the 1940s and José "Pepe" Figueres' *Partido Liberación Nacional*-PLN in Costa Rica, the Guatemalan revolution of 1944 and the subsequent governments of Arévalo and Arbenz, the "military populism" of Torrijos and Noriega in Panama and the Sandinist revolution in Nicaragua.

5 See appendix for the coding of populist regimes.

6 Thus, in Argentina universal male suffrage was implemented as a result of pressures by the Radical movement led by Yrigoyen whereas voting to female adults has been expanded by Perón.

7 Clientelism is a personalized relationship between partners of unequal status, a patron and a client. The relationship consists of an exchange of support (e.g. votes) by the client against the provision of access to scarce resources (state services, subsidized markets) by the patron.

8 In contrast to these two variants of modern clientelism traditional or agrarian clientelism typical for oligarchic regimes is less relevant for populist regimes.

9 Examples of clientelistic techniques are Belaúnde's policy vis-à-vis teachers and García's job creation program for urban poor in Peru, the provision of cheap foodstuffs, medical and legal advice by Argentine Radicals and Peronists, Estimé's favoring of his home region for U.S.-financed development projects in Haiti and Manley's "Land Lease" program for peasants in Jamaica.

10 A good example for the first possibility is the Jamaican system of two rather similar competing lower class-based populist alliances (i.e. Bustamante's JLP and Manley's PNP) of which both rely heavily on clientelistic techniques. The change of regime that occurred every second election has usually been associated with a massive shift of clients

between the two clientelistic networks (cf. Edie 1991). The second variant may be illustrated by García's APRA in Peru, which rapidly lost control over the urban poor after cutting its job creation program for them in 1987 due to economic and financial difficulties (cf. Graham 1991).

11 The necessity of implementing policies of incorporation has been emphasized by Perón in the following statement (cited in van Niekerk 1974: 150): "In order to prevent the masses, who have once shared in the essential and natural social justice, from making excessive demands, these masses must first be organised, so that under the care of responsible and properly led organisations they are dissuaded from taking the side of injustice, because the common sense of the organic masses is bound to prevail over the exaggerated demands of a few of their members. That, then, is the insurance: organisation of the masses."

12 Examples are post-revolutionary Bolivia (1952-64/69), Argentina under Perón, or the Venezuelan AD.

13 Further examples are the military populism and socialism of Torrijos and Noriega in Panama and of Toro and Busch in Bolivia and the period of the "Honorable Mission" in Chile (1924-31).

APPENDIX

List of well articulated populist regimes with type of mass support in brackets (L=Lower class populist regimes, M=Middle class populist regimes):
Argentina: Yrigoyen / Alvear, 1916-30 (M); Perón, 1943-55, 1973-76 (L); Frondizi / Illía, 1958-66 (M); Alfonsín, 1984-89 (M); Menem, 1989- (L). *Bolivia:* Saavedra, 1920-25 (M); Toro / Busch, 1936-39 (L); MNR, 1952-64 (L); Barrientos, 1964-69 (L); Siles Zuazo, 1982-85 (L). *Brazil:* Vargas / Dutra, 1930-54 (L); Quadros / Goulart, 1961-64 (L). *Chile:* Alessandri, 1920-25 (M); Ibañez, 1927-31, 1952-58 (L); Rad. Era, 1938-52 (L); Frei, 1964-70 (M); Allende, 1970-73 (L); Alwyn: 1990- (M). *Colombia:* Rojas Pinilla, 1953-57 (L). *Costa Rica:* Calderón / Picado, 1940-48 (L); PLN (Figueres ff), 1953-57, 1962-66, 1970-78, 1982-90 (M). *Cuba:* Grau San Martín, 1933 (M); Castro, 1959- (L). *Dominican Republic:* Bosch, 1963 (L). *Ecuador:* Ayora, 1925-31 (M), Velasco Ibarra, 1934-35, 1944-47, 1952-56, 1960-61, 1968-71 (L); Roldós / Hurtado, 1979-84 (M); Borja, 1988- (L). *El Salvador:* Araujo, 1931 (M). *Guatemala:* Arévalo, 1945-50 (M); Arbenz, 1951-54 (L). *Haiti:* Estimé, 1946-50 (?); François Duvalier, 1957-71 (?). *Jamaica:* Bustamante, 1962-67 (L); Manley, 1972-80 (L). *Mexico:* "Revolutionary coalition" / Cárdenas / PRI, 1920-81 (L). *Nicaragua:* Sandinista, 1979-89 (L). *Panama:* Torrijos / Noriega, 1968-89 (L). *Paraguay:* Febrerista, 1936-37 (?). *Peru:* Billinghurst, 1912-14 (L); Sánchez

Cerro, 1931-33 (L); Bustamante, 1945-48 (L); Belaúnde, 1963-68 (M); Velasco, 1968-75 (L); García, 1985-90 (L). *Uruguay:* Batlle y Ordóñez / Colorado, 1903-58. *Venezuela*: Trieno, 1945-48 (L), AD / COPEI: 1959- (L).
List of weakly articulated populist regimes: *Bolivia:* Paz Estenssoro, 1985-89; Paz Zamora, 1989-. *Cuba:* Batista, 1934-44, Grau San Martín, 1944-48; Prío, 1948-52. *Dominican Republic:* PRD, 1978-1986. *Ecuador:* Rodríguez Lara, 1972-76. *Jamaica:* Shearer, 1967-72; Manley, 1989-. *Mexico:* de la Madrid / Salinas, 1982-. *Panama:* H. Arias / A. Arias (PPA), 1931-35, 1940-41, 1949-51. *Peru:* Leguía, 1919-30.
Sources concerning the coding of regimes: The coding of regimes is based on the case histories cited in the text and on social science literature concerning individual countries. These sources are described in detail in Suter (1993).

REFERENCES

Basurto, Jorge (1969): "Populismo y movilización de masas en México durante el régimen cardenista," *Revista Mexicana de Sociología* 31: 853-892.
Basurto, Jorge (1982): "The Late Populism of Luis Echeverría," pp. 93-111 in: Michael L. Conniff (ed.), *Latin American Populism in Comparative Perspective.* Albuquerque: University of New Mexico Press.
Blanchard, Peter (1977): "A Populist Precursor: Guillermo Billinghurst," *Journal of Latin American Studies* 9: 251-273.
Birnbaum, Norman (1986): "Populismus, Reaganismus und die amerikanische Demokratie," pp. 106-132 in: Helmut Dubiel (ed.), *Populismus und Aufklärung.* Frankfurt a.M.: Suhrkamp.
Boyte, Harry C., Heather Booth and Steve Max (1986): *Citizen Action and the New American Populism.* Philadelphia: Temple University Press.
Canovan, Margaret (1981): *Populism.* New York / London: Junction Books.
Cardoso, Fernando Henrique, Enzo Faletto (1979): *Dependency and Development in Latin America.* Berkeley: University of California Press.
Conniff, Michael L. (1981): *Urban Politics in Brazil: The Rise of Populism 1925-1945.* Pittsburgh: University of Pittsburgh Press.
Conniff, Michael L. (1982): "Introduction: Toward a Comparative Definition of Populism," pp. 3-30 in: Michael L. Conniff (ed.), *Latin American Populism in Comparative Perspective.* Albuquerque: University of New Mexico Press.
Cueva Dávila, Augustín (1982): *The Process of Political Domination in Ecuador.* New Brunswick, NJ: Transaction Books.
Dandler, Jorge (1977): "Low Classness' or Wavering Populism? A Peasant Movement in Bolivia (1952-1953)," pp. 142-173 in: June Nash, Juan

Corradi and Holbart Spalding Jr. (eds.), *Ideology and Social Change in Latin America*. New York: Gordon & Breach.
di Tella, Torcuato (1965): "Populism and Reform in Latin America," pp. 47-74 in: Claudio Veliz (ed.), *Obstacles to Change in Latin America*. London: Oxford University Press.
Dix, Robert H. (1985): "Populism: Authoritarian and Democratic," *Latin American Research Review* 20 (2): 29-52.
Drake, Paul W. (1978): *Socialism and Populism in Chile, 1932-52*. Urbana: University of Illinois Press.
Drake, Paul W. (1982): "Conclusion: Requiem for Populism?," pp. 217-245 in: Michael L. Conniff (ed.), *Latin American Populism in Comparative Perspective*. Albuquerque: University of New Mexico Press.
Edie, Carlene J. (1991): *Democracy by Default: Dependency and Clientelism in Jamaica*. Boulder: Lynne Rienner.
Elfferding, Wieland (1986): "Rechtspopulistische Potentiale in der CDU/CSU," pp. 150-189 in: Helmut Dubiel (ed.), *Populismus und Aufklärung*. Frankfurt a.M.: Suhrkamp.
Ellner, Steven (1982): "Populism in Venezuela, 1935-48: Betancourt and Acción Democrática," pp. 135-149 in: Michael L. Conniff (ed.), *Latin American Populism in Comparative Perspective*. Albuquerque: University of New Mexico Press.
Erickson, Kenneth Paul (1977): "Populism and Political Control of the Working Class in Brazil," pp. 200-236 in: June Nash, Juan Corradi and Holbart Spalding Jr. (eds.), *Ideology and Social Change in Latin America*. New York: Gordon & Breach.
Germani, Gino (1978): *Authoritarianism, Fascism, and National Populism*. New Brunswick: Transaction Books.
Goodwyn, Lawrence (1976): *Democratic Promise: The Populist Moment in America*. Oxford / New York: Oxford University Press.
Hall, Stuart (1980): "Popular-democratic vs Authoritarian Populism," pp. 157-185 in: A. Hunt (ed.), *Marxism and Democracy*. London.
Hennessy, Alistair (1969): "Latin America," pp. 28-61 in: Ernest Gellner and Ghita Ionescu (eds.), *Populism: Its Meanings and National Characteristics*. London: Weidensfeld and Nicolson.
Hischier, Guido (1987): *Politische Regimes in Entwicklungsländern*. Frankfurt a.M.: Campus.
Hofstadter, Richer (1956): *The Age of Reform*. New York: Alfred A.Knopf.
Ianni, Octavio (1970): *Crisis in Brazil*. New York / London: Columbia University Press.
Ianni, Octavio (1975): *A formaçao do estado populista na América Latina*. Rio: Civilizaçao Brasileira.
Jeffries, Richard D. (1975): "Populist Tendencies in the Ghanaian Trade Union Movement," pp. 261-280 in: Richard Sandbrook and Robin Cohen (eds.), *The Development of an African Working Class*. London: Longman.
Keller, Felix (1992): *Die Empörung der "Schweigenden Mehrheit"*. Unpublished thesis. Sociological Institute, University of Zurich.

Laclau, Ernesto (1977): *Politics and Ideology in Marxist Theory: Capitalism - Fascism - Populism.* London: New Left Books.
Low, D. A. (1964): "The Advent of Populism in Buganda," *Comparative Studies in Society and History* 6: 424-444.
Lynch, John (1979): *Juan Manuel de Rosas, 1829-1852.* Oxford: Clarendon.
Mitchell, Christopher (1977): *The Legacy of Populism in Bolivia.* New York: Praeger.
Mendes, Candido (1977): *Beyond Populism.* Albany: State University of New York Press.
Navarro, Marysa (1982): "Evita's Charismatic Leadership," pp. 47-66 in: Michael L. Conniff (ed.), *Latin American Populism in Comparative Perspective.* Albuquerque: University of New Mexico Press.
Narkiewicz, Olga A. (1976): *The Green Flag: Polish Populist Politics, 1867-1970.* London: Croom Helm.
O'Donnell, Guillermo A. (1973): *Modernization and Bureaucratic Authoritarianism. Berkeley*: University of California.
Pantojas-Garcia, Emilio (1989): "Puerto Rican Populism Revisited: The PPD During the 1940s," *Journal of Latin American Studies* 21: 521-557.
Pfister, Ulrich and Christian Suter (1989): Comparing Political Regimes of the Third World: Types and Sequences. Paper presented at the Annual Convention of the International Studies Association, London, 28 March - 1 April 1989.
Pfister, Ulrich and Christian Suter (1991): "Politische Regimes und Staatsentwicklung in der Dritten Welt: Peru seit den 1950er Jahren," *Schweizerische Zeitschrift für Soziologie* 17 (2): 343-374.
Portes, Alejandro (1985): "Latin American Class Structures: Their Composition and Change During the Last Decades," *Latin American Research Review* 20 (3): 7-39.
Quintero, Rafael (1980): *El mito del populismo en el Ecuador.* Quito: FLACSO.
Rock, David (1975): "Radical Populism and the Conservative Elite, 1912-1930," pp. 66-87 in: David Rock (ed.), *Argentina in the Twentieth Century.* London: Duckworth.
Saul, John S. (1973): "On African Populism," pp. 152-179 in: Giovanni Arrighi and John S. Saul (eds.), *Essays on the Political Economy of Africa.* New York: Monthly Review Press.
Sharpless, Richard F. (1978): *Gaitán of Colombia: A Political Biography.* Pittsburgh: University of Pittsburgh Press.
Stein, Steve (1980): *Populism in Peru.* Wisconsin: The University of Wisconsin Press.
Stein, Steve (1982): "Populism in Peru: APRA, the Formative Years," pp. 113-134 in: Michael L. Conniff (ed.), *Latin American Populism in Comparative Perspective.* Albuquerque: University of New Mexico Press.
Stepan, Alfred (1978): *The State and Society: Peru in Comparative Perspective.* Princeton, NJ: Princeton University Press.

Suter, Christian (1992): *Debt Cycles in the World-Economy*, Boulder: Westview.
Suter, Christian (1993): *Populismus in der Dritten Welt: Eine vergleichende Analyse populistischer Regimes*. Unpublished manuscript. Sociological Institute, University of Zurich.
Tamarin, David (1982): "Yrigoyen and Perón? The Limits of Argentine Populism," pp. 31-45 in: Michael L. Conniff (ed.), *Latin American Populism in Comparative Perspective*. Albuquerque: University of New Mexico Press.
van Niekerk, A. E. (1974): *Populism and Political Development in Latin America*. Rotterdam: Rotterdam University Press.
Walicki, Andrzej (1969): "Russia," pp. 62-96 in: Ernest Gellner and Ghita Ionescu (eds.), *Populism: Its Meanings and National Characteristics*. London: Weidensfeld and Nicolson.
Weber, Max (1956) [1922]: *Wirtschaft und Gesellschaft*. Tübingen: J.C.B. Mohr.
Weffort, Francisco C. (1973): "Clases populares y desarollo social: contribución al estudio del populismo," pp. 17-169 in: Francisco Weffort and Anibal Quijano (eds.), *Populismo, marginalización y dependencia*. San José, Costa Rica: Editorial Universitaria Centroamericana.
Wiles, Peter (1969): "A Syndrome, Not a Doctrine," pp. 166-179 in: Ernest Gellner and Ghita Ionescu (eds.), *Populism: Its Meanings and National Characteristics*. London: Weidensfeld and Nicolson.
Worsley, Peter (1969): "The Concept of Populism," pp. 212-250 in: Ernest Gellner and Ghita Ionescu (eds.), *Populism: Its Meanings and National Characteristics*. London: Weidensfeld and Nicolson.

9 THE CAUSES OF LATIN AMERICAN SOCIAL REVOLUTIONS
SEARCHING FOR PATTERNS IN MEXICO, CUBA AND NICARAGUA

John Foran

The sociology of revolution has come of age in the last two decades, following the seminal work of Theda Skocpol (1979) on the causes of social revolution in France, Russia, and China.[1] The last fifteen years have seen a number of major comparative contributions on various cases from diverse theoretical perspectives. The best of these include the work of John Walton[2] and Farideh Farhi[3] on the Third World, Ian Roxborough[4] and, most recently and comprehensively, Timothy Wickham-Crowley[5], on Latin American social revolutions in particular. Each of these writers has fashioned a distinctive, multi-causal model of the origins of revolutionary movements. Walton, for example, works out a synthesis of "(1) the context of uneven development; (2) the conditions of protest mobilization; (3) modernization crises and coalitions; and (4) the role of the state."[6] Farhi bases her model on Skocpol's discussion of state autonomy, amended by a "broader under-

---

This article is drawn from the research project "Third World Social Revolutions: A Comparative Study" funded by the World Society Foundation. John Foran is Assistant Professor of Sociology, University of California, Santa Barbara, California 93106, U.S.A.

standing of ideology" and tailored for her Third World cases by a call for consideration of "the changing balance of class forces occasioned by uneven development of capitalism on a world scale."[7] Wickham-Crowley carefully compares instances of successful and failed guerrilla insurgencies in Latin America between 1956 and 1990, isolating five causal elements in the two successful cases of Cuba and Nicaragua: "(1) the attempt at guerrilla warfare, (2) guerrilla successes in securing high levels of peasant support, (3) guerrilla achievement of substantial military strength, (4) at the national level, the presence of a patrimonial praetorian regime, and (5) the withdrawal of U.S. support for that regime."[8]

Collectively, this work has advanced our understanding of the causes of social revolutions in the Third World. In particular, the key questions of *who* makes revolutions, *why* they make them, and *how* they succeed, now seem closer to adequate answers than a generation ago. While I am sympathetic to the approaches adopted by these students of revolution, various critical gaps can be noted in the state of the art. Underdevelopment, while signalled by Walton and Farhi, is absent in Wickham-Crowley's account; moreover, it remains to be explained what it is about dependency that makes certain Third World countries more vulnerable to revolution than others. Penetrating the complex ways in which culture, ideology, and world-views shape the actions of participants also remains more of a promise than a secure achievement in this literature. The combined effects of internal and external factors contributing to a revolutionary crisis are likewise sometimes hinted at, but not yet clearly specified.[9] In a general way, Farhi's effort to bring the state to the fore, and Wickham-Crowley's structuralist emphasis both tend to slight actors, including classes, to some degree; the need here is to bring state and society into a proper analytic balance, and to do this with sensitivity to the actions of people. Finally, despite the varied and significant contributions of all the writers mentioned here, the problem remains of how all of the "factors" proposed cohere into a *theory* of the causes of revolution.[10]

A Theory of Third World Social Revolutions

My own previous work on a variety of cases, most notably Iran, suggests a different, if related, conceptual framework.[11] Its starting point is the premise that Third World social revolutions have origins in the complexities of Third World social structures. These are shaped in two ways: the pre-existing rural and urban social formations, possessing their own dynamics, came into fateful contact with the world-economy from the sixteenth century onwards (in Latin America). They were thereafter changed in ways that have both internal and external determinants, with historically specific consequences in different regions and periods. In some places at some times, this took the form of what Cardoso, Faletto, Evans, and others have called *dependent development,* essentially a form of growth within limits.[12] That is, unlike earlier dependency theorists such as André Gunder Frank, who largely denied the possibility of industrialization and economic expansion, these cases exhibit significant gains in indices such as industrialization, trade, per capita GNP, and the commercialization of agriculture. At the same time, the process both creates new social classes and expands existing ones (urban and rural workers, capitalists, professionals, and urban marginals among them), and entails social costs in various areas, including health, education, housing conditions, inflation and wages. It should be stressed that this kind of dependency takes many forms, which may differ from one another,[13] but it does separate out one group of Third World countries – the more dynamic ones at given points in time – from the rest, and it also captures the complex social turmoil that certain generations experience in these countries.

Dependent development, whether in the shah's Iran, South Korea, Brazil, or elsewhere, often (though again not always) is coupled with a repressive state, one capable of containing the inevitable unrest generated by its effects. Recent research on the type of regime most vulnerable to revolution has isolated one particular kind of repressive state – a personalistic, non-democratic one – as most likely to provoke a deep movement for change.[14] The exclusion by such states of their own elites from politics, not to mention aspiring middle classes and the "dangerous classes" in the social order below, eventually provokes multiple demands for participation. The personalized, quasi-dynastic rule of dictators such as the shah, Batista, Somoza, Marcos, and their counterparts elsewhere focuses the attention of the opposition on the single person visibly responsible for the situation, often detaching him from the elite he would otherwise represent *(collective* military dictatorships, as in El Salvador, Guatemala, Brazil, Argentina, or South Korea, are less vulnerable, especially if they take steps in time to open up the political system). The two structural factors of dependent development and exclusionary, personalistic regimes, then, mark off a specific, limited subset of Third World countries where we might expect to see revolutionary movements.

Purely structural theories of revolution, however, too often overlook the simple fact that people make revolutions (even if not under circumstances of their own choosing, to paraphrase Marx). The resources people draw on to do so include material ones, as noted by Charles Tilly's and others' version of resource mobilization theory, but they are in large part *cultural* as well. I use the term "political cultures of opposition" to refer to the ways in which groups and classes undergoing dependent development in repressive situations fashion everything from simple slogans ("The shah must go!") to more elaborate ideologies of resistance (from Marxism and nationalism to liberation theology).[15] Such world-views and the perceptions and emotions that inform them are a crucial mediating link between structural determinants and the actual making of revolutions. While necessarily a broad concept, the underlying empirical referents must be accurate and powerful enough analyses and expressions of people's lived experiences to mobilize them, and flexible enough to hold them together until the regime is overthrown. Often several oppositional cultures will be articulated, entering into complex relations in the course of a struggle, and ultimately uniting for a time around the most basic demands and rallying images. While again of considerable variation across cases, two possible common denominators are the demands for the departure of the dictator and the elimination of foreign control; in this way political cultures of opposition possess an affinity for the structural problems of dependent development and internal dictatorship that they oppose.

The presence of the above factors might alone account for the outbreak of a revolutionary movement. One final factor making this more likely, and crucially, making success more likely, is the emergence of a dual crisis.[16] By this I mean the simultaneous occurrence of an internal economic downturn and a favorable international context for success. An economic downturn, coming on top of the problems characteristic of dependent development (and in part tied to the cycles of the world economy) sharpens the grievances that fuel the actions of various groups and classes.[17] This perceptible worsening of their condition for many constitutes the final straw that motivates them to translate anger into action. Chances for success are greatly facilitated too by the existence of "a tolerant or permissive world context", as Walter Goldfrank has termed the situation obtaining when the dominant external power or powers are unable or unwilling to intervene decisively against the revolution, for whatever reasons (distraction, rivalries, wars of their own).[18] I term this situation a "world-systemic opening" to indicate the second way in which the world-system plays an important role in the shaping of Third World social revolutions. The conjuncture of internal and external crises is a powerful one making outbreak more certain and success more likely.

The model elaborated above is schematically presented in diagram one, which suggests that the presence of dependent development, an exclusionary personalistic regime, political cultures of opposition, and a dual revolutionary crisis together account for cases of successful social revolution in the Third World.

DIAGRAM 1

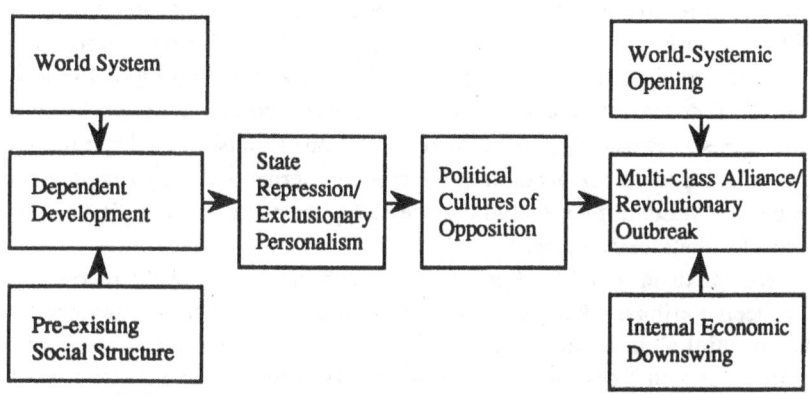

Such social movements tend to be multi-class in nature, for two reasons. One reflects the complexities of Third World social structure itself, which are such that no single class or sector (rural / urban) is likely to carry a revolution to successful completion. The other is the need for a wide coalition of forces to coalesce in order to overcome the repressive powers of the state (the story of what happens after seizing power typically requires analysis of the fragmentation of such coalitions, and is not our subject here). The present essay makes a preliminary assessment of this model through a look at the three full-fledged cases of social revolution in twentieth-century Latin America – Mexico 1910-20, Cuba 1956-59, and Nicaragua 1977-79.[19]

Mexico

The Mexican revolution was a complex, multi-sided event, and cannot be easily characterized. Interpretations abound: was it a bourgeois revolution overthrowing feudalism, or a failed socialist (or proletarian) revolution? The labels "peasant", "popular", "democratic", "nationalist", and "anti-imperialist" have been attached to it, while the outcome has been variously proclaimed a victory, a defeat, or a "permanent", "unfinished", or "interrupted" revolution leading up to the present.[20] All of these terms hint at the somewhat ambiguous, or mixed, outcome of the revolution. Our present task – sorting out the *causes* of the revolution – is complicated by the long duration of its course, which featured several prominent twists and turns: the 1910-11 uprising against Porfirio Díaz, the 1913-14 Constitutionalist movement against the dictator Huerta, and the bloody infighting of 1915-16 between the victors to that point. We will focus on the causal factors leading up to the successful revolt of Francisco Madero against Díaz, leaving, for reasons of space, a full account of the crucial aftermath of the struggle for a longer study. Let us then examine successively the elements identified by our model for the Mexican case.

The Mexican social (and political) structure on the eve of the revolution has been variously labelled – feudal, capitalist, oligarchic, autocratic, neocolonial.[21] In ethnic terms, creoles (often landowners and clerics of Spanish descent) dominated the top social positions, though they were yielding in some areas to the estimated half of the population classified as mixed-race mestizos. At the bottom of the social structure, about one-third of the population, were Indians of diverse cultures, and there were small black and Chinese populations. Alan Knight notes that ethnic categories represented fluid, sociocultural identities, based on "language, dress, income, food, literacy and domicile."[22] In economic terms, rural society was dominated by *hacendados* (large landlords), urban society by capitalists, merchants, and clerics. Peasants, the landless, and indentured rural workers were found at the bottom, their urban counterparts being workers, artisans, and the unemployed. There were middle-class ranchers in the countryside, and an intelligentsia and professionals in the cities. Women were located across the class structure, though structurally disadvantaged as well. Galeano claims: "In Mexico City, out of every ten young women, two engage(d) in prostitution."[23] Overall, in 1910: "Mexico's labour force was predominantly agricultural, secondarily artisan and only thirdly industrial; for every hundred rural workers, there were perhaps a dozen small farmers and a dozen artisans, four factory operatives (at least one a woman), three miners, one *ranchero,* and a quarter of 1% of an *hacendado.*"[24] Regional variations are central to Porfirian social structure too: the north was more industrialized and mining oriented, its land tenure based on ranching; the central valley more peasant; the south based on plantation work.

The dramatic transformation of this social structure during the reign of Porfirio Díaz from 1876 to 1910 constitutes a textbook case of dependent development. A few simple statistics demonstrate the remarkable growth that occurred: population grew by 1.4% a year to 25.2 million, while economic output rose by 2.7% annually and exports by 6.1%.[25] Foreign trade grew by three- or fourfold between 1888 and 1910, a great boom led by cotton, mining, and other raw materials. Railroads expanded from 666 kilometers of track in 1876 to 24560 by 1910. Sugar output rose five times, henequen eleven times.[26] Oil production climbed meteorically until Mexico ranked third in the world in 1911, with fourteen million barrels.[27] Mining thrived as well. Gross domestic product grew from 435 million pesos to 1184 million, 1877-1910. In aggregate terms, this meant growth from 513 pesos per capita in 1895 to 768 by 1910.[28]

Alongside these indices of growth, however, could be discerned characteristic limits, external and internal in origin and impact. In all, foreign capital controlled "90% of Mexico's eighty largest capitalized business concerns, including nine of the top ten."[29] Mexican capital still accounted for much agricultural and craft production, but textiles were 80% French and banking 94% foreign.[30] Great Britain had a large stake in the budding oil industry. Towering over the Europeans was the United States, with over $1 billion in investments by 1910, representing 80% of foreign investments and more than that of the entire Mexican bourgeoisie. American companies and individuals controlled about 80% of mining, owned over 100 million acres of land, provided 57% of imports and took 75.6% of exports in 1910. Railroads had a north-south orientation, reflecting American needs. These investments in Mexico came to 45% of all U.S. investments abroad.[31]

Internally, the most significant repercussions of dependent development were the crisis in agriculture and deteriorating urban conditions. Peasants were increasingly squeezed from their land and proletarianized as latifundios encroached on their communal holdings in places like Morelos, where sugar plantations grew rapidly. While no definitive regional figures exist, by one estimate 90% of central plateau people were landless on the eve of the revolution, and 67% in the provinces of Mexico, Michoacan, and Veracruz. Agricultural production grew at about 0.7% a year, less than population, and was shifting to export crops at the expense of subsistence staples like corn, whose output declined from 2.7 million tons in 1877 to 2.1 million two decades later.[32] In the urban economy, artisans lost jobs as foreign imports flooded markets, especially in textiles. By 1900, the railroad building spree was over, industry was contracting, and migrants crowded the cities. The cost of staples far outstripped the purchasing power of wages, which in real terms were the same in 1908 as a century before.[33] The squeeze on land and the rise of urban living costs would prove central to the grievances that fed the ensuing struggle; the argument advanced here is that these changes in the political economy and social structure as a whole can be attributed to the process of dependent development.

The authoritarian character of the Porfirian state has been well documented. Its slogan, *Pan y palo* ("Bread and the stick"), suggests the combination of cooptation and repression that undergirded it. Porfirio Díaz came to power in a popular movement in 1876 and ruled continuously till 1911, with the exception of 1880-84. Elections were regularly held but the results cynically manipulated: civilian politicians were controlled through a vast patronage machine that oversaw appointments from the level of village cacique to state governor, some of whom ruled for twenty or more years, enriching themselves in the process. The army could field 14 000 regular troops (there were 30 000 on paper), 2400 *rurales* to police the countryside, and several thousand irregulars, in addition to the local police. It was poorly fed and treated at the lower levels and its commanders were rotated at the top to ensure loyalty to Díaz. This force was increasingly called upon to do repressive duty as Díaz aged: 100 strikers were killed at the Cananea mine in 1905 and 200 at the Río Blanco textile mill a year later. In the provinces, the citizenry was subjected to "arbitrary fines, impressment, deportation, even ... murder".[34] The anarchist Partido Liberal Mexicano (PLM) was persecuted; its leaders fled. When Franciso Madero mounted a vigorous electoral challenge to Díaz in 1910, he was arrested and the opposition press shut down. The Porfirian state was clearly personalistic (focussed on Díaz); exclusionary of all serious challengers, including new elites; and repressive when all else failed.

Mexico on the eve of its revolution was rich in expressions of resistance to Díaz's rule, political cultures that included anarchism, agrarian populism, nationalism, and liberalism. Exiled Spanish anarcho-syndicalists brought their ideas to the textile mills of central Mexico. After an initial florescence in the 1870s they were forced underground by Díaz until a new upswing began around 1900, organized in part around the Flores Magon brothers who founded the PLM in 1905, calling for free speech, agrarian reform, and labor legislation. Local revolts in 1906 and 1908 failed and the Flores Magons had to operate outside the country. In the end anarchism was limited to a part of the working class and some intellectuals, and not capable of uniting opposition to Díaz, who repressed it forcefully, but its egalitarian ideals contributed to the anti-authoritarian leveling that appeared after 1910.[35] A rural counterpart took the form of *agrarismo* - an agrarian populism rooted in the long history of regional and local revolts that continued throughout the nineteenth century as hacienda encroachments touched more and more mestizo and Indian communities. Indigenous political culture was based on millenarianism, a return of social justice, restoration of lands, and expulsion of intruders. The veneration of saints in Sonora and Morelos added a religious cast to moral outrage. In the north and highlands everywhere, ranchers, smallholders, and communal villagers articulated an independent stand against central control that would evolve into the cross-class populism of the various stages of the revolution. There was widespread agreement with the sentiments of Cruz Chávez, "the Tomóchic leader of 1892, who told travellers that his people simply wanted that 'no-one should interfere with them, nor bother them for anything, nor meddle in their affairs'".[36] Once events started these feelings would permeate the vigorous, if socially distinct movements of Zapata and Villa. Behind both rural and urban grievances lay a growing nationalism generated in part by the Díaz clique's preference for things foreign, and fueled by the rural encroachments and industrial pay differentials between Mexicans and foreigners in mining, the railways, and elsewhere. The Mexico City newspaper *El Hijo del Ahuizote* had as its banner: "Mexico for the Mexicans", giving voice to these concerns.[37]

The embodiment of these diverse strands was the liberal-democratic ideology of the Madero revolt that touched off the first phase of the revolution. Francisco Madero, from a rich landed family, was educated in Paris and Berkeley in the 1890s and evolved a liberal, "spiritualist" humanism at that time. Government attacks on Liberal clubs in 1902-3 convinced him that the Díaz government would not reform itself, but had to be changed from without. Madero's early views on radical issues were vague and his later rule showed him to be a moderate, but in the period before the revolution he stood for the right to unionize, for improved conditions (if not a real land reform) in the countryside, stopping the onslaught of the large U.S. trusts (though not all foreign capital), and above all, for democracy and fair elections. His 1908 book against the re-election of Díaz and 1910 campaign for the presidency aroused the hope of discontented elements around the country, providing a temporary, if somewhat watered-down, fusion of strands of the pro-labor, pro-peasant, nationalistic, and democratic aspirations of a wide segment of the population: "The Maderista programme and philosophy were thus variably conjugated: for some, they implied a progressive, up-to-the-minute polity, well-governed, hard-working and prosperous; for some, a political housecleaning and overdue access to power; for some, a reassertion of old, heroic, liberal values; for some, agrarian restitution and / or village autonomy."[38] This amalgam would prove a significant political culture of resistance against Díaz in 1910, when the dual crisis provided an opening.

The internal aspect of this crisis took the form of a series of economic downturns between 1899 and 1911, the most severe between 1907 and 1910. The 1899-1904 financial crises in Europe hit Mexican investments hard, dampening the boom that had begun in the 1880s. In 1905-6, a fall in the price of silver led to less mining output, strikes, and unemployment.[39] The 1907 economic panic and recession in the U.S. brought severe short-term effects to Mexico – declines in economic output, shrinking tax revenues, rising foreign debt, and inflation. This was compounded by a two-year drought that began in 1908. Sugar production fell in Morelos and unemployed workers crowded city streets. Famine in the north and center due to the decline in corn crops meant five million pesos of corn imports in 1908, fifteen million in 1909, and twelve million in 1910. Cotton output fell, affecting textiles, where wages declined and unemployment rose. Imports plummeted by 50% from 1907-8 to 1908-9, and government income by 26% from 1905 to 1908. The state's fiscal conservatism prevented it from spending its way out of the crisis, as debt servicing grew to 25% of its budget.[40] Knight argues that aggregate data point to recovery by 1910, but the evidence is fragmentary, and the damage had already been done: the 1907-1909 crisis drove many into Madero's camp. Moreover, in early 1911, the economy turned down again and prices soared, especially in the north, just as the rebellion gathered steam. So while Knight rightly notes – "the timetable of middle-class protest was determined not, in some mechanical fashion, by the crises of the business cycle, but by the political chronology of the 1900s – the Creelman interview, the impending 1910 elections"[41] – this only highlights the powerful *conjunctural* effect of economic downturn and political cultures of opposition, both of which were present by 1910-11 where they had not been a decade earlier.

The final link in this chain of processes was the world-systemic opening at the time of Madero's uprising. To some degree, rivalries between Europe and the United States may have stayed American intervention in the 1910-11 crisis, but to a much larger degree the internal policy uncertainties of the Taft administration and the interests of individual American capitalists played a favorable role in Madero's victory. Conflicts arose between the Díaz government and the U.S. over naval manoeuvers in Baja in 1907, Mexican refuge for deposed Nicaraguan president Zelaya in 1909, oil contracts with British companies, and land disputes near the border in Texas. Taft personally would have liked to help Díaz but he moved rather slowly for various domestic reasons (the Democrats had just gained control of Congress in late 1910 and accused him of connections to Mexican capital).[42] Madero meanwhile activated numerous ties to wealthy American backers in San Antonio and New York, among them railroad tycoon H. H. Harriman, bankers Charles and James Stillman, and the Texas Oil Company.[43] Though Díaz called for Madero's arrest in Texas in late 1910, the U.S. took no action until February 1911, inadvertently aiding Madero. On March 6, 1911, Taft concentrated troops on the border for "routine" manoeuvers seemingly aimed at preventing more arms and men from crossing over to the rebels. Ironically, the action was perceived as an insult by Díaz and as a threatening message of no confidence in him to the Mexican public. Although a number of Americans were accidentally killed at El Paso when Madero's supporters took Ciudad Juarez just across the border in May, the U.S. again took no steps to help Díaz.[44] In the end, while the American government did not intervene for Madero, its studied neutrality hurt Díaz, and important financial interests backed the rebels.

These developments resulted in a fairly swift victory for the rebels under Madero's banner in the spring of 1911. Several "armies" responded to Madero's November 1910 call for an uprising to oust Díaz and restore democracy, led by Pablo Orozco and Franciso Villa in the north, Emiliano Zapata south of Mexico City, and numerous local figures elsewhere. By late May there was rebellion throughout Mexico, and the Federal army was stretched to the breaking point against up to 70,000 loosely organized insurgents. Díaz, in poor health and with no visible domestic or international support, resigned on 25 May, 1911, securing from Madero a compromise that preserved the army and much of the government.[45]

Who made this phase of the Mexican revolution? Victory was the product of a disparate, multi-class alliance of the social groups and classes that had been adversely affected by dependent development and the Porfirian repression. The political center of gravity in 1911 lay in the north, where excluded elites, hard-pressed ranchers, artisans, and miners, dispossessed peasant and Indian (Yaqui and Mayo) communities, and urban marginals all played a role. The middle classes everywhere wanted more responsible government; they were the natural core of Madero's movement. Women engaged in urban bread riots in 1911 and a few probably became *soldaderas* even at this early date. In the center, where hacienda encroachments had occurred but enough free villages still remained, as in Morelos, Puebla, and Tlaxcala, peasants engaged in land seizures and joined the rebel armies. These movements included Indian and mestizo villagers and smallholders. The plantation economy of the south, with its high proportion of peons and few free villages, did not become active to any comparable degree in this phase of the revolution. Throughout Mexico, while leaders tended to come from slightly higher class positions than the rank and file, they were local people in most cases, not outsiders. In two senses, then, the revolution was a multi-class affair, within each region, and across the country as a whole. In Knight's words: "... it was a complex, collective experience, to which many groups contributed in different ways and for different reasons".[46] No single social class, geographical area, or economic sector carried the movement by itself.

As is well known, the Mexican revolution did not end in 1911. While space does not permit analysis of its course from 1911 to 1920, my supposition is that the factors used in accounting for its outbreak and initial success would have continued relevance to making sense of its tortuous course and eventual outcome. Madero fell in 1913 after alienating both lower-class rebels and the U.S. A renewed multi-class coalition ousted the dictator Huerta from power in 1914, then fragmented into complex regional and cross-class movements that engaged in their own civil war. The timing and outcome of these struggles, I hypothesize, continued to have much to do with such factors as the contending political cultures, internal economic conditions, and the world-systemic conjuncture. The outcome was on the whole a defeat for the most radical forces unleashed in the course of events, even as it led to a stronger, more legitimate, and popular state than Díaz's had been. The cost, however, had been tremendous: a million dead and the foreclosure of a more radical social project in favor of a dependent capitalist and eventually authoritarian political economy and regime. This ambiguous outcome of Latin America's first twentieth-century social revolution must await telling elsewhere, however.

Cuba

The Cuban revolution presents the appearance of an almost wholly "willed" revolution: a small band of idealistic young revolutionaries overturning a military dictatorship through determination, bravery, and luck. And in good measure this is true, but it is not the whole story, even if it *is* an aspect we must not lose sight of. Much more than in Mexico, it seems a personalized, human-scale conflict, not a structurally-created one. This analysis will argue for the salience of both sorts of factors, and in one respect – the internal economic downswing – we will see the degree to which the Cuban rebels did create their own opportunity.

Cuban social structure presents some broad similarities with other patterns in Latin America, along with its own specific differences. The percentage of the population working in agriculture had dropped from forty-nine in 1919 to thirty-nine by 1959. Another 39% worked in the service sector, with 22% in industry (the fourth highest in Latin America at the time). The population of 6.5 million in 1958 was estimated to be 73% "white", 15% "mixed", and 12% "black".[47] At the top of the social structure, Cuba had more millionaires per capita than any other country of Latin America; "more Cadillacs were sold in Havana than any other city in the world in 1954".[48] Their major economic activities included rural landownership, urban real estate, construction, and tourism, often allied with American capital. This elite, however, played little independent economic or political role, caught between American influence and the dictatorial state. The middle classes included Spanish- and Chinese-born merchants, and native-born professionals. Another 11% – 186 000 in 1950 – were employed by the state. Its large overall size (22% of the employed population) was not matched by economic influence, nor, like the elite, by political representation in the weak party system.[49] Cuba's 400 000 unionized workers averaged $1600 or more in income a year, though this varied from $400 for a textile worker to $6000 for an electrical worker. The urban marginal class shaded upwards into the working class, with 250 000 servants, waiters, and "entertainers" in tourism, and downwards into the ranks of the 700 000 unemployed and underemployed.[50] Blacks and mulattoes, up to one-third of the population, were over-represented among the poorest, although racism arguably did not put down deep roots for historical reasons (no plantation economy, the presence of freed slaves).[51] Working women were likewise disproportionately poor: at ten to 15% of the labor force, the largest category was service workers (38% of all women workers), many of them domestics earning $8-25 a month, followed by office workers (20%), factory workers (20%), professionals (17%), and marginal occupations including prostitution.[52] In the rural sector there was a large landless proletariat due to the sugar industry, comprising 500 000 cane cutters and 50 000 mill workers. Small farmers were dependent on the mills to grind the cane and finance the crop.

Evictions in the 1940s and 1950s led to the displacement of many squatters into the cities or remoter hinterlands such as the Sierra Maestre mountains of Oriente province. This poorest, least healthy, and least educated group on the island engaged in the most land conflicts and would prove most receptive to the July 26 Movement's appeals.[53]

Underlying this social structure and shaping its dynamics was an almost textbook case of the process of dependent development. It is not always recognized that Cuba in the 1950s ranked as "one of the four or five most developed nations in Latin America, and the most developed tropical nation in the entire world".[54] Numerous indices of this development, based largely on sugar monoculture and a half-century of ties with American capital, can be found. Per capita income at $400-500 a year (depending on the estimate) was higher than all but Venezuela and Argentina within Latin America. Seventy pounds of meat were consumed annually per person, twice the level of Peru. Industry, which employed 22% of the labor force, had grown by 47% from 1947 to 1958. Cuba ranked fifth or sixth in Latin America in generation of electricity and production of cement, key items for "development". In terms of quality of life indicators, Cuba was second in hospital beds per person to Uruguay, had the lowest death rate in the Western hemisphere, and was fifth in literacy in Latin America.[55] The key to this growth, of course, was sugar: Cuba had been the world's largest producer since the early 1900s, and accounted for more than half the world market in sugar, amounting to 80% of Cuba's exports.[56] The health of the sugar sector determined the pace of development in industry, transport, banking, and trade, and the state of the economy generally.

Behind these positive statistics lay the dependent aspects of Cuban development. The United States had $1 billion invested in Cuba in 1958 (up from $657 million in 1952), second only to its investments in the Venezuelan oil industry and representing one-eighth of all U.S. investments in Latin America. American companies employed 160000 Cubans, owned nine of the ten largest sugar mills (and twelve of the next twenty), produced 40% of the sugar, held one-quarter of all bank deposits, ran the telephone system, refined all oil, and (with the mafia) controlled much of the hotel, gambling, and drug businesses. The U.S. Congress determined how much sugar Cuba could export to the U.S. (around 60% of Cuban output). The U.S. provided 80% of Cuba's imports, at low tariffs. This sweeping control was the legacy of fifty years of expansion following U.S. intervention in the 1895-98 Spanish-Cuban war, control of the party system into the 1920s, and support for Batista's rise in 1934 and 1952.[57]

The internal impact of this dependent development was likewise dramatic. Estimates of income inequality suggest that the poorest 20% got 2-6% of income, the richest 20% taking 55%. In terms of land tenure, the largest 9% of landowners had 62% of the land, while 66% at the bottom had only 7%. In the countryside, as a consequence of land concentration and proletarianization of the labor force, two-thirds of the population lived in thatched huts, 42% were illiterate (versus 12% in the cities), 60% were undernourished (this was 30 to 40% in urban areas). Only 4% of farmworkers ate meat regularly, 2% ate eggs, 11% drank milk. During the "dead season" in the countryside, which could stretch to eight or nine months, "families ate roots and bark to stay alive, hunted locusts, lived in woods, in caves".[58] Unemployment affected one-third of the population at some point during each year, reaching much higher in rural areas.

Holding this political economy together through various means was the state of Fulgencio Batista. The U.S. had blessed and abetted the rise to power of the army sergeant in 1933-34 as an antidote to the radical measures taken by the government of President Ramón Grau San Martín and revolutionary leader Antonio Guiteras. Batista was forced into "voluntary exile" in Florida when Grau surprisingly won the 1944 elections, returned in 1952 to run again, and instead seized power on March 10, 1952 after lagging in the polls. If his first administration had been forced into progressive measures and competitive elections by the tenor of the times, in his second he made sure that he remained firmly in control, partly through the vast patronage and corruption networks open to him, and partly through severe repression of opponents. He surrounded himself with a clique known as "the contractors", who plundered the treasury, public works, national lottery, and other patronage niches. The state, it will be recalled, employed one in nine Cubans; Eric Wolf sees it as a kind of multi-class coalition of its own, extending benefits to many social sectors, including labor.[59] This proved an ineffective substitute for political parties, especially as economic problems recurred, elections were perceived as meaningless, and repression mounted. An estimated 20 000 Cubans died between 1952 and 1959 at the hands of the police, army, intelligence service, Bureau to Repress Communist Activities, and hired thugs. The repression lost the government much legitimacy internally, and eventually would be a factor in weakening U.S. support for the regime, as we shall see. The army, however corrupt and low in morale, proved fairly capable of maintaining order in the cities, but even the most indiscriminate repressive practices failed to deter the small guerrilla movement that arose in 1957.[60] Batista's exclusionary, personalized control had weakened his military and alienated civil society, undermining the bases of his rule.

The precise current of oppositional culture at work in the Cuban revolution included a long history of rebellions, a tradition of nationalism, and the loose, radical amalgam ultimately fashioned by Fidel Castro's July 26 Movement. The first two fed the third. The Ten Years' War against Spain in 1868-78, the three-sided struggle with Spain and the United States from 1895 to 1898, and the failed 1933 revolution were national-level rebellions that cast long political shadows. The black population remembered with pride uprisings in 1812, 1827, 1843, 1879, and 1912, as well as participation in the other battles. The site of many of these movements was Oriente province, whose distinctive political economy was touched on above. The nationalist impulse came across in the anthem of the Ten Years' War (now the Cuban National Hymn): "Do not fear a glorious death, for to die for your country is to live. To live in chains is to live overwhelmed by shame and infamy."[61] The growth of U.S. influence and the seeming inability of Cuban politicians to withstand it made both nationalism and democracy appealing to diverse social strata. These perceptions had grown significantly since 1933, and in part this explains the greater success of the 1950s rebels.

A second major development was the unity ultimately provided by the message of the July 26 Movement. Fidel Castro was early influenced by nineteenth-century revolutionary hero José Martí's nationalism, humanism, and sympathy with the poor, as well as by his idol, Ortodoxo Party leader Eddie Chibas's dramatic suicide while on the air at a radio station in 1951, an event at which he was present. Chibas's death and Batista's coup convinced Castro that more radical forms of struggle were necessary. After the failed attack on the Moncada garrison in 1953, Castro regrouped his forces in Mexico, announcing the formation of the July 26 Movement there in 1955 and proclaiming it

> "...open to all Cubans who sincerely desire to see political democracy reestablished and social justice introduced in Cuba. ... Young and old, men and women, workers and peasants, students and professionals, can join its fighting groups, its youth cadres, its secret workers' cells, its women's organizations, its economic sections, and its underground distribution apparatus throughout the country."[62]

Though its specific positions were often deliberately vague and consciously kept moderate in 1957-58 to attract this diverse social base, it was undoubtedly understood by many Cubans as capable of providing the land reform it openly announced in October 1958, as well as more independence from the United States, and other radical goals.[63] Its ranks contained Marxists and others of more radical inclination than many of the supporting forces in the coalition. The democratic nationalism and populism of student and middle class organizations, such as Frank Pals's Acción Nacional Revolucionaria, was of decisive help. Lesser currents that were also present included Catholic social reformism, various tendencies within the labor movement (and more importantly, the general belief among workers that Batista was a dictator), and, late in the rebellion, the transfer of allegiance of a portion of the Afro-Cuban community and its religious symbols from Batista to Castro.[64]

The world-systemic opening that facilitated the success of the Cuban revolution came before the internal economic downturn. Batista, never particularly popular with the U.S. State Department, was still supported well into his reign as the only force that could hold Cuba together, thereby safeguarding U.S. interests there. From 1955 to 1957 there was still sentiment that he should be encouraged to liberalize the system (good advice, in light of our theory). Lower-level State Department criticisms of the regime's brutality were stifled in February 1957 by Secretary of State John Foster Dulles as problematic on the grounds that they "could be interpreted as US intervention in internal Cuban affairs".[65] By mid-1957 however a perception was growing that Batista was losing legitimacy in Cuba and might have to be abandoned.

The straw that broke the back of American support for the regime came when oppositional naval officers rose against Batista at Cienfuegos on September 5, 1957. Batista used substantial U.S.-supplied Military Assistance Program weaponry to crush the rebellion, in violation of American policy that such material be used only for external, hemispheric defense. The State Department began to back off from overt support for Batista, worried about "serious criticism from Congress and the United States public".[66] By late 1957 there was deep alarm that Batista might lose control of power, and the U.S. wanted to bring him and the (legal) opposition together to hold fair elections. Batista's failure to do this in February and then June 1958 led to cessation of all arms shipments and a studied neutrality in the civil war under way.[67] In the absence of a third alternative to Batista and Castro, U.S. policy floundered: some wanted to see free elections under Batista, others (such as U.S. ambassador Earl Smith) a renewal of arms to him, while others favored a military junta, and still others felt he could not be supported without losing all credibility in Cuba and the United States. Smith cabled in late March 1958: "At this time it would appear to me that we are in the position of a spectator watching the third act of a Greek tragedy."[68] Meanwhile, the July 26 Movement was well-financed by exiled, local, and American sympathizers, with some help from the Venezuelan interim revolutionary government of 1958, although U.S. diplomats saw no conclusive evidence that it was "Communist-inspired or dominated. ... if we had had conclusive information to this effect, our attitude towards the Cuban situation would have been altered considerably".[69] An eleventh-hour attempt to convene Latin American governments in the Organization of American States in December 1958 met with a lukewarm reception around the continent (with the exception of dictatorships in Nicaragua and the Dominican Republic): Latin American public opinion favored Castro and governments wanted no outside intervention.[70] Though American weapons continued to reach Batista through Nicaragua and the Dominican Republic, loss of support from the country with the greatest stake in Cuba crippled his ability to survive in office, providing a world-systemic opening for the July 26 Movement, whose swift final victory took the United States by surprise.

The internal economic downturn in the causality of the Cuban revolution is of special interest due to its timing. The Cuban economy, so dependent on sugar, was closely tied to its price on world markets, output in Cuba, and quotas in the U.S. In the decade leading up to the revolution, 1951 and 1952 were boom years, in part due to high sugar prices during the Korean War. 1953 and 1954 saw downturns in GNP and employment as the war ended; thereafter recovery set in. 1956 – the best year for the economy since 1952 – was not a good moment for Castro to launch a rebellion, and most economic indicators were satisfactory in 1957, at least by Cuban standards.[71] 1958 however started with large losses to tobacco and banana crops due to storms. The progress of the guerilla war thereafter created its own politico-economic dynamic. In the spring of 1958, U.S. losses due to the destruction of the sugar crop by the rebels amounted to $1.5 million. Rail transport began to be interrupted in Oriente province. World conditions now turned unfavorable too, as recession hit the U.S. market and the price of sugar dropped 20%. The failure of the April 1958 general strike provided a temporary pick-up through the summer and Havana, in particular, was kept relatively insulated from the turmoil. In the early fall, though, the economy went into an irreversible free fall as the rebels opened new fronts – industry, mining, sales, transport, and tourism all felt the effects of political disruption. By December, economic activity outside Havana had come to a virtual standstill and the coming sugar harvest was in serious jeopardy. Havana itself was now affected by inflation and unemployment, and tourism collapsed. The U.S. embassy reported: "In effect, Castro is creating a general strike in reverse. By playing havoc with the economic life of the country, he is forcing business and industry to shut down and thus shove workers into the streets."[72] The downturn, in the case of Cuba, was unique in that the sugar economy was vulnerable to political unrest. As rebellion spread this meant that the rebels could in some measure *create* the downturn needed to destabilize the government and enlist the population in a struggle for change. The theoretical implication is that rebels may start an uprising in the absence of an economic downturn, but popular support and success follow only with its eventual presence.

It remains to chronicle the making of the revolution itself. On the events, we may be brief: Castro's forces landed in December 1956 and spent a hard year building strength in Oriente province. In the course of 1958 they achieved growing success against the inefficient army opposing them, and by late in the fall had managed to open other fronts, cutting the island in two. Batista fled precipitously on New Year's Day 1959, leaving the field open to the rebels who secured Havana in early January, bringing his dictatorship to an end.

The more interesting question is who made the Cuban revolution. Most astute observers acknowledge its urban as well as rural component, making it another variant of our multi-class, populist coalition. Josef Gugler maintains that 60 to 80% of the guerrillas were of urban origin, while Wickham-Crowley on the other hand has it the other way around, guessing that the 600 rebel army members of summer 1958 were 50 to 70% peasant, the rest mostly middle class. O. Fernandez Rios puts the social composition of rebel columns at 31-51% workers, 31-39% peasants, and 39-51% "employees".[73] Among the rural population, the squatters of Oriente province provided crucial direct and indirect support, while the sugar proletariat and plains peasants did far less. The July 26 Movement also had a major urban following, especially in Santiago, among workers, the middle classes, and students. Some large landlords and businessmen were supportive, either out of anti-Batista feelings or as insurance in case of a rebel victory. Women were significant, too, both as fighters (about 5% of the rebels) and in urban demonstrations. Blacks, although held by many to have been pro-Batista, were also found in the rebels' ranks by various observers.[74] The Cuban revolution, then, like the Mexican, was made by a substantial multi-class population of aggrieved social forces, and succeeded when internal and external circumstances proved favorable in late 1958. Its roots, we have argued, lay in the dislocations produced by dependent development, an exclusionary state, and the articulation of a unifying culture of resistance.

Nicaragua

The third great social revolution in Latin American history has been the Nicaraguan one. For reasons of space and limited research to date, I will treat this case somewhat more briefly, but in enough detail to sketch in the relevance of the theory to the particulars of the case. Nicaragua, the poorest of the three countries under study here, has traditionally been primarily an exporter of agricultural products – first coffee, then cotton, cattle, and sugar. The Nicaraguan landed elite was economically divided by region and sector, and politically weakened by U.S. intervention from the 1910s to 1930s and then the Somoza dynasty until the revolution. Land concentration in the countryside and the beginnings of industrialization reduced the proportion in agriculture from 60% in 1960 to 44% in 1977. A heterogeneous middle class arose in the professions, state, and service sector (20 to 30% of the economically active), as did a modest-sized working class (16 to 18%), with a low level of unionization. Below them was a desperately poor underclass, often unemployed, and in part composed of landless migrants, many of whom returned to the countryside at harvest time. In the countryside, perhaps 30% of the economically active population were self-sufficient producers and owners, another third had some land but needed outside employment, and the rest worked as wage laborers when they could.[75]

The pattern of dependent development in Nicaragua is less pronounced than in Mexico or Cuba, but a case can still be made for its heuristic utility as a guide to the transformations accounting for the social structure sketched above. The first point to note concerns the sense in which Nicaragua has been *dependent* on outside forces. The U.S. has undoubtedly loomed large in Nicaraguan history, from outright interventions between 1909 and 1933, including prolonged military occupation, to the backing of the Somoza dynasty thereafter. The U.S. created the National Guard that fought Sandino's revolt, and handpicked Anastasio Somoza García to lead it: as F.D.R. is supposed to have said in 1939: "Somoza is an S.O.B. but he is our S.O.B."[76] Subsequent U.S. administrations supported his sons Luis and Anastasio Jr., the latter educated at West Point. U.S. control was primarily political, military, and strategic, rather than economic: the proportion of direct American investment was the lowest in Latin America, the economy was locally owned, and trade went as much to Europe, Japan, and Central America as to the U.S. Still, American multinationals accounted for 76% of all foreign enterprises, to which were added in the 1970s a shadier set of investors in hotels, casinos, and tourism.[77]

The second point to be raised is whether Nicaragua was at any time dynamic enough to be considered a case of *development*, for the country was poor even by Central American standards. The period which may sustain the claim is the 1950s to early 1970s, when agriculture was diversified and commercialized into large-scale cotton exporting as well as cattle, coffee, and sugar. The Somozas and other investment groups took advantage of the Central American Common Market in the 1960s and 1970s to extend the boom into light industries like food-processing, textiles, tobacco, and cement. Overall growth rates rose from good (5.6% annually in the 1950s), to very good (6.7% in the 1960s), with an outstanding 10.7% a year registered between 1960 and 1967. Exports rose 11.5% a year in the 1960s, tripling in volume. Inflation was kept to 1.7% annually in the 1960s. The 1972 earthquake also touched off a final construction boom in 1973-74.[78] On the other hand, this growth exhibited characteristic limits and negative features as well: food imports grew to 60% of exports in the 1970s, the foreign debt rose from $255 million in 1972 to $1 billion by 1978, and land concentrated in the hands of the top 1.5% of landowners who held 41.5% of the land, while 78.2% of rural families had but 17.4%. Per capita income likewise reached $966 in 1977, but this varied from $5409 for the top 5% to $286 for the bottom 50%. Peasants in the interior lost title to ranchers and cotton-growers and worked as a poor, landless proletariat or migrated to the cities to join the ranks of the marginal population there.[79]

The personalistic, exclusionary nature of the repressive Somozan state hardly needs extensive elaboration. The three Somozas controlled politics from 1933 to 1979, with only brief interludes when they governed behind the scenes, as for two months in 1947 and again in 1963-67. The fraudulent nature of elections is suggested by the returns for 1937, won by a vote of 107 000 to 169! In the process the family enriched itself to the point where the last Somoza was worth over $500 million, controlled 25% of agriculture (20 000 square kilometers of land), and as much industrial wealth. If his brother Luis had ruled with a reformist veneer from 1956 to 1967, Anastasio Jr. turned increasingly brutal and corrupt during his tenure. He personified the state in his roles as President, Director of the National Guard, and Supreme Leader of the (Liberal) Party.[80] Repression was the domain of the 7500-member National Guard, particularly its elite divisions. Although the U.S. trained 4119 officers between 1946 and 1973, the Guardia never represented a "professional" army, divided into desperately poor conscripts and the corrupt officers and privileged elite units who ran a good portion of the economy. It lacked training, mobility, and armor as well as morale at the lower levels. In the mid-1970s the Guardia terrorized society, killing at least 3000 peasants between 1974 and 1977. States of siege and censorship made the task easier. Through all this, the U.S. provided $1.8 million a year in military and $17.3 million in economic aid from 1967 to 1975.[81]

Dictatorship and dependence on the U.S. strongly shaped the emergent political cultures of opposition in Nicaragua. Sandino himself in the 1920s provided the aim – opposition to the oligarchy and U.S. domination – and the strategy – guerrilla warfare – later adopted by the revolutionaries. Weber describes the ideals that motivated him as "a form of petty-bourgeois nationalism, tinged with utopian socialist and spiritualist ideology, which grew increasingly radical in the heat of the guerrilla struggle itself".[82] Sandino's ideas and experiences were raised to the status of a national founding myth by the FSLN, created and named for him in 1961. One version of their updated blend of nationalism, socialism, and democracy was formulated by founder Carlos Fonseca from prison in 1964: "In my own thought, I welcome the substance of different ideologies: Marxism, Liberalism and Christian Socialism."[83] Strategically the FSLN evolved from a 1960s' emphasis on *foquismo* to a Vietnamese-style "protracted people's war" in the countryside, to a faction advocating a mass urban movement. In the 1970s, Daniel and Humberto Ortega, among others, favored a third, insurrectional tendency seeking wider alliances and a three-pronged tactic of mass uprising, military offensive, and general strike.

A second stream of oppositional culture flowed out of the liberation theology of the Christian base communities, study groups, and youth clubs that proliferated in the 1970s "to promote spiritual growth and community improvement through social and political action".[84] Both Che and Jesus could symbolize the new human being (and Jesus was "still the most revered example of love and sacrifice among the Christian poor").[85] These groups entered into a strategic alliance with the FSLN, who used the base communities to penetrate the urban barrios, as well as reach peasants and rural wage earners. To these oppositional cultures may be added the sentiments of a large section of the Nicaraguan bourgeoisie, whether motivated by Somoza's grasping monopoly of economic opportunities or his undemocratic hold on power. The best representative of the latter trend is publisher Pedro Joaquín Chamorro, leader of the Democratic Union for Liberation (UDEL), whose assassination by the regime in January 1978 outraged the population and further alienated the Nicaraguan elite from the regime. Nicaragua, in sum, presents probably the clearest case of the strength and efficacy of political cultures of resistance in the making of a multi-class revolutionary opposition.

The beginning of the end for Somoza started with the economic consequences of the December 25, 1972 earthquake, which killed over 10 000 people and destroyed 600 square blocks in Managua. Somoza cordoned off the old downtown, saying Managua would build on firmer ground. The new center had "similar seismological properties", however, but turned out to be on land owned by Somoza, who made enormous speculative profits, in the process alienating the old small business and service sector: "As one banker put it: 'He's violated the rules of the game that his father and brother had always followed'".[86] The Guardia helped itself to the spoils as well, further discrediting its image in the eyes of the people. Though there is some dispute about the precise timing of the economic downturn (Goodwin dates it only in 1978 during the disruption caused by the fighting), there are ample indications that a recession had started to set in by the mid-1970s. Construction boomed in 1973-74 as Managua rebuilt, but slacked off thereafter. Coffee prices rose, but by 1975 a prolonged drought led to a slump that lasted through 1977, compounded by low world prices for cotton, sugar, and meat. Inflation ran at 9.7% annually for 1971-76, then hit 11% in 1977. And, as in Cuba, by the latter stages of the insurrection, in the first half of 1979 the economy entered into crisis, with capital flight of $315 million, inflation skyrocketing to 75%, unemployment reaching 42%, and GDP falling by 25% for the year.[87]

The world-systemic opening that facilitated the Sandinista victory was likewise bound up with the timing of the insurrection itself. The U.S. faced conflicting policy imperatives in the wake of its defeat in Vietnam: on one hand there seemed to be a greater need than ever for regional allies to do the frontline work in containing communism; on the other, less trust was placed in authoritarian regimes as viable for that role. Jimmy Carter sought to make human rights abuses in Nicaragua *the* showcase for his new foreign policy, in part, perhaps, because in 1977 the FSLN still posed no serious threat (Israel, in any case, stepped in to provide up to 98% of Nicaragua's arms in the 1970s). Carter thereafter followed a confused policy of rebuke and support, complicated by bureaucratic cross-currents and compromise, as in Iran.[88] In January 1978, Somoza arranged the assassination of *La Prensa* editor Pedro Joaquín Chamorro. The U.S. put further restrictions on economic and military aid, and the Nicaraguan elite turned against Somoza, reasoning that no one was safe any more and resenting his heavy-handed economic competition. In August the FSLN staged a widely publicized taking of the National Palace, obtaining $5 million in ransoms for their 500 hostages, and the release of eighty-two prisoners, including founder Tomás Borge. U.S. concern to support Somoza now mounted: by November the middle class and elite Broad Opposition Front (FAO) had split up over American interference in its affairs, gradually losing credibility among the public as the FSLN's star rose and Somoza remained intransigent.

When the crisis deepened in early 1979, the U.S. found itself with minimal leverage, preoccupied with an even more traumatic revolution in Iran and in conflict with key Latin American states like Panama (over the canal) and Mexico and Venezuela (over the oil-induced recession). The Sandinistas meanwhile received material and logistic support from Costa Rica and Venezuela. On May 14, 1979 the IMF, with U.S. backing, incredibly granted Somoza a $65 million loan; Costa Rica, Panama, and Mexico lobbied against Somoza, Mexico breaking relations May 20. On May 28 the five Andean Pact presidents condemned Somoza and on June 16 they recognized the belligerent status of the FSLN. In June and July the final offensive moved to its costly victory (50 000 people – 2% of the population – were killed and material damage came to $1.3 billion). On June 24 the OAS rejected a U.S. proposal to send a peace-keeping force to Nicaragua, demanding Somoza's resignation instead. At the very end, the U.S. called for the expansion of the new governing junta by appointment of a general of the Guardia and a friend of Somoza's. The Sandinistas were now in a position to say no, with strong international backing and no credible alternative for the U.S. to support.[89] 1978-79 had proven an open world-systemic window of opportunity for their cause.

It remains to ask what social forces, precisely, made the Nicaraguan revolution. The FSLN itself numbered barely 200 members in 1977 and 500 when they entered Managua on July 19, 1979. Thousands more were active in its various organizations and tens of thousands fought Somoza spontaneously, recognizing Sandinista political authority. The identities of these concentric levels of participation varied somewhat. Roxborough, based on Carlos Vilas, finds that the "social composition of the revolutionaries" (presumably actual FSLN members) was 29% students (31% in the leadership), 22% artisans (17% in the leadership), 16% workers (18% in the leadership), 16% white collar (6% in the leadership), 7% professionals (17% in the leadership), 5% small traders (8% in the leadership), and only 5% peasants (13% in the leadership).[90] Farhi characterizes the FSLN army as consisting "largely [of] university dropouts".[91] Black maintains that "the core of the insurrection in each town was in the *barrios* of the working class and the migrant rural population".[92] Wickham-Crowley disputes the first part of this, and following Jeffery Paige places emphasis on marginal peasant squatters in the countryside and displaced rural migrants in the towns.[93] Goodwin judiciously notes three social bases: 1) peasants in north-central regions affected by the land enclosures of cattle ranchers, 2) rural workers on the Pacific coast, and 3) "a variety of petty producers and unsalaried workers in the cities – artisans, food vendors, carpenters, shoemakers, and the like".[94] He notes that supporting organizations also included student and labor groups, teachers, left-wing parties, and women's groups, to which we may add in the end the business organizations that joined the May-June general strike. Women made up an estimated 25 to 30% of the guerrilla columns' ranks.[95] There were also important spontaneous uprisings by indigenous communities in Monimbo (a suburb of Masaya) and Subtiava (part of León).[96] The Nicaraguan revolution, in sum, represented a third national multi-class coalition of social forces created or adversely impacted by dependent development from the 1950s to the 1970s, unified by Sandinista values and leadership into a broad-based opposition to the Somoza dictatorship.

Conclusions

We may conclude this long exercise with a short assessment. Diagram two summarizes the main findings for our three cases, adding in Iran as a fourth, non-Latin American instance of successful social revolution in the Third World, and El Salvador as a contrasting case of failed revolution.[97]

The successful cases all exhibit the combination of factors enumerated earlier as conducive to the success of social revolutions in the Third World: the structural features of growth and negative repercussions associated with dependent development and repressive, personalistic exclusionary states; the articulation and elaboration of multiple political cultures of opposition to these processes which unite people around basic demands for change; and the favorable context provided by the dual conjuncture of an internal economic downswing and a world-systemic opening. El Salvador exhibits some of these factors, but differs (for reasons beyond the scope of this essay) in some key ways, including a nonpersonalistic, less exclusionary state; a more narrowly Marxist oppositional culture; strong outside intervention; and a durable, painfully stable economic crisis. The result there has been prolonged stalemate on the battlefields and a recently negotiated end to hostilities, rather than a social revolution (though this is not a total defeat for the rebels either).

Many questions remain for further inquiry into the issues raised by the theory and case studies analyzed here. One key finding has been the variable timing and phases provided by the dual crisis: in Mexico, economic downturn preceded the outbreak of revolution more clearly than in Cuba, with Nicaragua somewhere in between. The world-systemic opening likewise deserves closer attention in this regard. The large question of the

DIAGRAM 2

	Social Structure	State and Elite	Political Cultures	Conjunctural Factors	Outcome
Mexico	Adversely impacted and diversified by dependent development	Diaz' Bread and Stick dictatorship / some elite conflict	Multiple oppositions	U.S. inaction 1910-12 and WWI / Deep recession 1907-1908	Broad-based coalition – Complex struggles
Cuba	Adversely impacted and shaped by dependent development	Batista's dictatorship/ some elite conflict	Multiple oppositions	U.S. non-support 1958/ economic decline 1950s	Broad-based coalition – Success
Nicaragua	Adversely impacted and diversified by dependent development	Somoza's repression/ elite conflict	Multiple oppositions	Carter human rights policy / Post-earthquake crisis, 1972-78	Broad-based coalition – Success
Iran	Adversely impacted and diversified by dependent development	Repressive Shah/ weak elite	Multiple oppositions	Carter human rights policy / End of oil boom, 1976-78	Broad-based coalition – Success
El Salvador	Internally divided by more classical underdevelopment	Repressive army rule with broad elite support	Guerrilla struggles	Carter-Reagan intervention / "Stable" crisis, 1970s-1980s	Prolonged civil war/ economic crisis – Negotiated settlement

exact mechanisms that lead dependent development to undermine political stability needs more work as well; one insight of the present comparison is that its combination with an exclusionary, personalistic state is particularly dangerous in the long run. The precise measure of this complex, holistic process too needs refinement. Finally, I have only been able to sketch lightly here the political cultures of opposition that connected large-scale structural processes and human actors in the making of these revolutions – much more remains to be done in this area. The present essay thus represents an initial stock-taking of a much vaster project, one which will attempt to bridge the gap a little further between theoretical elaboration and empirical research in the sociology of revolution.

NOTES

1 Theda Skocpol, *States and Social Revolutions. A Comparative Analysis of France, Russia, and China* (Cambridge: Cambridge University Press, 1979).

2 John Walton, *Reluctant Rebels. Comparative Studies of Revolution and Underdevelopment* (New York: Columbia University Press, 1984).

3 Farideh Farhi, "State Disintegration and Urban-Based Revolutionary Crisis: A Comparative Analysis of Iran and Nicaragua," pp. 231-256 in *Comparative Political Studies*, volume 21, number 2 (July 1988), and *States and Urban-Based Revolutions. Iran and Nicaragua* (Urbana and Chicago: University of Illinois Press, 1990).

4 Ian Roxborough, "Theories of Revolution: The Evidence from Latin America," pp. 99-121 in *LSE Quarterly*, volume 3, number 2 (Summer 1989), and "Exogenous Factors in the Genesis of Revolution in Latin America," a paper presented to the Latin American Studies Association, Miami (December 1989).

5 Timothy P. Wickham-Crowley, "Winners, Losers, and Also-Rans: Toward a Comparative Sociology of Latin American Guerrilla Movements," pp. 132-181 in Susan Eckstein, editor, *Power and Popular Protest. Latin American Social Movements* (Berkeley, Los Angeles and London: University of California Press, 1989); "A Qualitative Comparative Approach to Latin American Revolutions," pp. 82-109 in *International Journal of Comparative Sociology*, volume XXXII,

numbers 1-2 (1991); and *Guerrillas and Revolution in Latin America. A Comparative Study of Insurgents and Regimes since 1956* (Princeton: Princeton University Press, 1992).

6 Walton, op. cit., 161. Elsewhere, he describes his approach as a combination of theses on peasant revolts, world-system theory, Tilly's theory of multiple sovereignty, and analysis of the state: ibid., 21. Somewhere between these two formulations lies his own theory, never quite explicitly articulated in any capsule fashion.

7 Farhi, 1988 op. 1990 op. cit., 9-10.

8 Wickham-Crowley, "A Qualitative Comparative Approach," 82, abstract. See also *Guerillas and Revolution*, 318.

9 Farhi does note "the coincidence of internal crisis with a permissive world context" in both Iran and Nicaragua, but this is more an *ad hoc* part of her explanation of the cases than part of a formal model or theory.

10 I would like to register my debt to these rich analyses, and apologize for the necessarily schematic treatment they receive here. I have written more extensive - but still too brief - evaluations and critiques of the literature in two review essays: "Theories of Revolution Revisited: Toward a Fourth Generation?" *Sociological Theory*, volume 11, number 1 (Spring 1993), and "Revolutionizing Theory / Theorizing Revolutions: State, Culture, and Society in Recent Works on Revolution," *Contention* (1992).

11 On Iran, see John Foran, *Fragile Resistance. Social Transformation in Iran from 1500 to the Revolution* (Boulder: Westview Press, 1993). For a preliminary elaboration of the theory, see John Foran, "A Theory of Third World Social Revolutions: Iran, Nicaragua and El Salvador Compared," a paper presented to the International Sociological Association, Madrid, Spain (July 1990).

12 The key work in the literature on dependent development is Fernando Henrique Cardoso and Enzo Faletto, *Dependency and Development in Latin America* (Berkeley: University of California Press, 1979). Also important is Peter Evans, *Dependent Development. The Alliance of Multinational, State, and Local Capital in Brazil* (Princeton: Princeton University Press, 1979).

13 Roxborough perceptively suggests that these include political, investment, mono-export, and financial dependency: "Theories of Revolution," 111. I think others may be possible, and that while it is useful to disaggregate the procrustean concept of dependency, it is also important not to lose sight of its holistic context, as a process with multiple effects.

14 Robert H. Dix may have pioneered this insight in "Why Revolutions Succeed and Fail," pp. 423-446 in *Polity*, volume XVI, number 3 (Summer 1984). It has been developed further by Jeff Goodwin and Theda Skocpol, "Explaining Revolutions in the Contemporary Third World," pp. 489-509 in *Politics and Society*, volume 17, number 4

(December 1989), and Richard Snyder, "Explaining Transitions from Neopatrimonial Dictatorships," pp. 379-399 in *Comparative Politics*, volume 24, number 4 (July 1992). The terminology used to designate such states varies from "exclusionary personalism" to "neopatrimonial" "sultanistic", "autonomous personalist", and finally, Wickham-Crowley's evocative "mafiacracies". All denote roughly the same sort of regime.

15 My thinking on this topic has been influenced by A. Sivanandan, "Imperialism in the Silicon Age," pp. 24-42 in *Monthly Review*, volume 32, number 3 (July-August 1980), (first published in *Race and Class*, Autumn 1979). Of the authors already cited, Farideh Farhi is most sensitive to this dimension of social movements.

16 The question of the timing of this crisis remains an open one: must it precede the outbreak of revolt, or is it simply the factor whose appearance later seals the victory of the rebels? The suggestion that the latter is the case was made by an undergraduate student of mine, Markus McMillin, in an honors thesis on Algeria, and is further strengthened by consideration of the case of Cuba, below.

17 This factor in the making of revolutions has a pedigree going back at least to Alexis de Tocqueville, *The Old Regime and the French Revolution* (Garden City, New York: Doubleday and Company, Inc. 1955 [1856]). It was elevated to a single key factor by James C. Davies, "Toward a Theory of Revolution," pp. 5-19 in *American Sociological Review*, volume 27 (1962), and is noted also by Walton, *Reluctant Rebels*, 152.

18 Walter L. Goldfrank, "Theories of Revolution and Revolution Without Theory: The Case of Mexico," pp. 135-165 in *Theory and Society*, volume 7 (1979).

19 I am aware that other cases such as Bolivia in 1952 might arguably be found, and also that outcomes in Mexico and Nicaragua were far from clear-cut successes, in retrospect. But the three cases chosen for analysis possess the criteria of mass participation, with deep political and economic change that Skocpol proposes for a major, or "social" revolution. I am working on a full-fledged test of this theory, to include the non-Latin American case of Iran, as well as failed or reversed revolutions in El Salvador, Chile, and elsewhere. What follows is a first approximation of this theory to data - admittedly uneven - from the three Latin American cases.

20 For a sampler of the variety of views on the revolution, see Walter Goldfrank, "World System, State Structure, and the Onset of the Mexican Revolution," pp. 417-439 in *Politics and Society*, volume 5, number 4 (Fall 1975), 417. The interruption thesis is argued forcefully by Adolfo Gilly, *La revolución interrumpida,* (Mexico City: El Caballito, 1971).

21 Goldfrank, "World System, State Structure," 417-18.
22 Alan Knight, *The Mexican Revolution*, volume 1, *Porfirians, Liberals and Peasants* (Cambridge: Cambridge University Press, 1986), 3. See also Charles C. Cumberland, *Mexican Revolution. Genesis under Madero* (Austin: University of Texas Press, 1952), (hereafter referred to as *Mexican Revolution,* I), 4-6.
23 Eduardo Galeano, *Memories of Fire*, volume 111, *Century of the Wind* (New York: Pantheon Books, 1988), 23.
24 Knight, *The Mexican Revolution,* 79, citing *Mexican Year Book* (Los Angeles, 1922), 340-44.
25 ibid., 23.
26 John Mason Hart, *Revolutionary Mexico. The Coming and Process of the Mexican Revolution* (Berkeley and Los Angeles: University of California Press, 1987),131-34, 161.
27 Friedrich Katz, *The Secret War in Mexico. Europe, the United States and the Mexican Revolution* (Chicago and London: University of Chicago Press, 1981), 27.
28 John Womack, "Economy During the Revolution, 1910-1920: Historiography & Analysis," pp. 80-123 in *Marxist Perspectives,* volume 1, number 4 (December 1978), 94 table 1.
29 Hart, *Revolutionary Mexico,* 92.
30 Goldfrank, "World System, State Structure," 431.
31 On U.S. interests in Mexico, see Anita Brenner, *The Wind that Swept Mexico. The History of the Mexican Revolution 1910-1942* (Austin and London: University of Texas Press [1943],1971), 17; Charles C. Cumberland, *Mexican Revolution. The Constitutionalist Years* (Austin: University of Texas Press, 1972), 244 (hereafter cited as *Mexican Revolution,* II); Hart, *Revolutionary Mexico,* 47-50, 133; and Goldfrank, "World System, State Structure," 421 note 9.
32 Knight, *The Mexican Revolution,* 93-97. The classic study of these processes in Morelos is John Womack, Jr., *Zapata and the Mexican Revolution* (New York: Alfred A. Knopf, 1969).
33 Cumberland, *Mexican Revolution,* 11, 15; Hart, *Revolutionary Mexico,* 55.
34 Knight, *The Mexican Revolution,* 30. On the Porfirian state, see ibid., 15ff.; Cumberland, *Mexican Revolution,* I, 7-8; Goldfrank, "World System, State Structure," 427-428; Hart, *Revolutionary Mexico,* 176; and John Womack, Jr., "The Mexican Revolution, 1910-1920," pp. 79-153 in Leslie Bethell, editor, *The Cambridge History of Latin America,* volume V, c. *1870 to 1930* (Cambridge: Cambridge University Press, 1986), 83.

35 The classic studies of Mexican anarchism are John M. Hart, *Anarchism and the Mexican Working Class, 1860-1931* (Austin: University of Texas Press, 1978), and James D. Cockcroft, *Intellectual Precursors of the Mexican Revolution, 1900-1913* (Austin and London: University of Texas Press, 1968). I have drawn here on Hart, *Revolutionary Mexico*, 56-62, 91-94; Knight, *The Mexican Revolution*, 45-47; and Goldfrank, "World System, State Structure," 432.

36 Knight, *The Mexican Revolution*, 122. See also ibid., 113-27, 155-63, and Hart, *Revolutionary Mexico*, 28, 45.

37 ibid., 48.

38 Knight, *The Mexican Revolution*, 413. On Madero's ideas, see ibid., 55-56; Cumberland, *Mexican Revolution*, I, 30-46; and Katz, *The Secret War*, 41-42.

39 On these crises, see Hart, *Revolutionary Mexico*, 140, 145.

40 Data on the 1907-10 downturn is drawn from ibid., 163-68, 172-74; Cumberland, *Mexican Revolution*, 12-14; Goldfrank, "World System, State Structure," 434; and Knight, *The Mexican Revolution*, 93-94, 134-35.

41 Knight, *The Mexican Revolution*, 65. See also ibid., 130, 182, 206, 211.

42 On the U.S. and Díaz, see Goldfrank, "World System, State Structure," 433, 435; Hart, *Revolutionary Mexico*, 247-49; and Womack, "The Mexican Revolution," 84.

43 Hart, *Revolutionary Mexico*, 240-47; Katz, *The Secret War*, 39.

44 Cumberland, *Mexican Revolution*, I, 127-41. For a dissenting view arguing the insignificance of the U.S. in the events, see Knight, *The Mexican Revolution*, I, 184-86. *Non-action* is an important kind of world-systemic opening, however, when one has the power to do more to support an ally under siege.

45 The events are chronicled by Cumberland, *Mexican Revolution*, I, 119-50.

46 Knight, *The Mexican Revolution*, 335. To construct a picture of the social bases of 1911, I have drawn on ibid., 30, 60-63, 132-33, 175-78, 192-97, 223-27, 352, 426; and Hart, *Revolutionary Mexico*, 49.

47 These data are drawn variously from Susan Eckstein, "Restratification After Revolution: The Cuban Experience," pp. 217-240 in Richard Tardanico, editor, *Crises in the Caribbean Basin*, volume 9 of the *Political Economy of the World-System Annuals* (Beverly Hills: Sage, 1987), 228 table 9.2; Carmelo Mesa-Lago, "Revolutionary Economic Policies in Cuba," in Philip Brenner and William M. LeoGrande, editors, *The Cuba Reader. The Making of a Revolutionary Society* (New York: Grove Press, 1985), 64-65; and U.S. National Archives,

737.00/7-1758, State Department, "Cuba" (June 1958), (hereafter I will cite these archives as USNA).

48 Medea Benjamin, Joseph Collins, and Michael Scott, *No Free Lunch. Food & Revolution in Cuba Today* (New York and San Francisco: Food First and Grove Press, 1986), 5. On the elite see also Eric R. Wolf, *Peasant Wars of the Twentieth Century* (New York: Harper Colophon Books, 1969), 260.

49 Wolf, *Peasant Wars*, 261; Wickham-Crowley, *Guerrillas and Revolution*, 161-62.

50 Wolf, *Peasant Wars*, 261-62; Benjamin et al., *No Free Lunch*, 4-5.

51 Frank J. Taylor, "Revolution, Race, and Some Aspects of Foreign Relations in Cuba Since 1959," pp. 19-41 in *Cuban Studies*, volume 18 (1988), 22; Wolf, *Peasants Wars*, 252-54; Terence Cannon, *Revolutionary Cuba* (New York: Thomas Y. Crowell, 1981), 113.

52 Benjamin et al., *No Free Lunch*, 4; Johnetta B. Cole, "Women in Cuba: The Revolution Within the Revolution," pp. 307-317 in Jack Goldstone, editor, *Revolutions: Theoretical, Comparative, and Historical Studies* (San Diego: Harcourt, Brace, Jovanovich, 1986), 308-9; Republica de Cuba, Consejo Nacional de Economía, "Empleo y Desempleo en la fuerza trabajadora Agosto 1958," Informe Tecnico, Number 8 (Havana, 1958), 2 table 2.

53 Wolf, *Peasant Wars*, 256-57; Wickham-Crowley, *Guerrillas and Revolution*, 97, 132, 141.

54 Wickham-Crowley, *Guerrillas and Revolution*, 166.

55 Many of these data can be found in Benjamin et al., *No Free Lunch*, 1. See also Edward Gonzalez, *Cuba Under Castro: The Limits of Charisma* (Boston: Houghton Mifflin Company, 1974), 18; Mesa-Lago, "Revolutionary Economic Policies," 66; USNA, 837.00/2-2158, Foreign Service Despatch 673, Price, Havana, to State Department (February 21,1958); and 837.00/3-2058, Foreign Service Despatch 749, Gilmore, Havana, to State Department (March 20, 1958).

56 Benjamin et al., *No Free Lunch*, 9.

57 On U.S. interests in Cuba, see ibid., 10-11; *Foreign Relations of the United States, 1955-1957*, volume VI, *American Republics: Multilateral; Mexico; Caribbean* (Washington, D.C.: United States Government Printing Office, 1987), 870; Gonzalez, *Cuba Under Castro*, 18, 31; and Wolf, *Peasant Wars*, 256.

58 Cannon, *Revolutionary Cuba*, 41. Data in this paragraph are also drawn from Benjamin et al., *No Free Lunch*, 2-6, 12; USNA, 837.00/2-1056, Foreign Service Despatch 560, Boonstra, Havana, to State Department (February 10,1956); and 837.00/7-1356, Foreign Service Despatch 28, Price, Havana, to State Department (July 13, 1956).

59 Wolf, *Peasant Wars*, 265. On the evolution and corruption of the state, see Cannon, *Revolutionary Cuba*, 43-58; USNA, 737.00/2-1058, Foreign Service Despatch 615, Daniel Braddock, Havana, to State Department (February 10, 1958); 737.00/8-758, Memorandum of Conversation, Leonhardy, with Dr. Ioaquin Meyer, State Department (August 7, 1958); and Benjamin Keen and Mark Wasserman, *A Short History of Latin America* (Boston: Houghton Mifflin, 1988), 441-42.

60 On the repressive forces, see Cannon, *Revolutionary Cuba*, 109; Wickham-Crowley, *Guerrillas and Revolution*, 171-73; and USNA, 737.00/5-1958, Foreign Service Despatch 97, Paul Wollam, Santiago de Cuba, to State Department (19 May, 1958).

61 Quoted in Cannon, *Revolutionary Cuba*, 23. This paragraph also draws on Wickham-Crowley, "Winners, Losers, and Also-Rans," 154; idem, *Guerrillas and Revolution*, 132; Roxborough, "Exogenous Factors," 9; and Noelle Harrison, "Cuba: Making Sense of a Revolution," unpublished paper, Department of Sociology, University of California, Santa Barbara (Fall 1990),16-18.

62 Quoted in Cannon, *Revolutionary Cuba*, 67.

63 On Castro's views and the July 26 Movement's positions, see ibid., 54-57, 97; USNA, 737.00/8-458, Foreign Service Despatch 5, Park Wollam, Santiago de Cuba, to State Department (August 4, 1958), 11; "Ideario Económico del Veinte y Seis de Julio," found in USNA, 837.00/3-959, Foreign Service Despatch 982, Gilmore, Havana, to State Department (March 9, 1959); and Wickham-Crowley, *Guerrillas and Revolution*, 176-78.

64 Wickham-Crowley, "Winners, Losers, and Also-Rans," 164; idem, *Guerrillas and Revolution*, 38; USNA, 837.06/12-3055, Foreign Service Despatch 466, J. de Zangotita, Havana, to State Department (December 30, 1955); and 837.06/101457, Foreign Service Despatch 309, John F. Correll, Havana, to State Department.

65 Dulles is quoted in *Foreign Relations of the United States*, 841 note 3. See also ibid., 797-98, 799.

66 Ibid., 854. See also 845-46, 865 note 1, 869.

67 Countless State Department documents on Cuba make reference to the U.S. policy of non-intervention in the affairs of other countries. On the other hand, dozens of documents from 1957 and 1958 have been removed from the files.

68 USNA, 737.00/3-3058, Telegram 613, from Smith, Havana, to Secretary of State (March 30, 1958). For support of elections, see USNA, 737.00/9-2658, Foreign Service Despatch 320, Braddock, Havana, to State Department (September 26, 1958); for arms renewal, 737.00/7-1658, Telegram 79, Smith, Havana, to Secretary of State (July 16, 1958), and 737.00/10-2158, Telegram 386, Smith, Havana, to Secretary of State (October 21, 1958); for guarded intimations of support

for a military coup, 737.00/8-758, William G. Bowdler, Political Officer, Havana, Memorandum of Conversation with Sr. Vasco T. L. Da Cunha, Brazilian ambassador to Cuba (Confidential), (August 7, 1958); and for State Department doubts about continued support, 737.00/7-2458, Office Memorandum from C. A. Stewart to Mr. Snow (Secret), (July 24, 1958).

69 USNA, 737.00/10-3158, Memorandum of Conversation between Mr. Rubottom and U.S. businessmen, State Department (October 31,1958). On aid to the rebels, see Wickham-Crowley, *Guerrillas and Revolution,* 87.

70 See State Department correspondence in USNA for December 1958.

71 The details in this paragraph are based on a reading of numerous State Department economic reports found in the National Archives.

72 USNA, 837.06/12-458, Foreign Service Despatch 591, J. F. Correll, Havana, to State Department (December 4, 1958).

73 Josef Gugler, "The Urban Character of Contemporary Revolutions," pp. 399-412 in Josef Gugler, editor, *The Urbanization of the Third World* (Oxford: Oxford University Press, 1988); Wickham-Crowley, *Guerrillas and Revolution,* 26; O. Fernandez Rios, "El Ejército Rebelde y la dictadura democratico-revolucionaria de las masas populares," in *Revista Cubana de Ciencias Sociales* (1985), cited by Roxborough, "Theories of Revolution," 107 table 1.

74 Scattered data on the participation of all these social sectors is found in the U.S. National Archives.

75 This sketch of social structure draws on Edelberto Torres Rivas, "El Estado contra la sociedad: Las raíces de la revolución nicaraguense," pp. 113-143 in his *Crisis del Poder en Centroamerica* (Costa Rica: Editorial Universitaria Centroamericana, 1981), 115-16; Henri Weber, *Nicaragua: The Sandinist Revolution,* translated by Patrick Camiller (London: Verso, 1981), 28-29, 28 table 3; George Black, *Triumph of the People. The Sandinista Revolution in Nicaragua* (London: Zed Press, 1981), 70; Farhi, "State Disintegration," 235, 240; and idem, *States and Urban-Based Revolutions,* 73-74.

76 Quoted in Keen and Wasserman, *A Short History of Latin America,* 479. See also ibid., 476ff., and Torres Rivas, "El Estado," 142 note 5.

77 Weber, *Nicaragua,* 34, 34 note 11; Black, *Triumph of the People,* 37, 39, 41.

78 On the boom, see Farhi, *States and Urban-Based Revolutions,* 39; Weber, *Nicaragua,* 17, 24, 38; and Black, *Triumph of the People,* 62.

79 Weber, *Nicaragua,* 27, 27 table 2; Wickham-Crowley, *Guerrillas and Revolution,* 241-42.

80 Torres Rivas, "El Estado," 127 (for the 1937 election results), 139-40; Keen and Wasserman, *A Short History of Latin America,* 476-79;

Weber, *Nicaragua*, 17; Black, *Triumph of the People*, 43; Farhi, "State Disintegration," 235, 235 note 3.

81 Weber, *Nicaragua*, 32; Farhi, *States and Social Revolutions*, 58-59 note 22, 33-34, 46; Wickham-Crowley, *Guerrillas and Revolution*, 268-69; Black, *Triumph of the People*, 52; Jeff Goodwin, "Revolutionary Movements in Central America: A Comparative Analysis," Center for Research on Politics and Social Organization, Working Paper Series, Department of Sociology, Harvard University (1985), 21.

82 Weber, *Nicaragua*, 12.

83 Carlos Fonseca, *Desde la cárcel Yo Acuso a la Dictadura* (Managua: Carcel de la Aviación, July 8,1964), quoted by Black, *Triumph of the People*, 90.

84 Farhi, "State Disintegration," 247.

85 Farhi, *States and Urban-Based Revolutions*, 100. See further ibid., 81 note 43.

86 Dix, "Why Revolutions Succeed and Fail," 437 note 28, quoting Stephen Kinzer, "Nicaragua: Universal Revolt," in *The Atlantic Monthly* (February 1979), 12. See also Walton, *Reluctant Rebels*, 168 (on seismological properties); Farhi, *States and Urban-Based Revolutions*, 41; Roxborough, "Exogenous Factors," 10; and Black, *Triumph of the People*, 66.

87 Goodwin, "Revolutionary Movements," 11; Weber, *Nicaragua*, 38-42; Black, *Triumph of the People*, 67.

88 On U.S. policy see Farhi, "State Disintegration," 241-44, 254 note 9, and idem, *States and Urban-Based Revolutions*, 48-49. On Israel, Black, *Triumph of the People*, 56.

89 Weber, *Nicaragua*, 36-37, 47-48.

90 Roxborough, "Theories of Revolution," 109 table 2, based on Carlos Vilas, *Perfiles de la Revolución Sandinista* (Havana: Casa de las Americas, 1984), 176-78.

91 Farhi, "State Disintegration," 254 note 10.

92 Black, *Triumph of the People*, 134.

93 Wickham-Crowley, *Guerrillas and Revolution*, 209-210, 232-35, 275.

94 Goodwin, "Revolutionary Movements," 26. See also ibid., 30.

95 Weber, *Nicaragua*, 51; Wickham-Crowley, *Guerrillas and Revolution*, 215.

96 Wickham-Crowley, *Guerrillas and Revolution*, 214.

97 I discuss these last two cases in some detail in "A Theory of Third World Social Revolutions".

10 MEXICO'S UNSOLVED CRISIS

Hanspeter Stamm[1]

The Neglected Social and Political Dimensions of the Mexican Crisis

In August 1982, Mexico was everywhere in the headlines. The Mexican State, one of the largest Third World debtors, had surprisingly become insolvent and asked its foreign creditors for bridging loans, periods of grace and renegotiations of debt. This insolvency marked a turning point, not only for Mexico but for the whole world economy. The credit boom of the 1970s ended abruptly, to be succeeded by the debt crisis, with its drawn-out debt renegotiations, macro-economic adjustment programs and deep recession in the debtor countries.

Almost exactly ten years later, in the spring and summer of 1992, Mexico again hit the headlines. This time, however, the tone was optimistic: in connection with the signing of a treaty to create a common market with the United States and Canada (NAFTA) the improvement of Mexico's economic situation was emphasised. The country, it was judged, had overcome its crisis and would, thanks to the common market, at last find its way to stable

---

This forms part of the findings of the research project "Effects of Debt Problems on the Social and Political Conditions of Semi-peripheral Societies: A Case Study of Mexico 1982-88" funded by the World Society Foundation. Hanspeter Stamm took his Ph.D. from the University of Zurich and is senior staff member in Bornschier's research team at the University of Zurich. Address: Sociological Institute of the University of Zurich, Rämistrasse 69, CH-8001 Zurich.

growth. And in fact, from the end of the 1980s, the success of the economic efforts of the Mexican government became evident. Not only had foreign debt been substantially reduced but investment and growth rates exhibited clear upward trends while flight capital began to return from abroad and the balance-of-payments improved markedly.

The reverse side of the medal was not frequently mentioned in reports, for in the 1980s unemployment rose sharply while real wages were cut in half. In keeping with shrinking opportunities for making a living the slum belts around large cities extended and it became increasingly difficult for the public sector to carry out infrastructural and social programs to ease mass misery, in view of shrinking financial and personell resources. Most Mexicans are worse off today than they were a few years ago, despite economic recovery, and many question whether the economic upswing will make any difference to their precarious situations. For them, the 1980s with its developmental setbacks is really a "lost decade" which cannot easily be made good. Further, Mexico's political system is unstable. Despite widespread criticism the exercise of power remains strongly authoritarian. There is hardly an observer who does not believe that Carlos Salinas de Gortari only came to office in 1988 with the help of massive electoral fraud, yet real alternatives to the existing power structure are still lacking. Mexico's social and political situation has hardly dimmed the joy of those dazzled by economic growth and the prospects of investments under NAFTA. Where any attention at all is paid to non-economic problems optimistic assessments mostly prevail. In keeping with the reasoning popularized by modernisation theorists and neo-liberal thinkers that economic growth automatically improves standards of living it is submitted that the economic upswing is bound, in good time, to improve the lot of the masses. In this view, the setbacks of the 1980s represent an adjustment of economic and social conditions to reality. The decade, in this perspective, was not so much "lost" than it was a phase of cleaning up and removing structural problems and dubious developmental trends, current mass misery being the necessary sacrifice to attain health.

Here, it is proposed to question these positive assessments of the situation by reference to Mexico's social and political crisis. In this context, in opposition to modernisation theory and neoclassical economic thought, our point of departure is to be that economic success does not occur spontaneously but is conditional on cultural, socio-structural and political circumstances, which it also influences. Should this assumption prove true then it should be possible to show that the prevailing interpretation of the crisis as purely a debt and economic one is inadequate, and that the chosen strategy incurs excessive social costs by neglecting non-economic dimensions.

Such a demonstration, however, goes beyond our framework here. In what follows, therefore, only certain aspects of the social and political crisis are to be illustrated to show that a more cautious approach to the current situation is called for. On the basis of a few theoretical remarks about the links between economy and society and a historical summary of the development of Mexican society the long-term and general nature of the crisis of the 1980s is to be illuminated. Against this background we shall discuss under which political conditions the economic interpretation of the crisis and the solutions derived therefrom might be successfully carried through. This points to conflicts and changes in the political system which, like the social impacts of the crisis, are to be sketched out. All of which is to show that the crisis strategy occasions excessively high social and political costs which may well dim Mexico's prospects.

The Social Background to Economic Development

Though the assumption that there exists a systemic connection between economic, social and political elements is hardly new and has rarely been fundamentally challenged there is no agreement on how the different elements interact concretely. Yet the conception of how the linkage functions governs which situations are perceived as crises at all, which measures are adopted and how they work out.

The domination of neoclassical economic explanations for the Mexican crisis of the 1980s is striking. These are based on the idea that the economy is a relatively autonomous system which stands in a rather one-sided relation to the "rest" of society. In this perspective, economic behavior provides the bases for material welfare and functions largely independently of the social framework. Apart from references to democratic conditions and legal guarantees for business and investors as bases for a functioning market, the social background to economic behavior is hardly ever discussed in any detail, or assimilated in reductionist fashion to the rational behavior of "homo oeconomicus". The poor performance of markets is, in this perspective, blamed on backwardness, willful interventions or regulatory interferences by the State. Under crisis conditions, therefore, the freeing of the market from external constraints is required on the assumption that performing markets are automatically accompanied by improvements in general welfare.

Sociological and historical approaches, by way of contrast, underline the role of non-economic factors in economic development.[2] As part of a radical critique of the structurally inadequate economic perspective, the conflictual interrelations of historical, socio-structural, cultural, political and economic conditions, and the importance of distributional and power struggles are underlined. Here is not the place to pursue this discussion, even superficially. In what follows, therefore, it is merely proposed to sketch a model which does not assume any one-sided relationship between the economy and the "rest" of society. (cf. Stamm 1992: Chapters 2 and 3.)

Within the logic of such a model it may be assumed that, in countries like Mexico, economic modernization and growth processes must lead to increasing differentiation and dynamisation of social structures, to the creation and articulation of new needs and to a shift in the social distribution of power. Adherents to world systems and dependency theory, however, argue in this context, that these can be regarded as endogenous processes only to a limited extent since integration with the world market leads to unequal growth patterns and differentiation processes. In economic terms there is differentiation as between modern and backward sectors, which in socio-structural terms stimulates the emergence of new social groupings (workers, urban bureaucratic middle classes, new economic élites), while even traditional groupings with their own cultural and political interests continue to exist. Processes of differentiation and power shifts, however, cause (domestic) conflicts about the developmental strategy and the allocation of social wealth both within the élite and between it and subordinate groups. According to the strength of conflicting interests and how they are handled (organization of the political system) such conflicts may lead to the de-legitimation or (partial) re-organization of prevailing patterns, instability or a re-allocation of social resources to enhance legitimacy. Conflicts and conflict management thus also influence the economy, which reacts by adopting a wait-and-see attitude, while whatever is perceived as legitimate also encourages investment decisions. In this perspective, there are no pure, primarily endogenously generated economic crises, as claimed in economic theory. Economic problems are always co-determined by exogenous factors such as the developments in the social structure and the political system; in turn, they have their impact on the latter through regular backward linkage. In what follows, consequently, the point of departure will be the hypothesis that the crisis of the 1980s did not have economic causes only, but was equally determined by critical developments in the sphere of politics and social structure. As a result, the economic collapse may well have had far-reaching consequences for the political and social situation in Mexico.

The Long-Term Nature of the Mexican Crisis

A detailed analysis of the factors contributing to the onset of the Mexican crisis of the 1980s cannot be undertaken here. It must therefore suffice to refer briefly to some of the developments which show that Mexican society was in a "critical" situation well before the 1980s. Though certain of Mexico's current problems may be traced back to pre-Columbian times, developments originating in the 19th century are of primary contemporary significance. (cf. Meyer and Sherman, 1979, Mols 1981, Levy and Szekely 1987.) While, in the years after the Wars of Independence (1810 - 1821), the rigid power structure and ethnic segregation of the colonial regime were broken down, the economic expansion of the second half of the 19th century set in motion processes of differentiation in regional and socio-economic contexts. While the majority of the population remained in the agricultural sector and was thus scarcely touched by the growth process, there arose, apart from an industrial working class, the beginnings of a bureaucratic middle class, as well as business and financial élites which challenged the leadership of the big landowners and the Church.

Conflicts around appropriate economic and political participation were central to the Mexican revolution of the early 20th century. In retrospect, it was hardly a revolution by and for the masses but rather a successful experiment in the partial restructuring of power relations by the rising middle classes and élites. (Tobler 1984.) The most important characteristic of the post-revolutionary power structure was the "institutionalization of the revolution" whereby the ruling Partido Revolucionario Institucional (PRI) founded a corporatist order into which the industrial workers, certain parts of the urban middle class and the peasants were integrated.[3] So far as the exercise of power was concerned, paternalistic and authoritarian elements, along with Mexican *presidencialismo* and strictly hierarchical organisation of Party components were retained. Though the economic élite was formally excluded from this structure it was able, through informal contacts and economic pressure, to exercise political influence.

The post-revolutionary system of government demonstrated for some fifty years its ability efficiently to control and partly to satisfy the aspirations of the integrated groups. The consequent political stability formed the basis for an economic growth process undisturbed by violent conflicts, further buttressed by hopes of sharing in its success. Because politics were dominated by different political and economic interests of the élite it became possible to adopt a capitalistic developmental path which allowed Mexico upward mobility, within the framework of the world system, but at the price of extensive external dependency, reinforced by attempted import-substituting industrialization.[4]

Further, social development during the Mexican economic miracle *(milagro mexicano)* after the Second World War began increasingly to tax the integrative capacities of the political system (Aguilar Camin 1990, Basanez 1990). As in the 19th century, upheavals in the social structure were connected with economic growth. Thus a new political and economic élite arose around the PRI, which attempted to use the party and the state apparatus for its own purposes. The industrial workers and urban middle classes gained political weight and formulated their demands at the expense of the rural population, which became more and more marginalized. At the same time, the rising groups demanded a "fair" share of the fruits of growth, along with appropriate political participation. Increasing political mobilization was met by the régime, first, with repression in the late 1960s and then, from the early 1970s, with a drive to acquire fresh mass legitimacy.

The attempted governmental stabilization under President Luis Echevarría (1970-1976) combined several elements. (Cf. Levy and Szekely 1987, Basanez 1990.). In the economic sphere, these consisted of a shift to a developmental model to improve the distribution of incomes *(desarollo compartido)* and further comprised political and administrative reforms (democratization, campaign against corruption) as well as spot measures to regain the adherence of alienated middle class groups. Yet these reforms were contested within the élite. Political and administrative reforms threatened the power aspirations and privileges of the political élite, while economic reform ambitions met with resistance from the economic élite. The latter perceived a challenge to its traditional position and began to cut loose from its role as silent partner of the governing coalition in order to conduct actively oppositional politics through the liberal-conservative National Action Party (PAN) and its own organizations. (Luna 1985.)

The regime was thus caught between participatory demands from below and conservationist attempts from the established élite. As a result, political reforms were but partially implemented while business was to be mollified by extensive concessions (tax benefits, support for investment etc.). The redistribution program was replaced by neo-populist distribution and investment programs, largely financed by foreign loans and which hardly affected the situation of private business. Admittedly, the blunting of participatory demands by the middle classes and various segments of the industrial work force in order to create fresh mass legitimacy was only partly successful.[5]

These problems began to affect the economy, too. As early as the 1960s, the shortcomings of the import-substituting development model of the postwar era became evident, and growth slowed. These trends were reinforced in the 1970s through speculative investment, inflation, the flight of capital and increasing indebtedness, leading to a first "economic crisis".[6] In the mid-1970s, the Mexican peso had to be substantially devalued and in 1977 a first macro-economic stabilization program was agreed with the IMF. This, however, was soon abandoned in favor of forced investment measures as rich oil resources were discovered in the Gulf of Mexico. Oil-induced development promised to be a solution to economic and social problems by enlarging the cake to be distributed, though it did little to overcome the problems of participation and legitimacy. Further, expansion deepened socio-structural inequalities and led, via concentration of trade on oil and the huge needs for foreign financing, to greater external dependency. Thus, the government's ability to take independent economic decisions was reduced while the economic élite would only hesitantly allow itself to be mollified, despite the concessions made to it. In this perspective, the insolvency of 1982 represents but the latest in a long succession of regularly more acute problems. (Aguilar Camin 1990, Basanez 1990.)

The Interpretation of Crisis and Political Transformation in the 1980s

In the light of the foregoing it becomes questionable whether the crisis of the 1980s is to be considered as merely economic or debt-induced in nature. Rather, it should be seen as the so far last link in a whole chain of unresolved economic, political and socio-structural crises. Thus, the expression "crisis of the 1980s" is inappropriate: it would be better to refer to the "intensification of the general post-war system crisis".

The relevant discussions during the 1980s were, however, dominated by explanations awarding the central place to short-term liquidity problems arising from a combination of unforeseen fluctuations of world commodity prices and interest rates, profligacy by debtors and panicky over-reaction by creditors. Socio-political elements were mentioned only when they could be smoothly fitted into the neoclassical explanatory pattern. Reference was thus made to the loss of business confidence and the inefficiency and corruption of the public sector, to the neglect of problems of external dependency, distributional structures and government.

Against this background, a comparatively simple crisis strategy could be formulated: creditors should offer debtors, within the framework of debt rescheduling agreements, short-term payment facilities and fresh credits while the Mexicans should adjust exchange rates, improve their balance-of-payments, restrain demand, liberalize investment regulations for citizens and foreigners, curb State spending drastically and subject society to a process of "moral regeneration". (Alejo 1985, Villareal 1988, SHCP 1988.)

Other interpretations of the crisis might certainly also have been possible (Lustig 1989a). That they did not surface may have had three reasons. In the first place, the interpretation we have sketched labelled the immediate causes and characteristics of the crisis.[7] Different observers may indeed have believed at its outset that Mexico's problems were short-term and easily solvable.

In the second place, the interpretation is one which could gather a consensus amongst influential groups in Mexico and abroad, thereby mobilizing the support needed to pursue the measures identified as appropriate. Insolvency was a really major problem for foreign interests, threatening financial networks and, along with them, the entire world economic system with collapse under the weight of debt. (Suter and Stamm, 1992.) Whether debtor countries had other problems as well could hardly be expected to interest foreign economic circles while Mexico was equally endangered by a possible collapse of the world economy as by threatened exclusion from economic flows if it refused the measures suggested by the creditors.

Against this background, the sketched assessment of the situation also found support amongst the economic and parts of the political élite. For business, the liberal economic interpretation provided a guarantee of traditional positions. These circles thus needed to take no responsibility for problems and could even plead victimization by external circumstances and political mistakes which had shattered their confidence and created an unfavorable overall climate.

It is, at first sight, astonishing that the government was prepared to shoulder a good deal of blame. Yet one must recall the timing of the crisis. In December 1982, three months after its outbreak, Miguel de la Madrid came to power as the new president, to whom the confession of political error by the preceding government must have come rather easily, given that changes of government in Mexico are mostly accompanied by distantiation from the preceding administration, and promises of a fresh start. No later than September did de la Madrid's predecessor, José López Portillo, identify Mexico's business class as chiefly responsible for the crisis and nationalize the banks. Since Mexican financial and industrial interests are closely linked, this action constituted a painful blow to the economic élite which, as earlier in the 1970s, withdrew all support from the government and conducted various protests and media campaigns. (Aguilar Camín 1990, Basañez 1990.)

The new administration had the option in this situation to use the revolt of the business classes as the occasion for more severe measures, thereby turning to its advantage the enhanced legitimacy amongst wide sections of society acquired through the nationalization of the banks. But this would have incurred the danger of international isolation. Acceptance of the economic version, on the other hand, implied the stabilization of relations with foreign creditors and the domestic economic élite, even though the latter refused unconditional loyalty and kept its lines to the opposition and the North American media open.

The third explanation for the choice of interpretation is the absence of any powerful opposition to the dominant version. Apart from the traditionally marginal leftist opposition, which failed in its bid to obtain more severe sanctions against domestic and international economic interests, objections to government policy were voiced only in certain parts of the PRI. That the government succeeded in quashing intra-party resistance points to two important trends of change within the political system. These are, on the one hand, the progressive uncoupling of governmental might from the Party and, on the other, the partial restructuration of the ruling coalition on this basis, towards an exclusive élite alliance between government and economic leadership.

The uncoupling process had already begun in the 1970s and accelerated through the crisis. (Mols 1981, Bailey 1988.) At the administrative level this process consisted of the gradual replacement of old, clientistically bound Party stalwarts by so-called *técnicos* who had hardly any Party ties. Weak linkage with the Party apparatus gave the government a chance to cement alliances with groups external to the Party while simultaneously tackling bureaucratic and Party shortcomings without being itself associated therewith.

Tough opposition from the PRI spelt the danger for its leadership of being totally excluded from the governing coalition and of losing its traditional privileges, all the more so since the crisis undermined one of the Party's essential integrative and legitimation supports in the shape of the dispensing of jobs and material advantages. Silent countenancing of the government's economic policy, however, would have strengthened the thus far successfully controlled disintegration and reform tendencies at the base. In this context, the protest manifestos and strikes by the union movement at the end of 1982 and in the first half of 1983 are to be interpreted as attempts by the Party leadership to force the government into concessions to enhance legitimacy, thereby buttressing its own power base.[8] The fact that such concessions were coupled with requirements not to put the ongoing adjustment process into fundamental question is a strong indicator of the PRI's loss of influence. All through the 1980s, limited wage increases were granted within the framework of "social pacts" but these were always below the rate of inflation and thus did nothing to stop the erosion of real wages (see below).

That greater opposition did not arise from the official unions and other Party organizations under such circumstances was no doubt because the view prevailed within the integrated elements that small concessions were still better than none at all. This explanation is all the more realistic since, until the mid-1980s, no significant political alternative to the PRI existed while democratic experiments and approaches towards an opposition movement were systematically and often severely repressed by the traditional leadership.

Despite all problems of legitimation and integration, the PRI succeeded in maintaining its role as the strongest political organization and "mobilization machine" in Mexico, which the government could not entirely reject without provoking social unrest. This explains why the uncoupling process between government and the Party and the partial restructuration of power relationships did not lead to a full demobilization of the PRI nor to stronger authoritarianism or the general democratization of political life. These remarks describe the limits of the process of political change which ran its course in Mexico during the 1980s. True, opposition groups gained in influence and could occasionally swing the election of governors. A closer analysis of opposition in Mexico nevertheless reveals that it has not been able to offer any real alternative to the corporatist PRI system. Thus the liberal conservative PAN profited from the ideological rapprochement of the government with its own positions and its appealing critique of the authoritarian and corrupt PRI style. Further, it seems to have succeeded in recruiting the urban middle classes, underrepresented within the PRI and threatened by social demotion, to its side. Yet the PAN never disposed over sufficient ideological, personnell and organisational resources to challenge the PRI effectively. (Loaeza 1989.)

The same may be said of the attacks on PRI hegemony from the left and of the so far most dangerous opposition movement which emerged in the mid-1980s from the ranks of the PRI itself under the name of *corriente democrática*. After this group, which demanded comprehensive reform of the PRI, was neutralized it ran under its own banner in the presidential elections. Its candidate, Cuautémoc Cárdenas, might well have obtained a majority of votes, through a combination of personal popularity,[9] left-wing populism, democratic aspirations and electoral alliances had not manipulative emergency measures by the PRI defeated him. It is indeed questionable whether Cárdenas could have altered much in the Mexican situation since he and his program would inevitably have collided both with domestic business and foreign interests and his policies would not have benefited from the organisational backstopping of the PRI. In fact, the Party of Democratic Revolution (PRD), which he founded after the election of 1988, has encountered difficulties in presenting and promoting a coherent program, problems worsened by the well-aimed destabilization tactics of the PRI.

Notwithstanding, the process of decoupling between governmental and Party power continued under the new president, Carlos Salinas de Gortari. Salinas adhered to the macro-economic adjustment policy but complemented it from 1990 with a "social solidarity program" within the framework of which highly visible social projects were carried through, after the populist manner. The prospect of greater attention to social problems may, together with economic recovery,[10] have contributed to the calming of the tense situation after the elections of 1988 and endowed the present government retrospectively with a certain legitimacy.

Though liberal economic policy was not fundamentally changed, the social crisis of the late 1980s appears to have reached proportions which made concrete action imperative. In what follows it is hence proposed to dwell on the dimensions of social problems.

The Social Crisis

The concept of "social crisis", so often to be found in Mexican literature, refers to the fact that Mexican society of the early 1990s is characterized by great social inequalities. For what is true of the economic and political crisis also holds for the social one: it began to build up well before the 1980s. The period since 1982 must then correctly be regarded as the deepening of an already existing crisis. While the economic crisis is now judged to have been overcome, or at least controlled, and the political system has to an extent survived the pressures of crisis, there is as yet no sign of an end to the social crisis.

It is difficult to assess the extent of social problems with any precision since reliable data are not at hand. Table 1 illustrates at least certain dimensions of current social problems and compares these with developments during the 1970s. It should be noted that not all the data indicate a worsening. Most striking are developments connected directly with the economic situation. Thus the decline of real wages is clear, while underemployment (including unemployment), according to conservative estimates, affected around a quarter of the active population at the end of the 1980s (Table 1).

TABLE 1 Indicators of social development in Mexico, 1974-1988

	1974	1981	1988
Index of average wages (1980=100)	85.4	104.6	54.2
Rate of un- and underemployment	17.7	(5.7)*	25.3
Percentage share of labor in disposable national income	39.6	42.7	30.9
Pupils in primary schools as a share of age cohort 5-14	73.7	72.9	70.5
Hospital beds per 1000 population	.94	.95	1.11

* Due to a change in the calculation of unemployment rates, values before and after 1981 are not comparable.
Source: Stamm (1992: Appendix) on the basis of various Mexican sources.

These data imply a series of further problems, such as increases in crimes against property, and the extension of the informal sector and of the slums surrounding large cities, the inhabitants of which had even fewer prospects of regular jobs at the end of the 1980s than before. It is in this context that the slightly lower primary school attendance, shown in Table 1, is to be understood: as regular subsistence income opportunities shrank, so children were increasingly recruited into the economic sphere. Though the quality of education during the 1980s does not seem to have provably suffered, lower rates of school enrolment may, in the medium run, lead to greater barriers to mobility than before for certain groups. It would be wrong to blame these negative developments entirely on the economic adjustment and stabilization programs of the 1980s. Quite apart from the fact that marked inequalities and misery have always been essential characteristics of Mexican society, no serious attempts having ever been made to overcome them, the economic collapse would have had negative social impacts even without the adoption of the chosen adjustment policy. It must, however, be admitted that the liberal economic crisis strategy led to a lopsided allocation of adjustment costs. That, during the crisis, the share of the labor factor in disposable income diminished (see Table 1) is a strong indication that the crisis strategy led to a disproportionate burden on the dependent wage earners while those owning considerable capital were able to extend their share of disposable income. This argument is supported by tentative data relating to income distribution which became more skewed during the 1980s.[11]

Apart from such trends in income and wealth concentration it can also be demonstrated that the crisis did not hit all population groups to the same degree. Thus, for example, the agricultural population, which had hardly profited from post-war growth, was less affected than the bureaucratic middle class and the workers, both of whom saw their incomes and mobility opportunities increasingly blocked. The disproportionate losses of those who benefited from the *milagro mexicano* led to an effect described by Aguilar Camín and Meyer (1990: 269) as a trend towards "greater equality of poverty". By contrast to the data on employment and wages, those concerning medical services and infant mortality in Table 1 indicate that coverage by the public sector appears to have improved during the 1980s.[12] Though it is hardly possible to draw any conclusions about the quality of services thus extended from such aggregated data they do point to the fact that rationalization measures in the public sector had some effect, despite diminishing absolute social expenditures. This may be a reason for the enhanced legitimacy of the government, referred to above.

But it must further be remarked that the coverage of public services, despite certain improvements, remains inadequate and so far extends mainly to urban populations, while the marginalized rural population hardly enjoys them (Lustig 1989b). Moreover, certain subsidies (to food, transport) were abolished or greatly reduced. Thus, price increases of different basic foods lay well above the rate of inflation which, in view of shrinking real wages, must have worsened the already problematic nutritional situation of broad segments of the population (Lustig 1989b, Martinez 1989b). The public sector, despite all measures to improve its efficiency, was therefore finally in no position to stem the general decline into misery.

Prospects

We have referred to certain non-economic aspects of the Mexican crisis, to show that the widespread version restricting it to debt and the economic sphere is inadequate. Rather, the current crisis is the hitherto latest link in the chain of mutually interacting economic, political and socio-structural problems.

Beyond the obvious economic breakdown the crisis made unsolved political and social problems more acute. In socio-structural and political terms what may be detected is the immiseration of broad population strata, sharper social contradictions and a progressive loss of legitimacy of the governmental system. This loss, though, did not lead to the re-establishment of mass legitimacy but rather to a transformation of governing conditions in the direction of the exclusive exercise of power. The economic élite became more closely bound to the ruling coalition while the traditional political élite, and along with it the groups integrated with the PRI, lost influence. The PRI's loss of influence in turn led to the enhancement of the legitimacy of Carlos Salinas de Gortari's administration, which meant that it could conduct a relatively credible and efficient policy in disregard of traditional political interests.

It must be noted that the adjustment measures of the 1980s mainly mirror the interests and power potential of international creditors and the domestic economic élite. Though it would be mistaken to blame the economic crisis and adjustment measures alone for the decline in the living standards of segments of the population, it must nevertheless be remarked that, despite the declarations of economists and functionaries, these adjustment programs were not neutral in their distributional impacts. Overall, one may say that, while the rich got richer during the crisis years, those who had already suffered in previous decades were joined by other population groups.

To which must be added that the adjustment strategy attained its essential goals, beyond stabilization and financial relations, but partly and after several years of a recessive phase. Possible successes of the adjustment policies might well result less from real structural adjustment than from relative price changes arising over the recession of several years' duration. That, for example, manufactured exports could, in the second half of the decade be boosted seems to have been less the consequence of greater productivity than of the combined effects of exchange rate fluctuations and declining wages. While it may, in this connection, be correct to refer to relative prices as having reached a "realistic" level from a strictly economic viewpoint this argument is not bereft of cynicism in view of the level of underemployment and mass misery.

Since the economic, social and political restructuration of Mexico is not yet terminated it is risky to prognosticate about the country's prospects. A central feature should be the increasing economic, and therefore also political integration with the United States. NAFTA will enable Mexico – at least indirectly and more so than other countries – to participate in the world market. Integration should initially act absorptively, though this may make escape from dependency more difficult in the long run. Developmental possibilities should be determined even more than before by the needs of the great northern neighbor for whom Mexico will remain an important partner so long as it offers cheap raw materials and labor and promising investment opportunities. That would seem to define the limits of an improvement of the economic situation and of social conditions.

On the other hand, modifications of the political system in the near future seem eminently possible. There are two scenarios. Firstly, the continuation of an exclusive process of closure within the élite is possible which, over the medium term, should lead to greater repression. But political liberalization may also occur which, however, posits the emergence of a political alternative which can triumph over the resistance of the established élites. Integration with the United States may be decisive in this connection, inasfar as the northern neighbor might well serve as the model and promoter of processes of democratization in Mexico by securing its interests, but could equally try to consolidate the existing power structure. Whichever path is ultimately followed, a lasting solution to the social crisis hardly seems realistic in the foreseeable future. In view of greater external dependency and the continuing influence of particularist élite interests it is not likely that a developmental model directed at the greater satisfaction of mass needs has much of a chance of being adopted in the coming years.

NOTES

1 The author wishes to thank Michael Nollert and Jeannette Rüegg for their helpful comments.
2 One may mention sociological classics like Karl Marx and Max Weber, the contributions of critical or historically oriented economists (Karl Polanyi, Werner Sombart, John Maynard Keynes) as well as the extensive literature on dependency and world system theory. Currently, the embeddedness of the economy is being discussed mainly by the representatives of the "new economic sociology" (Swedberg 1987, Bornschier 1988, Etzioni 1988, Block 1990).
3 The PRI is less a political party in the Western, pluralistic sense than a great allocational coalition through which conflicting aspirations can be mobilized, reconciled wih each other and controlled (Mols 1981, Levy and Szekely 1987, Bailey 1988, Aguilar Camin and Meyer 1990).
4 Typical trade dependency already existed in colonial times when Mexico's revenues were derived mainly from the sale of ores and agricultural products. Lately, it has extended to technological and financial domains (foreign credits).
5 Thus, during the 1970s, rising rates of strikes may be observed. Dissatisfaction with political authoritarianism was also expressed through lower voter turnouts, despite the fact that the electoral laws were revised so as to give the opposition a higher, if still restricted voice in affairs.
6 Thus the annual average growth rate of GDP, which stood at over 7% in 1960-70, fell to 6% in 1970-76. The rate of inflation, however, which never fell below 10% from 1973, reached a peak of 30% in 1977. In the same year the proportion of external debt reached 35% of GDP, its peak to date. (Source of these and following data: Stamm 1992: Appendix.)
7 While the GDP growth rate was still barely 9% in 1981 it became negative (-0.6%) in 1982 and fell to -4.2% in 1983. Meanwhile, the rate of inflation between 1981 and 1983 rose from nearly 30% to over 100%

annually and remained at over 50% annually until the end of the 1980s. The proportion of foreign debt to GDP reached about 50% in 1982 to rise to 60% the following year. Only at the end of the 1980s did it become possible, on the basis of fresh debt renegotiation programs, which included substantial depreciations for the creditors, to reduce this proportion to under 50%.

8 Strikes reached a peak in 1982, to decline markedly in the following years while remaining more numerous in the 1980s than in the 1970s.

9 Cárdenas acquired the reputation of an honest politician during his term as governor of the State of Michoacán which strengthened him in his conflicts with the PRI. To this must be added that he could count on much sympathy and prominence as the son of the former revolutionary general and president, Lazaro Cárdenas. (cf. Zermeõ 1989, Aguilar Camín and Meyer 1990, Tamayo 1990.)

10 Thus growth and investment rates began to rise again, while inflation was kept down to 20% annually. The debt situation could also at last be controlled while in 1986, for the first time since 1973, flight capital began to pour back into the country.

11 While the Gini index for household income distribution had improved from 0.496 to 0.425 between 1977 and 1984 it rose again to 0.552 until 1987 (Stamm 1992: 15).

12 Similar results are obtained if the number of those covered by public insurance programs or indicators of the educational system are taken into account.

REFERENCES

Aguilar Camin, Hector (1990): *Después del milagro,* México, D.F.: Cal y Arena.

Aguilar Camín, Héctor, and Lorenzo Meyer (1990): *A la sombra de la Revolución Mexicana,* México, D. F.: Cal y Arena.

Alejo, Francisco-Javier (1985): "Racionalidad económica y política de los programas de estabilización económica," in Pablo González Casanova and Héctor Aguilar Camín (eds.), *México ante la crisis, Vol. I,* México, D.F.: Siglo XXI, 349-398.

Bailey, John (1988): *Governing Mexico. The Statecraft of Crisis Management,* New York: St. Martin's Press.

Basáñez, Miguel (1990): *El pulso de los sexenios. 20 años de crisis en México,* México, D.F.: Siglo XXI.

Block, Fred (1990): *Postindustrial Possibilities. A Critique of Economic Discourse,* Berkeley: University of California Press.

Bornschier, Volker (1988): *Westliche Gesellschaft im Wandel*, Frankfurt and New York: Campus.
Etzioni, Amitai (1988): *The Moral Dimension. Toward a New Economics*, New York: Free Press.
Levy, Daniel, and Gabriel Szekely (1987): *Mexico - Paradoxes of Stability and Change* (2nd edition), Boulder, Co.: Westview.
Loaeza, Soledad (1989): *El llamado de las urnas*, Méxiko, D.F.: cal y arena.
Luna, Matilde (1985): "Transformaciones del corporativismo empresarial y tecnocratización de la política", Revista Mexicana de Sociología, 47(1), 125- 137.
Lustig, Nora (1989a): "Seis versiones sobre las causas de la crisis mexicana de 1982," *El Trimestre Económico*, 56(4), 941-949.
Lustig, Nora (1989b): "Crisis económica y niveles de vida en Mexico: 1982-1985" in: Carlos Tello (ed.): *Mexico. Informe sobre la crisis*, México, D.F.: CIIH-UNAM, 421-445.
Martínez, Ifigenia (1989): "Algunos efectos de la crisis en la distribucion del ingreso en Mexico" in: Carlos Tello (ed): *México. Informe sobre la crisis*, México, D.F.: CIIH-UNAM, 373-420.
Meyer, Lorenzo, and Jose Luis Reyna (1989): "México el sistema y sus partidos: entre el autoritarismo y la democracía" in: Lorenzo Meyer and Jose Luis Reyna (eds.), *Los sistemas políticos de América Latina*, México, D.F.: Siglo XXI, 305-328.
Meyer, Michael C., and William L. Sherman (1979): *The Course of Mexican History*, New York: Oxford University Press.
Mols, Manfred (1981): *Mexiko im 20. Jahrhundert. Politisches System, Regierungsprozess und politische Partizipation*, Paderborn: Schöningh.
SHCP (Secretaría de Hacienda y Crédito Publico), (1988): *Deuda externa pública Mexicana*, México, D.F.: Fondo de Cultura Económica.
Stamm, Hanspeter (1992): *Krise und Anpassung in Mexiko. Eine Länderfallstudie zu Auf- und Abstieg in der Semiperipherie des Weltsystems*, Saarbrücken: Breitenbach.
Suter, Christian, and Hanspeter Stamm (1992): "Coping with Global Debt Crises," *Comparative Studies in Society and History*, 34(4): 656-689.
Swedberg, Richard (1987): "Economic Sociology: Past and Present," *Current Sociology*, 35(1).
Tamayo, Jorge (1990): "Neoliberalism Encounters Neocardenismo," in Joe Foweraker and Anne L. Craig (eds.), *Popular Movements and Political Change in Mexico*, Boulder, Co.: Lynne Rienner, 121-136.
Tobler, Hans Werner (1984): *Die mexikanische Revolution. Gesellschaftlicher Wandel und politischer Umbruch, 1876-1940*, Frankfurt a. M.: Suhrkamp.
Villareal, Rene (1988): "External Debt and Adjustment Policies: The Case of Mexiko 1982-1986," in Stephany Griffith-Jones (ed.), *Managing World Debt*, Harvester: Wheatsheaf, 40-63.
Zermeño, Sergio (1989): "El regreso del líder: crisis, neoliberalismo y desórden," *Revista Mexicana de Sociología*, 51(4), 115-150.

11 SOCIAL PERCEPTION OF ENVIRONMENTAL PROBLEMS
DESTRUCTION OF TROPICAL FORESTS AND ETHNIC PROTEST MOVEMENTS IN BOLIVIA

H.C.F. Mansilla

Introduction

Bolivia is a landlocked country extending over roughly 1.1 million square kilometers. According to the latest census (June 1992) its population is 6.3 million. Its socio-economic characteristics differ considerably from those of its neighbours to the south (Argentina and Chile) and resemble those of the Andean countries to the north, specially with regard to such indicators as per capita income, life expectancy and general economic development. Bolivia indeed exhibits poor modernization indices, the lowest among all Latin American countries except Haiti. This, together with a very low population density and a high emigration rate to foreign countries, must also be seen within the context of an ecological crisis.

This article is part of the research project "Social Perception of Environmental Problems; Destruction of Tropical Forests and Ethnic Protest Movements in Bolivia" funded by the World Society Foundation. Hugo Celso Felipe Mansilla took his Ph.D. and his Habilitation from the Free University of Berlin. He teaches social sciences at the Universidad Mayor de San Andrés de La Paz and is affiliated to the Centro Boliviano de Estudios Multi-disciplinarios (CEBEM), Casilla 2049, La Paz, Bolivia.

During Spanish colonial times, this territory was extremely important because of the silver production in Potosí. Until 1985 mining (tin, zinc, silver, gold) was still the central economic activity in Bolivia. Mining constitutes one of the most dangerous activities for the environment; in this case, Spanish methods of ore processing required an immense amount of energy, which was supplied by cutting down almost all the forests of the Western highlands and of the valleys of the Andes. Acid residues have polluted rivers and arable land for 450 years.

Low population density must be seen in connexion with these persistant environmental phenomena. The geographical position of the country (between the tropical zone and the desert belt of the southern hemisphere), the very high proportion of mountainous territory and the early human occupation of the Andean slopes have caused extensive – and almost irreversible – erosion processes in numerous regions of Bolivia. Although his figure may be somewhat exaggerated, a distinguished scientist and pioneer of Bolivian ecological research, Wagner Terrazas Urquidi, estimated that approximately 420 000 square kilometers (39% of the total surface) were already eroded by human agency in 1983[1]. In any case, Bolivia currently represents a case of dramatic environmental degradation, a very high degree of vulnerability of almost all soils, large parts of the country transformed into irretrievably eroded zones, destruction of the original ecosystems of the western mountainous region, and increasing clearing of the humid forests of the eastern lowlands. The relatively small population and its low density should, of course, not be considered to be a result of deplorable environmental conditions, but most probably is concomitant therewith. Public opinion in Bolivia disregards this complex relationship; it believes that a small population and low demographic density represent obstacles to accelerated modernization. Almost all social groups in Bolivia[2] continue to adhere to a traditional conception which perceives a large population and the occupation of the entire national territory to be preconditions for rational development.

The actual environmental situation has been complicated by the rise[3] of indigenous political movements, which pursue their own strategies and developmental models. The scarcity of arable land, the impoverishment of the small plots in the western regions (because of continuous partition and over-utilization), population growth among the Indian communities and the process of urbanization have compelled the western Indian peasants to migrate eastwards. Their ecological vision[4] is completely different from the environmental conceptions of the eastern lowland Indians of Amazonian origin. And amongst the latter there are also contradictory tendencies. None the less, the only socially and politically serious resistance to "normal" development (opening-up of the eastern lowlands, logging the humid forests, "rational" utilization of all resources, like timber, minerals, pasture lands, the building of means of transport and communication) is now coming from these Amazonian forest Indians. They constitute a confederation of tribes whose binding principle is precisely the defense of the tropical territories, including especially the forests, against all penetration from the (Bolivian) west. The celebration of the fifth centenary of America's discovery has intensified discussions among these Amazonian communities about their social and historical identity and their real chances of evolution[5].

The protest movement of these Indians is being supported by the Catholic Church and by certain groups (trade unions, political parties, university students, non-government organizations, etc.), which only a little while ago advocated the rapid modernization of the whole country – of course, under a socialist dispensation.

The ecological issue in Bolivia's eastern lowlands and forests is very complex and contradictory including ethnic demands, political manœuvers and rational drives. The following pages present a summarized analysis and interpretation of this socio-political topic, based on documentary sources and on a set of interviews with representative figures of the modern functional elites. Yet our findings are essentially provisional, for with regard to environmental issues public opinion, government behavior, public policies and the strategies of all involved groups are changing rapidly. Although scientific research on these matters in Bolivia has so far been very limited, published reports exercise a certain influence on the formulation of normative and programmatic goals by political and social movements.

The Context of a Generalized Modernization Ideology

On the basis of documentary sources it can be concluded that rapid modernization of all aspects of Bolivian life constitutes the major normative goal of every important ideological and political flow of public opinion. Almost all parties, pressure groups and functional elites consider that modernization efforts must have absolute priority over other considerations, like for instance ecological ones. This modernization drive is now a central element of national identity; its nation-wide cohesive function cannot easily be called into question. Its emotive content, which has the force and radiation of a religious belief, makes any attempt to consider it merely a passing fashion difficult. According to this general perception, environmental issues must be subordinated to development and modernization needs. Ecosystems are also assumed to have a very high capacity for absorbing loads, stress and utilization; their capacity for regeneration is considered to be almost unlimited.

With the exception of a few scattered articles in Bolivian newspapers (and of the testimonies of the Amazonian Indians of the eastern lowland forests), there are practically no publications on the complex ties between environmental problems and socio-political action patterns. The links between development processes and ecological disturbances are generally not perceived as problematic and thus not deserving of scientific research or public debate. This basically optimistic view of the whole situation tends to push ecological programs and conservationist measures to secondary place: they are seen as a luxury that poor countries cannot afford.

This was also the main argument of the few official Bolivian interventions at the Earth Summit (Rio de Janeiro, June 1992) and in the public debate in Bolivian newpapers. The position can succinctly be characterized as the adoption of a simplified version of the ideology of sustainable development anticipated by the Group of 77. The principal points are:

-the "inalienable right to development";
-"national sovereignty" over natural resources;
-the satisfaction of basic needs of the whole population as a fundamental criterion;
-the need for rapid growth for all national economies in a state of crisis;
-the major responsibility of industrialized countries for all global environmental disturbances;
-excessive consumption in Northern societies as the real cause of worldwide resources depletion;
-the "necessity" of placing ecological disturbances in tropical regions into a "global context" (which includes the "responsibility" of the industrialized nations for world-wide development) and, simultaneously, for world-wide policies to protect endangered ecosystems;
-the allocation of funds by the industrialized nations to compensate for the losses suffered by Third World countries through the protectionist policies of the former and through environmental conservation measures;

-the obligation on the industrialized countries to remove the obstacles to sustainable development in the South and hence to contribute indirectly but effectively to the conservation of ecosystems by reducing the external debt of Southern countries, raising the prices of raw materials, transferring technology and lowering tariffs on Southern products.[6]

Bolivian commentators agreed emphatically with the following pronouncements by Third World statesmen during the Rio Summit:

-Tanzania's President Ali Hassan Mwinyi: Today the dilemma of poor countries is to survive or to protect the environment.[7]

-Colombia's President César Gaviria: Industrialized nations have an "ecological debt" vis-à-vis the Third World, because they founded their economic development upon the environmental destruction inflicted on the Southern countries.[8]

-Guatemala'a President Jorge Serrano: The international ecological movement can become damaging to sustainable development and thus have a boomerang effect on the economic governments and peoples proposing to exercise their sovereign rights over natural resources.[9]

-João Baena Soares, Secretary-General of the Organization of American States (OAS): The protection of tropical forests should not imply any (additional) disadvantage to the urban poor.[10]

Bolivia's President, Jaime Paz Zamora, made only a short statement at the Rio Summit, which comprised the preceding arguments. He stressed the idea of an ecological debt, the creditors being the developing countries. No international environmental agreement should restrict Bolivia's right to unfold its economic potential.[11]

The subordinated position of ecological issues to development "needs" appears perfectly clearly in an article by a very distinguished Bolivian commentator on environmental affairs. In her report on the Earth Summit, Marthadina Mendizábal de Finot asserted that:

a) forest preservation is a "functional necessity" of industrialized societies in order to meet their oxygen demands.

b) Economic and social pressures run counter to the strict protection of tropical forests. Bolivia should preserve certain species, ecosystems and areas, but not all regions covered by tropical forests.

c) Most Bolivian forests must be incorporated into development projects because they are important national resources, which can contribute to the financing of an autonomous development model.[12] The idea is widespread that poverty, underdevelopment and backwardness are the real and profound causes of environmental disturbances.[13] The only rational way to avoid them is to speed up development, to industrialize and to extend the role of the State to all regions of Bolivia and to many activities which are still free of governmental presence.

Comprehensive development represents for the Bolivian functional elites the only realistic way to prevent the disintegration of tropical forests, subtropical savannas and other natural landscapes. They do not envision the possibility that industrialization and urbanization could also represent major factors of ecological destruction; thus they reject the opportunity of learning from the evolution and experiences of European and North American societies. Development is perceived as such an urgent social, political and historical need that ecological and conservation efforts are characterized as "the false ethics of developed nations".[14] This "double standard" creates ideologies and devices – like the "myth" of Amazonian forests as the "lung of humanity" – designed to keep the Third World in backwardness and dependence and to delay rapid modernization with social justice. Poor people in Bolivia are actually cutting down the trees just to survive; hunger, misery and underdevelopment must be unfailingly considered as the principal agents producing environmental damage. The best and most rational ecological concern of the rich, developed nations should consist in diminishing the gap between them and the Third World.[15] Bolivian newspapers commented very favorably on the statement of a Brazilian politician (the Vice-Governor of Amazonas State) when he said, while visiting Bolivia, that the developed nations of the North attempt to preserve the Amazonian region at the expense of human lives! We must exploit its resources in order to improve our general situation and especially that of the poorest, as if the Amazonian basin were just any area.[16] The director of the official agency for forestry development (Centro de Desarrollo Forestal) asserted that Bolivia should use its timber resources like any others to attain adequate development; the developed nations are in any case putting pressure on Bolivia to produce and sell products coming out of the tropical forests.[17] The problem does not lie in cutting down trees, but in the lack of appropriate public policies to handle forestry resources within a national perspective of accelerated development and healthy criteria of social justice.[18]

There are certain basic images underlying these popular opinions, images which have acquired the status of unquestionable truth. They support profound collective longings, particularly the conviction that all nations of the world can and should reach the higher evolution of the Northern countries.

Their consumption patterns, life styles and socio-economic structures have in the meantime become universal normative goals for every objective of "development" though there are, of course, different conceptions about the ways and means of attaining such objectives (for instance socialist models, nationalist strategies, etc.). Ultimately however there is no dispute about the anxiously pursued ends of historical development.

Apart from this almost mythical (hence generally and uncritically accepted) image of human evolution, there exists a set of other preconceived ideas about the links between development and ecology. In the Bolivian case such ideas are bound up with features like the existence of an indigenous Indian civilization, low population density and the emptiness of tropical regions. Amongst elements of this specific ideology are the following:

-The upsetting of the ecological balance is exclusively to be blamed on the European invasion after 1492. Indigenous societies in the New World – and especially in the Andean zone – had lived in reasonable harmony with their environment. Disturbances of ecosystems accompanied the European (and foreign) aggression against the indigenous communities for five hundred years; the moral and financial responsibility for this behavior and for the environmental damage caused by it remains chiefly with the Northern societies. This opinion has been frequently voiced and spread by Bolivia's President Jaime Paz Zamora.[19]

-There are practically no ecologically endangered landscapes in Bolivia, for this country constitutes one of the rare cases of an uninhabited territory. The "national problem" *par excellence* is how to populate the empty land and to colonize the supposedly fertile eastern tropical lowlands. In order to unfold its huge economic potential Bolivia should have some twenty million inhabitants; the government ought to promote foreign immigration through appropriate policies.[20] Attempts to restrict demographic growth rates are redundant as well as irrational, because our planet can support unlimited development, an ever-growing population and far more environmental strains than at present – on condition of adopting a well-designed program of sustainable development.[21]

-Latin America is not Africa, and Bolivia does not lie in the Sahel zone.[22] In Bolivia there is no serious threat to the tropical forests; the real problem lies in the expansion of forests and the concomitant reduction of pasture lands in the eastern lowlands. In the ten years since 1978 cattle herds have been reduced by half because of the lack of policies to transform "useless" forests areas into useful, socially serviceable pastures.[23] Conversationist ideas and environmental protection are creating an irrational and anachronistic taboo: forests and tropical landscapes run the risk of becoming sacred, of being converted into legally inaccessible zones, closed to human progress and utilization. The cutting down of trees is responsible for only trifling environmental damage in tropical regions.[24] The latter require "normal" opening-up, the construction of a transport and communication network and a set of policies favoring cattle raising, farming and export-oriented forestry.[25] Workers and employers of the tropical zones know already what they must do in order to protect nature and guarantee adequate human development without European, and particularly German advice, which is, of course, in the vested interests of the metropolitan societies.[26]

-European and North American experts tend to underestimate the regenerative capacity of tropical ecosystems, especially the forests. What Bolivia really needs is sustainable development without too many ecologist and conservational reservations, conditions and restrictions, a development strategy principally devoted to a "commitment to eliminate poverty and backwardness". Environmental protection must first consider that tropical regions "shelter economic, political, cultural and social realities", i.e. human settlements, which have an inalienable right to full development. This was, for instance, the fundamental argument of President Paz Zamora's speech at the Manaos Summit (Heads of State of the Amazon Pact, February, 1992, prior to the Earth Summit), which chimed with opinions prevailing amongst civil servants, political parties and other functional elites.[27]

Summarizing, we may say that government agencies, political parties and important pressure groups adhere to the Manaos Declaration: the preservation of tropical ecosystems (and particularly of the rain forests) should be subordinated to the so-called "commitment to the fight against poverty". The conservation of woodlands would favor the "vested interests" of the rich Northern countries. Protection – if really indispensable – should be financed entirely by the metropolitan societies because they have an ecological debt vis-à-vis the Third World.[28] The Bolivian delegation, which did not otherwise distinguish itself by any original contribution, declared that forest preservation was not a national priority, which could obviously change if Bolivia were to obtain the financial equivalent to the entire amount that could be earned by timber utilization.[29]

The social context is by no means static. Important changes have been taking place over the past years: a growing ecological consciousness among the middle and upper classes, international pressure on the Bolivian government and its agencies, the emergence of novel social movements (many of them with a vague environmental ideology)[30] and chiefly the new orientation of the Catholic Church and the revival of the Amazonian Indian communities of the eastern lowlands, who live mostly in the tropical forests. But revised perceptions of environmental problems remain politically weak and socially irrelevant.

Perception of Environmental Issues by the Bolivian Functional Elites

A significant change has undoubtedly occurred amongst a portion of the Bolivian elites as to the handling of the ecological issues approximately since 1988/1989, when international organizations like the World Bank and the International Monetary Fund began to require environmental components to almost all applications for development projects. This position refers specifically to the treatment of environmental degradation and not to a different conception of forests and other ecosystems. This new approach has, in effect, been forced upon the Bolivian elites by foreign institutions and by contemporary fashions; it did not spontaneously arise out of discussions which Bolivian politicians and scientists felt to be necessary. It remains at the intellectual (and not political) level, although it may, of course, acquire its own dynamics and become a socio-political force of some relevance over the long run.

This is not the place to discuss the nature and evolution of the Bolivian elites.[31] They followed the usual pattern of other elites in Latin America: they moved from land ownership and rural bases to an urban environment and private business[32], though a very high proportion of elite members still cling to State functions and bureaucratic positions, thus continuing the old tradition of a patrimonial, statist and centralized order.[33] That is insofar relevant to actual elite behavior as a major part of the Bolivian elite still derives its income, influence and even status from access to, and control of the state apparatus and firms, and not from the ownership of the means of production. In the Bolivian case, this patrimonial model includes a diffuse, variable borderline between public and private spheres, legal instability and a paternalistic-authoritarian political culture. All this implies that, despite contemporary liberal tendencies, civil society remains feeble vis-à-vis the State, private initiative plays a secondary role and the government and its agencies retain a crucial influence on development and therefore on environmental issues for the foreseeable future. The Bolivian bureaucracy is certainly not going to encourage any ecological policy which might endanger its comprehensive modernization efforts, the opening-up of the eastern lowlands, the search for new resources in the tropical areas or plans for the zones designated for settlement. Conservation efforts by small groups, private institutions or Indian communities must fight the vested interests of the bureaucracy, the so-called strategic plans of the government and the shortsightedness of the State.

In this context it is not surprising that the officials of the new government agencies for environmental protection adhere to the following principles:

-Most ecological trends are short-lived fashions, which obviously are not binding on the Bolivian government.

-There are not yet clearly-defined problems – and therefore options – concerning tropical rain forests. In this context the official agencies must move very cautiously.

-The ancient ecological balance of the pre-Columbian cultures was disrupted by European colonialism, which imposes a moral obligation to finance required environmental protection.

-A sustainable development program, under the wise guidance of government agencies, will avoid subsequent ecological damage.[34]

Although not representative of Bolivian elite thinking as a whole it is worth alluding briefly to the ideas of landowners and the military on environment issues. The association of Landowners and Cattle-Breeders of the eastern provinces has emphatically protested against any attempt to establish indigenous reservations with limited sovereignty to benefit the eastern Indian tribes of the tropical lowlands, and also against the enactment of new laws on environmental protection, because both measures would impair the principle of private property and perspectives of rapid economic growth.[35] Cattle-breeders oppose almost any project to restrict the logging of tropical forests which is said only to serve "European interests".[36] The creation of indigenous reservations and especially of protected areas closed to economic exploitation is considered by the military as unpatriotic, as treason against sacred developmental goals and as a betrayal of Bolivia's future. Since the restoration of democracy in 1982, Bolivian officers do not dare to air controversial opinions on basically political matters, but according to certain oral communications we can assume that they share the strictly anti-ecological viewpoint of their Brazilian colleagues.[37]

Bolivian elites perceive environmental problems as being a portion of a giant international distribution struggle concerning financial and technological resources.[38] Should an important transfer of funds to the developing countries to predispose them to possible environment protection programmes actually take place, it is very probable that these elites would appropriate such funds for private ends, evading all reform responsibilities.[39]

The perception of environmental issues by the Bolivian elites can be illustrated by the results of a small opinion enquiry among elite members from four sectors: private entrepreneurs (both owners and top managers of large private firms), well-known journalists (from newspapers, television and radio), trade union leaders (including some important advisers to the National Executive Committee of the Central Obrera Boliviana[40]) and senior officials of the Agriculture, Planning and Finance Ministries. Twenty-five persons from each sector were interviewed between February and April 1992 in La Paz. This opinion enquiry cannot claim to be fully representative but is rather indicative. It does, however, give a tolerably faithful reflection of the problem. In the case of the entrepreneurs almost all members of the Board of the Industry and Commerce Chambers were interviewed; relatively high representativeness was also achieved for the senior civil servants in the ministries related to development issues. Interviewed trade unionists did not include peasant leaders.[41] The enquiry being restricted to the modern functional elites, excludes the more traditional ones, like the military, the (Catholic) clergy and landowners.[42] Their social relevance and influence upon the government (and the formulation of public policies) are clearly diminishing.

One interesting outcome of the enquiry perhaps lies in the fact that differences in the positions of elite sectors concerning ecological-conservationist issues are ultimately not irreconcilable. According to some samples, journalists and entrepreneurs clearly exhibit an understanding of environmental problems which is slightly more reasonable and better informed than that of trade union leaders and civil servants. This difference should not be traced back to political or ideological positions, but to disparities in education and information.

It emerges from Table 1 that Bolivian elites assume by a truly overwhelming majority that the country disposes of a very rich endowment of natural resources (including energy sources), which can in the future guarantee a complete modernization process. The main obstacles to this accelerated development are perceived in cultural, political and social terms, i.e. factors, which can be overcome through human efforts (Table 2). Although not clearly specified, these factors can be roughly described as the imperialist threat and dependent capitalism (according to the leftists) or as the burden of a patrimonial-statist tradition and the weakness of private initiative (according to the rightists). As already mentioned, the peculiarities of Bolivian topography (an extremely high proportion of mountains, deserts and jungles), of the soils (thin humus layer in tropical regions and easily disintegrable soils on mountain slopes) and of the climate (irregular rainfalls, closeness to the southern desert belt) does not seem to influence the thinking of the elites or to affect their perception of the modernization drive in the long run. This may well change radically over the coming years, however, for the intense debate on environmental issues and increasing information about ecological dangers, which the Bolivian mass media are currently spreading, will most probably alter conceptions and even the developmental goals of all elite sectors (Table 4).

The goal of a thoroughly industrialized and urbanized society is shared by a majority of all elite sectors, but trade union leaders and civil servants accept it in a probably more uncritical manner than others. (Tables 3, 4, 9). Despite the sympathy of trade union leaders for the claims of Indian forest communities, they also assume that the accelerated economic development of the country – but in a socialist perspective – will automatically improve ("civilize") the conditions of all Indian groups. All elites take about the same positive attitude towards the rapid growth of towns (Table 5) as also an uncritical attitude towards demographic variables (Table 6). But we must note that a more subtle question about the consequences of demographic trends (Table 7) elicited more differentiated responses, especially from businessmen.

The emergence of Amazonian Indian tribes in national political life has caused a vehement reaction amongst the elites, particularly amongst entrepreneurs and civil servants, who strongly oppose the grant of limited sovereign rights to the forest Indian communities (Table 8). Trade union leaders show more insight into the fate of the "forest laborers", while businessmen are prone to understand the interests of timber industrialists. The idea of conferring wider autonomy on Indian communities is, indeed, not very popular among the elites, not even among the trade unionists (Table 9). The prevailing opinion is still that a reasonable modernization process will solve the problems of the "poor", including, of course, the Indians. Finally, we should point to the positive function of the mass media, which have aroused valuable public interest in environmental issues (Table 10), although more conventional viewpoints continue to predominate.

The Destruction of the Tropical Forests and the Emergence of the Amazonian Indian Communities

The rather uniform image of ecological and demographic[43] conditions – albeit with some important contradictions – by the Bolivian elite and public opinion, is being eroded by the following factors:

-Very fast opening-up and colonization of subtropical and tropical regions by people coming from the western highlands in an astonishingly short lapse of time (since 1953 at a slow pace and since 1970/75 at an accelerated one);

-The links between this and the coca/cocaine complex (together with its international ramifications):

-Growing ecological consciousness of the vulnerability of tropical ecosystems and dangers of erosion in tropical zones (together with increasing international concern for the fate of the rain forests); and

-The emergence of the Indian communities of the eastern lowlands, claiming their allegedly historical rights to their territories, life style and disposal over natural resources (since approximately 1990).

The last circumstance deserves special emphasis, not only because of the worldwide spreading of cultural relativism and the revival of indigenous cultures close to nature, but also because of the appearance of a pressure group defending the presumptive right of Indian communities to defend their lands and forests against "foreign" incursions and "modern" exploitation while asserting their ecology-friendly way of life.[44] These Indian communities began to protest against the invasion of the eastern lowlands by migrants when (a) their economic basis, the forests, became one of the preferred targets of the opening-up of the eastern regions[45], (b) the lowland Indian communities discovered the commercial value of the resources in their territories and claimed their share of the increasingly profitable timber business, and (c) when this whole process endangered their ancestral customs and life style, i.e. their collective identity.

Since roughly 1970 three groups of migrants have been invading the lowlands:

-Indian peasants from the highland communities of Aymaras and Quechuas[46], driven by progressive soil erosion on the mountain slopes and the high plateau, by population increase and the apparently greater earning prospects in eastern Bolivia.[47]

-The commercial search for valuable types of trees and for pastures by relatively large private firms.

-Prospection for gold, semi-precious stones and other minerals, conducted by small groups and co-operative societies.

It is impossible to ascertain precisely which group is actually causing major damage to the rain forests. Leftist parties and organizations tend to see in the timber and cattle-breeding industries the principal agents of environmental destruction. But it is the enormous and constantly growing crowds of Indian peasants from the western highlands moving towards and colonizing the tropical lowlands which constitute the single most important agents in the degradation of the rain forests.[48] It is known that the ancient Andean societies adopted rational and ecology-friendly techniques of agriculture and stock-farming (particularly cultivation on terraces and contour rows following the levels of the terrain) and that many peasant groups still adhere to these in the western mountain areas.[49] But when the same social groups are confronted with a completely different geographic and climatic setting (in this case with humid forests in tropical and subtropical zones), they adopt other behavior patterns. They perceive the new environment as decidedly hostile and strange, to be exploited in the most intensive manner over a short time, as if it were a mine – the non-agricultural economic reality peasants usually know in western Bolivia.[50] This makes it impossible to establish emotive bonds with the new environment, long-term investments and erect a stable community. The cultivation of coca in the newly colonized areas has dramatically worsened this situation.[51] The sacred plant, transformed into a common cash crop and removed from its Andean habitat, has become a major contributor to forest destruction and social disintegration in its new tropical surroundings. Coca is being cultivated after the burning of extended forest portions without any concern for the peculiarities of tropical or subtropical soils (on mountain slopes) and without laying out level strips, contour rows or terraces. Instead immigrant peasants apply in tropical zones the totally conventional slash-and-burn method. Because of the rapid fertility loss of all tropical soils, the peasants are compelled to abandon their original plots and move further into the jungle. This system of shifting cultivation leaves behind eroded steppes, ruined soils and the annihilation of fauna and flora.[52] Although leftists and nationalist parties, trade unions and pressure groups of the immigrants do not cease to praise the anti-imperialist character of coca cultivation and to emphasize the continuity of an allegedly sacred and genuinely local tradition, the coca monoculture has caused

(1) Environmental damage:

-cutting down or burning of forests at an exponentially increasing rate, far beyond the needs of the peasants for arable land for their coca plantations;

-water pollution because of the extensive utilization of chemicals in the first stages of cocaine preparation;

-erosion of soils on mountain slopes and washing away of loose earth with rainfalls;

-floods in the lowlands, the capacity of soils and the vegetation mantle of binding water in the upper reaches of the river basis having been drastically reduced.

(2) Social change:

-disruption of the traditional social and cultural fabric of peasant communities, especially of the prevailing behavior patterns of Andean origin (based on reciprocity);

-dissolution of the extended family and kinship systems;

-introduction of market and monetary relations[53];

-irrational consumption of fashionable goods, neglect of savings, lack of attention to educational and training issues.

(3) Political effects:

-decay of traditional political parties, especially the leftist ones;

-decline of the Marxist-oriented trade union movements;

-rise of populist parties without policy patterns;

-hostile reaction of the lowland Indian population to all these developments.

The listed ecological and social aspects are being increasingly perceived by the lowland Indians as endangering their habitat and resources: the highland Indian immigrants are now considered as part of the modernizing peril from the West[54], and no longer as a fraternal, ethnically related population. From the viewpoint of the lowland inhabitants, the so-called Andean logic has lost its connotations of reciprocity, ecology-friendly agriculture and immediate solidarity and is becoming a "normal" ideology of the market economy, resource exploitation and environmental devastation. By contrast, an Amazonian logic is slowly emerging. Two main events have so far contributed to mould its Bolivian version, which remains without a clear outline: the so-called Indigenous March for Land and Dignity *(Marcha Indígena por el Territorio y la Dignidad)* in the first half of September 1990 and the Inter-American Indigenous Congress on Natural Resources and Environments *(Congreso Indígena Interamericano de Recursos Naturales y Medio Ambiente)*, held in San Ignacio de Moxos (Beni, Bolivia), 2-7 December, 1991.

The core of this ideology consists of claims against the government and "modernization agent" from the West:[55]

-The concession (or rather: the recognition) of administrative, political and cultural autonomy for those tropical territories, inhabited or "customarily possessed" by the ethnic groups of the lowlands;

-the promotion of their own cultural and educational activities (with government funding);

-prohibition of logging or burning forests;

-participation in the profits of the timber industrialists so long as they operate.

The argument of the lowland Indians is based on the claim that they were the original proprietors of the whole eastern part of Bolivia; the bestowal of semi-sovereign rights upon these territories is considered by them as a long overdue restoration and as a case of historical justice. The Indigenous March for Land and Dignity, when thousands of Amazonian Indians walked from the eastern lowlands to La Paz, wrested from the government in September 1991 the declaration of four tropical areas as "indigenous territories"[56], in which the Indians are to have a certain autonomy in administrative and cultural fields and where logging was forbidden from January 1992.[57] This measure was contested from the very outset. In the Bolivian constitution and legal codes there is no mention of "indigenous territories" or "property rights"; the measure does not respect the property rights of persons and institutions in the zones concerned; ambiguity surrounds State property in rivers, forests and subsoil resources. The Chimane reservation in particular proved to be a most controversial issue. It lies very close to important roads, contains the best timber reserves and harbours different ethnic groups.[58] Many complaints arose about allegedly premeditated nonfulfilment of the treaty by government agencies and timber firms.[59] Institutions like the Agriculture Ministry were blamed for encouraging logging and extending additional concessions for forest exploitation in the indigenous territories protected by law.[60] In this field the Center for Forestry Development *(Centro de Desarrollo Forestal)*, a government organization for the protection of Bolivian forests, has earned an unenviable reputation: according to a German analysis, it is highly imcompetent technically and corrupt.[61] It has, for instance, granted concessions for logging in legally protected areas, in exchange for ridiculously trifling bribes.

In the entire sphere of environmental issues and Indian minority rights, the Bolivian State carries on a tradition dating from Spanish colonial times: laws have flexible validity being actually enforced only if they comply with dominant interests. Agreements are often made in order to ease certain momentarily troublesome pressures. This casual application of laws can be observed in the case of the national parks, wildlife reserves and sanctuaries: they exist on paper but often no attention or financing from the State exists. Although every economic (and in some, every human) activity is forbidden, the national parks are being colonized and, in some cases, used for coca plantations and cocaine refinement. This, for instance, is the fate of the Isiboro-Sécure National Park (established in 1965), a part of which has now been declared indigenous territory. In all of them intense logging and massive hunting of legally protected animal species are taking place – of course tolerated and often encouraged by government agencies.[62] All timber firms are by law obliged to re-afforest the exploited areas (two new trees for each felled tree), yet not a single case of re-afforestation is so far known.[63]

The Amazonian Indians (roughly 100000) do not constitute a major element within Bolivian society: they have no political or economic influence. Since they have so far not been able to generate a powerful solidarity movement effectively to support their claims, the Indian lowland communities remain in a vulnerable position. The central government knows well enough that it will not be seriously criticized for failing to carry through the agreement on indigenous territories; certain leaders of these lowland communities have also proven to be corruptible with governmental favors and gifts. The practical functioning of the indigenous territories since September 1990 suggests that strict environmental protection is not a goal shared by all community members. According to available information, the existence of two main tendencies among the Amazonian Indians can be distinguished. The first is an endeavor indeed to preserve the old traditions of living in and on the forests, rejecting modern conceptions of resource utilization and particularly the cutting down of trees. The second – which has a considerable and probably growing following – enlists the claims to autonomy (and the so-called Amazonian ideology) towards a very profane goal: to share in the highly profitable business of logging and timber exporting. The aim, presumably, is to obtain both property rights over the forests and a kind of wide autonomy within the eastern region, in order to escape burdensome controls by the central government and international organizations seeking to enforce ecological and conservation measures.[64]

At present the most important ally of the Amazonian Indians is the Catholic Church[65] which, in Bolivia, has abandoned its conservative positions and supports the grant of political autonomy and property rights to the forests to the lowland communities. It further favors the cultural and educational autonomy of the Amazonian tribes and the establishment of a special legal status for the indigenous territories. The Catholic Church is more cautious with regard to environmental issues; it gives no mention at all to the preservation of the forests, stressing instead the need for fresh investments in the tropical areas. The support of trade unions for the lowland Indians has followed the same pattern, although in a much more lukewarm way: they approve of the bestowal of cultural and administrative autonomy on the Indian communities, protest vehemently against "imperialist penetration of the tropical regions" and against the "capitalistic exploitation" of "national resources", but keep silent on environmental issues. The trade union movement has adopted an anti-establishment line, but at the same time avoids any utterance that might be interpreted as being against material progress, modernization and industrialization. The peasant unions furthermore favor the extension of the agrarian frontier into the tropical regions and the maintenance of the coca plantations, so that they do not seem very interested in the preservation of ecosystems. The support of trade unions and peasant movements (whose members are Indians from the western highland) of the eastern Amazonian tribes can be considered as mainly rhetorical.[66]

The demands of the Amazonian Indians have met the most outspoken opposition from private entrepreneurs. The Bolivian Federation of Private Entrepreneurs *(Confederación de Empresarios Privados de Bolivia)*[67], the cattle-breeders[68], timber industrialists[69], local pressure groups of the eastern regions[70] and forestry engineers[71] have harshly and steadily opposed them. The central points stressed by them are:

-Bolivia's sacred unity has been seriously endangered by the creation of autonomous territories; the country could be fragmented into little republics, making sustainable development impossible.

-The solution of social and cultural (i.e.: ethnic) problems must necessarily pass via economic measures and the attainment of continuous growth. Ecological considerations are out of place in the Bolivian context.

-Autonomous territories on an ethnic base will discourage investments while encouraging bureaucratic inefficiency and arbitrariness.

-The creation of ethnically defined territories implies a step backwards into a premodern form of societal organization through privileged treatment of small groups and regions to the disadvantage of the nation and its modernization process as a whole.

-These measures transgress the principle of private property. The State reneges on legal contracts with timber firms.

-The timber industrialists apply the most advanced technology and, of course, care for reafforestation; frustrating them implies technical backwardness, corruption and the loss of the already achieved level of civilization. Many of these arguments are those of vested interests, but some reflect a well-founded critique of the indigenous position.

A very complex topic does not permit us to draw simple conclusions, all the more because the available empirical data do not yield an unequivocal image and, since political options are at stake, options which represent the deeply felt aspirations of the majority of Bolivian society. These aspirations can, however, collide with ecological limits to ambitious development processes. It is for instance possible that, in Latin America "most land is seriously fragile"[72], although – according to certain authors – this is no permanent obstacle to degrees of development.[73] In any case, there are alarming reports[74] on the scope and rapidity of forest destruction, soil erosion and dissolution of life styles and societal models in Bolivia's tropical regions – all of which can affect human and natural diversity in the near future. Even though the survival of mankind and modern civilization may not yet depend on the fate of the tropical forests, it is not too early to call attention to an impending catastrophe in a vast part of South America.[75]

TABLE 1 Question: *Bolivia disposes of a very rich endowment of natural resources (including energy sources, minerals, arable lands, pastures and promising uninhabited territories). Please comment on this statement.* (Figures in percentages, N=100)

	private entre- preneurs	journa- lists	trade union leaders	civil servants	total
Basically correct statement	88	80	96	92	89
Basically erroneous statement	8	16	4	4	8
no answer	4	4	0	4	3
					100

TABLE 2 Question: *Bolivian society is aspiring to an all-round modernization process. Which are the most serious obstacles to it?* (Figures in percentages, N=100)

	private entrepreneurs	journalists	trade union leaders	civil servants	total
A relatively poor endowment of natural resources and fragile soils	8	12	0	4	6
Foreign pressures and dependence on the world market	36	56	60	44	49
Inappropriate social and political structures	56	28	36	52	43
no answer	0	4	4	0	2
					100

TABLE 3 Question: *What should be the final goal of the current modernization process and of the developmental efforts of Bolivian society?* (Figures in percentages, N=100)

	private entrepreneurs	journalists	trade union leaders	civil servants	total
An industrialized and urbanized society, with high consumption and education levels	64	64	72	68	67
A mixed society, with an important agricultural sector and with indigenous communities pursuing their own developmental models	24	20	20	16	20
no answer	12	16	8	16	13
					100

TABLE 4 Question: *Processes of industrialization and urbanization could in the long run cause environmental pollution, strains on the ecosystems and destruction of forests. Please comment on this statement.* (Figures in percentages, N=100)

	private entre-preneurs	journa-lists	trade union leaders	civil servants	total
This is the unavoidable price of material progress. In the Bolivian case, conservationist considerations are exaggerated.	64	60	80	68	68
Policies should prevent environmental degradation caused by modernization processes.	24	28	16	24	23
no answer	12	12	4	8	9
					100

TABLE 5 Question: *Bolivian towns have in recent times undergone a rapid modernization process, drastically expanding their housing and industrial areas without providing their inhabitants with adequate educational opportunities and public services (drinking water, electricity, etc.). Please comment on this statement.* (Figures in percentages, N=100)

	private entre-preneurs	journa-lists	trade union leaders	civil servants	total
Despite difficulties and shortages urban development is a positive feature and attests to Bolivia's material progress.	60	64	64	60	62

Bolivian towns are ugly, disorderly and too rapidly growing agglomerations offering a diminishing quality of life.	28	32	24	24	27
no answer	12	4	12	16	11
					100

TABLE 6 Question: *According to the last census (June 1992) the population stands at 6,3 million. Population density is one of the lowest in Latin America. What is the meaning of these demographic data with regard to development strategies and goals?* (Figures in percentages, N=100)

	private entre- preneurs	journa- lists	trade union leaders	civil servants	total
We need a larger population and higher density in order to use resources better.	76	68	80	80	76
A relatively small population and low density mean fewer strains on the ecosystems and fewer development problems.	16	20	8	16	15
no anwer	8	12	2	4	9
					100

TABLE 7 Question: *International organizations and well-known scientists plead for programs to restrict population growth in Third World countries. Does this apply to Bolivian reality?* (Figures in percentages, N=100)

	private entre- preneurs	journa- lists	trade union leaders	civil servants	total
Over-population is an imperialist invention; checking population growth must be opposed.	12	20	32	20	21
Because of the low density and declining demographic growth rate such programs are unnecessary.	36	32	44	42	36
These programs may be supported because they can diminish strains on the ecosystems and alleviate the situation of the unemployed.	44	32	16	40	33
no answer	8	16	8	8	10
					100

TABLE 8 Question: *In 1991 the Bolivian government conferred on some Indian communities of the eastern (Amazonian) lowlands limited sovereign rights to organize and exploit forest reserves according to their own customs and norms. What do you think of this?* (Figures in percentages, N=100)

	private entre- preneurs	journa- lists	trade union leaders	civil servants	total
This measure can endanger the unity of the country and all development efforts in the eastern region; it affects rights to private property.	84	52	52	72	65

This measure constitutes an act of historic justice; it can contribute to an original development model.	4	32	40	12	22
no answer	12	16	8	16	13
					100

TABLE 9 Question: *What is the appropriate response to the autonomy claims of the Indian communities in the eastern lowlands?* (Figures in percentages, N=100)

	private entre-preneurs	journa-lists	trade union leaders	civil servants	total
Grant of extensive autonomy; transformation into a federal nation.	0	16	24	4	11
Grant of restricted autonomy; transfer of some economic powers to the Indian communities.	8	16	32	16	18
Accelerated economic development of the whole country will automatically improve the condition of the Indian communities.	48	40	44	48	45
Maintenance of the present situation.	28	20	0	24	18
no answer	16	8	0	8	8
					100

TABLE 10 Question: *The mass media increasingly report on the destruction of the rain forests by human agency and on the very vulnerable character of tropical soils. Please comment on this statement.* (Figures in percentages, N=100)

	private entre- preneurs	journa- lists	trade union leaders	civil servants	total
These reports overstate the case; the opening-up of the tropical zones must continue.	48	36	60	44	47
These reports actually reflect reality; they must be taken seriously.	36	52	28	4	40
no answer	16	12	12	12	13
					100

NOTES

1 Wagner Terrazas Urquidi, *La supervivencia de los bolivianos*, La Paz: Sociedad Boliviana de Ecología 1983, p. 11; Terrazas Urquidi, *Bolivia, país saqueado*, La Paz: Carlinghi 1973, p. 82.

2 Cf."Los (medio) ambientes de la ecología", in: *Revista Unitas*, La Paz, Nr. 6, June 1992, pp. 27-32; Ricardo Cox Aranfbar, "Nuestro ambiente y medio", in: ibid., pp. 68-72.

3 Cf. "Il Congreso Indígena Interamericano de Recursos Naturales y Medio Ambiente", San Ignacio de Moxos, December 1991, in: *Revista Unitas*, Nr. 5, March 1992, pp. 89-92; "Declaracion Kari-Oca y la Carta de la Tierra de los Pueblos Indígenas, in : *Habitat*, La Paz, Supplement of July 1992, pp. 11-17.

4 Cf. Olivier Dollfus, *Territorios andinos. Reto y memoria*, Lima: IFEA / IEP 1991, passim.

5 Cf. Guido Chumiray Rojas, "Kuruyuki cien años despues", in: *Revista Unitas*, Nr. 6, June 1992, pp. 73-80; Avecita Chicchón, "Can

Indigenous People and Conservationists be Allies?", in: *TCD Newsletter*, vol. 23, February 1991, pp. 1-5.

6 "Sin iniciativa ni trabajo previo: Bolivia asiste a la Cumbra de la Tierra sólo para firmar", in: *Presencia* (La Paz), June 10th, 1992; "Temor en los países pobres: ecología podría ser un bumerang", in: *Presencia*, June 15, 1992; "Grupo 77 se pronuncia sobre ecología y desarrollo", in: *Presencia*, March 6, 1992.

7 "Temor en ...", op. cit. (note 6).

8 Ibid. - President Gaviria belongs to the traditional Liberal Party of Columbia.

9 Ibid. President Serrano belongs also to a liberal, right-wing party.

10 Baena Soares: "defendió la tesis de que la protección de las selvas no debe hacerse a costa de los pobres de las ciudades", in: *Presencia*, June 12, 1992.

11 "Temor en ...", loc. cit. Cf. the report by Carlos Cardoso, "Un futuro promisorio para la Tierra", in: *Habitat* (La Paz), Nr. 17, September 1992, p. 3 sq.

12 Marthadina Mendizábal de Finot, "La Cumbre desde Bolivia. Preservación versus conservación de bosques en la CNUMAD", in: *Presencia*, June 12, 1992.

13 Marthadina Mendizábal de Finot, "La Cumbre desde Bolivia. Pobreza a medio ambiente en discusión", in: *Presencia*, June 7, 1992.

14 "Una Amazonia de carne y hueso", in: *Presencia*, June 8, 1992.

15 Alberto K. Bailey Gutiérrez, "Conciencia verde durante dos semanas", in: *Presencia*, May 31, 1992.

16 Vice-gobernador del Estado de Amazonas: "países desarrollados quieren conservar la Amazonía a costa de vidas humanas", in: *El mundo*, (Santa Cruz), March 5, 1992.

17 "Cumbre de la Tierra": Bolivia asiste, pero tiene sus dudas (Interview with Jaime Cardozo), in: *Presencia*, May 31, 1992.

18 "Los dilemas del Nuevo Mundo", in: *Presencia*, May 31, 1992.

19 Javier Palza Medina, "Pueblos indígenas y medio ambiente", in: *Presencia*, August 24, 1992.

20 Ricardo Ocampo Castro, "El País vacío", in: *Ultima Hora*, (La Paz), September 8, 1991.

21 "El desarrollo infinito", in: *Presencia*, May 31, 1992; "De la conciencia a la acción! El estado del medio embiente en Bolivia. Propuestas políticas y programáticas", La Paz: Liga de Defensa del Medio Ambiente 1992, p. 31 sqq. 41 sq.

22 José Gutiérrez Basadre, "El desafío europeo nos conducirá al suicidio ecológico", in *Presencia*, August 7, 1991. - Gutiérrez Basadre, a

representative of the landowners of eastern Bolivia, has published regularly on environmental issues, attacking ecological efforts and asserting that Latin America has nothing to do with the situation of Africa or Asia.

23 Ibid. - Cf. José Gutiérrez Basadre, "El humo, el cólera y la ley del medio ambiente", in: *Presencia*, August 30, 1991.

24 "Deforestación resultado de conversión de los bosques a tierras agrícolas", in *El Diario* (La Paz), August 26, 1992. Critical of this position: Lincoln Quevedo, "Atropello a la naturaleza bajo la consigna de generar divisas", in *Presencia*, June 5, 1992.

25 José Gutiérrez Basadre, "La Declaración de Manaos en el Senado Nacional", in: *Presencia*, March 11, 1992.

26 J. Gutiérrez Basadre, "El desafío ...", op.cit. (note 22), loc. cit.

27 "Amazónicos unidos contra pobreza", in: *Presencia,,* February 12, 1992.

28 "En defensa de bosques países amazónicos hacen causa común", in: *Presencia*, June 5, 1992; Marthadina Mendizábal de Finot, "La Cumbre vista desde Bolivia. El informe de Bolivia", in: ibid.; "La fiebre de conservar lo que aun queda", in: ibid.

29 Marthadina Mendizábal de Finot, "La Cumbre desde Bolivia. La defensa de bosques en la CNUMAD", in: *Presencia*, June 6, 1992.

30 The thinking of these movements has been decisively influenced by international Non Governmental Organizations. - Cf. "Opinión mayoritaria de las ONGs para el éxito de la reunión cumbre sobre medio ambiente y desarrollo", in *Habitat* (Liga de Defensa del Medio Ambiente), La Paz, Nr. 16, May 1992, pp. 3-6: This document includes some reasonable principles about the protection of ecosystems, but is in large part devoted to the usual economic demands on the developed world. - Cf. also: "Resultados Carta de la Tierra de la ONGs" in: ibid., p. 10; "Tratado entre Pueblos Indígenas y ONGs", in: ibid., pp. 20-21.

31 For the general Latin American discussion of this issue cf. José Luis de Imaz, "Los que mandan", Buenos Aires: *EUDFBA* 1964; E. Bradford Burns / Thomas E. Kidmore, "Elites, Masses and Modernization in Latin America", Austin: Texas U.P. 1979; Günter Endruweit, *Elite und Entwicklung. Theorie und Empirie zum Einfluss von Eliten auf Entwicklungsprozesse*, Frankfurt / Bern: Lang 1986; Hans-Dieter Evers / Tilman Schiel, *Strategische Gruppen. Vergleichende Studien zu Staat, Bürokratie und Klassenbildung in der Dritten Welt*, Berlin: Reimer 1988.

32 José L. Havet, *The Diffusion of Power. Rural Elites in a Bolivian Province*, Ottawa 1985; Salvador Romero Pittari, *Notas sobre la estratificación social en Bolivia*, La Paz: Universidad Católica de Bolivia 1974.

33 Cf. Claudio Véliz, *The Centralist Tradition of Latin America*, Princeton U.P. 1980; Howard J. Wiarda (ed.), *Politics and Social Change in Latin*

America. The Distinct Tradition. Amherst: Massachusetts U.P. 1982; René Antonio Mayorga, "De la anomia política al orden democrático?", La Paz: CEBEM 1991; Guillermo A. O'Donnell / Philippe Schmitter, *Transitions from Authoritarian Rule: Tentative Conclusions about Uncertain Democracies*, Baltimore: Johns Hopkins U.P. 1986; James M. Malloy / Eduardo A. Gamarra, "The Transition to Democracy in Bolivia", in: J.M. Malloy / M. Sellingson (eds.), *Authoritarians and Democrats: The Politics of Regime Transition in Latin America*, Pittsburgh: Pittsburg U.P. 1987; René Antonio Mayorga, "Democratización y modernización del Estado en Bolivia", La Paz: CEBEM 1991; Jorge Lazarte, *Cambios en los paradigmas del accionar político*, La Paz: ILDIS 1988; Jerry R. Ladman (ed.), *Modern Day Bolivia: Legacy of the Revolution and Prospects for the Future*, Tempe: Arizona U.P. 1982.

34 Director del PAAB (Jorge Cortés). "Con desarrollo sostenido se puede preservar los recursos naturales", in: *Presencia*, August 26, 1992; "El deterioro del medio ambiente es causa de mayor pobreza", in: *Presencia*, April 21, 1992 (Interview with Carlos Arze, Director of LIDEMA = Liga de Defensa del Medio Ambiente (League for the Protection of the Environment).

35 "Ganaderos en contra de leyes de medio ambiente e indígena", in: *Presencia*, September 25, 1991.

36 José Gutiérrez Basadre, "Asesores europeos distorsionan realidad del Beni", in *Presencia*, March 23, 1992.

37 "Brasil: militares impedirán que ONU preserve Amazonía", in: *Presencia*, August 29, 1991; "Dilema en torno a la Amazonía", in *Presencia*, July 20, 1991.

38 Cf. the excellent analytic forecast of the Earth Summit in Rio devoted to this theme: "Festival der Heuchelei", in: *Der Spiegel* (Hamburg), vol. 46, Nr. 21, May 18, 1992, p. 246.

39 Hans Mathieu / Joachim Gottschalk, "UNCED II and Beyond: The Politics of the Global Environment", in: *Vierteljahresberichte der Friedrich-Ebert-Stiftung*, Nr. 128, June 1992, p. 114.

40 Central Obrera Boliviana (=COB) is the Bolivian Trade Union Federation, known for its radical leftist positions.

41 The (Indian) peasants of the western highlands have their own union, the Confederación Sindical Unica de Trabajadores Campesinos de Bolivia (=CSUTCB), which is both within and outside the COB.

42 Since the Agrarian Reform (1953) there are white (non-Indian) landowners only in the eastern lowlands.

43 On demographic issues, there is still virtual unanimity among the most varied political and social sectors to deplore the "meagre" results of the census of June 1992. - Cf. Ana María Fabbri, "Control de población: cuatro gatos y ahora estériles", in: *Presencia*, June 14, 1992. - Some

interesting insights in: Washington Nováes, "Amazonien und der Nord-Süd-Konflikt", in: *Vierteljahresbericht der Friedrich-Ebert-Stiftung*, Nr. 128, June 1992, pp. 119-127.

44 Cf. the excellent article by Carlos Navia Ribera, "Reconocimiento, democracia y control de Territorios Indígenas: situación y experiencias en Bolivia", in: *Revista Unitas*, Nr. 5, March 1992, pp. 38-48; Miguel Urioste, "Desarrollo rural, Estado y modernidad", in: ibid., pp. 60-66.

45 Cf. Javier Fernández / Pablo Pacheco, "Los cambios en la Amazonía central y su impacto ambiental", in: *Revista Unitas*, Nr. 6, June 1992, pp. 42-56.

46 On the causes of the partially seasonal migration of the highland Indians cf. Jane L. Collings, "Labor Scarcity and Ecological Change", in: Peter D. Little / Michael M. Horowith / A. Endre Nyeres (eds.), *Lands at Risk in the Third World: Local-Level Perspectives*, Boulder / London: Westview 1987, p. 28 sq.

47 Cf. David A. Eastwood, "Planned Colonization in Bolivian and Ecuadorian Amazonia. The Need for a Re-Assessment of Successful Planning Policy", in: *Revista Europea de Estudios Latinoamericanos y del Caribe*, Nr. 50, June 1991, pp. 115-134; Michael Painter, "Unequal Exchange: The Dynamics of Settler Impoverishment and Environmental Destruction", in: Little / Horowith / Nyeres (eds.), op. cit. (note 47), pp. 164-191, especially p. 185 sq.

48 Cf. the very early testimony: "Conclusion de simposio: el hombre provoca los peores daños a la ecología del país", in: *Presencia*, May 17, 1982; *Ecología y recursos naturales*, Cochabamba: Centro Portales 1983, pp. 13-22; on the causes of this process cf. "Tierras del altiplano, valles y llanos en peligro de desertificación", in: *Presencia*, June 20, 1989; "Más de un 80% de tierras erosionadas en el Altiplano", in: *Presencia*, July 20, 1992; Joan Martínez-Alier, "Ecology and the Poor: A Neglected Dimension of Latin American History", in: *Journal of Latin American Studies*, vo. 23, Nr. 3, October 1991.

49 Cf. Olivier Dollfus, op. cit. (note 4), pp. 105-119; Stephan Rist, *Etica, naturaleza y desarrollo en los Andes*, Cochabamba: AGRUCO 1992, p. 4 sqq., 11 sqq.; Hans Ellenberg, *Desarrollar sin destruir*, La Paz: Instituto de Ecología 1981, passim; about similarities with the idea of ecodevelopment cf. Bernhard Glaeser (ed.), *Ecodevelopment. Concepts, Projects, Strategies*, Oxford: Pergamon 1984, passim.

50 José Blanes, "Migraciones, colonización y narcotráfico en Bolivia", in: *Desarrollo amazónico: una perspectiva latinoamericana*, Lima: CIPA / INANDEP 1990, p. 225, 233; Rainer Stolz et al., *Posibilidades de utilización de los recursos tropicales forestales del Norte y del Este de Bolivia considerando aspectos ecológicos*, Bonn: Bundesministerium für wirtschaftliche Zusammenarbeit 1986, p. 255.

51 Cf. C. Allen, *The Hold Life Has. Coca and Cultural Identity in an Andean Community*, Washington; Smithsonian Institution 1988; "La coca provoca catástrofe ambiental en el Chapare", in: *El Deber* (Santa Cruz), February 22, 1992; Jorge Giusti, *Producción, tráfico y consumo de drogas: su significación económica y social*, Santiago de Chile: CEPAL 1991, p. 115 sqq.; cf. also Marc J. Dourojeanni, *Impactos ambientales del cultivo de la coca y la producción de cocaína en la Amazonía peruana*, Lima: Universidad Nacional Agraria 1990, p. 286.

52 Cf. S. Hecht / A. Cockburn, *The Fate of the Forest. Developers, Destroyers and Defenders of the Amazon*, London: Verso 1989; Rainer Stolz et al., op. cit. (note 50), p. 49; Marianne Schmink / Charles H. Wood, "The 'Political Ecology' of Amazonia", in: Little / Horowitz / Nyeres (eds.), op. cit. (note 46), pp. 38-57; Eduardo Bedoya Garland, "Intensification and Degradation in the Agricultural Systems of the Peruvian Upper Jungle", in: ibid., pp. 292-295.

53 José Blanes, op. cit. (note 50), p. 233; Ana María Vera, "Droga y ecología: un duelo a muerte", in: *Ultima Hora* (La Paz), April 12, 1991; Henry oporto Castro, "Bolivia: el complejo coca / cocaína", in: Diego García-Sayán (ed.), *Coca, cocaína y narcotráfico, Laberinto en los Andes*, Lima: Comisión Andina de Juristas 1989, pp. 171-174; Kevin Healy, "The Boom within the Crisis: Some Recent Effects of Foreign Cocaine Markets on Bolivian Rural Society and Economy", in: D. Pacini / C. Franquemont (eds.), *Coca and Cocaine: Effects on People and Policy in Latin America*, Peterborough (N.H.): Cultural Survival 1986, pp. 101-143.

54 Cf. Teresa Flores Bedregal, "Los cambios en el movimiento indígena mundial. Diálogo con José María Iñet, indio mocoví", in *Presencia*, May 31, 1992; Edwin Chacón Aramayo, "Bolivia tiene responsabilidad a revindicaciones territoriales indígenas", in *Presencia*, June 15, 1992; *INFORME R*, vol. XI, Nr. 228, 1-15 October, 1991 (special issue: "Parchando los daños ecológicos").

55 "Il Congreso ...", op. cit. (note 3), pp. 89-92; cf. also the preparatory document: "La casa que se llama bosque", La Paz: ILDIS 1990.

56 The four territories (all located in the Beni department) are: Isiboro-Sécure (1.1 million hectars and 7000 inhabitants); the "multi-ethnical territory" (355 000 hectares and 2000 inhabitants); Chimane (392 000 hectares and 4000 inhabitants - the most important because of its wood resources and excellent soils); El Iviato / Sirionó (80 000 hectares and 1000 inhabitants). For a description and a map of the new territories cf. Carlos Navia Ribera, op. cit. (note 44), p. 39, 46.

57 "Gobierno declara 'Territorios Indígenas' zonas en las que nacieron y viven etnies", in: *Presencia*, October 18, 1991; Guillermo Rioja Ballivián, "Conquista del pueblo chimane, pilón lajas, territorio indígena", in: *Presencia*, May 10, 1992.

58 Cf. Carlos Navia Ribera, op. cit. (note 45), p. 46; Rainer Stolz et al., op. cit. (note 50), p. 80; cf. also the contradictory reports: "Reducen volumen de corte de madera en bosque Chimán", in: *Presencia*, April 12, 1992; "Coordinadora indígena: Madereras continúan explotación ilegal del bosque de los Chimanes", in: *Ultima Hora*, July 14, 1992.

59 "Gobierno no cumple con decretos de respeto a territorios indígenas", in: *Presencia*, October 30, 1991: "Siguen destruyendo el bosque Chimanes", in: *Aqui* (La Paz), May 29, 1992; "Gobierno incumplió acuerdos suscritos con grupos indígenas", in: *Presencia*, March 17, 1991.

60 "MACA violó decreto de reservas forestales", in: *Presencia*, August 26, 1992; "Empleados de YPFB se dedican a depredar bosques", in: *Presencia*, April 12, 1992.

61 Rainer Stolz et al., op. cit. (note 51), pp. 83-92, 256. - This report to the German Ministry of Economic Cooperation (and similar studies) has not been contested at all by government officials.

62 On the national parks and wildlife reserves cf. Stolz et al., ibid., pp. 178-181, 259, 289-296, 302; cf. the still valid study: Peter H. Freeman et al., *Bolivia: State of the Environment and Natural Resources. A Field Study*, McLean / West Virginia: JRB Associates 1980, p. 26.

63 Stolz, ibid., p. 256.

64 Carlos Navia Ribera, op. cit. (note 44), p. 45. - Cf. the very informative report by a Catholic bishop on the "treachery" perpetrated by the leaders of the Chimane community: "Obispo califica acuerdo sobre Bosque Chimano como una traición", in: *Presencia*, September 15, 1992.

65 "Obispos piden respeto al 'derecho de aquellos que poseen la tierra' ", in: *Presencia*, September 16, 1990 (official declaration of the Bolivian Episcopal Council of the Catholic Church); cf. also "Explotación y menosprecio por los pueblos originarios continúan", in: *Presencia*, February 1, 1992 (declaration of general Assembly of Bolivian Clergy and Monks).

66 "Pronunciamiento emanado de la consultiva realizada en la ciudad de Trinidad (...) el 13 de septiembre de 1990", in: *Presencia*, September 16, 1990.

67 Confederación de Empresarios Privados de Bolivia, "Los grupos étnicos y el desarrollo del país", in: *Presencia*, September 14, 1990; CEPB, "Ley indígena conformará 'republiquetas' dentro del país y frenará el desarrollo", in: *Presencia*, September 25, 1991.

68 "Lo que debe saber el gobierno y el pueblo de Bolivia sobre las demandas de territorios en las etnías", in: *Presencia*, September 15, 1990.

69 "La demanda indígena y su solución", in: *Presencia*, September 12, 1990; "Empresarios forestales aguardan negociación compensatoria", in: *La Razón* (La Paz), September 30, 1990.

70 "Gobierno sentó un funesto precedente al dividir el territorio para las etnías", in: *Presencia*, September 27, 1990.

71 Sociedad de Ingenieros Forestales de Bolivia "Marcha indígena: manipulaciones ponen en riesgo el más avanzado plan de manejo forestal del país", in: *Presencia*, September 11, 1990.

72 William M. Denevan, "The Geography of Fragile Lands in Latin America", in: John O. Browder (ed.), *Fragile Lands of Latin America. Strategies for Sustainable Development*, Boulder / London: Westview 1989, p. 24. - Denevan is the author of the classical work: *The Aboriginal Cultural Geography of the Llanos de Moxos of Bolivia*, Berkeley: California U.P. 1966 (concerning the eastern lowlands).

73 David Gow, "Development of Fragile Lands: An Integrated Approach Reconsidered", in: J.O. Browder (ed.), ibid., p. 40: "There is no essential contradiction between sustainable economic development and conservation of the natural resource base. The environmental community increasingly realizes and accepts that conservation and economic development are complementary concerns, particularly in the case of those people, often already marginal, who are trying to live off fragile lands".

74 "Es alarmante destrucción de bosques en el país", in: *Presencia*, June 5, 1989; "Explotación irracional de los bosques causa inmenso daño", in:*Presencia*, December 21, 1989; "En dos ó tres años se agotarán bosques de mara y roble en la Chiquitanía", in: *Presencia*, July 6, 1989; "Bolivia perderá la riqueza de sus bosques hasta el año 2000", in: *Presencia*, June 13, 1992; "Depredación sin límites efectúan colonizadores y madereras", in: *Presencia*, September 13, 1992.

75 In any case it is important to remark that ecological consciousness may be still underdeveloped within the western Indian community in Bolivia. The distinguished economist of Aymara origin, Fernando Untoja, asserted that ecology is a mere ideology of the rich, fright-ridden societies of the North. F. Untoja, "Ecología: una ideología?", in: *Presencia*, September 21, 1991.

12 BETWEEN REFORM AND DISASTER: OPTIONS FOR SUB-SAHARAN AFRICA IN THE EMERGING GLOBAL ORDER

Julius O. Ihonvbere

It is now obvious that sub-Saharan Africa is increasingly being marginalized in the global system. The monumental developments in the global system in the past decade as well as the region's unenviable performance show very clearly its powerlessness in global relations and its vulnerability to external pressures, penetration and manipulation. Despite political and ideological experimentation, regime changes, foreign aid and countless declarations, charters and cooperation schemes, the region remains the most marginal, the most poverty-stricken, the most debt-ridden (in per capita terms), the most-politically unstable and the least attractive to

---

This article draws on the research "Africa as a Threat to World Peace and Security: Implications of Deepening Socio-economic Crisis" funded by the World Society Foundation. Julius Omozuanvbo Ihonvbere was born in Oyo, Nigeria, and took his Ph. D. in political economy from the University of Toronto, Canada. His research was started in Nigeria while he was a senior lecturer at the Faculty of Social Science, University of Port Harcourt, Nigeria. Due to the 1990 political disturbances he had to flee and now lives in Canada where he is professor at the University of Toronto, Department of Political Science, 100 St. George Street, Toronto, M51 1A1.

donors and investors. As the Economic Commission for Africa (ECA) has noted, the deepening crisis of the region is "manifested not only in abysmal declines in economic indicators and trends, but more tragically and glaringly in the suffering, hardship and impoverishment of the vast majority of African people".[1]

How did a sub-continent, with about 600 million people (about 12% of the world's population), some 53-odd states, with a landmass second only to Asia, and containing huge reserves of several space-age minerals[2] get to this point? The answer can be found in Africa's historical experience, the consequences and implications of that experience, and in post-colonial alignment and re-alignment of class forces in a direction which has culminated in the fragmentation of society, waste, corruption, mismanagement, the suffocation of civil society and the general inability to reverse the distortions and disarticulations of the colonial experience.

In this article, we explore, first, the background to the African predicament; second, we discuss the specifics of the crisis in order to highlight the contemporary consequences of Africa's historical experience; third, we examine responses to the African crisis, paying particular attention to structural adjustment and political conditionality; and finally, we locate Africa in the contemporary world system and make projections for the future.

Background to the African Predicament

Africa's contact with the forces of Western imperialism left it structually distorted and disarticulated. It lost the capacity for endogenous development and, as Aimé Cesaire would put it, all "extra-ordinary possibilities" were stultified, halted or destroyed.[3] The colonial experience left legacies which till this very day continue to have direct or indirect impacts on politics, production and exchange relations. The relationship between the state and civil society, the role of the bureaucracy and the military, the power of foreign capital in the local economy, the character of the dominant local classes and the dynamics of primordial conflicts have some relationship to the impact and implications of years of foreign colonial domination and exploitation. As the Organization of African Unity (OAU) noted in one of its major documents in 1986, "the colonial economic structures inherited by most African countries have proved difficult to be changed radically for African development ... These colonial economic legacies have been compounded by a host of other related international factors ... "[4] Earlier, in the *Lagos Plan of Action,* African leaders traced the origins of their woes to "the disastrous effects of natural and endemic diseases of the cruellest type ... settler exploitation arising from colonialism, racism and apartheid".[5] Yet such explanations have been conveniently silent on the *internal* dimensions of the African crisis.

To be sure, the colonial experience left Africa with a) non-hegemonic and unstable states; b) a corrupt, weak, fractionalized and unproductive dominant class; c) deep-rooted ethnic, regional and religious antagonisms and conflicts; d) a weak and marginal industrial sector with little or no linkages to other sectors of the economy; e) a foreign-dominated economy especially in the extractive and financial sectors; f) an inefficient, exploitative and corrupt bureaucratic sector designed to serve the interests of an elite; g) an excessive culture of economic and political commandism, with the state determining all economic, social and political policies and relations; h) a culture of non-accountability of the state, its agents and agencies to the needs of the people and reliance on manipulation, repression and the initimidation of communities; i) concentration of rural producers on cash as against food crop production and exports, thus laying the foundation for a food dependency; j) the accentuation of spatial inequalities through the concentration of power, resources, opportunities and facilities in a few selected urban centers; k) a uni-directional external trade structure designed to consolidate dependence on the centers of imperialism and make the dominated social formation easy to penetrate, dominate and exploit; l) the bastardization of educational, social and cultural forms and traditions thus creating an inferiority complex, an alien world-view, taste dependence, distaste for local products and a neo-colonial mentality; and m) the structured incorporation into and marginalization of Africa in the global division of labor.

However, African elites have, since political independence in the late 1950s, contributed significantly to the consolidation and reproduction of these inherited distortions and conditions of crisis. They have depoliticized the masses, appropriated the privileges of the former colonial officers, intimidated and harassed popular groups, taken corruption to legendary proportions, wasted limited scarce resources, and suffocated civil society. African leaders, in spite of the creation of the OAU in 1963, have remained grossly incapable of sponsoring viable development projects, challenging the region's marginalization in the world capitalist system, or strengthening intra-African trade relations which remains at about 5% of its total visible trade. At all levels of development, the African region has simply moved from crisis to crisis.

Specifics of the African Crisis

The record of decline and the manifestations of the African predicament are so severe and graphic that they have generated a wave of cynicism and pessimism about the chances for recovery in the region. It is impossible to drive home the desperate dimension of African reality without highlighting the dismal statistics. The usual error in most existing analyses is the tendency deliberately to downplay or overlook the causes of the manifestations outlined in the earlier section. Hence, public policy and other prescriptions, especially those of the World Bank, the IMF and Western donors, tend to respond to the manifestations, rather than to the causes of the African crisis. Thus, regimes and social classes directly responsible for the current crisis and which have, and continue to benefit from it, are expected to suddenly experience a change of heart and adopt different policies simply because they are dictated from abroad. The structural roots of the problem are ignored, the class dimensions are ignored being treated as a moral, emotional or philanthropic issue. The net result, as the World Bank admits in its 1989 report in relation to the failure of more than half of its projects in Africa is the intensification of the crisis and the further marginalization of the region in the global division of labor.[6]

Observers agree on certain facts: that the population is growing too fast; that the foreign debt burden is unmanageable; that exports, investment and employment have stagnated or fallen; and that agriculture has underperformed. In the 1986 *African Priority Programme,* the OAU expressed its concern at the "continuing deterioration of our economies which have been severely affected by the deep world economic recession and penalized by an unjust and inequitable international economic system". The Organization went on to draw attention to the fact that the region's crisis was "aggravated by drought and natural calamities, compounded by the problem of refugees and displaced persons, thus making almost half of the Member States of our Organization dependent on food aid". Finally, the OAU catalogued problems as including:

"deteriorating terms of trade and the consequent reduction in export earnings for debt servicing, unprecedented rise in interest rates, sharp exchange rate fluctuations, deteriorating terms of borrowing and the reduction in the flow of concessional resources, the combined effects of which result in the net capital outflow from most of our Member States. In this regard, the 26 African LDCs have been the most seriously affected."[7]

In spite of these realizations and public confessions, African leaders hardly altered the patterns and structures of power, politics, production and exchange in their respective economies. The OAU blamed the crisis on outside forces; the ECA, until very recently, blamed the crisis on the debt burden and IMF/World Bank-sponsored orthodox adjustment programs; and the World Bank, again, until 1989, blamed the crisis exclusively on poor domestic *economic* policies.

The complaints by the OAU and the ECA about unfavorable external conditions are hardly new. The world system, right from the era of the slave trade through colonialism to contemporary neo-colonialism, has never favored Africa. The region has historically been marginal to the outside world in terms of their priorities and it has been nothing more than a source of cheap labor, raw materials and a dumping ground for outdated and second-rate products. International organizations like the World Bank and the IMF practically had the same attitude. Africans were never perceived as capable of handling their own affairs. Hence, though the "World Bank employs the services of management consultants" to work on Africa, of the "80 000 expatriate consultants ... less than 0.1% are Africans".[8] Transnational corporations have always treated weak African economes as pawns in their global calculations bringing in little or no capital, sourcing their investment capital locally, using few or no local raw materials, not promoting local research and development, corrupting politicians and transfering more resources than they bring in from abroad.

Finally, even during the Cold War, Africa did not benefit from conflict. While a country like South Korea, in addition to internal reforms, benefited from the East-West struggle, there is not one country in the African region that moved from the periphery to the semi-periphery. For Africa, the rewards of the Cold War included, "the militarisation of continental and national conflicts, which festered endlessly because neither side possessed or was allowed a decisive military advantage; regimes that were politically and administratively weak acquired and came to rely disproportionately on military capability; regimes as diverse as Zaire and Ethiopia, sustained by foreign patrons, refused to reach the necessary accommodations with their national populations".[9]

Despite these clear indicators of global disinterest[10] African leaders systematically ran down their economies, human rights were wantonly abused, political parties were banned, students and youths were massacred, debt-profiles shot up dramatically, coups and counter-coups became the order of the day, trade relations deteriorated, politics became warfare, intellectuals and business persons emigrated abroad, corruption became institutionalized, while accumulation shifted completely from production to distribution. In addition, the various leaders relied on propaganda, rhetoric, defensive radicalism, the manipulation of primordial loyalties in order to divide the opposition, and reliance on foreign aid. As the Economic Commission for Africa noted in its 1989 *Economic Report on Africa* "the cumulative impact of the economic crisis in Africa during the 1980s has been a continued drop in the standard of living of the average African, so much so that today, his or her per capita income is only about 80% of what it was at the beginning of the decade".[11]

Today, Africa's foreign debt stands at about $300 billion. The region's debt "equals 102.3% of its GNP and more than 300% of its total exports", while over "30% of the continent's export earnings is used to service debt".[12] For Zambia, the debt has grown from 40% of GDP in 1975 to 400% of GDP by 1986.[13] Of the 47 Least Developed Countries in the world, 32 are in Africa with many more waiting to join the club. According to Fantu Cheru, "Seventy out of every 100 Africans are either destitute or on the verge of poverty, with annual per capita income ranging from $59 to $115. One out of every four Africans has access to clean water. Of the 33 million people added to the work force during the 1970s, only 15 million found remunerative employment".[14] Adult literacy levels remain very low as well as life expectancy. In countries like Nigeria, Zaire and Zambia, increasing disillusionment, poverty, inflation and unemployment have led to riots, violence and coups. In the 16 countries in Southern and Eastern Africa, 40 million people are facing famine as a result of drought and political crisis.[15] The International Research Office of the U.S. Census Bureau has estimated that about "70 million Africans could become infected with HIV, based on data from 36 sub-Saharan countries. This could bring the annual number of AIDS-related deaths to 4.6 million".[16]

According to the ECA, per capita income declined by 1.7% annually between 1980 and 1989 and in the same period gross fixed capital formation fell by 1.9%; export volumes declined by 3%; unemployment experienced a fourfold increase; investment as a proportion of GDP declined from 25% in 1970 to 15.8% in 1988; debt-servicing obligations ranged from 35% to 125%; the number of unemployed persons reached 30 million and underemployed persons increased to 95 million. In Africa today, over 1000 children die daily (excluding deaths recorded in Somalia and the Sudan) and some 45 million are starving; average annual expenditure on health and education declined from 26% of total budgetary allocations in the early 1980s to less than 19% in 1988; 34 million Africans are suffering from malnutrition and the region's share of world trade declined from 4.7% in 1980 to 2.2% in 1989. Africa accounts for 18 of the 20 lowest ranking nations listed in the UNDP's Human Development Index and it is estimated that the region has "lost a third of its skilled people to Europe".[17]

In 1992 Africa, it is difficult to identify a single nation that can be said to be on the path to growth and development, where there is policy-consistency and where the basic needs of the people are being met. The region accounts for half of the world's refugees "most of them fleeing drought or war or both";[18] food production is about 35% lower than it was in the early 1970s and while the economic growth rate is only 1.5% (the lowest in the world), the population growth rate is 3.2% annually, higher than Asia and Latin America with 1.8% and 2.1% respectively.[19] This dismal performance compelled the ECA to declare the 1980s to have been "Africa's lost decade".[20]

Responses to the African Crisis: Structural Adjustment and Democracy

There have been several broad and specific responses from African international organizations, donors, Scandinavia, international financial institutions and so on, to the deepening crisis in Africa. Beyond the prescriptions of import substitution industrialization in the 1960s, the early 1980s witnessed prescriptions of structural adjustment programs as the only solution to the deepening crisis of the region. By the mid-1980s, largely as a result of deepening crisis in the Soviet Union and Eastern Europe, the West and other donors added new "political conditionalities" by requesting committment to democracy or political pluralism as preconditions for further assistance to adjusting African economies.[21] This latest demand has complicated the patterns of restructuring in Africa, especially in the context of deepening contradictions and conflicts generated by the implementation of orthodox adjustment programs. One point that needs to be made, however, is that African regimes were forced into adopting structural adjustment programs as a result of massive capital flight, increasing bankruptcies, the closure of credit lines, declining flows in foreign investment and foreign aid, and inability to service growing foreign debt. Creditors, donors and other suppliers, made the adoption of the IMF stabilization and the World Bank structural adjustment programs almost inevitable for "normal business".

The content of Africa's adjustment programs have not differed in any way from the standard IMF/World Bank package. They have in general included a) reduction in the size of the public sector; b) elimination of price distortions in all sectors of the economy; c) trade liberalization through the total opening up of the economy; d) control of the money supply and credit; e) a floating interest rate policy designed to promote domestic savings and the rational allocation of resources; f) exchange rate adjustment through currency devaluation; g) deregulation of prices of goods and services; and h) the commercialization and/or privatization of public parastatals. These policies have been accompanied by debt-equity swap policies of converting debts into equity share holdings in privatized public corporations; the massive repression of popular forces; the imposition of new fees, levies, tariffs and taxes on already marginalized groups; the retrenchment of hundreds of thousands of able-bodied workers; and the general marginalization of the people in decision-making. For the World Bank, Ghana is the only successful case of structural adjustment in Africa, though this claim is disputable.[22] In all other cases, it has been one tale of woe after the other.

According to Adebayo Adedeji,

> "the orthodox structural adjustment programmes, by their very design, assume that the classical instruments of control of money supply, credit squeeze, exchange rate and interest rate adjustments, trade liberalization etc. which may be valid in well-structured economies, could bring about positive results in African economies characterized by weak and disarticulate structures. However, there is documented evidence that in many cases sustained economic growth has not materialized, the rate of investment rather than improve has tended to decrease, budget and balance of payments deficits have tended to widen after some temporary relief and debt service obligations have become unbearable".[23]

Adedeji further notes that the objectives of structural adjustment in Africa, "cannot be achieved without addressing the fundamental structural bottlenecks of African economies".[24] This is exactly the contradiction of adjustment programs as a response to Africa's deepening crisis. They pay little or no attention to the region's historical experience; overlook the distorted character and relations of politics, power, production and exchange; overlook the available room for manoeuvre for local elites; ignore the desperate conditions of vulnerable groups (at least until recently) who are already at the margins of survival and are often the first victims of harsh public policies; pay little attention to questions of corruption, political repression, elite mismanagement and the record of waste and poor policy implementation; and ignore the power of certain constituencies to resist adjustment especially when pushed to the verge of survival. Also, donors and the Bank ignore the fact that in virtually every instance, orthodox adjustment policies had to be imposed through massive repression. By ignoring the people, who are the direct victims of the difficult policies, adjustment programs in Africa stood few chances of success. They pushed Africa further to the margins of a grossly unequal international division of labor.[25]

In its 1990 economic report on Africa, the ECA reached the conclusion that "conventional adjustment programmes, have failed to address the fundamental issues in Africa's development; hence their failure to arrest the downward trend, less reverse it and bring about a sustainable process of development and transformation".[26] In the *African Charter* the ECA and OAU also noted their "disapproval of all economic programmes, such as orthodox structural adjustment programmes, which undermine the human condition and disregard the potential and role of popular participation in self-sustaining development". [27] Such criticisms recently forced the World Bank to admit its failures, and to acknowledge the *political* dimensions of the African crisis. Consequently, the Bank prescribed a check on corruption, the empowerment of the people, the decentralization of the bureaucracy, the mobilization of the people and the creation of an "enabling environment" to facilitate the effective implementation of adjustment. Further, the Bank emphasized the need to protect vulnerable groups in the process of implementing adjustment programs.[28]

While structural adjustment was generating deeper contradictions and conflicts between regimes and the people, donors, Western governments and finance institutions threw a new conditionality into the reform arena:

the demand for democratization and political pluralism as preconditions for further support. This dimension has generated fresh debates and disagreements between African policy makers and the financial institutions. For the West, democracy is interpreted as the adoption of free-market economic policies and Western political models. "Democracy" also means an acceptance of the Western way of life, and in a restructured global order dominated by the United States, to be democratic means to support American initiatives in a so-called "new world order".[29]

To many African leaders and policy-makers, "political conditionality" is a mere attempt at justifying the direction of investment and aid away from Africa and an excuse to impose Western political models on African states.[30] More importantly, the West continues to support repressive regimes in Africa, and expects such regimes, which have maintained their hold on power through corruption and repression, to begin to democratize. Further, an unmediated linkage is established between democracy and development, even with human rights. In this regard, the impression is conveyed that, irrespective of structural deformities and the implications of a marginal location and role in the global division of labor and power, all that is required for African states to become "developed" like the West, is democracy. Yet, the United States has not put up any agenda to support popular organizations which have demonstrated commitment to such restructuring.

Yet the West continues openly to demonstrate its preference for Eastern Europe over Africa. As Lance Morrow notes in a recent special report in *Time*, "in the face of political instability and disintegrating roads, airports and telephone networks, and other disincentives, investors from Europe, America and Japan are withdrawing from sub-Saharan Africa and looking elsewhere". Morrow notes that, after all, "neglecting Africa carries no immediate, urgent threat to the world. Black Africa has no nuclear powers".[31] Private investment in sub-Saharan Africa not only declined from $2.3 billion in 1982 to $900 million in 1989, but British transnational corporations withdrew 31% of their investments from the region between 1979 and 1989.[32] With the emergence of new markets and a renewed interest in Eastern Europe, Asia and the Middle East, Africa will have to struggle hard to attract investors.

Increasing Western disinterest in Africa is evidenced in several recent developments. A few examples: in its few years as an independent nation, Russia alone has received more aid, pledges and material assistance than most of the nations in sub-Saharan African combined. Gehbray Berhane, Secretary-General of the African Caribbean and Pacific (ACP) group has argued that "West Europe is devoting more and more resources to promote not only industry and agriculture in East Europe and the CIS, but also technical assistance and institution building and there is less emphasis on these things for Africa".[33] When the State of Alaska announced that it had excess fish, it shipped the surplus to Russia. Starving nations like Somalia, Mozambique, The Sudan, Ethiopia and Chad were hardly considered. Poland continues to be treated with kid gloves when it defaults on its loans. Though the economic restructuring of Boris Yeltsin is as yet achieving very little, there is hardly much criticism of it in the Western media. In FY91, the 47 countries in sub-Saharan Africa received only $616 million in foreign assistance from the United States while Eastern Europe received $900 million, Nicaragua and Panama, $720 million and Israel alone, $3.5 billion.[34]

The Commonwealth of Independent States (CIS), in its short existence on the global map has received $34.88 billion from Germany, $5.85 billion from Italy, $4.08 billion from the United States, $3.88 billion from the European Community, $2.72 billion from Japan, $1.36 billion from Spain, $1.22 billion from France, $0.07 billion from the UK and $14.01 billion from other sources.[35] The G7 have also promised a $24 billion aid package to Russia while the United States announced a Special Marshall Fund to help the CIS. It is obvious that the West is more interested in the political and economic recovery of Eastern Europe than it is in construction efforts in Africa. The responses to African civil wars, the faint comments on developments in South Africa including the September 1992 massacre in the Ciskei and refusal to make political concessions at the global level to African states, support this observation. The West and the United Nations have never demonstrated in Africa the recent interest in peace, in containing repressive leadership, and in protecting oppressed peoples they are demonstrating in Eastern Europe and in the Middle East.

The reality in today's Africa is that adjustment programs are faltering and regimes have devised several ingenious ways to meet expectations so as to attract more foreign aid. This is not to minimise the increasing organization and mobilization of non-bourgeois forces across ethnic, regional and religious lines, the growing power of civil society, on-going popular struggles demanding more participation in the political process, accountability of leadership and respect for human rights. Several dictators and sit-tight rulers have fallen, from Benin to Zambia; military juntas are being forced to organize transitions to civil rule, from Ghana to Nigeria; and new perspectives of development planning, the role of the state in the economy and strengthening of productive (as against distributive) sectors of the economy are going on all over the region.[36] As Lance Morrow has noted, "In 1990 more African nations introduced multiparty politics than in all the previous 25 years. When the Berlin Wall fell in 1989, 38 of Africa's 47 states were ruled by one party or by military juntas; today about half those countries have held free elections or adopted democratic reforms. Many Africans are talking about a second revolution".[37] But the opposition is very divided; several discredited elements of yesterday have emerged today as leaders of pro-democracy movements; in many cases the focus on the visible instruments of democracy diverts attention from the salience of *democratization;* and there are too many efforts to ape the West. In addition, political posturing, opportunism, the lack of alternative and credible programs for organizing socio-economic and political relations; the excessive personalization of the struggle for power and the tendency to confuse the capture of governmental power with the capture of state power, continue to divide, weaken and confuse the pro-democracy movements. Yet, this is where we must anchor the hopes for Africa's future.

The Emerging Global Order and the Future of Africa

The reality of the contemporary global order is that the apparent de-ideologization of global political relations has not eliminated the gulf between the North and the South. As Perez de Cuellar has noted, "We cannot forget that while the iron curtain has been brought down, the poverty curtain still separates two parts of the world community".[38] Given that Africa is the most crisis-ridden of the world's continents, the general conclusion today is that "unless African countries seize the initiative in their international relations, the rapproachment between the two superpowers may well lead to the continent's further marginalization in world politics and international economic relations ... The blurring of the ideological divide arising from superpower rapproachment has greatly diminished that space for manoeuvre and this may also lead to the shifting of "Big Power" attention away from Africa's security and economic problems".[39] The question to ask is: is this marginalization and declining interest really bad for Africa?

The United States and other Western powers have, before and since political independence in the 1960s, struggled against civil society in Africa and supported undemocratic, repressive and corrupt regimes as in Zaire, Nigeria, Liberia, Kenya and Malawi. The West has bastardized indigenous cultures and diverted the tastes and interest of Africans away from their own indigenous products. Western governments have recognized military regimes which had no iota of regard or respect for human rights and accountability. Minority regimes in Southern Africa received their support from Western governments. Though the vast majority of African regimes remained subservient to their former colonial exploiters and expressed open admiration for the Western way of life and institutions, the region never received corresponding attention from the West. Western support for democracy in Africa has been lukewarm, its aid policy to Africa has historically been concentrated on a handful of nations and its mass media shows almost no interest in the region.

In the contemporary world order however, it would seem that Africa has an unprecedented opportunity to take advantage of increasing disinterest and reduced interference in its internal affairs. Such an opportunity indeed presented itself in the early years of political independence, but the new leaders depoliticized the populace and appropriated the privileges of the departing European elite. As Yoweri Museveni of Uganda noted recently, "A little neglect would not be bad. The more orphaned we are, the better for Africa. We will have to rely on ourselves".[40] Now that African elites have expended all opportunities for diversion, manipulation, bribery, foreign aid and playing the East against the West, and the West as well as investors are showing little interest in Africa, it is the appropriate time to return to basics and redefine local socio-economic and political relations to reflect African realities and priorities. The end of the Cold War provides an ample opportunity to terminate on-going meaningless political conflicts. The restructuring of the global system spells a need to restructure the OAU and make it more efficient, effective and relevant to the needs of contemporary Africa. Also, new opportunities are opening up around the world especially in Eastern Europe. The emerging trade blocs call for a new realism, since the trade blocs, despite the Lomé Conventions, are bound to redirect policies and interest away from Africa. The reality is that Africa will not just be marginalized but also discriminated against around the world. Yet, it is our contention that this is perhaps Africa's greatest chance to reconstruct, restructure and reconstitute political, social and economic relations at the domestic and international levels.

Without doubt pressures from failed restructuring experiments and from the emerging global order will push African nations along paths of economic, political and ideological innovation and experimentation. This is why they have all opted for structural adjustment at great cost and pain. Yet, adjustment must remain on track with modifications to make it reflect the misery, sacrifices and aspirations of the people.[41] It may be doubted that Africa can rely on the United Nations under the new world order to address its problems. To all intents and purposes the UN right now appears to exist only to implement policies which reflect and extend Western and US interests, largely because the "essential ingredient of the 'new world order' is the uncontested military power of the United States".[42] This is where the danger lies for weak, unstable, dependent and foreign dominated countries like those in Africa. They have, in the course of the Gulf crisis, in the context of the disintegration of the Soviet Union and the pro-Western posture of Russia, and the collaboration of other Western powers, lost to the United States the only really global base they had for advancing their opinions and putting pressure on the developed nations.[43] For Africa, this means a major loss and if the United States continues its opposition to UN agencies like UNESCO, the prospects for continued technical and special assistance to the poor countries of the region will become very gloomy.[44]

These developments indicate an urgent need to look inwards and map out programs for self-reliance, mobilization and increased productivity. Fortunately for the region, the required responses already exist and are embodied in documents, Charters and Declarations from the OAU and the ECA.[45] The task for the 1990s, if Africa is to escape continuing marginalization and deepening crisis, is to develop the political will required to implement these programs. Africa cannot afford to sit idly by and complain about Western neglect and lack of foreign aid and investments. The ways in which it executes its own political and economic restructuring programs, and the ways in which it creates an enabling environment for democracy, productivity and stability, will dictate the extent to which it is taken seriously and can therefore attract investors.

In specific terms, a new national order must be established in all African states for the region to reap concessions in a new world order, however constituted. This will be an order where there is social justice, planning, investment in productive ventures, constitutionally guaranteed rights, in particular the rights to organize and of free speech, accountability of the leadership, independence of the judiciary, limits to the terms of political leaders, and open checks on political irrationality, intolerance and corruption. African regimes must develop the capability to collect taxes, reduce military expenditures, promote agriculture especially food production, and increase intra-regional trade. The current plan to put an African Economic Community (AEC) in place in AD 2025 hardly demonstrates any serious appreciation of the urgency of the African predicament.[46]

The size of African armies needs to be reduced, academic freedom and the autonomy of the academy must be respected, there should be constitutional bans against military coups and provisions to bring insurrectionists to trial for illegal seizure of power even after they leave office, and as the *African Charter* rightly notes, "there must be an opening up of political process to accommodate freedom of opinions, tolerate differences, accept consensus on issues as well as ensure effective participation of the people and their organizations and associations".[47] The ECA, OAU and African NGOs must map out an indigenous economic and political recovery plan which differs from what the West, donors, the IMF and the World Bank are imposing on them.

There are opportunities opening up in other regions of the world – Asia and the new markets of Eastern Europe. Africa must shift its cultural and economic dependence on the West to a new agenda for exploiting fresh openings in Eastern Europe. The technology required for African development can easily be obtained in Asia and Latin America at lower prices. Of course, if African investors fail to go beyond their national and at best sub-regional boundaries the new opportunities will be seized by investors from Asia and Latin America. In any case, only a dominant elite that recognizes the importance of long-term investment, develops a credible business ethic and relies less on state patronage can operate effectively beyond its frontiers. This is the challenge for African investors in the 1990s.

It is all too easy to draw up a long list of what the West should do to aid Africa. Perhaps, it is such strategies in the past that have culminated in Africa's dependence on foreign aid, tastes and values and made the region extremely vulnerable to external pressures. While emergency foreign aid, an international debt conference, regard for African prescriptions to solve its crisis, improved terms of trade, lower interest rates, increased investments and the democratization of the Security Council and other international organizations like the IMF and the World Bank would be excellent starting points for the West, Africa, and Africa alone, bears the ultimate responsibility to resolve its problems. Leaving the region alone to look inwards, for the people to challenge themselves, their leaders and governments, for the people to take stock and work out alternatives based on the desperate realities currently confronting them in a hostile and exploitative global order would be a major contribution by the West. But the world does not function according to morals or the requirements of weak and vulnerable nations. This means that while internal restructurings are proceeding, Africa must be prepared to confront the West, through unity and new programs at the global level in the 1990s.

NOTES

1. ECA, *African Charter for Popular Participation*, (Addis Ababa, ECA, 1990) p.17.

2. According to the OAU's *Lagos Plan of Action* Africa has "97% of world reserves of chrome, 85% of world reserves of platinum, 64% of world reserves of manganese, 25% of world reserves of uranium and 13% of world reserves of copper, without mentioning bauxite, nickel and lead; 20% of world hydro-electrical potential, 20% of traded oil in the world (if we exclude the United States and the USSR); 70% of world cocoa production; one-third of world coffee production and 50% of palm produce, to mention just a few." p. 3.

3. See Aimé Cesaire, *Discourse on Colonialism* (New York and London: Monthly Review Press, 1972).

4. Organization of African Unity (OAU), *The African Priority Programme for Economic Recovery 1986-1990* (Addis Ababa: OAU, 1986), p. 13.

5. OAU, *Lagos Plan of Action for the Economic Development of Africa 1980-2000* (Geneva: Institute for Labour Studies, 1981), p. 3.

6. See Claude Ake, *A Political Economy of Africa* (London: Longman, 1981) and Haskell G. Ward, *African Development Reconsidered: New Perspectives from the Continent* (New York: Phelps-Stokes Institute, 1989).

7   OAU, *Africa's Priority Programme for Economic Recovery 1986-1990* (Addis Ababa: OAU, 1986), p. 5.
8   George B.N. Ayittey, "Why Structural Adjustment Failed in Africa," *TransAfrica Forum* Vol. 8 (2) (Summer 1991), p. 48.
9   Eboe Hutchful, "Eastern Europe: Consequences for Africa," *Review of African Political Economy* (50) (March 1991), p. 53. See also Julius O. Ihonvbere, "The dynamics of change in Eastern Europe and their Implications for Africa," *Coexistence* (29) (1992).
10 See Thomas Callaghy, "Debt and Structural Adjustment," *Issue* Vol. 16 (2) (1988); Timothy M. Shaw, "Africa in the 1990s: From Economic Crisis to Structural Readjustment," *Dalhousie Review* Vol. 68 (1-2) (Spring/Summer 1988); and Adebayo Adedeji, "Economic Progress: What Africa Needs," *TransAfrica Forum* Vol. 7 (2) (Summer 1990).
11 Economic Commission for Africa, *Economic Report on Africa 1989* (Addis Ababa: ECA, 1989), p. 2.
12 Ibrahim Babangida, Address to the 46th Session of the UN General Assembly, New York October 4, 1991.
13 Therese Sevigny, *From Crisis to Consensus: The United Nations and the Challenge of Development*. Keynote address, University of Ottawa, Canada, 14 November 1990, p. 6.
14 Fantu Cheru, *The Silent Revolution in Africa: Debt, Development and Democracy* (Harare and London: Anvil and Zed, 1989), p. 2.
15 Roy Laishley, "Drought dims hope of faster recovery," *Africa Recovery* Vol. 6 (2) (August 1992), p. 1.
16 "AIDS: a calamity in the making," *Africa Recovery* Vol. 5 (1) (June 1991), p. 6.
17 "Improved 'global governance' demanded," *Africa Recovery* Vol. 6 (2) (August 1992), p. 13.
18 Lance Morrow, "Africa: The Scramble for Existence," *Time* (September 7, 1992), p. 42.
19 Ibid.
20 ECA, *Economic Report on Africa 1990* (Addis Ababa: ECA, 1990), p. 3.
21 See Julius O. Ihonvbere, "Political Conditionality and Prospects for Recovery in Sub-Saharan Africa," *International Third World Journal and Review* Vol. 3 (1-2) (1992); Carol Lancaster, "Economic Restructuring in Sub-Saharan Africa," *Current History* Vol. 88 (538) (May 1989); "Donors Demand Political Reforms," *Africa Recovery* (July-September 1990); Salim Lone, "Africa: Drifting Off the Map of the World's Concerns," *International Herald Tribune* (August 24, 1990); and "Link National, International Democratization: OAU's Salim," *Africa Recovery* (July-September, 1990).

22 See Baffour Ankomah, "Ghana's reform programme: How long will it be before the patient is cured?" *African Business* (March 1990) and Daniel M. Green, "Structural Adjustment and Politics in Ghana," *TransAfrica Forum* Vol. 8 (2) (Summer 1991).

23 Adebayo Adedeji, "Foreward," to ECA, *African Alternative Framework to Structural Adjustment Programmes for Socio-Economic Recovery and Transformation* (Addis Ababa: ECA, 1989), p. i.

24 Ibid, p. ii.

25 See Julius O. Ihonvbere, "Economic Crisis, Structural Adjustment and Social Crisis in Nigeria," *World Development* (January 1993); "Assessing adjustment's social impact," *Africa Recovery* (August 1992); Adotey Bing, "Ghana: devaluation brings little gain," *Africa Recovery* (June 1991); April Gordon, "Economic Reform and African Women," *TransAfrica Forum* Vol. 8 (2) (Summer 1991); and Olusegun Obasanjo, "Our Situation is Desperate," *TELL* (Lagos) (March 23, 1992).

26 ECA, *Economic Report on Africa 1990*, op. cit., p. vii.

27 ECA, *African Charter for Popular Participation in Development*, op. cit., p. 19.

28 See World Bank, *Sub-Saharan Africa: From Crisis to Sustainable Growth*, op. cit.

29 See Julius O. Ihonvbere, "Africa and the New World Order," *The Iranian Journal of International Affairs* (Summer 1991); "Is There a New World Order?" *U.S. News and World Report* (March 11, 1991); Ibrahim Gambari, "Africa's Role in the Emerging New World Order," paper at the conference on Nigeria's National Development and Foreign Policy, New York, August 9, 1992.

30 For details on the OAU's response to political conditionality, see Salim Lone "Africans Challenge Nature of Prescriptions: Donors Demand Political Reforms," *Africa Recovery* (July-September 1990).

31 Lanca Morrow, "Africa: The Scramble for Existence," loc. cit., pp. 42-45.

32 Michael Chege, "Remembering Africa," *Foreign Affairs* Vol. 71 (1) (1991-92), p. 157.

33 Cited in Tim Wall, "Soviet demise brings Africa new challenges: competition for financial resources and markets compounds loss of aid," *Africa Recovery*, Vol. 6 (1) (April 1992), p. 14.

34 David S. Wiley, "Academic Analysis and U.S. Policy-Making on Africa: Reflections and Conclusions," *Issue*, Vol. XIX (2) (1991), p. 40.

35 *Newsweek* (March 30, 1992), p. 9.

36 See Michael Clough, "Africa Finds Reasons to Hope for Democracy's Future," *The New York Times* (March 22, 1992); "Democracy in Africa," *The Economist* (February 22nd 1992); David Vick, "Democratic tide turns Africa towards a new economic era," *African Business* (January 1992); Karl Maier, "Nigeria: Voodoo Democracy?" *Africa Report* (January-February 1992); and Salim Lone, "Political liberalization builds in Africa," *Africa Recovery* (October-December 1990).

37 Lance Morrow, "Africa: The Scramble for Existence,"op. cit., p. 46.

38 Javier Perez de Cuellar, United Nations Day Message, October 1990. See also The South Commission, *The Challenge to the South* (London: Oxford University Press, 1990), and Commonwealth Heads of Government, *The Kuala Lumpur Communique October 1989* (London: Commonwealth Secretariat, 1989).

39 Ibrahim A. Gambari, "Africa's Role in the Emerging New World Order." Paper at the Annual Conference on Nigeria's National Development and Foreign Policy, New York, August 9, 1992.

40 Yoweri Museveni quoted in Lance Morrow, loc. cit., p. 46.

41 See Adebayo Adedeji, "Economic Progress: What Africa Needs," op. cit; and Robert Browne, "The Continuing Debate on African Development," *TransAfrica Forum* Vol. 7 (2) (Summer 1990).

42 Salim Mansur, "The United Nations and the Gulf war", *Perspectives* (Canadian Institute of International Affairs) Vol. 5 (2) (March 1991), p. 3.

43 Kim Richard Nossal, "The Gulf war and the Future of the UN," *Perspectives* (Canadian Institute of International Affairs) Vol.5 (2) (March 1991), p. 5.

44 It is on record that until the Gulf War, the United States never had much regard for the UN and international law. Its attack on Libya, its invasion of Grenada and Panama to mention a few, were all against international law and without the approval of the UN. The same United States which has suddenly come to see the UN as an important organization is the world's largest debtor to the UN owing some $733 million. It did not consider paying its 1992 dues to the organization until ten months (October) after they fell due. See *U.S. News and World Report* (October 5, 1992), pp. 20-21 and 25.

45 See OAU, *Cultural Charter for Africa* (1976); *The Lagos Plan of Action for the Economic Development of Africa 1980-2000* (1981); *African Charter for Human and People's Rights* (1981); and the *African Economic Treaty* (1991). See also the ECA's *African Alternative Framework to Structural Adjustment Programmes for Socio-Economic Recovery and Transformation* (1989) and the *African Charter for Popular Participation in Development* (1990) among other documents.

46 See "Summit of deep concerns," *West Africa* (10-16 June, 1991); Ernest Harsch, "Africa seeks economic unity," *Africa Recovery* Vol. 5 (1) (June 1991) and Julius O. Ihonvbere, "Towards an African Common Market in AD 2025?: The African Crisis, Regionalism and Prospects for Recovery." International conference on "Africa and Eastern Europe: Similarities and Parallels," Kingston, Ontario, Canada, April, 1992.

47 ECA, *African Charter for Popular Participation,* op. cit., p. 19.

III

SOCIAL AND LABOR CONFLICTS

13 THE GLOBALIZATION OF SOCIAL CONFLICT

James H. Mittelman

What sets the context for conflict at the end of this millennium is the globalization process, which is paradoxically integrating and yet multipolarizing. Although the character of any given conflict has many sources, globalization establishes the conditions of conflict within which choices are made. By no means all the cases where there is conflict lead to violence and war, but the pressure of globalization provides one, though not the only, basis of future social conflicts.

Briefly, my core argument is that world society is entering a new era in the relationship between conflict and the division of labor, which is now globalized. If that is so, in what respects is the global division of labor a source of conflict at the close of the twentieth century? To answer this question, I will first explore varied meanings of the concept of the division of labor and the multilevel character of the globalization process. The next section anchors the discussion by examining one region – East Asia – within this framework. This section is obviously not a detailed account but a synopsis of the impact of globalization on a specific regional division of

---

This article is drawn from the research project "The Global Division of Labor" funded by the World Society Foundation. James H. Mittelmann is professor of political science and chairman at the Department of Comparative and Regional Studies, School of International Service, The American University, 4400 Massachusetts Ave., N.W., Washington, D.C. 20016-8071, U.S.A.

labor. Finally, I will turn to the seeds of future conflict sown by globalization and, also, the implications for adaptation to a rapidly changing and highly competitive environment.

Globalization

In *The Great Transformation,* Karl Polanyi analyzed the socially disruptive and polarizing tendencies in the world economy driven by what he called the self-regulating market, not a spontaneous phenomenon but the result of coercive power in the service of a utopian idea. He traced the tendencies in the global economy that generated the conjuncture of the 1930s and produced – out of a breakdown in liberal-economic structures – the phenomena of depression, fascism, unemployment, and resurgent nationalism, collectively a negation of economic globalization, leading to world war.[1] A Polanyian framework of "double movement" encapsulates unprecedented market expansion entailing massive social dislocation and a sharp political reaction in the form of society's demands on the state to counteract the deleterious effects of the market. Perhaps similar to the global economy of the 1930s, the contemporary globalization process appears to be approaching a conjuncture in which renewed liberal-economic structures will generate large-scale disruptions as well as sustained pressure for protection. The globalization of conflict is an integral part of this contradiction.

Globalization is a worldwide phenomenon which allows the economy, politics, culture and ideology of one country to penetrate others. An economically driven process, globalization is a rubric for varied trends: the interpenetration of industries across borders, the spread of financial markets, the diffusion of identical consumer goods to distant countries, massive transfers of labor primarily from the South and the East to the West, and an emerging worldwide preference for democracy. The chain of causality runs from the spatial reorganization of production to international trade and to the integration of financial markets.[2] Not only is economics globalized, but also politics and culture are central to this process. The concept of globalization interrelates multiple levels of analysis – economics, politics, culture – and encapsulates the compression of time-space relations in the contemporary world system.

To comprehend the globalization process, the choice of an avenue of inquiry is crucial because it sets one's sights on research questions and provides a perspective on data. An appropriate starting point, I believe, is the allocation of work and its products at a global level, for conflicts between capital and labor, commerce and consumer tastes all reflect what is produced and how it is produced. Hence, attention must focus on how whole societies and their constituent groups try to influence and adjust to changes in the organization of production.

Although first studied by classical political economists and then their followers, with implications for comparative advantages in trade, the global division of labor nowadays differs radically from the allocation of work and its reward in Adam Smith's time. In *An Inquiry into the Nature and Causes of the Wealth of Nations*, Smith contrasted the isolated producer and modern industry. He posited a subrational or nonutilitarian origin for specialization (but not its intensification) in a "propensity to truck and barter" innate in humankind. A novel form of specialization, modern industry separates the production process into compartments, each one performing a different task, with implications for the rates of profit. To the extent that these separated producers, buyers and sellers are identified with nations, the international division of labor refers to the specialization of a country in a particular trade or product – e.g., Portugal in wine and England in textiles.[3] Hence, the international division of labor highlights a set of relationships associated with an exchange of goods produced by individual units, namely nation-states. As the old international division of labor evolved, a small number of industrial countries provided capital and consumer goods to exchange for the Third World's primary products.

However, a basic change in the international division of labor occurred in the 1960s: a restructuring involving the formation and expansion of a world market for both labor and industrial sites. Beginning in the 1960s, Asia's "Four Dragons" achieved spectacular economic growth by exporting, not raw materials but manufactured goods. As an empirical study by Giovanni Arrighi and Jessica Drangel shows, in the period from 1965 to 1980, the "core" deindustrialized in terms of (a) the average percentage of the labor force employed by industry and (b) the average share of manufacturing in the Gross Domestic Product (GDP). By the late 1970s, the "semiperiphery" – an intermediate tier of countries – actually surpassed the "core" in share of GDP generated by industry.[4] Manufactures relative to export volume in East Asia jumped 13.2% per year from 1980 to 1985, 19.3% in 1986, 23.8% in 1987, and 11.2% in 1988.[5] With industrial upgrading, the Newly Industrializing Countries (NICs) sought to transform their structures of production from an emphasis on labor-intensive to capital- and technology-intensive goods, centering on high value-added products. No longer was there a dichotomy between a small number of industrial countries and a Third World providing primary products. An emerging world market for labor and production entailed massive industrial relocation, the subdivision of manufacturing processes into multiple partial operations, major technological innovations, large-scale migratory flows, and the feminization of labor. From Asia's export processing zones to Mexico's *maquiladora* program (assembly plants as subsidiaries or subcontracting firms for the manufacture of export-oriented goods), a barometer of the changing character of the labor force is the increasing number of women employed in manufacturing. Jobs take on characteristics identified with female employment: a minimum level of skills, low wages, and limited possibilities for promotion.

To explain this restructuring, scholars have devised the construct of "the new international division of labor." – the title of a seminal study by Folker Fröbel, Jürgen Heinrichs, and Otto Kreye. This thesis focuses on the "overriding pressure of competition" as the mainspring of a distinct set of conditions for global capital accumulation. These authors hold that observable changes in the international division of labor – the transfer of plants to the Third World, the fragmentation of production processes, etc. – are the result of "the conditions for the valorization and accumulation of capital".[6]

> This new international division of labour is an institutional innovation of capital itself, necessitated by changed conditions, and not the result of changed development strategies by individual countries or options freely decided upon by so-called multinational companies.[7]

For these authors, national strategies and the policies of multinational corporations are consequences, not causes, of new conditions, especially the need for additional industrial sites around the world.

This thesis centers on the expansion of capital and hence production as the motor force behind an international division of labor that is deemed new in that it restructures the classical division of labor between hewers of wood and drawers of water – Third World countries – and industrialized nations. Emphasis is placed on the spatial reorganization of production and increasing differentiation within the Third World. Clearly this mode of explanation advances understanding by providing a novel way to examine the relationships between developed and developing countries. However, some of the key tenets of the concept of the new international division of labor are flawed.

To begin with, exactly what is new about the new international division of labor? The claim that industrialization in the Third World is new overlooks the establishment of import-substituting industries in Argentina, Brazil, and Mexico in the 1930s and 1940s. In fact, industrial growth in some parts of Latin America stems from the interwar period.[8] Additionally, the new international division of labor has not replaced the old one. Properly understood, they coexist. In countries such as Mexico, jobs in export industries account for less than 10% of total employment. In many parts of the Third World, the share of primary goods in exports is more than half of all exports. The variance in job allocation among and within regions is sufficiently large to call into question the concept of the new international division of labor. What is more, to stress that cheap labor drives the movement of capital around the globe runs the risk of a mechanical and economistic explanation. It depoliticizes production.

By focusing so strongly on the logic of capital to the detriment of local social forces, the new international division of labor mode of inquiry is too abstract, too top-down. It is a useful starting point for investigation, but neglects a fine-grained analysis of different spatial divisions of labor within various industries and sectors. Innovation and technological developments take place in certain industries and sectors but also transcend national boundaries. Within a globalizing division of labor, technological and managerial cores form specifically regional divisions and redivisions of labor, and generate their own peripheries subject to both constraints and developmental opportunities.[9] Distinct regional divisions of labor – a phenomenon ignored by new international-division-of-labor theorists – provide diverse modes of coordinating capital flows, but are ultimately subordinate to the globalization process. Macro regions – the European Community, the North American Free Trade Area, and Asia-Pacific – may be regarded as loose spatial units larger than the state with some political and cultural bonds, however tenuous and sometimes conflictual. As we shall see, states – and indeed the interstate system – while diminished in scope in a global division of labor, may not be treated as mere epiphenomena.

Production, the State, and New Social Movements

The global division of labor may be conceived in a Braudelian manner as a system of interactions on a world scale. The French economic historian Fernand Braudel indicated that the whole world is not the ontology of world society but those entities, individual and corporate, that interact with global structures. He proposed that different axes be established corresponding to "social orders", hierarchy, time, and space. Along these axes, one can imagine divergent positions, such as those pertaining to evolving divisions of labor. To discern the implications of the global division of labor for social conflict, one may then identify interactions among production, the state, and social forces.[10]

(1) Economic globalization and the state. In recent decades, several states sought to protect the domestic economy against external forces and to limit the net outflow of surplus by acts of economic nationalism: the nationalization of industries, indigenization decrees, requirements for local incorporation of foreign capital, etc. Certain other states (e.g., China under Mao, Burma, and Tanzania) adopted a more radical course of selfreliance as a means of insulation from the world system. Today, however, there is little to commend strategies of economic nationalism or delinking, for transborder flows (migration, communications, knowledge, technology, etc.) have circumvented the globe and permeate the state.

The scope for state autonomy – a concept which drew considerable attention from scholars in the 1970s and 1980s – is reduced in the context of economic globalization. Additionally, the drive to bring the state back in to the forefront of social theory requires fresh analysis in the light of globalization.[11] In a globalized division of labor, the state no longer serves primarily as a buffer or shield against the world economy. Rather, the state itself seeks material gains from globalization. Put differently, the state increasingly plays an integrating role in facilitating globalization, and is itself an agent in globalization.[12] Surrounded by impersonal and nonaccountable forces beyond their control, leaders no longer lead.[13] Statecraft, tested as it is by non-state actors, is reduced in efficacy relative to transnational forces.

The state is at risk because of challenges to sovereignty at the end of the Cold War. With the disintegration of socialist regimes came the eruption of subsurface tensions formerly stifled by the state. Now, state borders are subject to revision.[14] East Germany has disappeared, the 15 republics comprising the former Soviet Union have achieved independence, and

Yugoslavia, now dismembered, is riven with ethnic conflict. Separatist movements in Quebec, Northern Ireland, the Basque country, and Corsica are challenging the status quo. While North Korea could be absorbed by South Korea, Balkanization is always a danger in Africa, where colonizers arbitrarily drew borders without regard to ethnic distribution and natural frontiers such as rivers and mountains. Hence, Ethiopia as a unified country is a dubious proposition.

(2) Pressures on the state. This explosion of pluralism involves a renewal of historical forces – a maze of religious loyalties, ethnic identities, linguistic differences, and other forms of cultural expression. As noted, the state, especially in the former Soviet Union and eastern Europe, had restrained these tensions. While globalization limits state power, there is a reassertion of historical forces. Just as globalization gives impetus to cultural homogenization (e.g., the diffusion of standard consumer goods throughout the world), so, too, does a global thrust undermine state power and unleash subterranean cultural pluralism.

This contradictory process merges with a dialectic of subnationalism and supranationalism. Many polities are disrupted by sub-state actors and simultaneously seek advantage in global competition through regionalization. Despite the past failings of regional groupings, regional cooperation is widely regarded as a way to achieve mobility in the changing global division of labor. Thus, the state is being re-formed from below by the tugs of subnationalism and from above by the pull of economic globalization.

(3) Globalization and democratization. To accommodate the new pluralism, the state must allow for demands for political reforms. With the revolution in eastern Europe, the release of Nelson Mandela from prison, and the assertiveness of the human rights movement, the drive toward democratization has won legitimacy. Equally important, pro-democracy forces have gained confidence. But what type of democracy is appropriate for the late twentieth century? While democracy is a universal concept, there are different versions of democratic theory.

From a liberal perspective, democracy centers on the principle of accountability: in some manner the right to rule should be based on the consent of the governed. Liberal democracy calls for public influence on government through such institutions as political parties, regular elections, and an alternation in power. However, critics point out that in practice, liberal democracies exclude some groups both from meaningful participation in politics and the distribution of economic benefits. In the Third World, it is often recognized that democracy is necessary for development, if democracy is understood to imply increasing social equality – an ingredient missing from ethnocentric and Western conceptions of democratization.[15]

A restricted type of democracy has emerged in Latin America, most notably in Brazil and Argentina, which have experienced authoritarian and democratic phases of development. Authoritarian democracy – other qualifying adjectives ("limited", "guided", and "protected") are also sometimes attached to the term democracy – is an expression of the state's efforts to expand its links to civil society. In view of a regime's lack of legitimacy and weak economic performance, proponents of authoritarian democracy advocate a more flexible system of political representation and gradual liberalization. Class alliances are broadened and the state makes concessions to pressure groups. However, such attempts to modernize the state leave the basic structures of power and domination unchanged. Programs for slow democratization typically include measures to restrain calls for social equality so that they can be accommodated by the political system. Armed with the power to enforce order, the state wields the means of coercion to safeguard the nation against "chaos". The transparency of this domination and its social ramifications engender mounting conflict: protests against abuses of human rights and demands for the pursuit of substantive justice.[16]

A challenge to democracy as an ideology of domination emerges from the mobilization of social movements seeking to assert popular control. The self-aggrandizing individualism characteristic of liberal and authoritarian democracy, coincident to the lack of accountability integral to economic globalization, is rejected in favor of a belief that the individual depends on society for development. The liberal-economic conceptualization of globalization allows for tolerance of social inequality, a formulation which critics regard as inconsistent with democracy, understood as the provision for all people to develop their potential.[17] In terms of actual performance, the ultimate test of democratization is whether a party will relinquish its preeminent role in political life, disengage from the state, and permit real dissent. The alternative preferred by some, popular democracy, while noble in theory, has yet to be proven viable at the national level, surely because of a combination of internal and external pressures. These pressures coagulate into one seemingly supreme challenge: how to both manage the socially disruptive costs of economic reform and democratize. Put differently, the major problem is how to make economic revitalization compatible with democratization.

(4) Resistance to globalization. In the drive for rapid economic growth, the East Asian NICs placed severe restraints on democratic rights. These states retained authoritarian controls to try to prevent the eruption of social tensions. Little dissent was tolerated, and the strong state touted as a prerequisite for good government and modernization.

Citing the examples of Taiwan, Singapore, and South Korea, Deng Xiaoping and his cohorts sought to justify their contention that restraining democratic rights is essential for successful economic development. In crushing the pro-democracy movement in 1989, the Dengists held that too much freedom promotes disruption and impedes economic reform. Silent on the matter of political reform, the leaders voiced concern that, given the chaos and turmoil experienced by China in this century, disorder is the gravest threat to development. In the absence of effective links between the state and civil society, the regime could only rely on guns and terror. In fact, the economic reform program required more flexible political structures to deal with increasingly autonomous groups in civil society – families detached from cooperatives by decollectivization, private entrepreneurs and industrialists, international traders, and students and intellectuals attracted by novel ideas entering China's open door.[18]

Just as autonomous groups are emerging in Chinese society, so too are new social movements bringing pressure to bear in global civil society. The globalization of civil society precipitates resistance from disadvantaged strata in a changing division of labor. The losers in global restructuring seek to redefine their role in the emerging order. In the face of the declining power of organized labor and revolutionary groups, the powerless must devise alternative strategies of social struggle. They aim to augment popular participation and assert local control over the seemingly remote forces of globalization. New social movements – women's groups, environmentalists, human rights organizations, etc. – are themselves a global phenomenon, a worldwide response to the deleterious effects of economic globalization. With the globalization of social conflict, observers have been quick to celebrate the formation of autonomous movements within civil society. Relatively little attention has been paid to the coalescence of these movements. Coordination is a crucial matter precisely because the proliferation of new social movements can splinter civil society, perhaps culminating in the Lebanonization of political life. The push for regional autonomy in areas such as Kurdistan has the potential to open a global Pandora's box. Another reason for caution is that new social movements can have a repressive side – e.g., the resurgence of Islamic fundamentalism in Africa and Asia and of anti-Semitism in the former Soviet Union and Eastern Europe. Before the disintegration of socialist regimes in 1989, the Soviet Union and its eastern European allies adopted anti-Zionist and anti-Israeli policies. Although the state did not sanction popular expressions of anti-Semitism, Jews were subject to discrimination in the bureaucracy. With the demise of socialism, however, anti-Semitism is flagrantly exhibited at many levels, with little sign of restraint, the impetus coming from autonomous groups in civil society. In sum, not only production and the state, but also civil society itself is being globalized.

Regionalism and Globalism: East Asia

Paradoxically, regionalism both shields domestic society from, and integrates it into, the global division of labor, as evident in East Asia. Although each regional division of labor has its distinctive features, all regional experiences are tethered to the global division of labor. The linkages differ substantially from one region to another and provide an important comparative basis for the better understanding of globalization.

As noted, one common element among diverse regions is that the state is increasingly a mechanism in the globalization process and, thus, intervenes directly in the economy to promote capital accumulation. Outflanked by transnational flows partly beyond its control, the state adapts to a changing global division of labor by tightening the fit between the local economy and technological innovation, R & D, and natural resource exploitation. With a lessening of the state's ability to control external forces, there has been a strengthening of regional groupings, largely a *de facto* process spearheaded by the private sector in the Pacific Rim, primarily a *de iure* process in Europe, and a mix of the two in North America, Mexico, and the Caribbean. The effects of regional cooperation as a means to enhance participation in globalization are not yet known. But it is clear that many Asian countries and firms look to improve regional cooperation for access to a burgeoning regional market and as a sound base for sharing in globalization.[19] The economic growth generated by the Japanese-led "flying geese" pattern of regional integration, involving countries at very different levels of development, suggests important distinctions among generations of countries to have penetrated global markets in diverse industries and sectors. In East Asia, there is a highly stratified division of labor among Japan, the Four Dragons, the countries comprising ASEAN (the Association of Southeast Asian Nations), Southern China, and Indochina.

In the Japanese model of state capitalism, the government subsidizes favored industries and shields them from market forces, especially imports. The state acts more by guidance than by edict, giving capital a major role in setting directions. As is well known, the state helps coordinate industries, the financial system, and technological innovations. Remarkable economic gains by Japanese business have prompted corporations in other countries to experiment with switching from a "just-in-case" manufacturing system to a *kanban* or "just-in-time" method. This method requires precise synchronization and continual supply of materials in order to reduce storage and other overhead costs as well as to improve productivity. Importantly, in terms of the regional division of labor, the "just-in-time" method places a premium on spatial proximity between suppliers and producers. In other words, it is a system that seeks advantage through spatial hierarchies. With this form of managerial and technological upgrading, Japanese industry has fanned out in East Asia in search of low-cost manual labor for such tasks as assembly operations.

Having negotiated financial and technological alliances between private capital and the state, other manufacturers in the region are attempting to follow in Japan's footsteps to establish protected domestic and expanding international markets. In the light of the Japanese experience, the Hong Kong government initially sought to keep labor costs low, partly by its welfare provisions in such areas as public housing and also through its policies of taxation, a form of indirect subsidies. Moreover, there was little history of militancy in Hong Kong's trade union movement. Hong Kong also had the advantage of being able to deliver highly skilled technical engineering at a cost considerably below that of the advanced countries. In terms of sourcing, there emerged a cluster of components, materials, and skilled labor in Hong Kong.[20]

Another city-state, Singapore, has similarly followed a path from low-cost, labor-intensive production to capital-intensive industries, and is now attempting to convert its economy to a knowledge center. As Singapore climbed the value-added ladder, it invested increasingly large sums in R & D activities. The state, especially its Economic Development Board (EDB) arm, has created a propitious zone for foreign investment, a catchment for transnational corporations offering ready technologies. As one EDB official summarized Singapore's development strategy, "Inner globalization", or regionalization, "and outer globalization benefit each other. Outer globalization improves inner globalization."[21] Too small to be anything but a regional power, Singapore lacks economies of scale to build large industrial parks and extensive facilities for a scientific culture. Unable to be on the cutting edge of R & D, Singapore emphasizes the D component, refining what others have invented. In other words, its technological capacity is borrowed, not indigenous. Singapore is a global power only to the extent that it has a transnational-driven economy. With a large concentration of transnational corporations, numbering over 3,000 in 1992, Singapore is an attractive location for banking, finance distribution networks and telecommunications operations. Optimizing its spatial advantages as a crossroads, Singapore has developed excellent infrastructure and state-of-the-art industrial services, making it a regional maintenance center which repairs equipment and provides aircraft services. Today, Singapore offers global technology, but its own products are competitive primarily in regional markets.[22]

To gain advantage, Singapore promotes subregional integration. Within ASEAN, there is a move to link three nodes – the city-state of Singapore, Johore state in peninsular Malaysia, and Indonesia's Riau Islands – in a Growth Triangle. This strategy of subregional integration seeks to combine Singapore's highly skilled, human capital and well-developed infrastructure, Johore's land and semiskilled labor, and Riau's land and low-cost labor. The Singapore-Johore-Riau Growth Triangle is partly derived from the experience of the twinning of Hong Kong and Shenzen, reputedly China's fastest growing city. Also to pull subregional entities into a tighter web are the plans for twinning the city-states of Hong Kong and Singapore. Thus, while Singapore upgrades its industrial and technological capacities, low value-added activities are shifted to neighboring countries, not unlike the strategy pursued by Hong Kong and Taiwan.

In addition to triangular ties among Hong Kong, Taiwan, and China's provinces of Guangdong and Fujian, the "Greater China Economic Zone" includes the participation of the ASEAN countries, with their powerful Chinese business communities, as investors in South China. An emerging Chinese transnational division of labor builds on Hong Kong's and Taiwan's extensive kinship networks with Guangdong and Fujian. The fusion of these networks and subregional culture forms strong economic linkages among Hong Kong, Taiwan, the ASEAN countries, and South China. The frequent movement of population, industry, and capital across borders is establishing a "transfrontier metropolis". China's economic integration with the region is furthered by its coast-oriented development strategy, most notably granting specially favorable conditions to select provinces and designating 14 coastal "open cities" further to attract Direct Foreign Investment (DFI).[23]

In a changing regional division of labor, China faces competition from other low-wage countries such as the Philippines and Indonesia, while some of the Four Dragons' neighbors, particularly Malaysia and Thailand, are experiencing remarkable economic growth. While the latter countries increasingly serve as magnets for DFI, questions are nevertheless raised about the NICs' future viability as industrial societies. Until recently viewed as the next Japan, South Korea is losing competitiveness in some key industries. Industries that fueled South Korea's economic dynamism, such as shoes, clothing, and simple consumer products, are now relocating in countries with lower wages. The shift from low-tech, labor-intensive industries is being hastened by democratic reforms demanded by formerly suppressed workers. Strikes in the 1980s led to a tripling of wages in some industries, causing Nike, Reebok, and other big firms to seek alternative production sites. Similarly, exports of personal computers from South Korea plummeted more than 57% in the first half of 1992 from the comparable period in 1991.[24] The policy debate now rife in South Korea, just as in Singapore and other NICs, is how to jump the elusive last hurdle in the race toward developed nation status. The challenge is to move up in the technological division of labor, which requires indigenous, not merely imported, capacity for innovation.

Meanwhile, resistance to restructuring is mounting, not least in South Korea from critics who challenge government assistance to a few huge conglomerates, known as *chaebol*. There are complaints about state policies subsidizing the *chaebol* and protecting them from imports, especially short of any reform of the financial system. In Hong Kong, worker mobility, most apparent among women in factories, is a sign of discontent. Notwithstanding economic growth for the country as a whole, Singapore faces disquiet among various ethnic groups and social movements. With English as the national language, and given a highly westernized culture, many Chinese-educated members of Singapore's Chinese community feel that they have been left behind in economic development. The share of wealth accruing to Singapore's Indian community, relative to that of the country's other ethnic groups, has declined in recent years. Singapore's Malays have found it hard to break into Chinese businesses, upper echelons of the civil service, and the military. Flanked by two predominantly Islamic countries, Malaysia and Indonesia, Singapore has established barriers for its Malays who seek to join the air force. Some Singaporean Malays claim to be caught in a spiral: poverty lessens the opportunity for education, and a low level of education begets poverty. Not surprisingly, Singapore's ethnic and Christian fundamentalist movements are gaining following.[25]

The developmental routes mapped here are unlikely to be replicated elsewhere, because global trends articulate with regional conditions in very different ways. The Four Dragons integrated into a "new international division of labor" during a period when the world economy was robust and when the Cold War generated not only extraordinary superpower conflict but also material assistance for allies in a strategically key region. On the fringes of the Third World, meanwhile, a strategy of subsidizing non-existent infant industries and protecting small markets within the ambit of heavy debt structures is of little use.[26] Although the external and domestic obstacles encountered by *parvenus* are now greater than in the past, the nature of the interactions between the contemporary globalization trend, which has superseded the "new international division of labor" of bygone decades, and social conflict offers important lessons for the future.

Future Directions

I began this study by suggesting that it is impossible to understand contemporary conflict without embedding the nation-state and social strata in a world society propelled by the unparalleled productive capacities of economic globalization. Formulating the problematic of conflict in this way directs attention to a Polanyian method of focusing on an expansion of the market and responses from those entities, regional and local, which directly encounter its disruptive and socially polarizing effects. This article has tried to extend Polanyi's conceptualization to a world scale, showing the interactions between globalization and social conflict.

Further, I have argued that the evolution of the theory of division of labor provides a key to comprehending the globalization of conflict. The discussion of this theory has concentrated on two theses, while taking the opportunity to propose a third and alternative conceptualization. First, classical political economy focused on efficiencies stemming from specialization of functions, with implications for developing particular products for trade and thus deriving comparative advantages of the international level. Although Adam Smith adumbrated a notion of interest-based politics centering on the division of labor, as did David Ricardo and Karl Marx, the concept of division of labor remained largely dormant and notwithstanding Max Weber's and Emile Durkheim's contributions to sociological theory, did not advance significantly until the second half of the twentieth century.

A conversation over "the wealth of nations" began anew in the 1960s. The emergence of the NICs sparked interest in the prospects for mobility in the international division of labor. Setting forth a structural analysis, the new international division of labor theorists sought to explain the shift of manufacturing from advanced capitalist to developing countries. In their view, the process is driven by declining profits in industrial centers, causing firms to seek new investment opportunities where labor costs are cheap. Hence, manufacturing operations are fragmented, with low-skilled tasks being transferred while the bulk of R & D activities are retained in the industrial heartlands. To this day, technological development, especially basic research, continues to be far less globalized than are manufacturing and sales.[27]

As we have seen, the new international division of labor thesis underlines the supposed logic of capital itself, but does not examine the interactions between global trends and varied local circumstances. In fact, during the 1980s global restructuring entailed a novel correlation of economic forces, political power, and social structure. Along with a change in emphasis from a Fordist model of mass production and mass consumption to a post-Fordist system of flexible production for niche markets came important technological innovations in certain industries, enabling NICs to move into higher value-added and upgraded operations, deepening the production structure in select countries, partly as a result of their own initiatives, and opening the way for integrated industries. The decomposition of the production process was accompanied by technological devolution to the NICs in crucial sectors revolving around transport and communications: major strides in containerized shipping making the spread of production facilities more profitable, improved engineering techniques speeding operations, and pervasive computer applications enabling instantaneous data processing to augment the efficiency of global business.[28] Important in this trend is the relatively "borderless" nature of technology and of a region, where complementary operations can easily be mounted and, if need be, transferred from country to country.

Beyond a "new" international division of labor, there have been remarkable changes in the global political economy in the past decade. In the emerging global division of labor, there are regional coordinating centers in specific industries in such hubs as Hong Kong and Singapore, with offshore assembly and natural resources situated in neighboring countries. The regional centers have upgraded and have leapfrogged into even higher value-added operations. They have sought to gain a technological edge by investing in R & D capacity. Although there is no technological quick fix for adjusting to a highly competitive global environment, raising spending on research and development promotes access to highly trained scientists and engineers, enhanced facilities for the reproduction of this form of labor, as well as other sources of investment in local universities and research institutes.[29] A handful of countries have used the impetus of the market and have tried to cushion its full impact. Nonetheless, upward mobility in the global division of labor remains relatively limited. It still takes place at the margins of the global political economy, and may be only partially determined by policy initiatives.

Globalization encompasses contradictory trends. On the one hand, the nonaccountable forces of globalization – cross-border flows of undocumented workers, modern communications with their faxlike speed, and the like – are largely beyond the control of effective state regulation. The state responds by becoming a transmission belt in the globalization process, more fully integrating the domestic economy into the world system. On the other hand, the state pulls in the opposite direction by using a variety of government interventions to create a competitive edge. All countries industrializing late rely on large-scale interventions, most importantly direct involvement in the production process, establishment of social and economic infrastructure, generous terms of credit, and material support for shifting from imitative to indigenous technological capacity. The options are clearly restricted, and the question is not whether the state should intervene in the economy, but what type of interventions are most appropriate in a specific context? And policy initiatives in whose interest? Will state intervention be subject to popular control? Given the limits on state policies and the promise of unprecedented productive capacity, new small states such as Georgia, the Baltic countries, Slovenia or Croatia can do no better than negotiate the channels of globalization, recognizing that freer markets entail greater social costs and hence must be popularly controlled. For these new countries, as for all others, globalization is not a matter of choice. Only within its ambit may policy decisions be made.

As countries manoeuver for position within the global division of labor, conflicts emerge anew, because the opportunity for ascent is quite constrained. It is constrained precisely because in a post-Westphalian and post-Cold War world, there is one, and only one, meta-structure – capitalism – establishing the rules for mobility, whether upward or downward. Intra-regional inequality is spearheaded by increased levels of interaction with the global economy. Hence, contradictions and conflicts have emerged among the Asia-Pacific countries, with heightened regional disparities, new competitors, and changing spatial orientations. Within China itself, the uneven distribution of DFI, interacting with state policies of encouraging some areas and localities to be more integrated in the global division of labor, have either exacerbated economic differences or reconfigured them. Empirical research shows that the overwhelming proportion of DFI in China is directed to coastal provinces and municipalities, with the vast interior beset by uneven development.[30] The global division of labor is also marked by inter-regional differences centered on three axes: Asia-Pacific, Europe with the possible participation of erstwhile socialist countries, and North America joined by Mexico and the Caribbean. The emergence of competing regional blocs could lead to increased global conflict, probably originating with instability in the Third World. Poverty and nondemocratic rule are the main sources of such instability. A host of proximate issues could ignite regional and global conflict – among others, a resurgence of ethnic or religious rivalries, a crisis of legitimacy, and the proliferation of advanced weaponry. In the absence of superpower restraints that were meant to head off a confrontation between the United States and the Soviet Union, regional powers now have greater leeway to pursue their own agendas. (Hence, Iraq marched into Kuwait partly because Saddam Hussein sought to fill what he regarded as a power vacuum.) Paradoxically, globalization engenders the regionalization of conflict.

In this post-hegemonic configuration, power is dispersed among more actors, and inter-regional competition is heightened. Given the instability characteristic of triads, an alliance between two of the three macro regions is a likely outcome. With the vast size of the European single market, the United States and Japan represent counter-balancing economic power. Currently first and second in size of GNP, the United States and Japan have mutual interests in a new world order. However, a new world order based on military superpower cannot be sustained by outside financing. The world's largest debtor nation, the United States derives jobs and investment capital from Japan, which in turn relies on its North American ally for innovation in industry and military power to guarantee the supply of vital resources, especially oil from the Middle East.

Yet for large numbers of people, there is no hint of a new world order or upward mobility in a changing division of labor. Rather, life is marked by a deep divide between rich and poor. The mosaic of globalization reflects a transformation of poverty in which three continents were most adversely affected by globalization to the marginalization of a single world region and of enclaves in other regions. According to projections by the World Bank, in Asia, the number in poverty will fall from 805 million in 1985 to 435 million by the end of this century; and in Latin America and the Caribbean, from 75 million to 60 million in the same period. In Sub-Saharan Africa, the number of poor will rise by 85 million, to 265 million in the year 2000. Thus, Asia's share of the world's poor will decline to 53% from 72% in 1985; Latin America's and the Caribbean's will drop to 11.4% from 19.1%; and Sub-Saharan Africa's will double from 16 to 32%.[31] In other words, there are holes in the global mosaic. Truncated globalization debars the bulk of Africa from gaining access to world society's productive processes. For the countries of Africa, the greatest challenge is to demarginalize when national options are severely constrained by the forces of globalization.

Against a backdrop of transformation from a hegemonic and state-centered structure to a multipolar and politically decentered world system, globalization is both an agent and product of social conflict. Globalization sets in train conflicts amongst competing capitalisms, deeper or reconfigured intra-regional disparities, engenders inter-regional rivalries among neo-mercantilist coalitions, and has combined with local forces to consign, at the end of this millennium, 265 million people on one continent to poverty, with little hope for escape in sight. The foremost contradiction of our time is the conflict between the zones of humanity integrated in the global division of labor and the ones which are excluded from it.

NOTES

1. Karl Polanyi, *The Great Transformation: The Political and Economic Origins of Our Time* (Boston: Beacon Press, 1957).
2. A valuable contribution to the discussion of the impetus for globalization is Keith Griffin and Azizur Rahman Khan, *Globalization and the Developing World: An Essay on the International Dimensions of Development in the Post-Cold War Era* (Geneva: United Nations Research Institute for Social Development, 1992).
3. Adam Smith, *An Inquiry into the Nature and Causes of the Wealth of Nations* (Middlesex: Penguin Books, 1970). I am drawing on James H. Mittelman, "Global Restructuring of Production and Migration," in Yoshikazu Sakamoto, ed., *Changing World Order and Structural Change* (Tokyo: United Nations University Press, 1993).
4. Giovanni Arrighi and Jessica Drangel, "The Stratification of the World-Economy: An Exploration of the Semiperipheral Zone," *Review* 10, 1 (Summer 1986): 55-56; and Gary Gereffi, "Paths of Industrialization: An Overview," in Gary Gereffi and Donald L. Wyman, eds., *Manufacturing Miracles: Paths of Industrialization in Latin America and East Asia* (Princeton: Princeton University Press, 1990), pp. 8-9.
5. World Bank, *World Development Report 1989* (New York: Oxford University Press, 1989), pp. 148-50. The figures for 1987 and 1988 are projected and, hence, represent estimates.
6. Folker Fröbel et al., *The New International Division of Labour: Structural Unemployment in Industrialised Countries and Industrialisation in Developing Countries,* trans. by Pete Burgess (Cambridge: Cambridge University Press, 1980), p. 46. An important extension of this work is Alain Lipietz, *Mirages and Miracles: The Crisis of Global Fordism,* trans. by David Macey (London: Verso, 1985). Cf. Alice H. Amsden, "Third World Industrialization: 'Global Fordism' or a New Model, " *New Left Review* 182 (July/August 1990): 5-31.
7. Fröbel et al. , op. cit., p. 46.
8. Gereffi, "Paths of Industrialization, " p. 3.
9. Robin Cohen, *The New Helots: Migrants in the International Division of Labour* (Brookfield: Gower, 1987); and Jeffrey Henderson, *The Globalisation of High Technology Production: Society, Space and Semiconductors in the Restructuring of the Modern World* (London: Routledge, 1989), pp. 22 and 27.
10. Fernand Braudel, "Unity and Diversity in the Human Sciences, " in Fernand Braudel, *On History,* trans. by Sarah Matthews (Chicago: University of Chicago Press, 1980), p. 55; and Eric Helleiner, "Fernand Braudel and International Political Economy," *International Studies*

Notes 15, 3 (Fall 1990): 74; Robert W. Cox, "Social Forces, States and World Orders: Beyond International Relations Theory," in Robert 0. Keohane, ed., *Neorealism and Its Critics* (New York: Columbia University Press, 1986), pp. 204-54; and James H. Mittelman, "Global Restructuring of Production and Migration."

11 See Peter Evans et al., eds., *Bringing the State Back In* (Cambridge: Cambridge University Press, 1985).

12 Robert W. Cox, *Production, Power, and World Order: Social Forces in the Making of History* (New York: Columbia University Press, 1987), pp. 253-65.

13 The inability of leaders and governments to deliver, as well as the effects of pluralism, are themes suggested by Thomas L. Hughes, *"Pro Patria Per Orbis Concordiam"* (remarks at the Carnegie Endowment for International Peace Trustees' Dinner, Washington, D.C., November 18, 1990).

14 Fred Halliday, "The Crisis of the Arab World: The False Answers of Saddam Hussein, " *New Left Review* 184 (November/December 1990): 69-74.

15 Maria Helena Moreira Alves, "Democratization Versus Social Equality in Latin America: Notes for Discussion" (paper presented to the Conference on Comparative Politics: Research Perspectives for the Next 20 Years, City University of New York Graduate School, September 7-9, 1988), pp. 9-13.

16 This argument is derived from James H. Mittelman, "The Dilemmas of Reform in Post-Revolutionary Societies," *International Studies Notes* 15, 2 (Spring 1990), especially p.67. Also, Alves, "Democratization Versus Social Equality," pp. 9-13.

17 C . B . Macpherson, *The Life and Times of Liberal Democracy* (Oxford: Oxford University Press, 1977); and Mittelman, "The Dilemmas of Reform," p. 67.

18 Ibid., p.68, citing Roderick MacFarquhar, "The End of the Chinese Revolution, " *New York Review of Books* 36, 12 (July 20, 1989): 8.

19 Organisation for Economic Cooperation and Development, *Programme of Research 1990-1992* (Paris: OECD, 1989), pp. 10-11 and 26.

20 I am borrowing from Henderson, *The Globalisation of High Technology Production*, pp . 102-17.

21 Interview with the author: Lee Suan Hiang, Director, Industry Development Division and Marketing Support Division, Economic Development Board, Singapore, December 10, 1991.

22 Interview with the author: Wong Chin Yeow, Director, Training, Research and Public Relations Division, Singapore Manufacturers Association, Singapore, December 18, 1991.

23 Xianming Chen, "China's Economic Cooperation with Major AsiaPacific Countries: Subregional and Local Dimensions, Determinants, and Consequences" in Arif Dirlik, ed., *What Is in a Rim? Critical Perspectives on the Pacific Region Idea* (Boulder: Westview, forthcoming); and *ibid*, citing Lawrence A. Herzog, *Where North Meets South: Cities. Space, and Politics on the U.S.-Mexico Border* (Austin: University of Texas Press, 1990).

24 "After Stall, Koreans See Need for Economic Reform, Too," *New York Times*, December 15, 1992.

25 Interviews with the author. Correspondents for Singaporean newspapers, Singapore, December 15, 1991.

26 For an elaboration of this argument, see James H. Mittelman, "Marginalization and the International Division of Labor: Mozambique's Strategy of Opening the Market," *African Studies Review* 34, 3 (December 1991): 89-106.

27 Comparing present-day trends to "the decades of American technological hegemony," the *New York Times* ("Technology without Borders Raises Big Questions for the U.S.," January 1, 1992) reports that despite various transnational flows, only 10% of U.S. corporate research and development funds is spent overseas. Motorola, for instance, derives half its revenue from international sales, stations 40% of its work force abroad, but only 20 to 25% of product development and 5% of basic research are conducted outside the United States. In a related article on U.S. technology policy, "Costs May Be Too High for All-American Chips," the same issue of the *New York Times* notes a surge of transnational partnerships and explains "what is driving the alliances," some of which are termed "politically explosive," "is not politics, but money."

28 An incisive discussion of these technological developments may be found in Ankie Hoogvelt, "The New International Division of Labour," in Ray Bush et al., eds., *The World Order: Socialist Perspectives* (Cambridge, England: Polity, 1987), pp. 65-86.

29 See Ian Chalmers, "International and Regional Integration: The Political Economy of the Electronics Industry in ASEAN," *ASEAN Economic Bulletin* 8, 2 (November 1991): 194-209; and Henderson, *The Globalisation of High Technology Production*, especially p. 45.

30 Chen, "China's Economic Cooperation with Major Asia-Pacific Countries," in Dirlik, ed., *What Is in a Rim?*

31 World Bank, *World Development Report 1990* (New York: Oxford University Press, 1990), p. 139.

14 CYCLES OF HEGEMONY AND LABOR UNREST IN THE CONTEMPORARY WORLD SYSTEM

Beverly J. Silver

Labor-Capital Conflict and World-Systems Analysis[1]

The role played by social conflict in general (and labor-capital conflict in particular) in explaining the origins and historical evolution of the capitalist world-economy remains an important, but underexamined aspect of the modern world system. This remains true despite the fact that there has been in recent years a growing effort to integrate class conflict as a central process into historical and theoretical accounts of long-term, world-scale social change. As Peter Waterman (1989: 301) notes in a review of the literature in international labor studies, those working from a world-systems perspective have shown an "increasing interest in labour and other social movements, seen in relation to the shaping and transformation of the contemporary world

---

This text is drawn from Giovanni Arrighi's research project "World-Scale Patterns of Labor Unrest" funded by the World Society Foundation. Beverly J. Silver was co-principal investigator of the research undertaken at the Fernand Braudel Center, State University of New York at Binghampton N.Y. She is now assistant professor of sociology at the Johns Hopkins University, Department of Sociology, Baltimore, MD 21218, U.S.A.

order." And he cites a series of recent essays by Arrighi, Hopkins and Wallerstein (1989) which "present social movements in general and labour movements in particular as co-creators with capital of the contemporary world-order."

The late 1970s and 1980s witnessed the publication of numerous books and articles which also suggested a causal link between long-term, large-scale social change and labor-capital conflict. In particular, various theories were proposed linking successive transformations in the organization of production (from craft production via "Fordist" production to "post-Fordism") to successive waves of labor militancy. This surge of intellectual interest was no doubt prompted by the end of the postwar boom and the simultaneous upsurge in labor militancy throughout much of the core in the late 1960s and 1970s, followed shortly by an intensive worldwide restructuring of production, focused in large part on restoring profit levels by cutting labor costs and increasing labor productivity.[2]

These studies provide many useful tools for an analysis of the links between labor unrest and social change. But they are all either theories of the evolution of "national" societies or general theories based on the experience of a few core states. They draw the boundaries of social systems at the borders of the nation-state; none take the historical development of the *world* social system as their unit of analysis.

The weakness of both the national and cross-national comparative approaches is that they presume that what goes on *within* one national case can be accounted for by processes specific to that national case, independently of what goes on elsewhere. This assumption has been subjected to a thorough critique by dependency and world-systems theorists, especially with regard to the concept of "national development".[3] This critique applies equally to the conceptualization of labor-capital conflict. The world-scale division of labor and interstate system link national labor movements to each other in a chain of causation. Just as "development" and "underdevelopment" have been interpreted as two sides of the same world-historical process, so too can we re-interpret the divergent experiences of national labor movements as part of a single world-scale historical process of labor-capital conflict.

During the 1980s, the proposition that global economic processes (especially the international mobility of capital) link workers and their movements across the globe gained broad acceptance. Deindustrialization, plant closings, expanding informal sector activities and declining union strength in the core have been (more or less explicitly) linked to industrialization, rapid urbanization, and the creation of new (in large part female) working classes in the so-called NICs (newly industrializing countries). The literature on the new international division of labor and globalization of production portrays the world as increasingly one single, giant labor market. In the words of one commentator, the "degree of actual and potential competition between labour in high and low-wage economies [is] now such that national labour organizations can no longer plan their strategies on the assumption that each is operating in a separate national labour market" (Godfrey 1986: 28).[4]

This literature has focused mainly on world-scale economic processes; and it has dealt primarily with the last several decades. However, the intensification of global economic competition in the 1970s and 1980s also spawned another literature focused on long-term cycles in world-scale political processes. This literature has portrayed the intensification of global economic competition as one of many indicators of a relative decline of US world power. Moreover, the US decline is conceptualized as part of a long-run cyclical process of rise and decline of world powers or world hegemonies, with three or more cycles (of hegemony / rivalry / world war) spanning the history of the capitalist world system.[5]

Unlike many of those writing during the rivalry / world war phase of the last cycle of world hegemony (that is, in the first half of the twentieth century), the contemporary literature rarely relates labor-capital conflict (and social conflict more generally) to these long-term global political processes.[6] Yet the central methodological premise outlined above – that is, that national labor movements are linked to each other in a chain of causation by the existence of a world-scale division of labor *and* an inter-state system – leads us precisely in the direction of linking the long-term world-scale patterning of labor-capital conflict to long-term global political processes. The third section of this essay will suggest a theoretical framework and provide some empirical evidence in support of the existence of such linkages.

Before proceeding with such a project, however, it was necessary to create new data sources. A major barrier to progress in the study of labor militancy (conceptualized as a world-scale historical process) has been the limitations of existing sources of information. Collections of data on labor unrest (as on other social phenomenon) tend to be nation-state-specific. Moreover, long time series (for example, covering at least one full cycle of world hegemony) are limited to a handful of core states. As part of an effort to overcome the limitations of existing sources of data, the World Labor Research Working Group at the Fernand Braudel Center set out in the early 1980s on a major project designed to create a database on world labor unrest that would allow us to construct reliable indicators of the patterning of world-scale labor unrest from the late nineteenth century to the present. The next section of this essay describes this project and its results to date. In the third and final section, indices constructed from the World Labor Group Database will be used to assess the plausibility of hypotheses about the relationship between world-scale labor unrest and cycles of world hegemony and rivalry.

The World Labor Group Database

The World Labor Research Working Group's project has involved the collection of information on incidents of labor unrest throughout the twentieth century as reported by the major newspapers of the two world hegemonic powers of the nineteenth and twentieth centuries – *The Times* (London) and *The New York Times*. Members of the research team read through the Indexes of *The Times* (London) and *The New York Times*, and recorded any act of labor unrest[7] anywhere in the world reported by these papers. Among the types of reported incidents included are strikes, riots, slowdowns, factory occupations, sabotage, and demonstrations. The result of this process is a complete census of all mentions of labor unrest around the world in the indexes of our two newspaper sources from 1906 to the present.[8] The resulting database contains over 80 000 reports from 156 countries.

Tapping major newspapers as a source to construct indexes of protest has become a fairly widespread and developed practice in the social sciences.[9] As Burstein (1985: 202) writes: "In recent years ... a small but growing group of social scientists has concluded that valid time-series data on many of the more visible aspects of politics could be collected by drawing on an obvious but hitherto untapped data source – major newspapers..." Burstein collected data on civil rights demonstrations and other protest activities from *The New York Times* and concluded that the data from this source "convey a generally accurate picture of the events and time trends analyzed ... and are far better than any other actual or potentially available data". Likewise, the Tillys (1975: 315) concluded from their study of collective violence in France that "newspaper scanning provides a more comprehensive and uniform sample of events than any alternative source available to us".

These studies use information gleaned from national newspapers to measure occurrences of protest within that state. What is innovative about the World Labor Group's project is that we claim one can use the major newspapers of the world's hegemonic powers to create reliable indicators of world-level labor unrest.

The World Labor Research Working Group has carried out extensive reliability studies which have substantiated the plausibility of this claim. The results to date are discussed in detail elsewhere (*Review 1993* and Silver 1992b). These results will be summarized in the remainder of this section.

Reliability studies on the geographical spread of the World Labor Group Database (and hence its suitability for building world-scale indicators of labor unrest) have shown that both newspaper sources (1) have had world-level information-collecting capabilities throughout the period of our study; (2) have used, those capabilities to report on labor unrest worldwide; (3) each have regional reporting biases which are to a large extent compensated for by the different regional reporting biases of the other source. The world-scale nature of the database is indicated by the fact that it includes reports on labor unrest in 156 countries, and that for 67 of these there is a minimum of 80 reports of labor unrest from at least one of the two newspaper sources.[10]

Wave years of labor unrest – years of exceptionally high militancy – were identified for each of the 67 countries that meet this 80-year-report threshold. Two criteria had to be met for any year to qualify as a wave in any given country: (1) the number of reported incidents of labor unrest in that year had to be 50% greater than the average of the preceding five years (cf. Shorter and Tilly 1974) and; (2) the number of mentions of labor unrest in that year had to be greater than the mean number of mentions for that country over the entire 80-year period.

Reliability studies comparing the wave years identified through the above process with the years identified as major periods of labor militancy by either official strike statistics and/or histories of the various national labor movements have confirmed the reliability of the database as a tool for identifying major waves of labor militancy. Country reliability studies carried out by members of the World Labor Research Working Group (see *Review*, 1993) found that, for all the cases examined (Argentina, China, Egypt, France, Germany, Italy, Poland, South Africa, and the United States), the major peaks of labor unrest as identified by either official statistics and/or the secondary historical literature were also wave years in the World Labor Group Database. Moreover, the World Labor Group Database identified some major waves of labor unrest that are missed by the official statistics because of gaps and weaknesses.

For example, based on an examination of the time series of mentions of labor unrest for Italy constructed from the World Labor Group Database, Arrighi (in *Review*, 1993) concludes that the latter is "highly reliable in the identification of minor and, above all, major national waves of labor unrest". The waves and peaks identified by the World Labor Group Database are years that are important, "not just from a quantitative point of view, but as watersheds in labor-capital relations".

The conclusion that the World Labor Group Database is an extremely useful tool for identifying major waves of labor unrest, and especially those years that represent turning points in labor-capital relations, is further supported by Dubofsky's analysis of the US data (in *Review*, 1993). 1937 emerges as the overall peak of labor unrest in the World Labor Group time series for the US. While 1937 is not the peak in the official statistics, it is the major turning point in labor relations in the US in the twentieth century: the wave of sit-down strikes in 1937 led to the recognition of unions in mass production industries for the first time.

The other country studies confirm the conclusion: we can be fairly confident about the ability of the World Labor Group Database to identify major waves of national labor unrest – and in particular those that represent turning-points in labor-capital relations. Major waves of labor unrest are, in turn, important determinants within theories which link long-term, large-scale social change and labor unrest. Elsewhere (Silver 1992a) we have analyzed the relationship between the world-level patterning of these major waves of labor unrest and long waves of capital accumulation (Kondtratieff cycles). In the final section of this essay, we will analyze the inter-relationship between the world-level patterning of these major waves of labor unrest and cycles of world hegemony and world war.

Labor Unrest and World Hegemony

The figures and charts used in this essay show a time series (constructed from the World Labor Group Database) indicating the geographical spread of major waves of national labor unrest in any given year from 1911 through 1985: that is, it shows the percentage of countries in the world experiencing a wave of labor unrest (as defined above) in any given year.[11]

TABLE 1 Patterns of world labor unrest

	Rivalry 1911-1948	Hegemony 1949-1985
Average annual % of countries w / waves of labour unrest	14 %	18%
Explosiveness: standard deviation	8.8	4.9
Major explosions	1919, 1946	none
Abnormal deviations from the trend		
High:	1919-1920 1945-1948	none
Low:	1914, 1940-1942	1968

FIGURE 1 The Geographical Spread of Waves of Labor Unrest – "World"

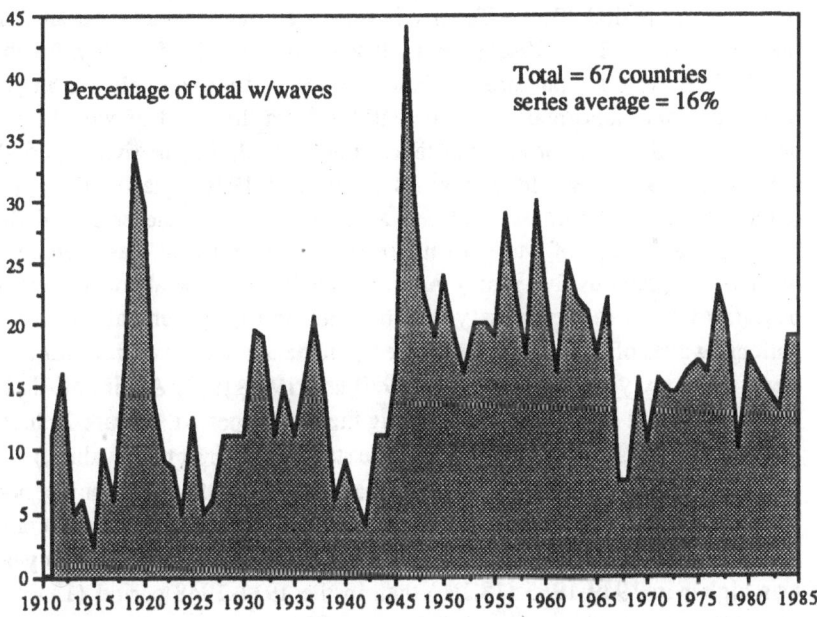

Two contrasting patterns emerge when we divide this 75-year series into two periods – roughly corresponding to the period of rivalry and world wars (1911-1948) and to the period of US hegemony (1949-1985). Figure 1 charts the world-level series over time. Table 1 summarizes the main differences. The picture of world-scale labor unrest from 1911-1948 is dominated by the two world wars: each brings about a sudden contraction in the geographical spread of major waves of labor unrest followed by violent explosions as the wars end. The Second World War contraction and explosion replicates the experience of the First, but with far greater severity in terms of the number of countries involved. In 1919 34% of the countries experience waves of labor unrest. In 1946 (the overall peak for the 75-year series) 44% are simultaneously contributing to the world-scale explosion of conflict.

In contrast to the sudden and severe contractions and explosions in world-scale labor unrest which characterized the rivalry period (1911-1948), the hegemony period (1949-1985) is characterized by a pattern in which the number of countries in any given year experiencing waves of labor unrest remains high but relatively stable – i.e., waves of labor unrest across the globe do not tend to cluster disproportionately in particular years as they had in the rivalry period. This difference is suggested by the greater variance in the series for the 1911-1948 period (standard deviation = 8.8) than for the 1949-1985 period (standard deviation = 4.9.) Moreover, all the major explosions and abnormally high deviations from the trend of world-scale labor unrest identified through this time series occur during the rivalry period. Only the two post-world war years (1919 and 1946) qualify as major explosions of labor unrest (defined as years in which the series of the geographical spread of waves of national labor unrest is at least twice the mean of the previous five years). Additionally, if we define abnormally high deviations from the trend as years in which the geographical spread of national waves of labor unrest is greater than the average deviation from the trend, only six years qualify: 1919-1920 and 1945-1948. Again, all these abnormally high deviations occur during the rivalry period. (Figure 2 charts the detrended world-level series minus the standard error of the y values.)

The less explosive nature of world-scale labor unrest in the hegemony period does not mean that there were fewer labor unrest waves. Rather, the average number of countries experiencing waves of labor unrest in any given year was higher in 1949-1985 (18.1%) than in the 1911-1948 period (13.6%). The difference is that the national waves of labor unrest did not cluster

FIGURE 2 The Geographical Spread of Waves of Labor Unrest Deviations from the Trend – "World"

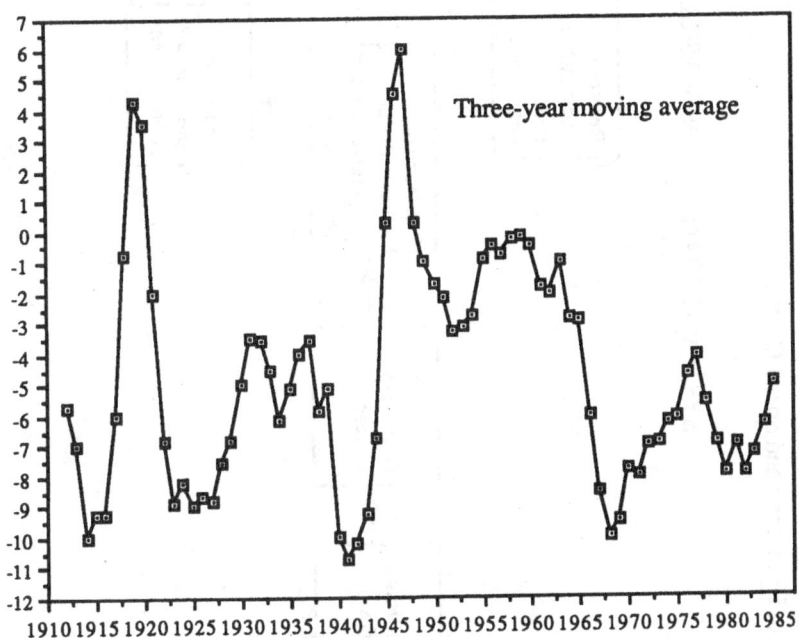

into simultaneous, worldwide challenges to the capitalist world-system as they had during the rivalry period.

The transformation in the world-level pattern of class conflict from one of increasing severity and explosiveness in the first half of the century to one of relatively high levels but decreasing explosiveness in the second half of the century can be explained in terms of global political processes – that is, phases of world hegemony and rivalry. Elsewhere (Arrighi 1990, Silver 1992b) we have put forward a conceptual framework suggesting a procyclical relationship between world labor unrest and cycles of hegemony. In periods of rivalry, a vicious circle operates: labor unrest both feeds and is fed by the increasing social chaos and violent interstate conflicts that characterize periods of rivalry. In periods of hegemony, in contrast, a virtuous circle operates as the hegemon successfully re-establishes the conditions for social peace (or at least contained class conflict) and for the expanded reproduction

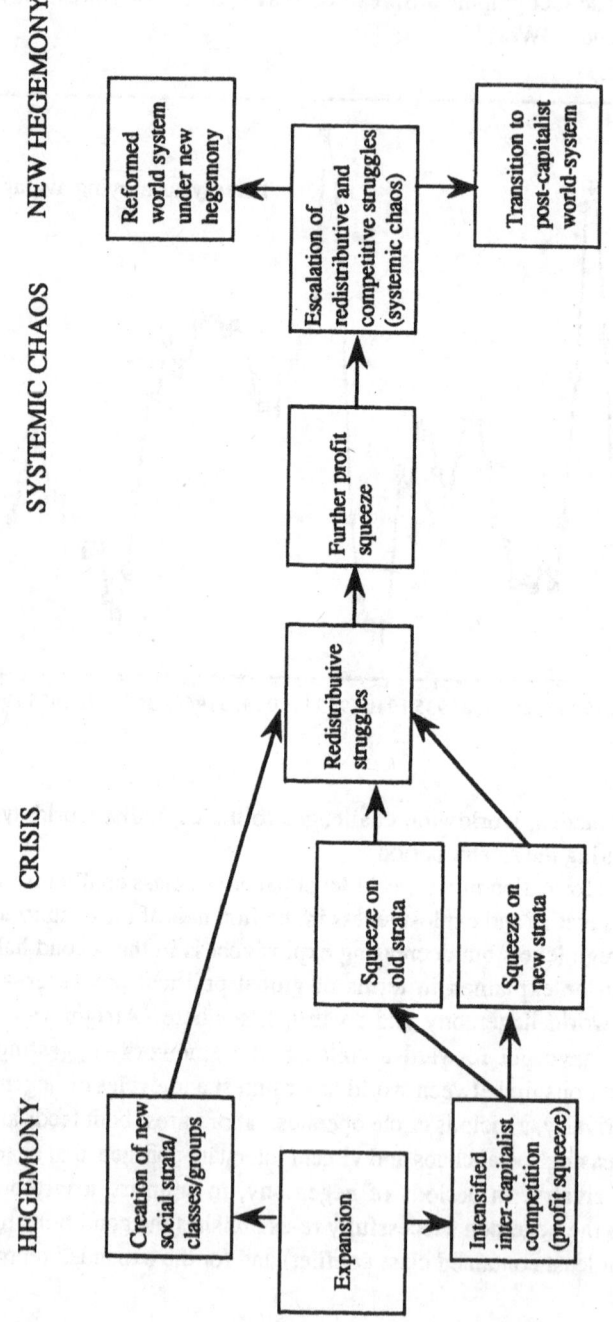

FIGURE 3 Cycles of Hegemony and Social Conflict

of capital on a world-scale. Expansion over time undermines the favorable conditions for further expansion, and a new period of global rivalry and explosive social conflict ensues. Figure 3 summarizes graphically this cycle of hegemony and social conflict.

At the beginning of the hegemony phase, economic power is concentrated in the hegemonic state; the expansion is primarily based on complementary / interdependent relations in the economic sphere, bringing about a general prosperity for the allies. However, the expansion itself sows the seeds of its own demise. Over time the allies catch up with or overtake the hegemonic state in trade and production leading to an escalation of competitive pressures and a concomitant squeeze on capitalist profits. Competitive pressures may lead the hegemonic state (or capitalists generally) to attempt to break expensive social compacts on which consent between classes and states had been based. The response from those being squeezed by capitalists and / or the state may well lead to an escalation of struggles. Intensifying struggles puts a further squeeze on profits, and provides an additional blow to the hegemon's continued dominance.

The most important source of social conflict may not, however, come from previously incorporated classes or strata. Each expansion takes place on a given social base (e.g., the class allies of the British-sponsored world order were the propertied middle classes of the West.) However, the expansion itself creates new social strata which either were not or cannot be accomodated within the world social contract of the hegemon (e.g., the core factory proletariat born of the 19th century expansion). As competition among capitalists increases, capitalists tend to increase the pressure on these new social strata (e.g., harder work, lower pay). But, as the new social strata grow in size and power, they become more and more likely to respond to increased pressure with struggles aimed at fundamentally transforming their position within the system. These struggles, in turn, further squeeze profits, and increase competitive pressures. The crisis of hegemony is announced by a simultaneous escalation of competitive struggles among capitalists and redistributive struggles between labor and capital. These struggles feed each other until a situation of systemic chaos characterizes the world-economy.

As competitive and redistributive struggles escalate, states tend to redouble their efforts to protect the interests and livelihood of their subjects, and historically the outcome has been generalized (world) war. At first, as war breaks out, ruling groups and classes attempt to enlist the support of subordinate classes (e.g., hard work both in factories and battlefields). Overt expressions of labor unrest are brought under control through a combination of repression and "political exchange" – e.g., tri-partite agreements among representatives of the workers, capitalists and the state in which labor quiescence for the duration of the war is exchanged for actual or promised benefits ("when we win"). However, towards the end of wars labor unrest tends to explode as "political exchanges" break down. Capitalists and states attempt to free themselves from expensive commitments made to labor during the war. Workers, in turn, seek to redress accumulated grievances now that militancy is no longer so easily de-legitimated or repressed. Moreover, where the war has been lost (and even sometimes where it has been won), revolutionary situations are fostered by the deterioration in economic and social conditions. For all these reasons, waves of labor unrest tend to cluster at the end of the two world wars, as shown in Figure 1.

Systemic chaos (wars, revolutions, etc.) disrupts networks of accumulation. The expanded reproduction of capital on a world scale can only take off again if a new hegemony is established capable of bringing the systemic chaos to an end. Historically, a partial pre-condition for the emergence of a new hegemony has been the concentration of economic and military power in a single state. However, this has not been sufficient. The previous round of expansion (and struggles) always transforms the world. New social groups are created and incorporated into the world division of labor, some of which are too powerful to ignore. They demand to be taken into account in the new set-up.

Without social peace there can be no new round of accumulation. But struggles do not subside and social peace cannot be restored unless a reformist solution to the social upheavals is found. Each new hegemon has thus been forced to transform the system in order to save it from its own contradictions. In this sense, then, each hegemony has come to define not just a cycle in the history of the modern world system, but also a stage in its evolution.

Labor unrest in the hegemony phase is less explosive, in part because the hegemon successfully implements reformist solutions to the revolutionary challenges posed during the previous rivalry phase. But labor unrest also becomes less explosive as favorable conditions for the geographical mobility of capital on a world scale are restored. The greater spatial mobility of capital in periods of hegemony allows capitalists to relocate production away from areas of labor militancy, weakening labor movements in the sites of

TABLE 2

TABLE 2(A) Average annual % of countries with waves of labor unrest

	World	Core	Periphery	Semiperiphery
Rivalry: 1911-1948	14%	21%	8%	15%
Hegemony: 1949-1985	18%	16%	21%	21%

TABLE 2(B) Explosivness (standard deviation)

	World	Core	Periphery	Semiperiphery
Rivalry: 1911-1948	8.8	11.3	9.7	10.8
Hegemony: 1949-1985	4.9	8.9	9.3	10.7

TABLE 2(C) Major Explosions

	World	Core	Periphery	Semiperiphery
Rivalry: 1911-1948	1919, 1946	1912, 1918-20, 1932, 1947	1946-47	1919, 1946
Hegemony: 1949-1985	none	none	1953-57, 1962-64, 1966, 1974, 1981	1959, 1965, 1985

TABLE 2(D) Deviations from trend

	World	Core	Periphery	Semiperiphery
Rivalry:				
High:	1919-20, 1945-48	1918-20, 1946-49	1946-48	1919-20, 1946-47
Low:	1914, 1940-42	1914-15 1923	1942-43	1940-42
Hegemony:				
High:	none	none	1953-56, 1963	1958-60, 1985
Low:	1968	none	1983-34	1967-70

disinvestment, but strengthening movements over time in the new sites of investment. This process can be seen during the period of US hegemony as capital successively relocated production in response to labor militancy: first, from the United States in response to the consolidation of union victories after the Second World War; then from Western Europe in response to the late 1960s resurgence of class conflict, and now from the semiperipheral locations which have experienced mass waves of labor unrest in the 1980s (e.g., South Korea, South Africa, Brazil and Poland). This successive relocation of capital has had the effect of containing the labor movement in the region from which capital emigrates, but strengthening it (over time) in the areas to which capital migrates (Arrighi and Silver 1984; Silver 1991, 1992b). This has meant a decline in labor unrest waves in the core but an increase in the semiperiphery, adding up to the high but fairly stable worldwide trend typical of periods of hegemony.

Table 2 disaggregates the world-level series of labor unrest into three groups: core, periphery and semiperiphery.[12] The results provide further support for the hypothesis that distinct world-level processes are at work in the hegemony and rivalry periods.

As already mentioned, the average annual percentage of countries in the world experiencing waves of labor unrest increases from 14% in the rivalry period to 18% in the hegemony period. However, this world-level increase is composed of:

a) a *decline* in the core (from 21% to 16%);

b) an *increase* in both the periphery (from 8% to 21%) and semiperiphery (from 15% to 21%).

This is consistent with the argument that the geographical relocation of production from core to semiperiphery and periphery has been followed by a geographical relocation of labor unrest from core to semiperiphery and periphery. Table 2 also reveals divergent regional patterns in the explosiveness of labor unrest (as measured by the standard deviation of the series) which decreases from 8.8 in the rivalry period to 4.9 in the hegemony period. It is, however only the core aggregate that experiences a decrease (from 14.8 to 8.9), while the peripheral and semiperipheral aggregates remain equally explosive in both periods. At the same time, they form a larger percentage of the total volume of world-level waves of labor unrest (as mentioned above). Thus, the world-level decline in explosiveness cannot simply be attributed to a decline for the various parts.

Instead, a different type of interaction among the parts has characterized the hegemony and rivalry periods. In the rivalry period, waves of labor unrest in the three different aggregates tended to cluster in the same years. Thus, 1919-1920 are "abnormally high deviations from the trend" for both core and semiperiphery; 1946-1947 are abnormally high deviations from the trend for all three aggregates – core, periphery and semiperiphery. The intensifying systemic chaos and global warfare associated with the crisis of hegemony promotes simultaneous, worldwide explosions of labor unrest, which in quantity and quality, represent major challenges to the capitalist world system.

In contrast, during the hegemony period, abnormally high deviations from the trend never occur simultaneously in more than one of the aggregates. The waves do not cluster in time. Instead, they counterbalance one another, contributing to the relatively flat profile of world-level labor unrest waves during the period of US hegemony. In part, the new hegemon's reformist solutions to the revolutionary challenges brings unrest under control. But in part, it is the re-establishment of the necessary conditions for world-scale capital accumulation which accompanies the establishment of a new hegemony (including the transnational mobility of capital) which keeps labor unrest waves from escalating into simultaneous, worldwide and revolutionary challenges to the system.

Thus, the period of US hegemony has been characterized by a decline in labor unrest in the core (see Table 2). This decline is rooted in two main processes: (1) the incorporation of the core working classes as subordinate members of the hegemonic project through the promise of mass consumption; (2) the successive relocation of capital away from areas of trade union strength leading to the weakening of core labor movements.

The period of US hegemony has also been characterized by a downward trend in labor unrest in the periphery. While the average annual number of countries experiencing waves of labor unrest in the periphery grew from 8% in the rivalry period to 21% in the hegemony period (see Table 2), most of the major explosions of labor unrest in the periphery were concentrated in the early decades of US hegemony. According to the World Labor Group time series, labor unrest waves begin to spread throughout the periphery in the early 1920s, explode in the late 1940s and then remain at extremely high levels throughout the 1950s and early 1960s. Labor militancy escalated together with national liberation struggles throughout Asia and Africa. But from the early 1960s onward, an overall downward trend in labor unrest has prevailed. The decolonization process sponsored by the US and the UN succeeded in channeling the nationalist movements into paths that could be absorbed by a reformed capitalist world system. The new states were incorporated into the world-hegemonic project as subordinate members of the hegemonic project through the promise of self-determination and development. Once nationalist movements controlled state power, workers' struggles inevitably lost much of their former support from other classes in society. The "battering ram of the masses" – having accomplished the goal of state power – was fairly easily repressed.

In contrast, the semiperiphery is the only one of the three aggregates that shows no decline in labor unrest throughout the period of US hegemony. It can be argued that the contradictions of the core were being shifted to the semiperiphery, as the relocation of capital weakened labor movements in the core, but created and strengthened new working classes in the semiperiphery.

A new pattern emerges in the post-1968 decades. Since 1968 there has been an upward trend in waves of labor unrest, for the world as a whole and for each of the three aggregates taken separately. The year 1968 shows up as an abnormally low deviation from the trend – the calm before the storm, so to speak. And while there is a relative upsurge of labor unrest after 1968, there is no world-scale decline in the late 1970s and 1980s. At the present time the World Labor Group Database ends in 1985. However, there is every reason to expect that these upward trends will be confirmed and strengthened once the data collection is extended into the early 1990s – especially given the escalation of conflict in the semiperiphery, ranging from South Korea and South Africa to Eastern Europe and the former USSR.

It is interesting to note that the period since 1968 has also been identified as one of latent crisis of US hegemony, analagous to the late nineteenth century crisis of British hegemony. The success of the US in reestablishing the preconditions for profitable accumulation on a world scale after the Second World War led, within just a few decades, to intense intercapitalist competition as Western Europe and Japan caught up with the United States' economic lead.

According to the conceptual framework suggested here, this concurrence between a rising trend in labor unrest and a crisis of hegemony is not an historical accident. Rather, if the analysis put forward here has any relevance to the future evolution of the world system we should not be surprised if: (1) labor unrest and other struggles on a world scale spread as the crisis of US hegemony deepens; (2) the protagonists of these struggles are primarily strata, groups or classes which were created by the latest post-Second World War expansion of the system; (3) the new protagonists of these struggles generate new kinds of demands which only a reformed or transformed system can accommodate.

NOTES

1 This chapter reports on the work of the World Labor Research Working Group at the Fernand Braudel Center (State University of New York, Binghamton). A more detailed account of the project is forthcoming as a special issue of *Review: Fernand Braudel Center*. The members of the World Labor Group are: Giovanni Arrighi, Mark Beittel, John Casparis, Jamie Dangler, Melvyn Dubofsky, Roberto Patricio Korzeniewicz, Donald Quataert, Mark Selden and Beverly Silver. We are grateful to the World Society Foundation for a termination grant which has allowed us to bring this work to fruition.

2 Among those who proffered theories linking labor militancy to cycles and stages in the organization of production Aglietta (1979), Boyer (1979), Burawoy (1985), Coriat (1980), Cronin (1979, 1980), Edwards (1979), Gordon, Edwards & Reich (1982) and Mandel (1980).

3 For a methodological critique of the national-case study and comparative-national approaches, see Hopkins 1982.

4 Among the extensive literature that deals with the globalization of production processes see: Froebel et al., 1980; Bluestone and Harrison 1982; Nash and Fernandez-Kelly 1983; Scott and Storper 1986; Caporaso 1987; Lipietz 1987; Sassen 1988; MacEwan and Tabb 1989; Portes, Castells and Benton 1989; Ward 1990; Rothstein and Blim 1992.

5 See, e.g., Arrighi 1983, 1990; Bergesen 1983; Bousquet 1980; Chase-Dunn 1989; Gilpin 1975, 1981; Goldstein 1986; Hopkins 1990; Kennedy 1988; Modelski 1978; Wallerstein 1984.

6 Both Polanyi (1944) and E.H. Carr (1945) emphasize the role of the expanding free trade world order characteristic of British hegemony in provoking profound worldwide social dislocations which promoted the militancy of various social (and especially labor) movements in their demands for protection from their respective national governments, which in turn contributed to a deepening of the crisis and the turn toward world war, which thereupon increased the militancy of worldwide labor protest. For Lenin (1916: 175) the stage of imperialism (that is,

generalized warfare among the core powers) intensifies all the contradictions of capitalism, and thus, "Imperialism is the eve of the social revolution of the proletariat".

7   See *Review* (forthcoming) and Silver (1992b) for an elaboration of the conceptualization of labor unrest which guided the data recording process, as well as for a detailed discussion of the project, including data collection procedures and results of data analysis.
8   1906 was the first year that *The Times* (London) is indexed.
9   Among those who have used the newspapers to construct indexes of protest, see the writings by Burstein 1985; Danzger 1975; Franzosi 1987; Jenkins and Perrow 1977; Korzeniewicz 1989; McAdam 1982; Paige 1975; Snyder and Kelly 1977; Snyder and Tilly 1972; Sugimoto 1978a, 1978b; Tarrow 1989; Tilly 1978, 1981, 1986; and Tilly et. al. 1975.
10 We should emphasize that the data collection project was *not* designed to produce a count of *all* incidents of labor unrest that have taken place in the world over the last century. The newspapers report on only a small fraction of the labor unrest which takes place. Instead, the procedure is intended to produce a measure that reliably indicates *the changing levels* of labor unrest - when the incidence of acts of labor unrest are rising or falling, when they are high or low - *relative to* other points in time or locations in space.
11 The "world" includes the 67 countries that met a threshold of 80 mentions of labor unrest in either or both newspaper sources.
12 For present purposes, the core, periphery and semiperiphery aggregates were composed as follows: a core group composed of fifteen countries (Northwestern Europe, North America, Australia and New Zealand); a peripheral group composed of fifteen countries (sub-Saharan Africa except South Africa, and Asia except Japan and South Korea); and a semiperipheral group composed of twenty countries (Latin America, Southern Europe except Italy, and South Africa). This corresponds in large part to the Arrighi and Drangel (1984) classification, albeit with simplifications.

REFERENCES

Aglietta, Michel (1979). *A Theory of Capitalist Regulation: the US Experience*. London: New Left Books.
Arrighi, Giovanni (1990). "The Three Hegemonies of Historical Capitalism." *Review*, 13:3, Summer, 365-408.

Arrighi, Giovanni (1983). *The Geometry of Imperialism*. London: Verso.
Arrighi, Giovanni & Jessica Drangel (1986). "The Stratification of the World-Economy: An Exploration of the Semiperipheral Zone," *Review*, X, 1, Summer, 9-74.
Arrighi, Giovanni, Terence K. Hopkins, & Immanuel Wallerstein (1989). *Antisystemic Movements*. London: Verso.
Arrighi, Giovanni and Beverly Silver (1984). "Labor Movements and Capital Migration: The US and Western Europe in World-Historical Perspective," in Charles Bergquist (ed) *Labor in the Capitalist World-Economy*. Beverly Hills, CA: Sage.
Bergesen, A. (1983). "1914 Again? Another Cycle of Interstate Competition and War," in P. McGowan and C.W. Kegley, Jr. (eds.) *Foreign Policy and the Modern World System*. Beverly Hills: Sage.
Bluestone, B. & Harrison B. (1982). *The Deindustrialization of America: Plant Closings, Community Abandonment, and the Dismantling of Basic Industry*. New York: Basic Books.
Bousquet, Nicole (1980). "From Hegemony to Competition: Cycles of the Core?" in T.K. Hopkins and I. Wallerstein, eds., *Processes of the World System*. Beverly Hills: Sage, 46-83.
Boyer, Robert (1979). "Wage Formation in Historical Perspective: The French Experience." *Cambridge Journal of Economics*, 3, 99-118.
Burawoy, Michael (1985). *The Politics of Production: Factory Regimes Under Capitalism and Socialism*. London: New Left Books.
Burstein, Paul (1985). *Discrimination, Jobs and Politics*. Chicago: Chicago Univ. Press.
Caporaso, James A. (1987). *A Changing International Division of Labor*. Boulder, CO: Lynne Rienner Publishers.
Carr, Edward H. (1945). *Nationalism and After*. London: Macmillan.
Chase-Dunn, Christopher (1989). *Global Formation*. Cambridge, MA: Basil Blackwell.
Coriat, Benjamin (1980). "The Restructuring of the Assembly Line," *Capital & Class*, No. 11, Summer.
Cronin, James (1980). "Stages, Cycles and Insurgencies: The Economics of Unrest." In T.K. Hopkins and I. Wallerstein (eds.) *Processes of the World-System*. Sage Publications: Beverly Hills, CA.
Cronin, James E. (1979). *Industrial Conflict in Modern Britain*. London: Croom Helm.
Danzger, Herbert M. (1975). "Validating Conflict Data", *American Sociological Review*, XL, 5, 570-84.
Edwards, Richard (1979). *Contested Terrain: The Transformation of the Workplace in the Twentieth Century*. New York- Basic Books.
Franzosi, Roberto (1987). "The Press as a Source of Socio-Historical Data," *Historical Methods*, XX, 1, Winter.
Frobel, F., Heinrichs, J. & Kreye, 0. (1980). *The New International Division of Labor*. Cambridge: Cambridge Univ. Press.
Gilpin, R. (1981). *War and Change in World Politics*. Cambridge: Cambridge University Press.

Gilpin, R. (1975). *US Power and the Multinational Corporation.* New York: Basic Books.
Godfrey, Martin (1986). *Global Unemployment: The New Challenge to Economic Theory.* B righton Press.
Goldstein, Joshua S. (1986). *Long Cycles: Prosperity and War in the Modern Age.* New Haven: Yale Univ. Press.
Gordon, D.M., Edwards, R. and Reich, M. (1982). *Segmented Work, Divided Workers: The Historical Transformation of Labor in the United States.* Cambridge: Cambridge University Press.
Hopkins, Terence K. (1990). "Note on the Concept of Hegemony." *Review,* 13, 3, Summer, 409-411.
Hopkins, Terence K. (1982). "The Study of the Capitalist World-Economy: Some Introductory Considerations." In Terence K. Hopkins, Immanuel Wallerstein & Assoc., *World-Systems Analysis: Theory and Methodology.* Beverly Hills, CA: Sage.
Jenkins, J.C. & Perrow, C. (1977). "Insurgency of the Powerless: Farm Worker Movements," *American Sociological Review,* XLII, 2, 249-67.
Kennedy, Paul (1988). *The Rise and Fall of Great Powers.* New York: Random House.
Korzeniewicz, Roberto P. (1989). "Labor Unrest in Argentina, 1887-1907," *Latin American Research Review,* XXIV, 3.
Lenin, V.I. (1971) [1916]. *Imperialism, the Highest State of Capitalism.* In V.I. Lenin *Selected Works.* New York: International Publishers.
Lipietz, Alain (1987). *Mirages and Miracles: The Crises of Global Fordism.* London: Verso.
MacEwan, Arthur and William K. Tabb, eds. (1989). *Instability and Change in the World Economy.* New York: Monthly Review Press.
Mandel, Ernest (1980). *Long Waves of Capitalist Development: The Marxist Interpretation.* Cambridge: Cambridge Univ. Press.
McAdam, Doug (1982). *Political Process and the Development of Black Insurgency, 1930-1970.* Chicago: Univ. of Chicago Press.
Modelski, George (1978). "The Long Cycle of Global Politics and the Nation-State," *Comparative Studies in Society and History,* XX, 2, 214-38.
Nash, June & Fernandez-Kelly, Maria Patricia eds., (1983). *Women, Men and the International Division of Labor.* Albany, NY: State University of New York Press.
Paige, Jeffery M. (1975). *Agrarian Revolution.* New York: Macmillan.
Polanyi, Karl [1944] (1957). *The Great Transformation: The Political and Economic Origins of Our Time.* Boston: Beacon Press.
Portes, Alejandro, Manuel Castells and Lauren Benton, eds. (1989). *The Informal Economy.* Baltimore: Johns Hopkins University Press.
Review: A Journal of the Fernand Braudel Center. Special Issue: Labor Unrest in the World-Economy (by the World Labor Research Working Group.) 1993.
Rothstein, Frances and Michael Blim (1992). *Anthropology and the Global Factory.* New York: Bergin and Garvey.

Sassen, Saskia (1988). *The Mobility of Labor and Capital*. Cambridge: Cambridge Univ. Press.
Scott, Allen J. & Storper, Michael (1986), eds., *Production, Work, Territory*. Boston: Allen & Unwin.
Shorter, E. and Tilly, C. (1974). *Strikes in France: 1830-1968*. Cambridge University Press, Cambridge.
Silver, Beverly (1992a)."Class Struggle and the Kondratieff 1870 to the present." In: A. Kleinknecht, E. Mandel, I. Wallerstein (eds.) *New Findings in Long Wave Research*. London: Macmillan
Silver, Beverly (1992b). "Labor Unrest and Capital Accumulation on a World Scale." PhD Dissertation: State University of New York, Binghamton. (Ann Arbor: University Microfilms International.)
Silver, Beverly (1991). "World-Scale Patterns of Labor-Capital Conflict." In I. Brandell (ed.) *Workers in Third World Industrialization*. London: Macmillan.
Snyder, D. & Kelly, W. (1977). "Conflict Intensity, Media Sensitivity, and the Validity of Newspaper Data," American Socioloqical Review, XLII, 1, 104-23.
Snyder, David & Tilly, Charles (1972). "Collective Violence in France," *American Sociological Review*, XXXVII, 5, Oct., 520-32.
Sugimoto, Yoshio (1978a). "Quantitative Characteristics of Popular Disturbances in Post-Occupation Japan (1952-1960)," *Journal of Asian Studies*, XXXVII, 2, Feb., 273-91.
Sugimoto, Yoshio (1978b). "Measurement of Popular Disturbance," *Social Science Research*, VII, 284-97.
Tarrow, Sidney (1989). *Democracy and Disorder: Protest and Politics in Italy, 1965-1975*. Oxford: Oxford Univ. Press.
Tilly, Charles (1986). *The Contentious French*. Cambridge, MA: Harvard University Press.
Tilly, Charles (1981). "Computing History," in C. Tilly, *As History Meets Sociology*. New York: Academic Press, 53-83.
Tilly, Charles (1978). *From Mobilization to Revolution*. Reading, MA: Addison-Wesley.
Tilly, Charles; Tilly, Louise & Tilly, Richard (1975). *The Rebellious Century 1830-1930*. Cambridge, MA: Harvard Univ. Press.
Ward, Kathryn, ed. (1990). *Women Workers and Global Restructuring*. Ithaca, NY: ILR Press
Waterman, Peter (1989). "From the Liberation of Internationalism: A Long March Through the Literature," *Alternatives*, XIV, 5-47.
Wallerstein, Immanuel (1984). "The Three Instances of Hegemony in the History of the Capitalist World-Economy," in I. Wallerstein, *The Politics of the World-Economy*. Cambridge: Cambridge University Press.

15 GOVERNMENTAL BUDGETING: A COMPUTER MODEL OF CONFLICT AND BARGAINING

Georg P. Müller

Introduction

Governmental budgeting is the allocation of money by state authorities to societal goals such as defense, education, social security, etc. Even this simple definition immediately raises two important questions about the nature of governmental spending:

a) Who is involved in decisions about the governmental budget? The government itself, the civil service, external interest groups, or all of them?

b) How are conflicts which arise from diverging expectations about governmental spending resolved? By bargaining among the interested groups, by proportional cuts in budget claims, or by other decision making mechanisms?

The answers to these questions differ from theory to theory. Some theories[1] focus mainly on the first question, others[2] deal primarily with the second, hardly any adequately answers both.

This text is drawn from the research project "Determinants and Effects of Budgetary Policy Options" funded by the World Society Foundation. Georg P. Müller took his Ph.D. in sociology from the University of Zurich. He works as a lecturer and researcher at the University of Fribourg, Institut de Travail Social, Rue St. Michel 6, 1700 Fribourg, Switzerland.

The regime theory of F. Castles[3] for example is focused on the influence of interest groups directly participating in government, but says hardly anything about allocations if there is a conflict of interest between different pressure groups. Institutional analysts such as J. P. Crecine[4] adequately describe the governmental decision-making process, but provide hardly any reasonable answer to questions about different influence strengths between interest groups on the governmental budgeting process.

In the following three sections a mathematical model is presented, designed to answer both questions by means of a bargaining approach.

An Overview of the Model

The bargaining model presented here is a synthesis of an interest group approach on the one hand and the political cybernetics paradigm on the other. Hence it is conceptualized as a feedback loop between

a) a submodel of *governmental decision-making* and
b) a submodel of *interest group claims*.

FIGURE 1 An overview of the components of the model

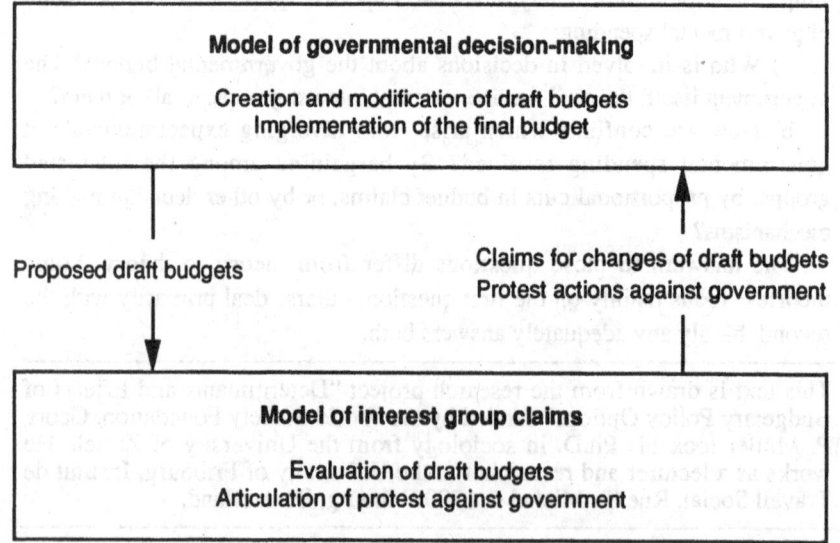

As Figure 1 shows, the claims of the interest groups model is used for the evaluation of governmental draft budgets by different interest groups. The claims resulting from this evaluation are transmitted to the governmental decision-making model where they are used appropriately to modify the current budget proposals. The modified budget is then transmitted to the claims-of-interest-groups model for a fresh evaluation. This process of evaluating and modifying budgets is repeated until the decision-making resources are exhausted or a budget is found which satisfies the expectations of the relevant interest groups. The result of this feedback process is either a compromise between conflicting expectations about budgets or the breakdown of the regime.

The following two sections contain a more detailed description of each of the two submodels.

The Model of Interest Group Claims

The claims of the interest groups model are based on the assumption that society is composed of interest groups able to influence governmental budget decisions. Among others, the military, the civil service, farmers' associations, labor unions, and business lobbies are examples of interest groups in this context. Although the interests of these groups are quite heterogeneous we hypothesize that at a certain level of abstraction they are all structured similarly.

a) An interest always refers to a *budget dimension* such as social security expenditures or military outlays.

b) A budget dimension always has a *valence* in terms of Kurt Lewin's social topology.[5] The valence of a budget dimension is positive if the interest group favors increased spending on it. The valence is negative if the interest group favors decreased spending on the budget dimension. And finally the valence is zero if the interest group has no stake in it.

c) If a budget dimension has a valence other than zero interest in it always implies the existence of a *level of expectations* with regard to future budgets. It separates the levels of spending that are acceptable to an interest group from those which are not acceptable. Following the theory of revolution of J. Davies[6] we hypothesize that the level of expectations depends in the following way on past budget dynamics: if the sign of the past growth of a budget dimension corresponds to the sign of its valence then the level of expectations is based on the continuation of past percentage growth (see Figure 2). However, if the past growth on this budget dimension does not correspond to its valence, the level of expectations is based on zero-growth which permits at least the maintenance of the current level of spending (see Fig. 3). Expressed in a formula this reads:

$E_{t+1} = B_t * \max((B_t / B_{t-1}), 1)$ if valence > 0
and
$E_{t+1} = B_t * \min((B_t / B_{t-1}), 1)$ if valence < 0,
where
E_t = Level of expectations for year t
B_t = Budget for year t.

FIGURE 2 Level of expectations for budget *growth* > 0 and valence > 0.

FIGURE 3 Level of expectations for budget *growth* < 0 and valence > 0

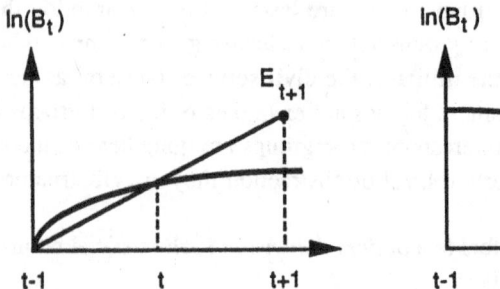
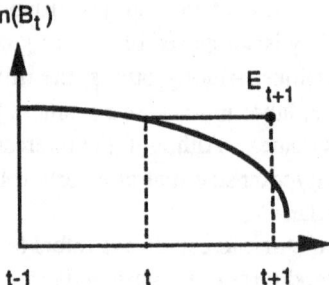

As long as the budget proposals of the government satisfy the levels of expectations of an interest group we hypothesize that the group has no complaints about the proposed budget. However, as soon as there is a *performance gap* between the proposed budget and the level of expectations, group claims are raised for increasing or decreasing allocations. The strength of these claims depends on the size of the gap: there is a *tolerance for performance gaps* which separates acceptable performance gaps from inacceptable ones (see Figure 4); i.e., as long as the performance gap is narrower than this tolerance level only *minor claims* occur which primarily result in the articulation of dissent or in minor protest actions which do not harm the

FIGURE 4 Performance gaps and claims of interest groups

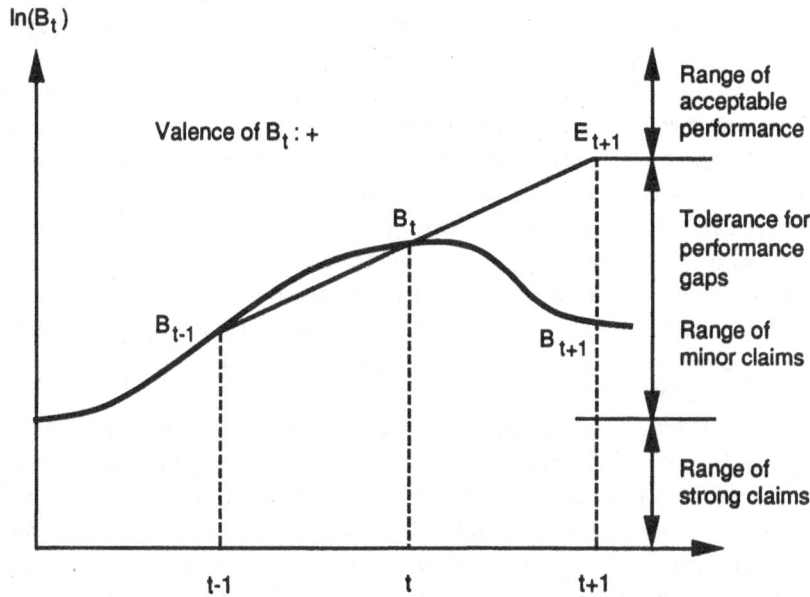

government. However, if the performance gap becomes wider than the tolerance level, *severe claims* occur, leading frustrated interest groups to overthrow the government by a coup d'état, a political strike, violent protest, or just by the withdrawal of political support.

We hypothesize that the tolerance for performance gaps mainly depends on two factors:

a) On the *relevance of the budget dimension* to which the tolerance level refers. The higher this relevance, the more costly is a performance gap for the concerned groups and the lower its tolerance.

b) On the *power of the interest group*. The more power an interest group has, the easier for it to overthrow the government and the lower is the tolerance of this group for governmental performance gaps.

The Model of Governmental Decision-Making

The governmental decision-making model represents government as a cybernetic system[7] with two facets. It can be seen:

a) As a *control system* which attempts to maintain externally disturbed parameter values within a target range.

b) As an *information processing system* which reaches decisions on the basis of information continuously acquired from its environment.

Government as a control system has two goals:

a) It tries to prevent overthrow by its political enemies, by among other things conflict management through an appropriate spending policy.

b) It tries to satisfy the levels of expectations of the regime supporters, i.e. the expectations of those interest groups which directly participate in governmental power.

As an information processing system government is confronted with the difficulty of making decisions in a highly complex political environment. There are many interest groups and budget dimensions to be considered and sometimes also very rapid changes of the political environment happen. Since the information-processing capacity of governmental organizations is limited, they must rely on appropriate mechanisms to reduce the complexity of their environment. Following Simon's idea of bounded rationality[8] our model assumes that governmental decision-making is based on the following mechanisms to simplify the processing of information about its environment:

a) It is assumed that the search for a new budget always starts from the *budget of the preceding year*.[9] In a stable environment the budget of the preceding year is a good precedent that often needs no more than some fine tuning to meet the requirements of the political situation of the current year.

b) It is assumed that the search for a new budget is a *trial-and-error process:* randomly generated budgets are presented to the interest groups and the claims of these groups are used for further modification of the budget.[10] By using this trial-and-error feedback, government is able to make reasonable decisions without being omniscient.

c) It is assumed that the governmental decision-making process aims at *solutions that are satisfying but not optimal*.[11] Among other things this means that government aims at the satisfaction of the levels of expectations of the regime supporters and not at the optimization of the budget with regard to these expectations. Obviously it is easier to find a satisfying solution than an optimal one, especially if there are conflicting expectations about the budget.

Figure 5 A flow chart of the governmental decision-making model.

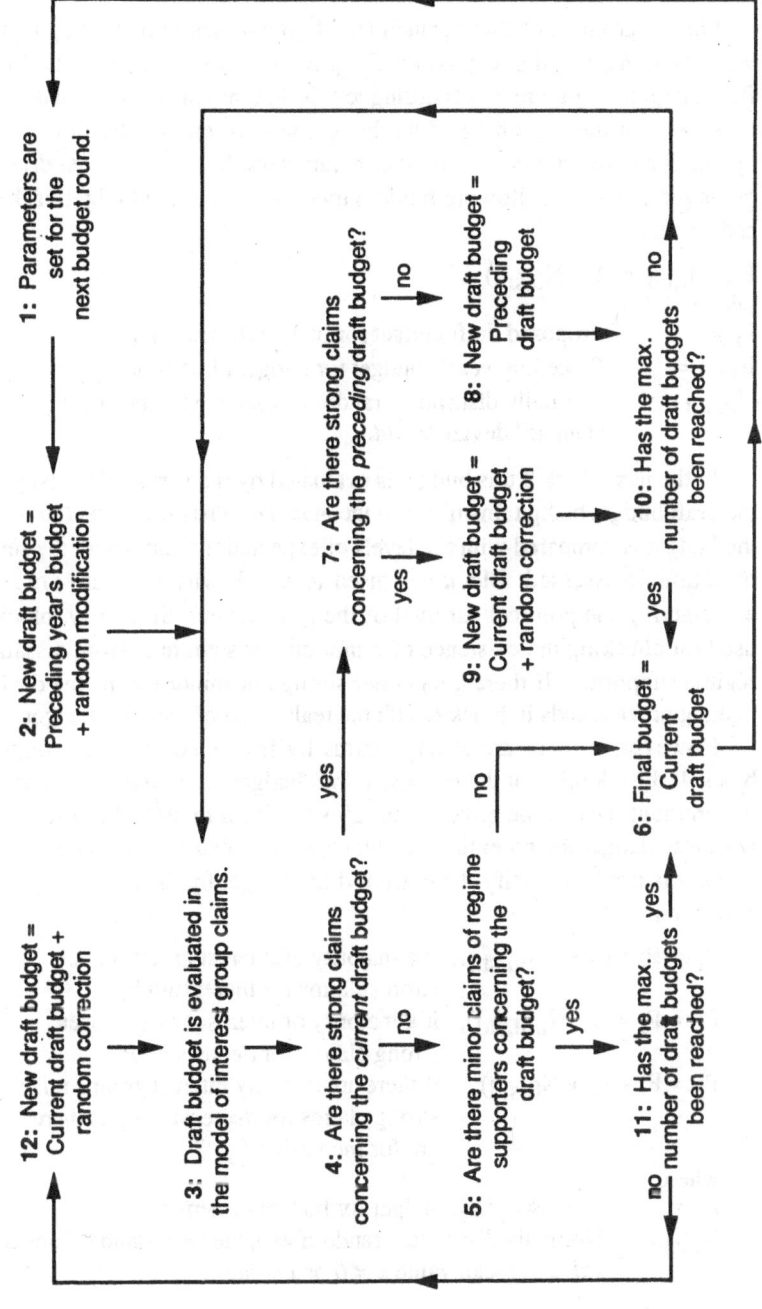

On the grounds of these principles of governmental budgeting behavior we have constructed a decision-making model which is represented by the flow diagram in Figure 5. According to this diagram the decison-making process starts at the beginning of the budget year in block 1 by initiating and updating clocks, counters, and other parameters. In block 2 a first draft budget is set up by the following random modification of the budget of the preceding year:

$P_i = B_{i,t-1} * (1 + N_{0,std})$
where
$P_i =$ Proposed draft budget for budget dimension i
$B_{i,t-1} =$ Preceding year's budget for budget dimension i
$N_{0,std} =$ Normally distributed random variable with mean value 0 and standard deviation *std*.

In the next block 3 this budget is evaluated by the various interest groups, the draft budget being transmitted to the *model of interest group claims* where the budget is compared with the levels of expectations and where the severity of claims is assessed. Block 4 is used to check whether there are claims endangering the political survival of the government. Similarily, block 5 is used for checking the existence of minor claims stemming from dissatisfied regime supporters. If there are neither strong nor minor claims the decision-making process ends in block 6 with the realization of the draft budget.

However, if there are strong claims by frustrated interest groups (see block 4) the adoption of the proposed draft budget might result in a change of government. Hence the government tries to return to an earlier draft budget with less dangerous potential (see block 8). If no such solution is available block 9 is used to modify the current draft budget by the following random correction:

$P_i := P_i * (1 + N_{mu,std})$, if a majority of interest groups raises strong claims for *in*creasing P_i,

$P_i := P_i * (1 - N_{mu,std})$, if a majority of interest groups raises strong claims for *de*creasing P_i,

$P_i := P_i * (1 + N_{0,std})$, if there are as many interest groups raising strong claims for *de*creasing P_i as there are for *in*creasing P_i,

where
$P_i =$ Proposed draft budget for budget dimension i
$N_{x,std} =$ Normally distributed random variable with standard deviation *std* and mean value $x = 0$ or $x = mu$.

So long as the maximum number of budget drafts has not yet been reached the draft budget created in block 8 or 9 is transmitted to the claims of the interest groups model in block 3. However, if decision-making resources are already exhausted the draft budget is adopted even if it entails a change of government. Many draft budgets give rise to minor claims by dissatisfied regime supporters. In such a situation block 5 branches off to block 11. If block 11 shows that the decision-making resources are already exhausted the draft budget is adopted even if it dissatisfies some regime supporters. If the maximum number of trials has not yet been reached the draft budget is modified in block 12 by a random process analogous to the one used in block 9. Afterwards the modified draft budget is transferred to block 3 for further evaluation by the various interest groups.

Simulating the Behavior of the Model

Since the model outlined is relatively complex we decided to use stochastic computer simulation instead of deductive reasoning to obtain further insights into its behavior.[12] Below, we present some of the results of these simulations applied to calculate, for the time span between 1972 and 2002, three types of time series describing conflict and budgeting behavior:
 -Annual mean numbers of dissatisfied groups of regime supporters as a measure of internal conflict.
 -The percentage of governments surviving the attacks of their political enemies till a given year in the simulated time span, an indicator which points to the severity of budget conflicts.
 -Means and standard deviations of budget forecasts.
Due to the stochastic nature of the model all these measures are based on 100 repetitive simulation runs. Since it was too costly to perform them for all possible *combinations* of parameter values the study was confined to the effects of the following principal parameters:
 -The composition of the regime in terms of groups supporting the government.
 -Past growth rates of the budget variables.
 -Tolerance for performance gaps.

FIGURE 6 Mean values of simulated growth rates of a budget for different types of regime

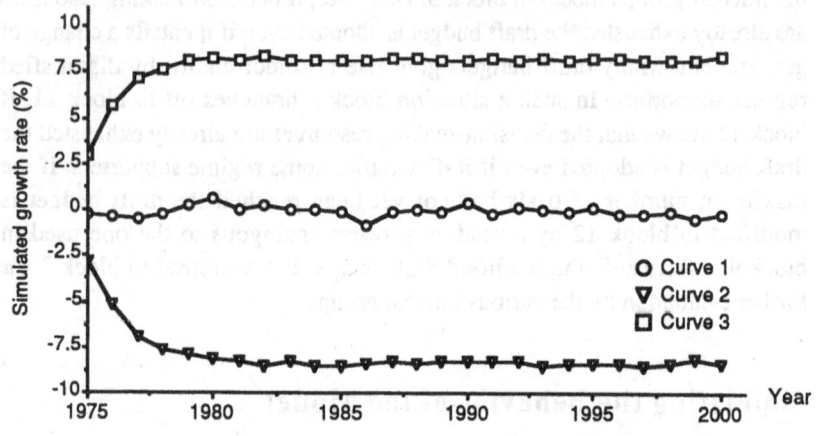

Legend:

Parameter	Curve 1	Curve 2	Curve 3
Valence for group 1	-1	-1	-1
Valence for group 2	+1	+1	+1
Regime support by group 1	yes	yes	no
Regime support by group 2	yes	no	yes
Gap tolerance of group 1	.10	.10	.10
Gap tolerance of group 2	.10	.10	.10
Past budget growth rate	0%	0%	0%

Consequently, all *other* parameters were assigned *constant values* so that it was possible to analyze the simplest nontrivial conflict situation with *one budget dimension* and *two interest groups* with opposing valences:
- Number of repetitive simulation runs: 100
- Number of budget dimensions: 1
- Number of interest groups: 2
- Valence of the budget dimension for group 1: -1
- Valence of the budget dimension for group 2: +1
- Maximum number of draft budgets: 10
- Mean value *mu* of the random variable $N_{mu,std}$: 0.05
- Standard deviation *std* of the random variable $N_{mu,std}$: 0.025

FIGURE 7 Simulated number of regime conflicts for different types of regime (Legend see Figure 6)

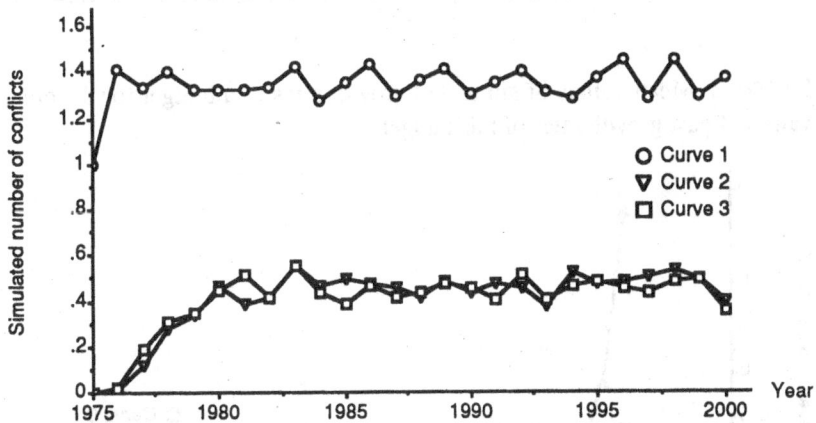

In a political system with only 2 interest groups there are theoretically $2^2 = 4$ patterns of participation each corresponding to a different type of regime. Since a government without any support can hardly exist we have studied the effects of the *composition of the regime* only for three types of regimes:

a) For a single-party government supported by one interest group which favors *in*creased spending (see Figures 6, 7, curves 3). Since the group not integrated in the regime prefers decreased spending, there is a potential external conflict between the regime and this interest group.

b) For a single-party government supported by one interest group which favors *de*creased spending (see Figures 6, 7, curves 2). As for the first type of regime, there is a potential external conflict with the group which is not integrated in the regime.

c) For a broad coalition government supported by two interest groups each favoring a *different* spending policy (see Figures 6, 7, curves 1). Due to this difference with regard to spending policy there is a potential internal conflict within the regime.

As Figure 6 shows there are considerable differences between the budgeting behavior of the three regimes. The three patterns of simulated growth rates of the budget correspond to what regime theorists would predict. Obviously, the policies of the single-party governments are heavily influenced by the preferences of the ruling interest group while the broad coalition governments seem ambivalent about their spending policy. Among others, this ambivalence is indicated by the oscillations of the growth rates of the budget (see curve 1), resulting from the cross-pressures which force the

FIGURE 8 Mean values of simulated growth rates of a budget for different values of past growth rates of this budget

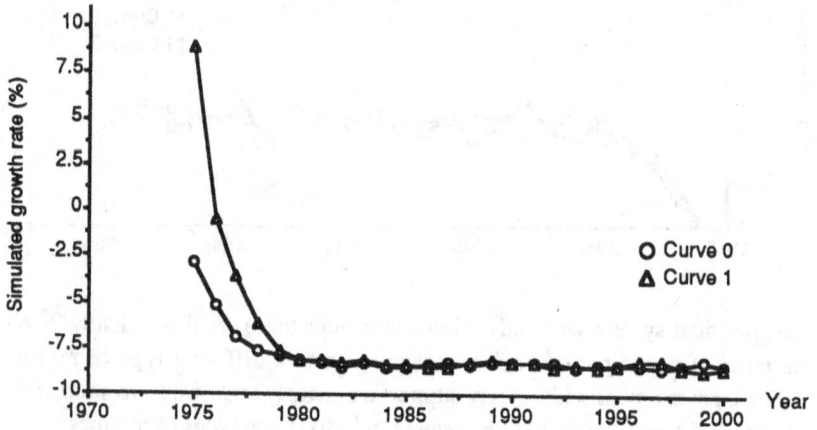

Legend:

Parameter	Curve 0	Curve 1
Valence for group 1	-1	-1
Valence for group 2	+1	+1
Regime support by group 1	yes	yes
Regime support by group 2	no	no
Gap tolerance of group 1	.10	.10
Gap tolerance of group 2	.10	.10
Past budget growth rate	0%	20%

government to follow a zigzag policy. As curve 1 in Figure 7 shows, this zigzag policy is rather expensive in terms of regime conflict: about 1.3 of the 2 groups are unhappy with the budget decisions of the government. However, also about half the budget decisions of single-party governments do not satisfy the expectations of the regime supporters, apparently due to rising expectations. As long as government is able to increase (decrease) the growth rate of the budget, conflicts are relatively contained. After the stabilization of the growth rates government has difficulties in keeping pace

FIGURE 9 Mean values of simulated growth rates of a budget for different tolerance for performance gaps

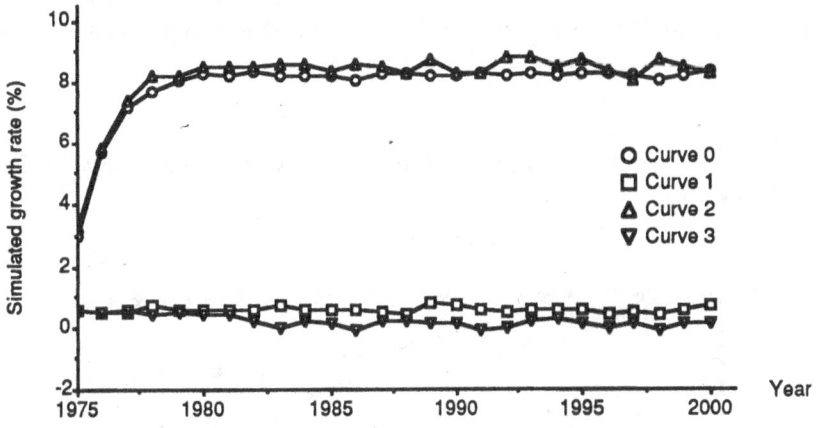

Legend:

Parameter	Curve 0	Curve 1	Curve 2	Curve 3
Valence for group 1	-1	-1	-1	-1
Valence for group 2	+1	+1	+1	+1
Regime support by group 1	no	no	no	no
Regime support by group 2	yes	yes	yes	yes
Gap tolerance of group 1	.10	.02	.10	.02
Gap tolerance of group 2	.10	.02	.02	.10
Past budget growth rate	0%	0%	0%	0%

with the expectations of its supporters and conflicts become more acute (see Figures 6 and 7, period after 1979).

Since the *past growth rates of the budget* influence the dynamics of expectations it seems reasonable to assume that they also influence governmental budget decisions. To test this hypothesis we have simulated two budgets with two different histories. The first had an original growth rate of 0% (see Figure 8, curve 0), the second originally grew at an annual rate of 20% (see Figure 8, curve 1). As Figure 8 shows, both budget simulations soon converge to the same level of growth. This means that, in the long run, the initial growth rates of the budget variables have no influence on budget dynamics. However, for the first few years the inertia effects of past budget policies are clearly visible in Figure 8. It is obvious that these inertial effects have important consequences for political change. If the composition of a regime is changed for one reason or other it can take several years for the new regime fully to implement its political program.

FIGURE 10 Simulated regime survival rates for different tolerance for performance gaps (Legend see Figure 9)

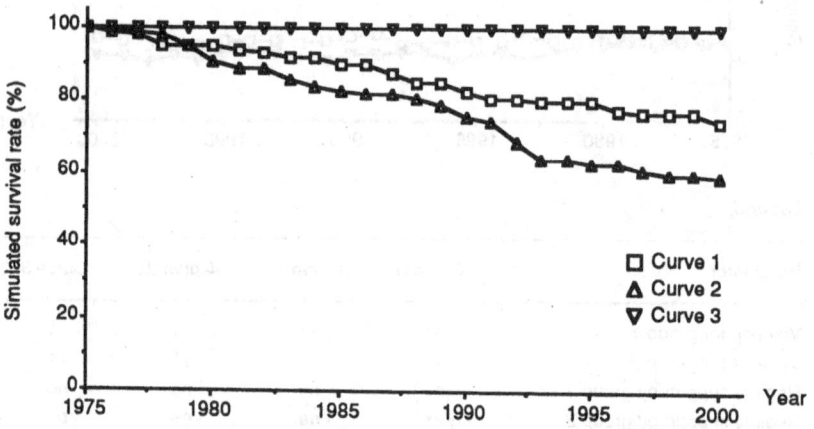

The *tolerance for performance gaps* as the third parameter to be analyzed in this study is negatively correlated to the power of a group. The more power an interest group has, the *lower* is its tolerance for performance gaps with regard to a given budget dimension. Consequently, questions about the importance of the power of interest groups on the budget and conflict dynamics can be answered by simulation runs for different levels of tolerance for performance gaps.

If the power of the *regime supporters* is increased without changing the power of the other interest group, there is only a slight increase in the growth rate of the budget, as represented in Figure 9 by a relatively small difference between curve 0 and curve 2.

If the power of the *opposing group* is increased without an increase in the power of the regime supporters, the situation may change completely. As shown by curve 3 in Figure 9 this is a situation where government is no longer able to follow its own preference for increased spending. Perhaps this experimental result explains why, in many countries, there is hardly any difference between the politics of different types of regime.[13]

Finally, curve 1 in Figure 9 shows a stalemate situation caused by a heavy but symmetric increase in the power of *both groups*. It is obvious that the corresponding decrease of tolerance for performance gaps makes governmental bargaining relatively difficult. According to our computer simulation government tries to find a compromise between contradictory expectations by slightly increasing the budget in order to satisfy its supporters without excessively provoking its enemies. As the regime casualty curve 1 in Figure 10 shows, this policy is not always very successful. Surprisingly however, a *symmetric* increase of power entails *less* regime casualties than an *asymmetric* increase of power in favor of regime supporters (see Fig. 10, curve 2). This peculiarity is probably the result of the rapid growth of the budget shown by curve 2 in Figure 9. On the one hand a rapidly growing budget gives rise to very strong claims of the opposing group which favors decreased spending. On the other hand a rapid growth rate may also trigger rising expectations by the regime supporters. Obviously both processes are politically dangerous, thus leading to a relatively high regime casualty rate.

Summary and Outlook

In this article we have tried to outline the structure of a new model of governmental budgeting. It is based on the idea of conflicting spending expectations by interest groups mediated by a governmental bargaining process. Our preliminary investigation of the behavior of the model to explain the dynamics of expenditures, internal conflicts, and the casualties of regimes are, in most cases, very promising. However, it is obvious that the model needs further testing and exploration. Among other things, the behavior of the model must be analyzed for more realistic scenarios with several budget variables, three or more interest groups, and with exogenously triggered changes of the political regime.

NOTES

1. See e.g. the regime theory approach, exemplified by F. Castles, "The Impact of Parties on Public Expenditure" (in F. Castles, ed., *The Impact of Parties*, London, 1982, pp. 21 ff.) and C. van Arnhem and G. Schotsman, "Do Parties Affect the Distribution of Incomes?" (in F. Castles, ed., op. cit., 1982, pp. 283 ff.).
2. See e.g. the institutional analyses of J. Crecine, "A Computer Simulation Model of Municipal Budgeting" *Management Science,* July 1967, pp. 786 ff. and of O. Davis et al., "A Theory of the Budgetary Process" *American Political Science Review,* 1966, vol. 60, pp. 529 ff.
3. See F. Castles, op. cit.
4. Op. cit.
5. K. Lewin, *Field Theory in Social Science,* New York, 1964.
6. J. Davies, "Toward a Theory of Revolution"*American Sociological Review,* 1962, vol. 27, pp. 5 ff.
7. For a good description of the governmental cybernetics paradigm see K. W. Deutsch, *The Nerves of Government,* New York, 1967.
8. See e.g. H. Simon, "Theories of Bounded Rationality" in: C. McGuire and R. Radner (eds.), *Decision and Organization,* Amsterdam, 1972, pp. 161 ff.
9. O. Davis et al., op. cit., successfully used this idea to explain the federal budget of the United States.
10. For a similar idea see G. Miller et al., *Plans and the Structure of Behavior,* New York, 1960.
11. See H. Simon, op. cit.
12. For a discussion of the method of computer simulation for constructing and exploring social theories see R. Hannemann, *Computer-assisted Theory Building,* Newbury Park, 1988.
13. For empirical investigations see F. Castles, op. cit. and M. Schmidt, *Wohlfahrtsstaatliche Politik unter bürgerlichen und sozialdemokratischen Regierungen,* Frankfurt, 1982.

16 POLITICAL CONFLICT AND LABOR DISPUTES AT THE CORE
AN ENCOMPASSING REVIEW FOR THE POST-WAR ERA

Volker Bornschier and Michael Nollert

Introduction

From the data on social conflict in the OECD countries, two pieces of empirical evidence emerge in the post-war era. (1) After a phase of decreasing social unrest, crime and suicide rates after World War II, the core countries experienced a phase of protest mobilization against political authorities, of increasing delinquency and self-damaging behavior in the late 1960s (Bornschier, 1988). (2) Though many characteristics of Western countries' social structures have been converging since World War II (Kaelble, 1987), the cross-country variations in political and industrial conflict increased markedly in the 1970s (Nollert, 1992).

This review article draws on a paper presented at the Inaugural Pan-European Conference in International Relations, Sept. 1992, Heidelberg, Germany. Volker Bornschier is professor of sociology at the University of Zurich and President of the World Society Foundation. Michael Nollert took his Ph.D. from the University of Zurich and is a senior member of Bornschier's research team. Address: Sociological Institute of the University of Zurich, Rämistrasse 69, CH-8001 Zürich, Switzerland.

Previous summaries of research on political conflict show perplexity concerning explanatory schemes. Ekkart Zimmermann, an expert in the field, concludes that "we know little about predictors of (violent) political conflict in Western European countries and the determinants of political stability" (Zimmermann, 1989: 192), which applies also to the whole OECD area (Zimmermann, 1988: 67). While explanations for the obvious country differences seem to be lacking we observe that diachronic analyses have been rare despite variations that should have attracted more research endeavor.

Since much earlier research on social conflict fails simultaneously to account for these diachronic variations and country differences we offer together with our review, a synthesis on the basis of our own research which may fill the gap. Unlike most of the research, we cover simultaneously two areas of social conflict, i.e. political conflict and labor disputes.

Our starting point is a summary of the trends in political and industrial conflict at the core in the post-war period on the basis of major data sources. Three figures below as well as tables presented elsewhere (Bornschier, 1988; Nollert, 1992) suggest wide differences over space and time, which definitely contradicts the familiar convergence assumption of the "logic of industrialism" (Kerr *et al.*, 1964; see also Kaelble, 1987). In the second part of the article we briefly evaluate major approaches in conflict research which however fail to explain both cross-temporal and cross-national variations

In the third part, after reviewing the hardly promising controversy between anomie, deprivation and resource mobilization theories, we propose an encompassing causal model. First, we refer to an explanation based on a world system approach (Bornschier, 1988: ch. 7) which offers an explanation for the observed patttern of political and industrial conflict at the core. Over the lifespan of what we term *societal models* no general increase or decrease of conflict is expected. Instead, the career of a societal model produces a U- or W-shaped pattern of social conflict. In a second subsection we focus on cross-national differences and suggest integrating the neo-corporatist paradigm, which argues that political and industrial conflicts reflect a lack of incorporation of societal interests into the process of policy formation. Furthermore, we propose to combine deprivation and mobilization theory. Our argument for explaining longitudinal variations in conflict is that collective articulation of discontent is most probable in phases when either material deprivation is extremely high or the availability of resources is high. As to cross-national variations we argue that the level of deprivation and the availability of resources reflects not only the phase of the societal model but also the mode of interest intermediation and world economic and political constraints. At the end of the discussion we suggest a comprehensive causal model which predicts that the level of deprivation and resource availability in a country at a specific time depends on the phase of the societal model and its system of interest intermediation. The latter is also determined by the country's position in the world system and the power distribution between moderate left-wing and bourgeois parties.

Conflict at the Core in the Post-War Era

Core countries, as democratic market economies, belong in many ways to a single type of society since they share many crucial institutional features. This would suggest the following methodology: to look in a first step at the overall pattern of conflict in the aggregate and to explain differences between individual countries in a second step. But core countries are at the same time differentiated. One crucial aspect of this differentiation in the post-war era was the split between the hegemon, the United States, and the other core member states, of which we consider here the 17 stable democracies (Australia, Austria, Belgium, Canada, Denmark, Finland, France, Germany, Ireland, Italy, Japan, Netherlands, New Zealand, Norway, Sweden, Switzerland and the United Kingdom).

A hegemon enjoys devices of conflict management which ordinary core members do not have at their disposal. This suggests that the hegemon should be treated separately. In more detail the argument is as follows. After World War II only the U.S. was able to externalize internal conflicts (particularly those resulting from race discrimination) by way of military involvement in the Third World (see Russett, 1990), whereas the small European countries had to prevent domestic insurgency by welfare policies. However, as the Civil Rights Movement and anti-Vietnam War protest in the 1960s indicate, this "rallying 'round the flag" strategy may fail in the long run if wars are not quickly fought out (see Bornschier, 1988: 174). This argument also holds in the context of the former East bloc. In contrast to the Polish and Rumanian regimes, the Soviet hegemon was able – at least over the short run – to externalize internal tensions in its final phase to Afghanistan.

The data on political conflict we employ in this review are from the *World Handbook of Political and Social Indicators* (Taylor, 1985). The number of six indicators, covering 35 years of systematic observation (1948-1982), was reduced by factor analysis. For the whole period the often replicated two-factor structure is apparent which distinguishes between three indicators of moderate protest and three of high violence (cf. Hibbs, 1973 and Zimmermann, 1980). Figures 1 and 2 show how the two additive indices "collective protest" (annual number of riots, political strikes, protest demonstrations) and "internal war" (annual number of armed attacks, political assassinations, political deaths) distribute over time. As argued above, we treat the hegemon separately and therefore present the trend patterns of conflict for the U.S. and the other 17 core countries in two figures. In Figure 1, the sum of those events, which can be classified as *internal war*, is divided by 10 for the purpose of graphic presentation.

FIGURE 1 Collective protest and internal war events in 17 core countries (aggregated), 1948-1982

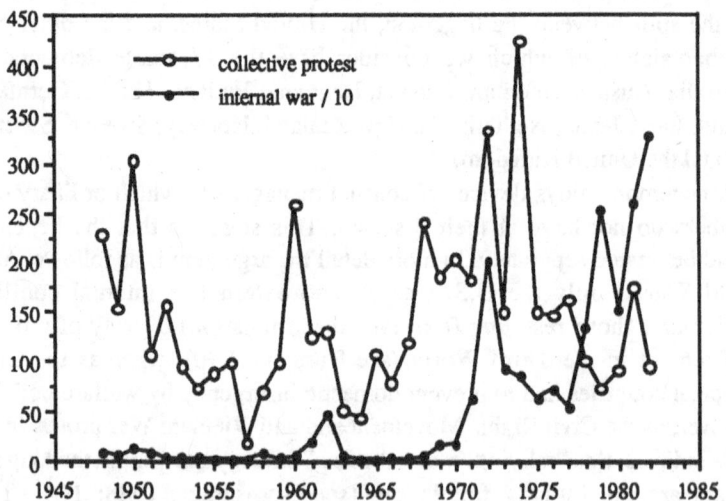

For the 17 non-hegemonic countries political conflict markedly decreased from the late 1940s until the late 1950s. Since the level again declined after a peak around 1960, we refer to the phase around 1960 as the interim peak (Bornschier, 1988). This description also makes sense in view of the renewed and marked rise of political conflict in the 1970s. The phase of rising and high conflict, which lasts until the beginning of the 1980s (the end of our data series), began with the student revolts in the late 1960s. After 1970 political conflict changed character insofar as violent events became more frequent.

At a first glance the pattern for the United States seems to be different (see Figure 2). This impression changes when we look at it as displaced in time. The lead of the U.S. developments – after the New Deal in the early 1930s – was, by contrast to most other core members, uninterrupted by the war. The earlier start into the new societal model of the Keynesian epoch offers an explanation (Bornschier, 1988). The dynamic of conflict in the U.S. should have run in advance of the other core countries and have reached the first

FIGURE 2 Collective protest and internal war events in the United States, 1948-1982

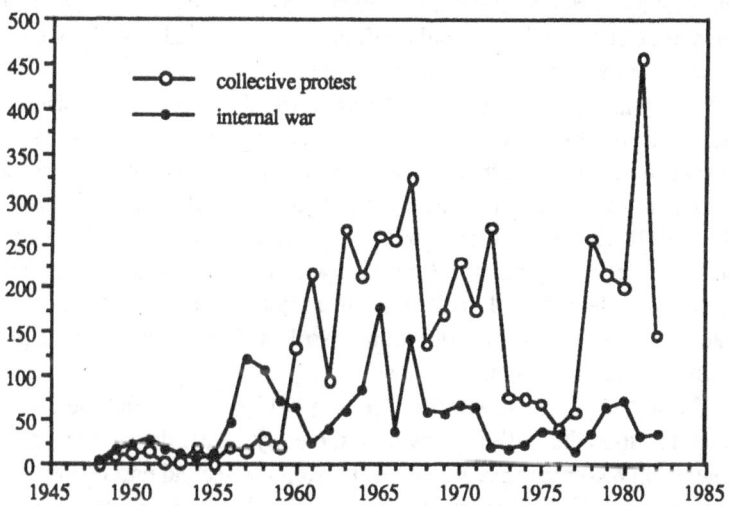

trough as early as the end of the 1940s (cf. Kerbo and Shaffer, 1992). If this holds then – contrary to the aggregate of the 17 core countries – the first descending line of the W-shaped pattern for the U.S. cannot, of course, appear in the data available only from 1948.

This view is supported by the fact that the U.S. had already passed its peak of conflict at the time of the worldwide student revolts. The latter started in the U.S. already in the early 1960s. On the other hand, the level of conflict in the other core countries began to climb considerably only after 1968. We conclude that the patterns for the two groups are displaced in time with a lead of the United States of about one decade. Another difference becomes apparent. In the U.S. the number of collective protest events exceeds the number of violent ones, while in the other 17 core countries - especially due to the inclusion of the United Kingdom, Ireland, France and Italy (see Nollert, 1992: 253) internal violence dominates by far. As an explanation we suggest that the hegemon was able to displace violent conflict into the interstate sphere (cf. Russett, 1990).

According to both sets of figures, the level of political conflict at the core fluctuates considerably over the whole post-war era. Furthermore, both levels - collective protest and internal war - appear to follow a W-shaped pattern, part of which is not observable in these data for the U.S. In line with Tilly's et al. (1975) work on nineteenth century movements and Tarrow's study on trends of political and industrial conflict in post-war Italy (1989) we observe cycles in the magnitude of political conflict.

The deviant pattern of the U.S. both in trend and level of conflict is also evidenced in the course of industrial conflict. The statistics of the International Labour Organization offer the number of strikers and of working days lost as indicators for industrial conflict. Data on the years before 1948 and after 1982 would be available, but we wish to compare trends and levels of industrial conflict with those of collective protest and internal war. Number of strikers as an indicator has certain shortcomings since it does not control for duration of strikes. Therefore, Figure 3 presents the time series on working days lost.

The severity of labor conflict declines between 1948 and the late 1950s, except for sporadic outlying years. In the early 1960s the severity generally remained at a comparatively low level. From the second half of the 1960s on a leap occurred in the level of working days lost. After 1968 the level of conflict was higher than in the 1950s and early 1960s. This leap was more pronounced in the aggregate of 17 core countries than in the USA. The data suggest that industrial conflict decreased until the middle of the 1960s and then began to rise again. This observation supports the argument of Pizzorno (1978) that conflict research should pay attention to cycles of social conflict (see also Tarrow, 1988: 433). We must mention also the research of

Giovanni Arrighi and Beverly Silver on labor unrest who however employ a world sample (see Silver in this volume) and thus go beyond the focus of this article.

FIGURE 3 Working days lost (in thousands) in 17 core countries (aggregated) and in the USA, 1948-1982

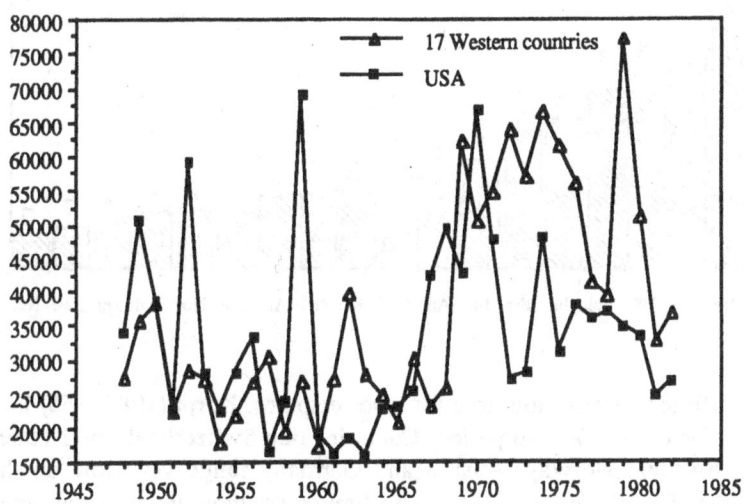

Concluding this portrayal of the trends in political and industrial conflict between 1948 and 1982 we stress the wide differences between countries in our sample. Indicators are presented in detail elsewhere (Korpi, 1983; Paldam and Pedersen, 1984; Zimmermann, 1988, 1989; Nollert, 1992) and remain very substantial when weighted. In order to convey an impression Figure 4 shows all events of political mass protest per million population in the 1948-1982 period.

For political violence (internal war) the differences are even more pronounced – in some cases due to exceptional constellations (like the conflict in Ulster) – the rounded figures for the number of armed attacks per million population are: 235 in Britain, 59 in France, 48 in Ireland, 15 in Italy, 12 in Germany, 9 in Canada, 7 in the U.S., 6 in Belgium, 5 in Austria, 4 in Switzerland, 3 each in the Netherlands and Australia, 1 each in Norway, Denmark, Japan, Sweden, New Zealand and Finland.

FIGURE 4 Events of political mass protest per million population for 18 core countries 1948-1982

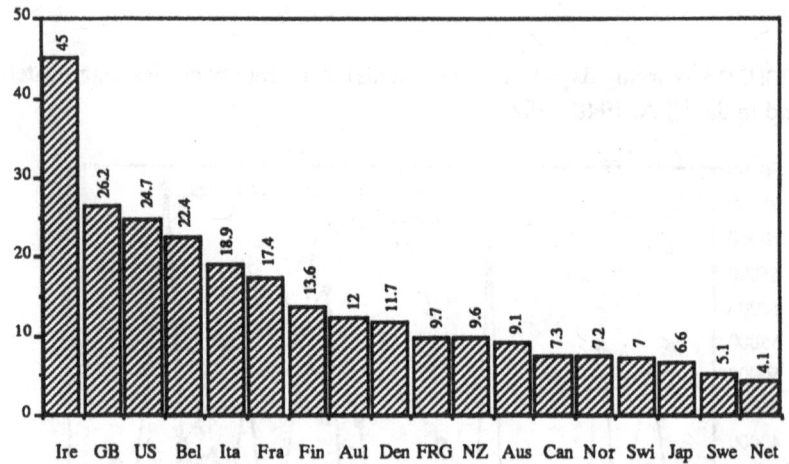

Huge differences also hold true for labor disputes. Korpi (1983: 165) lists figures for the 1946-1976 period. Countries like Switzerland, the Netherlands, Sweden, Norway, Austria and Germany range very low on the indicator of working days lost – with figures (in thousands) in the range between 11 and 90. This can be compared to the strike-loss-prone group of the United States, Finland, Ireland, Canada and Italy with figures for the same indicator between 509 and 631.

Furthermore, despite frequently observed tendencies of convergence among core countries (see Kaelble, 1987), cross-country variations in levels of conflict have not become less pronounced over time. Quite the contrary. Country differences in political conflict and in intensity of labor disputes instead of withering away increased in comparing the conflict-prone phase between 1968-1982 with the 1950s and 1960s (cf. Nollert, 1992: ch. 9). So much for our review of certain crucial facts. Now we turn to an evaluation of theoretical explanations.

The Poor Answer of Theories Prominent in the Field

Reviews of sociological research on political and labor conflict are rarely concerned with the extent to which current theories are able to explain at the same time the observed long-term cycles in the four conflict indicators *and* cross-country variations. Furthermore, political rather than labor conflict has been at the center of interest. While Zimmermann (1980, 1982, 1988, 1989), Muller (1985), Muller and Seligson (1987), Boswell and Dixon (1990) propose and test global causal models explaining cross-national variations in political conflict, the debate on longitudinal trends at the core has largely been dominated by theoretical work on social movements and case studies (e.g. Korpi, 1983; Screpanti, 1984). The starting point of this separation of cross-national analysis and research on mobilization of discontent was the finding that grievances were not the major preconditions of the collective protest and political violence which started in the late 1960s. Hence, students of social conflict in the 1970s focussed on those factors supporting or hindering the mobilization of discontent. Yet, Tarrow (1988) who enlarged this research strategy by stressing the connection between politics and collective action finally avowed that "cycles of protest" are "triggered both because of a changing grievance structure and when the structure of political opportunities expanded." (Tarrow, 1989: 337).

Nevertheless, the debate on conflict in core countries in the 1970s and 1980s actually paid more attention to individual motivation, attitudes and opportunities of actors, leadership strategies and organization than to structural features. This change of focus was paralleled by a switch away from structuralism towards methodological individualism. Previous introductions to sociological conflict research (Oberschall, 1978; Eckstein, 1980; Zimmermann, 1982) thus emphasized the metatheoretical controversy between "breakdown" theories, assuming the cause of social unrest to lie in characteristics of social structure, and "solidarity" theories, seeing political and industrial conflicts as the results of successful processes of collective mobilization (cf. Tilly *et al.*, 1975). The classical breakdown theories are divided into two main streams. The stream with the longest tradition encompasses all those theories relating to the concept of *anomie*. In the early 1960s the concept of *relative deprivation* was launched as a theoretical alternative. Both lines of breakdown theory are contrasted in the early 1970s with the *resource mobilization* approach, or more specifically the *political process* perspective. Since there are numerous synopses of theories of social conflict (see references above), we will dispense here with a detailed presentation of their arguments. Instead we will focus on what the theories can tell us about variations in the level of political and industrial conflict over time and between the 17 non-hegemonic core states.

According to Emile Durkheim (1964 [1893]) political and labor conflict may reflect a lack of normative regulation and integration: *anomie*. Although Durkheim discussed several outcomes of anomie such as class struggle, increasing crime and high suicide rates, he did not suggest how "lack of social integration" could be measured. Methodologically, it is therefore not appropriate to propose testable hypotheses on the relationship between anomie and social conflicts, let alone expect an answer to our question on the cause of the differences between countries.

In Merton's (1949) extended concept, anomie is not only a state of societal disorientation (goal anomie), but rather a cleavage between cultural goals and means available in the social structure to achieve these goals. Above-average political and industrial disputes should therefore be observed in societies which provide actors with below-average opportunities to realize their aspirations. In the same way, it can be postulated that variations in the level of conflict over time reflect the differences in the gap between individual demands and the capacity of the society to provide ways and means for realizing these demands. Unlike Durkheim's formulation, the revision of the anomie concept by Merton makes it possible to formulate hypotheses and test them empirically. In considering the mobilization of social protest in the 1960s, some theorists argue that the student generation at that time suffered particularly from a closure of opportunities to realize their professional goals. Further variables, which could be conceived as predictors of anomic conflict, are unemployment and inflation rates. The loss of jobs, as well as dwindling purchasing power, implies forfeiting the means of reaching culturally defined goals. Correspondingly, it could be expected that unemployment, inflation and real wage increase correlate positively with conflict across countries and time. Even if anomie theory belongs to the classic sociological tradition, weighty theoretical arguments as well as data presented below speak against, rather than for, the notion that anomie is transformed into political and labor conflict. On the theoretical side, the lack of indicators for Merton's anomie concept is problematic. Correspondingly it makes no sense methodologically to declare manifest conflict both as being a result *and* as evidence of anomie.

Furthermore, one can question the premise that, in general, all members of a social group share and strive with the same intensity after the same cultural goals. On the contrary it makes sense to suggest that modern societies differ from traditional ones not least in the diversity of cultural goals. It can be argued that people with high social status, for instance, pursue different cultural goals from those with low status (cf. Hyman, 1953). As a result it could be supposed that the majority of the conflicts documented in the three figures above simply reflect diverging cultural goals and not the gap between goals and the means for achieving them. On the other hand the assumption that commonly shared values contribute *a priori* to a lower conflict level must also be queried, since it neglects the fact that commonly shared values can also contain a conflict potential. For this assumption ignores the fact that personal goals can often only be reached by disregarding the interests of other actors. Furthermore, as is illustrated by the low conflict level in multi-cultural Swiss society, diverging cultural goals can neutralize each other and thereby contribute to reducing conflict, provided the cultural conflict lines criss-cross (cf. Simmel 1908) and do not run parallel.

Empirical research so far provides hardly any guidelines for the validation of such theses. Thus it may make sense to explain the differences observed over time and space as results of differing anomie levels. Yet, as long as no anomie indicators are at our disposal, anomie theory cannot be falsified (cf. Opp 1976: 414f). Nevertheless, aside from the shortcomings regarding the premises and empirical evidence, the notion of the gap between culturally predefined demands and the means provided by society as occasionally triggering the conflict appears plausible enough to include it in an integrative approach. The student revolts which peaked at the end of the 1960s are cases in point.

By contrast, *deprivation theory* is more informative than anomie theory, since it is more falsifiable. Certainly the most popular hypothesis is that *absolute* deprivation, indicated by low economic growth rates, high inflation and high unemployment levels, contributes to a high level of political conflict (e.g. Jagdozinski, 1983; Boswell and Dixon, 1990). A great deal more ambitious than this concept of absolute deprivation is the idea of *relative* deprivation. The starting point here is the fact that social systems which provide actors with means to realize their goals do not necessarily show an egalitarian distribution of wealth and income. While anomie theory expects that even extreme material inequalities would be tolerated as long as ambitious persons have the opportunity of attaining a higher position in one of the various dimensions of social stratification systems, the concept of relative deprivation implies that underprivileged persons cannot be pacified simply by the prospect of individual advancement. Rather, they would compare themselves with affluent members of their reference group (Runciman, 1966) and revolt if they feel an unbearable discrepancy between what they think they are entitled to and what they are actually getting (Gurr, 1970). Starting from this premise, social conflicts would reflect the gap between societal demands and their realization rather than the gap between cultural goals and the *chance* of individual realization. Nation-states, which for example are not in a position to fulfil the demands of the population for welfare and equitable distribution of goods, therefore suffer from an above-average level of conflict, even if people have generally sufficient opportunities to improve their individual situation. As to variations among non-hegemonic core states, it can be expected that economic performance and low inequality in the distribution of societal rewards would run parallel with low social unrest. Regarding the longitudinal perspective, social conflict was expected to increase on the one hand, during periods of economic crisis and, on the other hand, during phases in which social inequality intensifies.

Such cross-national studies as are limited to core countries and indicators of *objective* deprivation do at least support this hypothesis. Empirical findings of Zimmermann (1989) and Nollert (1992) indicate that political and industrial conflict during the 1968-1982 period is most intensive in countries with poor economic performance and high income inequality. In the longitudinal perspective, however, there is no consistent empirical support for the hypothesis. Yet the years of crisis following 1929 are characterized by an increase in collective action (see Zimmermann, 1985; Kerbo and Shaffer, 1992). Furthermore, the thesis is rejected by the findings of Screpanti (1984) on waves in class struggle and by our Figures 1 to 3. The evidence in these figures indicates that in the postwar period both industrial conflict as well as political conflict increases in the late 1960s, i.e. in a phase of economic prosperity and of equalizing income distribution (see Kraus, 1981).

The paradigm of *resource mobilization* was launched during the 1970s by the work of Oberschall (1973), Tilly (see Tilly *et al*, 1975; Tilly,1978), and Zald and McCarthy (1979) (cf. Jenkins, 1983). It originated partly as a response to the historical fact that waves of protest in the late 1960s did not follow a period of increasing deprivation but one of prosperity. In fact, not persons of low rank but the comparatively privileged students, as well as affluent workers not menaced by unemployment, took to the streets. Proponents of this approach suggest that neither deprivation nor discontent are sufficient conditions of collective action (see Gurney and Tierney, 1982).

Deprived actors, they claim furthermore, are only prepared to express their discontent if resources are available and the articulation of the conflict does not cost too much. Based on this premise, resource mobilization theory even expects conflicts to originate under relatively privileged circumstances.

Though the resource mobilization approach has pointed to shortcomings of deprivation theory, like anomie theory it is unable to explain differences in observed conflict levels across societies and over time. Thus the approach predicts less variance than the deprivation theory if the level of resources is crudely operationalized by level of economic development and school enrolment ratios (cf. Nollert, 1992). In addition, it can also not explain why political and industrial conflict increased in the early 1930s. Finally, it fails to explain – for example – why class conflict does not rekindle in each core country after 1968 (cf. Crouch and Pizzorno, 1978), nor why, in the crisis years of the 1930s, discontent was expressed by the fascist movement as well as by radical and moderate left-wing parties.

Introduced by the case study of Piven and Cloward (1977) and Gamson's longitudinal findings (1975), in the 1980s an emphasis within resource mobilization theory emerged to focus more on *political opportunities* for insurgents to express their grievances than on their cognitive and monetary resources (see Tarrow, 1988). According to Tarrow's (1988, 1989) "political process model" of social movements, political and industrial conflict generally reflect a favorable political environment and open opportunity structures. As for the student revolts in 1968, some theorists would reject anomie and deprivation as explanatory schemes by arguing that there was not a shortage but rather an abundance of opportunities. All in all, proponents of the concept establish that grievances alone do not trigger the rise of political and industrial conflict (e.g. Tarrow, 1989) but that an opening of the opportunity structure does. However, even if we assume that in the 1930s and the 1960s the political opportunity structure might have been comparatively open (Tarrow, 1989) we get no empirical answer to questions such as whether it was more closed in Finland than in the United Kingdom, or whether it was more closed during the 1970s than in the 1920s and the 1950s.

Towards an Integrative Theoretical Approach

The preceding paragraph demonstrates that the major theoretical approaches hardly explain the presented longitudinal and cross-national data on political and industrial conflict. From this it seems obvious that an encompassing approach is desirable, one which takes into account U- or W-shaped trends of conflict at the core as well as inter-country differences within the core. Having taken into consideration the merits and shortcomings of breakdown and solidarity approaches, we will first return to some of the integrative efforts made in connection with the varying occurrences of conflict over time. Subsequently we will refer to arguments from functionalist conflict sociology, the neo-corporatist paradigm and a power mobilization approach, which leads us to expect that a low level of social conflict mirrors world economic constraints, the mode of interest intermediation and strong democratic left-wing parties.

In this article we thus propose an encompassing approach which more than any of the single theories suggested so far can claim to explain intertemporal and international variations in the level of conflict. Apart from deprivation theory arguments and critical objections from the resource mobilization approach, the resulting causal model also integrates long wave and world system arguments, functionalist conflict sociology and the neo-corporatism-paradigm's criticism of the ungovernability-thesis.

Downswings and Upswings in the Trend of Conflict

A first attempt to integrate the various theoretical arguments for an explanation of ups and downs in social unrest is made by Charles, Louise and Richard Tilly in their book, *The Rebellious Century, 1830-1930* (1975), on the social and economic history of France, Italy and Germany. Although their argument rejects the idea that *structure* is directly connected to the extent of conflict, their approach does not preclude that structural change may hinder or favor the organisation and mobilization of interests: "The argument ... treats structural change as affecting collective violence profoundly but only indirectly, through the creation, transformation, and destruction of groups with common interests ..." (Tilly *et al*, 1975: 244). In contrast to the arguments put forward by the breakdown approaches, it is thus assumed that an increase in deprivation is not sufficient to provoke collective action but can weaken solidarity between groups and thereby indirectly contribute to a reduction in the level of conflict. However, we have just mentioned that Tilly *et al.* cannot explain why conflict also increased in phases of extreme deprivation. Hence, Sidney Tarrow (1989: 48) added: "Since periods of prosperity and periods of crisis alike produce cycles of protest, it seems logical to expect that the factors responsible for generating protest can be present in both, although they are obviously not going to be equally present in all periods of history." In sum, he states that actors would protest both when deprivation is unbearable and when the political environment offers fresh opportunities for insurgent mobilization.

Although hardly recognized in comparison with Tarrow's work, a similar view was already offered by Harold Kerbo (1982). It implies that both extreme deprivation and economic affluence may stimulate collective action. Issuing from the fact that the two important waves of political conflict in this century, the late 1920s and the 1970s, followed a phase of economic crisis and a phase of prosperity respectively, he suggests integrating relative deprivation and resource mobilization theories. According to Kerbo, political conflict thus indicates material deprivation as well as sufficient provision with relevant conflict resources. Correspondingly, a curvilinear relationship between economic performance and social conflict is to be expected, whereby in historical phases of extreme economic recession (e.g. in the early 1930s) as well as in phases of economic prosperity (e.g. in the early 1960s) an above-average level of conflict can be found. As to leaps in conflict levels, Kerbo allots the responsibility (taking into account the overall economic situation) either to movements of crisis groups whose material life situation is in danger (e.g. the workers' movement) or to movements of affluent actors who are distinguished by above-average financial, time and cognitive resources (e.g. the New Social Movements).

A fourth attempt to explain the observed cycles of social conflict stems from Volker Bornschier (1988: ch. 7). Contrary to the approaches mentioned above, his attempt focuses on the evolution of Western social structure in general. The main assumption as to conflict is that its longitudinal pattern does not follow a linear trend but oscillates similar to *long waves* in economic development. Nevertheless, in contrast to theories of long cycles, the ups and downs in conflict are not explicitly linked to cycles in socioeconomic performance (cf. Screpanti, 1984). Rather, trends in conflict are seen as the outcome of a historical interaction between normative theories, technological and political factors.

In the pattern of conflict, four sources of conflict are distinguishable: (1) the regulated conflict over distribution (2) the unregulated conflict over distribution (3) the conflict over values and (4) the realization conflict. During the stages of a *societal model,* stretching over about 50 to 60 years similar to the Kondratieff cycles in economic development, the sources of conflict vary in importance. In a first phase, in which the societal model is formed, the conflict over values (or, in the terminology of anomie theory, the goal anomie) dominates. In the course of this phase the importance of this source of conflict is reduced, while the realization conflict (that is, in terms of anomie theory, the goal/means anomie) gains in importance on the one hand and the regulated conflict over distribution on the other hand. Only with the saturation of the societal model is this trend stopped. The realization conflict therefore loses in importance versus the value conflict, while the conflict over distribution now becomes unregulated, because it is no longer supported by a generally binding basic consensus.

According to the degree of legitimacy of the societal model, one must in addition distinguish between a basic consensus phase and a dissension phase, assuming that in both phases other factors also contribute to the explanation of conflicts. In the basic consensus phase, conflicts are primarily the result of legitimacy deficits, which among other things can point to a situation of deprivation. By contrast, in the dissension phase conflicts indicate the ability of social groups to mobilize relevant conflict resources.

The legitimacy of the societal model is strengthened in the phase of basic consensus by two factors: firstly, the new technological style offers new and attractive goods and the diffusion of the technological style provides for structural upward mobility. Secondly, the capacity of the politico-economic regime to satisfy societal demands increases parallel to the fair distribution of the above-mentioned new goods in the population.

However, as the rise and decline of the *technological style* (Perez, 1983) occurs several years in advance of the rise and decline of the *politico-economic* regime, the result is not simply a U-shaped pattern in the level of conflict in the course of the societal model. Yet it is expected that the level of conflict starts to climb in the short term after saturation of the technological style and before the full development of the politico-economic regime. This interim high, which is also evident in the three figures, suggests a W-shaped conflict pattern in the course of a societal model.

This approach has a higher information content and is more testable than that of Tilly *et al.*, which does not claim an ability to be tested empirically:

"We have not stated the arguments in a way that could be tested directly through cross-national analyses of the Hibbs-Gurr variety." (Tilly *et al.*, 1975: 298). In addition, the theories of Bornschier and Kerbo are quite compatible. Even if Kerbo – in contrast to Bornschier – does not refer to long waves in societal development, both theories lead one to expect that, in the first stage of the new societal model (e.g. Sweden and the USA in the early 1930s), the thematic determinants dominate as factors of explanation both in anomie theory (goal anomie) and in deprivation theory (material deprivation). In Figure 5, which underlines the compatibility of the theories of Kerbo and Bornschier, we have graphically combined the most important features of conflict, which distinguish the two main phases in the career of a societal model. Both approaches assume that with each long-term economic boom the

FIGURE 5 Pattern of conflict over the career of a societal model

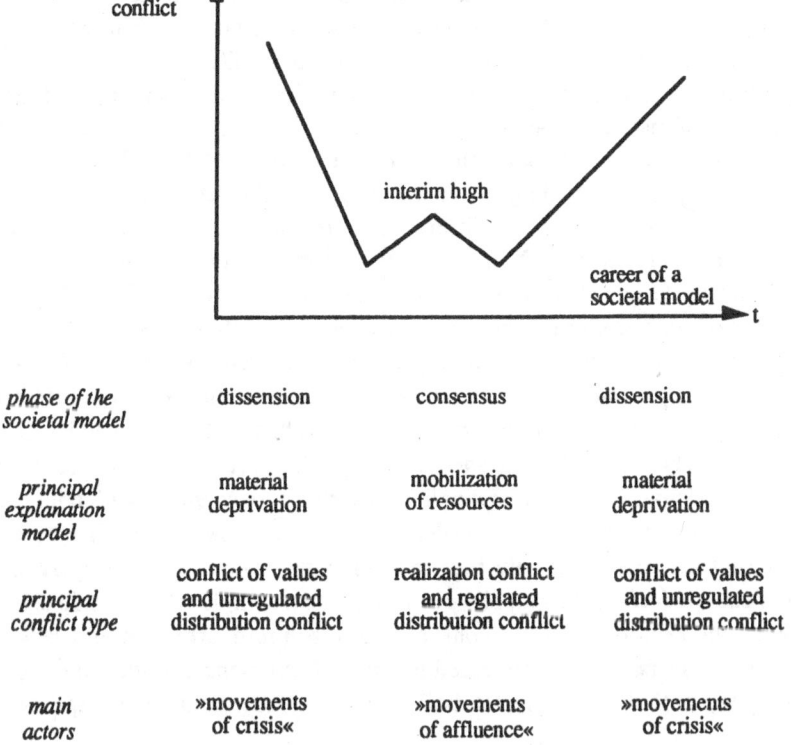

phase of the societal model	dissension	consensus	dissension
principal explanation model	material deprivation	mobilization of resources	material deprivation
principal conflict type	conflict of values and unregulated distribution conflict	realization conflict and regulated distribution conflict	conflict of values and unregulated distribution conflict
main actors	»movements of crisis«	»movements of affluence«	»movements of crisis«

traditional movements of crisis will also continually lose ground. Conflict becomes virulent again, however, in the dissension phase, and especially after a continued phase of economic prosperity (e.g. the end of the 1960s). Therefore "new" movements of affluence especially can be observed here. Furthermore, one expects that conflicts in the phase of basic consensus are initiated mainly by deprived people, whereas in the dissension phase those who have sufficient resources at their disposal are the basis of insurgency.

Towards an Explanation of the Cross-National Variations

Figures 1 to 3 above, as well as various country patterns (see Bornschier, 1988: 178-185) suggest that the level of conflict in all Western countries does in fact develop more or less according to the W-hypothesis displayed in Figure 5. That leaves us to predict the level at which individual countries traverse this W-shaped pattern. Following our argumentation and the empirical results available, two variables can easily be integrated which may directly affect the level of political and industrial conflict.

First, as touched on already in the discussion on the current paradigms, the level of material deprivation theory should definitely be considered in any integrative theoretical approach (see Zimmermann, 1980, 1992). According to Nollert's (1992) findings a substantial part of the variance in the level of conflict can be explained by differences in the distribution of income and in economic performance. Yet, it is important to note that political and labor conflicts presuppose far more cognitive and material resources than deviant behavior such as murder, suicide or drug abuse. Conflict thus only occurs if resources and political opportunities, as well as agencies who can mobilize those with grievances, are available. Since core countries, in contrast to peripheral and former socialist ones, are indeed highly developed and dispose of a variety of mobilizing agencies (political parties and interest group organizations), it would in principle follow that core countries with both high levels of relative and of absolute deprivation traverse the W-shaped pattern of conflict at a comparatively higher level. Since low *absolute* deprivation indicates insufficient availability of resources, a complex relationship arises. Thus the relation between conflict and absolute deprivation and lack of resources respectively – measured in terms of economic development – is U-shaped, with high levels at both extremely low and high degrees of deprivation. In consequence, in phases of crisis, high absolute deprivation is assumed to promote social unrest, while it should lessen conflict in phases of prosperity.

Second, cross-national research suggests that the mode of interest intermediation was also linked to the level of social unrest in the post-war era. Thus it can be expected that a broad incorporation of encompassing business and labor organizations and particularly political interests into the process of policy formation (neo-corporatism) (see Lehmbruch and Schmitter, 1982) would help to smooth both political discontent and labor disputes. Indeed, the findings of Schmitter (1981) and Nollert (1992) indicate an inverse relation between corporatism and both political and industrial conflict. This fact corresponds to Zimmermann's (1992) observation that Austria, Switzerland, the Netherlands and the Scandinavian countries – where political elites co-operate rather than competing – showed low levels of unrest.

Our hypothesis, according to which countries with corporatist interest intermediation should show lower degrees of insurgency, originally stood in contrast to deprivation theory and the concept of "ungovernability". For one thing, Schmitter in his pioneering article (1981) rejects the idea that the opening of the gap between claims of the population and the ability of the state to satisfy these needs, contributed decisively to the increase in conflict at the end of the 1960s. Furthermore, he refutes the warnings of conservative authors that excessive claims make Western political societies ungovernable (see Crozier et al., 1975). Following the empirical finding that the countries are clearly randomly scattered on various indicators for ungovernability, the institutionalized participation of interest groups in formulating and implementing politics may contribute to a high degree of governability.

We agree at least with Schmitter's criticism of the concept of *ungovernability* and suggest that incorporating interest groups indeed increases governability, which is reflected in lower levels of political and industrial conflict. Since the advantage of corporatism vis-à-vis pluralist interest intermediation rests in a wider legitimation basis (that is, a consensus supported by as many interests as possible) we argue that corporatism reduces the gap between claims in the population and the intermediation potential of the state to satisfy them. Yet, a lot of empirical findings suggest that neo-corporatism goes together with low unemployment and inflation rates (e.g. Schmidt, 1986; Castles, 1987) and lower income inequality (e.g. Nollert, 1990). It therefore seems plausible to expect pluralist interest intermediation to aggravate conflict indirectly and not directly, as Schmitter assumed (see Nollert, 1992).

The fact that corporatist countries are characterized by a below-average level of industrial and political conflict does not imply that neo-corporatism in general reduces social conflict. As for the transformation of deprivation into collective action, core countries, in contrast to peripheral ones, are better able to make resources and political opportunities available to underprivileged actors. However, corporatism limits political opportunities by including only major business and labor organizations.

In addition, the opacity of the process of policy formation has impacts for individual actors. They are less likely to localize the cause of failures in socio-political power relationships but rather tend to personalize problems. It can thus be argued that people in countries with neo-corporatist interest intermediation tend to view their problems as the result of wrong personal behavior rather than due to shortcomings in the social structure.

Finally, corporatism with its affinity to consensus, *social partnership* and *consociational democracy* tends to stigmatize interpersonal conflicts. While under pluralism conflict is viewed as an innovative force, corporatism connotates political dissent negatively. In countries with corporatist interest intermediation more self-damaging behavior is predicted.

FIGURE 6 Levels and patterns of different types of conflict according to the mode of interest intermediation

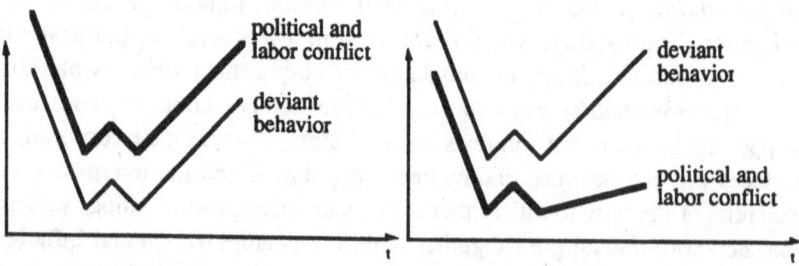

Legend: time (t) refers to the career of the societal model as discussed above, see also Figure 5.

The hypothesis presented in Figure 6 receives support from empirical findings: firstly, the levels of political conflict correlate in an inverse and linear way with suicide rates; secondly, countries classified as corporatist do in fact suffer in general from an above-average suicide rate (see Nollert, 1992). As to the long-term pattern of conflict, corporatism does not completely suppress the rise of conflict in the phase of dissension, but mitigates and postpones its increase (not represented in Figure 6). The limits of problem-solving capacity in the corporatist countries will be reached later than in pluralist ones. This also suggests that the consensus phase of a new societal model can be pioneered by pluralist countries through social innovations (see Bornschier, 1988: 154-157). The New Deal in the USA was a case in point.

While deprivation and the availability of resources respectively are to a large extent determined by the mode of interest intermediation, cross-national research also suggests that corporatism itself is determined by interparty politics and the position of a country in the world system (see Western, 1991; Nollert, 1992).

Two arguments speak for the hypothesis that corporatism reflects a strong political weight of social democratic parties: firstly, since the state ultimately guarantees adherence to exchange arrangements, employers and employees should be the more willing to collaborate if their "political arm" is part of the government. Concerning the interests of the employees, the unions' willingness to cooperate is ensured first and foremost if moderate labor parties participate in power. Secondly, participation in government presupposes a deradicalization of party ideologies, which in turn facilitates cooperation. Under such conditions workers no longer aim at defeating the "class enemy", but prefer to bargain within a "social partnership" for a fair share of economic progress (see Jessop, 1979; Korpi 1983: ch. 2 and Pzreworski and Wallerstein, 1984).

Apart from the distribution of power among domestic political agencies, the international distribution of power is also responsible for an increase in the willingness to cooperate within the framework of corporatist arrangements. The functionalist conflict theory, for example, points to this hypothesis. Following Georg Simmel's arguments in the chapter *Der Streit* (1908b), Lewis A. Coser's ninth proposition in *The Functions of Social Conflict* (1956) states that the more a group is threatened by other groups, the higher the propensity to cooperate among their members. Hence, larger and more powerful societies can afford more internal conflict than smaller and less powerful ones. For a comparison of countries one can postulate that employers and employees in small states which are politically and militarily weak, and at the same time usually highly integrated into the world market, are forced to cooperate more closely than those in major powers to preserve international competitiveness (see Katzenstein, 1985).

This view is quite compatible with the world system approach, locating the sources of conflict in inter- and transnational dependency and power relationships. However, two remarks should be added that point to the structural position in the world system. First, it is important to be aware that dependency on imports and exports at the periphery is more likely to incite than to reduce insurgency (see Boswell and Dixon, 1990). Second, our argument for the core implies that a weak position in the world system works not directly but indirectly – mediated by corporatism and a favorable socio-economic performance – in mitigating internal conflict.

For one thing the resulting theoretical model proposes that the level of political and labor conflict in a given country at a certain point in time depends both directly and indirectly on the phase of the societal model. In short, the level of conflict decreases during the formation phase and definitely increases after an interim high during the disintegrational phase of the societal model. Linked to the phase of the societal model is the extent of aggregate deprivation and the availability of resources, respectively. The climax of legitimacy which promotes prosperity – connected with a relatively even distribution of economic progress – is reached in the full development of the societal model following the formation phase. Distinguished from this is the disintegration phase of the model which eventually leads to an economic depression connected with a more uneven distribution of wealth. Correspondingly we expect that, at the end of the full development of the societal model, movements of affluence emerge, while at the end of the disintegration phase conflict is initiated by movements of crisis fighting for redistribution of social rewards. Also affected by the phase of the societal model is the mode of interest intermediation. Introduced by the New Deal in the United States and the Folkhem-project in Sweden in the 1930s, the consensus phase at the core was characterized by the formation of a politico-economic regime encompassing corporatist arrangements and redistributive social policies. This *Neo-corporatist Keynesian societal model* (see Bornschier, 1988: ch. 6) was fully developed in the 1960s and started to disintegrate in the 1970s. At the turn of the 1980s this societal model began to dissolve. Landslide electoral victories of neo-liberal forces in the USA (Reaganism) and the United Kingdom

(Thatcherism) requiring deregulation paved the way for a revitalization of pluralism.

By contrast, cross-national differences reflect the status of a nation-state in the world system and the internal political power constellation. As a result, both variables are assumed to indirectly affect the level of conflict via the mode of interest intermediation and its influence on the degree of deprivation and the availability of resources (see also Korpi, 1974). A low level of conflict is therefore to be expected in countries that are geopolitically weak and closely linked to the world economy and where left-wing parties are relatively strong. Both attributes then should be linked to a high incorporation of societal interests in the process of policy formation and implementation, which in its turn guarantees lower degrees of deprivation and social conflict.

Figure 7 summarizes all our theoretical arguments. The level of conflict in a country at a time is considerably affected by (i) the phase of the societal model, (ii) the status of the country in the world system and (iii) the internal political constellation of power. Both the status in the world system and the political power distribution indirectly affect the level of conflict by structuring interest intermediation and the levels of "absolute" and "relative" deprivation. Several studies indicate that corporatism is indeed linked to high economic performance and low income inequality (e.g. Nollert, 1992). In other words: conflict should be lowest in countries with corporatist interest intermediation during the formation phase of the societal model, whereas the highest level appears in countries classified as pluralist during the disintegration phase.

FIGURE 7 An encompassing approach to the explanation of variations in the level of conflict

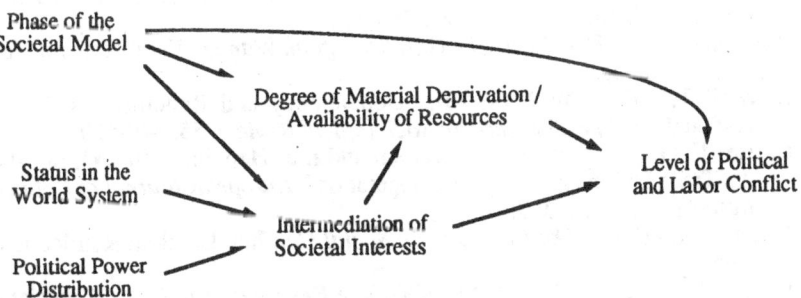

Even if we do not perform rigorous statistical tests here, the data presented in our figures and further empirical findings not presented (Bornschier, 1988: ch. 7; Nollert, 1992: ch. 9) support our theoretical approach. Furthermore, the patterns of conflict in the USA underline that a budding hegemonic power runs through the phases of the new societal model earlier, as a kind of forerunner. Figures 1 to 3 document that both political and industrial unrest decreased in the 17 non-hegemonic countries until the mid-1960s and then increased. Also in line with our argument is the fact that the lowest level of political conflict is to be found in Finland, which since the end of the 1960s can be classified as corporatist. In contrast, the United Kingdom and Italy whose interest intermediation is classified as pluralist in the literature are characterized by the highest level of conflict. Finally, corporatist countries (e.g. Austria, Norway, Switzerland) definitely evidence clearly lower levels of industrial conflict than pluralist countries (e.g. Italy, Australia, New Zealand).

To sum up: the available data on both forms of conflict in the post-war era affirm that structural properties of nation-states (phases of a societal model, status and position in the world system, internal power distribution, mode of interest intermediation, economic growth rate, social inequality) substantially predict collective action.

REFERENCES

Bornschier V., Chase-Dunn C. (1985): *Transnational Corporations and Underdevelopment*. New York: Praeger.

Bornschier V. (1988): *Westliche Gesellschaft im Wandel*. Frankfurt and New York: Campus.

Boswell T., Dixon W J. (1990): "Dependency and Rebellion: A Cross-National Analysis." *American Sociological Review*, 55: 540-559.

Castles F. G. (1987): "Neocorporatism and the 'Happiness Index', or what the Trade Unions get for their Cooperation." *European Journal of Political Research*, 15: 381-393.

Coser L. A. (1956): *The Functions of Social Conflict*. London: Routledge & Kegan.

Crouch C., Pizzorno A. (eds.) (1978): *The Resurgence of Class Conflict in Western Europe since 1968*. London: Macmillan.

Crozier M., Huntington S., Watanuki J. (eds.) (1975): *The Crisis of Democracy*, New York: NYU Press.
Durkheim E. (1964 [1893]): *The Division of Labor in Society*, New York: Free Press.
Eckstein H. (1980): "Theoretical Approaches to Explaining Collective Political Violence." Pp. 135-166 in Gurr T. R. (ed.) *Handbook of Political Conflict*, New York: Free Press.
Ellis D P. (1971): "The Hobbesian Problem of Order: A Critical Appraisal of the Normative Solution." *American Sociological Review* 36: 692-703.
Gamson W. A. (1975): *The Strategy of Protest*. Homewood, Ill.: Dorsey Press.
Gurney J. N., Tierney K J. (1982): "Relative Deprivation and Social Movements: A Critical Look at Twenty Years of Theory and Research.", *Sociological Quarterly*, 23: 33-47.
Gurr T. R. (1970): *Why Men Rebel*. Princeton: Princeton University Press.
Hibbs D. (1973): *Mass Political Violence*. New York: Wiley.
Hyman H H. (1953): "The Value System of Different Classes." Pp. 426-442 in R. Bendix, S M. Lipset (eds.) *Class, Status and Power*. New York: Free Press.
Jagodzinski W. (1983): "Ökonomische Entwicklung und politisches Protestverhalten." *PVS Sonderheft 'Politische Stabilität und Konflikt'*, Pp. 18-43.
Jenkins J. C. (1983) "Resource Mobilization Theory and the Study of Social Movements.", *Annual Review of Sociology*, 9: 527-553.
Jessop B. (1979): "Corporatism, Parliamentarism and Social Democracy." Pp. 185-212 in P. C. Schmitter, G. Lehmbruch (eds.) *Trends Toward Corporatist Intermediation*. London: Sage.
Katzenstein P. (1985): *Small States in World Markets. Industrial Policy in Europe*. Ithaca, N.Y.: Cornell University Press.
Kaelble H. (1987): *Auf dem Weg zu einer europäischen Gesellschaft*. München: Beck.
Kerbo H. (1982): "Movements of 'Crisis' and Movements of 'Affluence'. A Critique of Deprivation and Resource Mobilization Theory." *Journal of Conflict Resolution*, 26: 645-663.
Kerbo H., Shaffer R A. (1992) "Lower Class Insurgency and the Political Process: The Response of the U.S. Unemployed, 1890-1940." *Social Problems*, 39: 139-154.
Korpi W. (1974): "Conflict, Power and Relative Deprivation." *American Political Science Review*, 68: 1569-1578.
Korpi W. (1983): *The Democratic Class Struggle*. London: Routledge & Kegan.
Kraus F. (1981): "The Historical Development of Income Inequality in Western Europe and the United States." Pp. 187-236 in P. Flora, A J. Heidenheimer (eds.) *The Development of Welfare States in Europe and America*, New Brunswick N.J.: Transaction Press.
Lehmbruch G., Schmitter P. (eds.) (1982): *Patterns of Corporatist Policy-Making*, London: Sage.

Merton R. K. (1949): *Social Theory and Social Structure*. Glencoe: Free Press.
Muller E. N. (1985): "Income Inequality, Regime Repressiveness, and Political Violence." *American Sociological Review*, 50: 47-61.
Muller E. N., Seligson, M A. (1987): "Inequality and Insurgency." *American Political Science Review*, 81: 425-451.
Nollert M. (1990): "Social Inequality in the World System: An Assessment." Pp. 17-54 in V. Bornschier and P. Lengyel (eds.): *World Society Studies Vol. I*, Frankfurt am Main: Campus.
Nollert M. (1992): *Interessenvermittlung und sozialer Konflikt*. Pfaffenweiler: Centaurus.
Oberschall A. (1973): *Social Conflict and Social Movements*. Englewood Cliffs, NJ: Prentice Hall.
Oberschall A. (1978): "Theories of Social Conflict." *Annual Review of Sociology*, 4: 291-315.
Opp K-D. (1976): *Methodologie der Sozialwissenschaften*. Reinbek: Rowohlt.
Paldam M., Pedersen P J. (1984): "The Large Pattern of Industrial Conflict – A Comparative Study of 18 Countries, 1919–79", *International Journal of Social Economics*, 11: 3-28.
Perez C. (1983): "Structural Change and Assimilation of New Technologies in the Economic and Social Systems.", *Futures*, 15: 357-375.
Piven F. F., Cloward R. (1971): *Regulating the Poor: The Functions of Public Welfare*, New York: Pantheon.
Przeworski A., Wallerstein M. (1984): "The Structure of Class Conflict in Democratic Societies." *American Political Science Review*, 76: 215-238.
Runciman W G. (1966): *Relative Deprivation and Social Justice*. London: Routledge & Kegan.
Russett B. (1990): "Economic Decline, Electoral Pressure, and the Initiation of Interstate Conflict." Pp. 123-140 in C. Gochman, A N. Sabrosky (eds.) *Prisoners of War*. Cambridge, Mass.: Ballinger.
Schmidt M. G. (1986): "Politische Bedingungen erfolgreicher Wirtschaftspolitik - Eine vergleichende Analyse westlicher Industrieländer." *Journal für Sozialforschung*, 26: 251-273.
Schmitter P. C. (1981): "Interest Intermediation and Regime Governability in Contemporary Western Europe and North America." Pp. 285-327 in S. Berger (ed.) *Organizing Interests in Western Europe*. Cambridge: Cambridge University Press.
Screpanti E. (1984): "Long Economic Cycles and Recurring Proletarian Insurgencies." *Review* VII, S. 509-548.
Simmel G. (1908a): "Die Kreuzung sozialer Kreise." Pp. 403-453 in *Soziologie. Untersuchungen über die Formen der Vergesellschaftung*. Berlin: Duncker & Humblot.
Simmel G. (1908b): "Der Streit." Pp. 247-336 in *Soziologie. Untersuchungen über die Formen der Vergesellschaftung*. Berlin: Duncker & Humblot.

Tarrow S. (1988): "National Politics and Collective Action: Recent Theory and Research in Western Europe and the United States." *Annual Review of Sociology*, 14: 421-440.
Tarrow S. (1989): *Democracy and Disorder. Protest and Politics in Italy, 1965-1975*, Oxford: Clarendon Press.
Taylor C. L. (1985): *World Handbook of Political and Social Indicators. Third Edition ZA No. 1130-1132*. Köln: Zentralarchiv für Empirische Sozialforschung.
Tilly C., Tilly L., Tilly R. (1975): *The Rebellious Century, 1830-1930*. Cambridge, Mass.: Harvard University Press.
Tilly C. (1978): *From Mobilization to Revolution*. Reading, Mass.: Addison-Wesley.
Western B. (1991): "A Comparative Study of Corporatist Development.", *American Sociological Review*, 56: 283-294.
Zald M. N., McCarthy J. D. (eds.) (1979): *Dynamics of Social Movements: Resource Mobilization, Social Control and Tactics*, Cambridge, Mass.: Winthrop.
Zimmermann E. (1980): "Macro-Comparative Research on Political Protest." Pp. 167-237 in T R. Gurr (ed.) *Handbook of Political Conflict*. New York: Free Press.
Zimmermann E. (1982): *Political Violence, Crises, and Revolutions: Theories and Research*, Cambridge, Mass.: Schenkman.
Zimmermann E. (1985): "The 1930s World Economic Crisis in Six European Countries. A First Report on Causes of Political Instability and Reactions to Crisis." Pp. 84-127 in P. M. Johnson, W. R. Thompson (eds.) *Rhythms in Politics and Economics*. New York: Praeger.
Zimmermann E. (1988) "Political Unrest in OECD Countries: Trends and Prospects." *World Futures*, 25: 43-80B
Zimmermann E. (1989) "Political Unrest in Western Europe: Trends and Prospects." *West European Politics*, 12: 179-196.
Zimmermann E. (1992) "Mechanismen der Konfliktregulierung in liberalen Demokratien." (forthcoming) in O. W. Gabriel (ed.) *Verstehen und Erklären von Krisen und Konflikten in der nationalen und internationalen Politik*, Baden-Baden: Nomos.

WAVES, FORMATIONS AND VALUES IN THE WORLD SYSTEM
WORLD SOCIETY STUDIES VOLUME 2
311 pages • 1992 • ISBN: 1-56000-056-2

Volker Bornschier and Peter Lengyel, Editors

    INTRODUCTION: THE END OF THE POST-WAR ERA, *Volker Bornschier* and *Peter Lengyel*
1. LONG WAVES IN THE WORLD SYSTEM, *Volker Bornschier* and *Christian Suter*
2. THE CHANGING ROLE OF CITIES IN WORLD-SYSTEMS, *Christopher Chase-Dunn*
3. REALPOLITIK AND MULTISTATE SYSTEM STABILITY, *Thomas R. Cusack*
4. THE STRUCTURING OF SOCIAL PROTEST IN MODERN SOCIETIES: THE LIMITS AND DIRECTION OF CONVERGENCE, *S.N. Eisenstadt*
5. THE SOCIALIST SOCIETIES: RISE AND FALL OF A SOCIETAL FORMATION, *Jakob Juchler*
6. THE INTERNATIONAL CIVIL SERVICE IN PERSPECTIVE, *Peter Lengyel*
7. THE POWER AND LIMITS OF STATES: STRUGGLES FOR DOMINATION BETWEEN STATES AND SOCIETIES, *Joel S. Migdal*
8. THE EMERGING EUROPEAN-WIDE HUMAN RIGHTS REGIME: TOO MUCH OF A GOOD THING? *Philip Alston*
9. NUCLEAR CONFRONTATION: AMBIVALENCE, RATIONALITY AND THE DOOMSDAY MACHINE, *J. David Singer*
10. THE PROBLEM OF RELIGIOUS POLITICS AND ITS IMPACT ON WORLD SOCIETY, *William H. Swatos, Jr.*
11. STRUCTURAL SITUATION AND WORLD VIEW: THE CASE OF SWITZERLAND, *Walter Schönl* and *Heinrich Zwicky*

Transaction Publishers
New Brunswick (U.S.A.) and London (U.K.)